DESIGNING AMERICA:
CREATING URBAN IDENTITY

DESIGNING AMERICA:
CREATING URBAN IDENTITY

*A Primer on Improving U.S. Cities for a Changing Future
Using the Project Approach to the Design and Financing
of the Spaces Between Buildings.*

Joel B. Goldsteen

Cecil D. Elliott

VNR VAN NOSTRAND REINHOLD
_____ New York

Library of Congress Catalog Card Number 93-3265
ISBN 0-442-01111-3

I(T)P   Van Nostrand Reinhold is an International Thomson Publishing company.
ITP logo is a trademark under license.

Printed in the United States of America.

Van Nostrand Reinhold   International Thomson Publishing Germany
115 Fifth Avenue   Konigswinterer Strasse 418
New York, NY 10003   53227 Bonn
                                         Germany

International Thomson Publishing   International Thomson Publishing Asia
Berkshire House, 168-173   38 Kim Tian Rd., #0105
High Holborn, London WC1V 7AA   Kim Tian Plaza
England   Singapore 0316

Thomas Nelson Australia   International Thomson Publishing Japan
102 Dodds Street   Kyowa Building, 3F
South Melbourne 3205   2-2-1 Hirakawacho
Victoria, Australia   Chiyada-Ku, Tokyo 102
                                         Japan

Nelson Canada
1120 Birchmount Road
Scarborough, Ontario
M1K 5G4, Canada

16 15 14 13 12 11 10 9 8 7 6 5 4 3 2 1

Library of Congress Cataloging in Publication Data

Goldsteen, Joel B.
    Designing America : creating urban identity / Joel B. Goldsteen,
Cecil D. Elliott.
        p.   cm.
    Includes index.
    ISBN 0-442-01111-3
    1. City planning—United States. 2. Open spaces—United States.
I. Elliott, Cecil D. II. Title.
HT167.G67 1993
307.1′216′0973—dc20
                                                    93-3265
                                                      CIP

CONTENTS

funds and grants, donor contributions, federal and state
funds, commercial funding, self-funding mechanisms,
direct city funding, unexpected revenues, tax
abatement, tax increment financing, exactions, impact
fees, enterprise zones, public-private participation,
special district designation, city districts and economic
concerns, planned unit developments, historic districts;
selecting a financing alternative, funding techniques,
city plans, spaces, and timing, plans and budgets,
incremental projects, development organizations and
teams, design review committees, public-private
negotiation, citizen participation, balancing interests
and equity; economics and esthetics.

PREFACE

The spaces between buildings are the major elements of urban settings. Individual interests and legal tradition are inclined to consider the open space of a site as its original condition, upon which decisions about construction are imposed. Within and between buildings and the lines that limit the ownership of property, smaller spaces are made on each site. The observed reality, nevertheless, is that urban space is not so much a matter of private ownership as the community perception of places as they are defined by forms of the buildings themselves, rather than by legal limitations. Increasingly, regulations have been used to exercise community interests in the spaces of cities as perceived by the eye, rather than as defined and limited by site property lines. For the common interest, civic ownership of certain spaces, particularly streets, has been recognized from the beginning of history. However, in recent times the interrelationship of spaces on private properties has been legislated in terms both physical and emotional. This book is about such spaces, and describes the ways in which spaces are designed, financed, and developed in the United States.

Any community interest is of concern to an amazing variety of individuals and groups. Residents, elected officials, city staff, designers, social scientists, business leaders, and others are constantly making decisions affecting outdoor spaces. For that reason, we have included many distinctly different points of view that can be assumed when considering the most advantageous designs for urban spaces. All readers, because of the backgrounds from which they approach the matter, will probably find that one or more of the chapters treat familiar ideas. We hope that a fresh look at such material will be helpful, along with an introduction to many new and unfamiliar topics.

Our own design preferences have been intentionally subdued in preparing the text and illustrations. We believe that the design of urban places can follow many paths to success, that style and fashion are of much less importance than the spirit with which a spatial project is conceived and constructed. The need for imagination as well as logic seems obvious; and it is our hope to stimulate imagination rather than to proselytize for a particular style. In addition, we believe that the creative pursuit of spatial projects that improve city identity is inevitably an interaction of many minds, not just an individual's flash of inspiration. Because these projects are undertaken through group enthusiasm and group participation, it seems evident to us that many participants must contribute their insights, individually and jointly, if a design is to achieve lasting success.

The visual traditions of American cities have been stressed in these pages, because we are convinced that they merit more attention. In the past, American urban design understandably has been so dependent on the forms and practices of European precedent that it has been difficult to identify American forms that are easy to follow. Yet there is a spirit of the American place that is distinctive and can be adapted to present-day conditions.

The reader will detect in our descriptions waves of popularity for certain functional and visual forms in the design of urban spaces. It has not been possible to develop this aspect of our subject, but we recommend it as a field of study by others. Festival market places, a new idea in the 60s, will be succeeded by other solutions, and it is useful to speculate on the manner in which this succession may take place.

On maps and site plans, north is toward the top unless noted. In order to attempt to accommodate readers from different disciplines, technical language was avoided in the manuscript.

JBG

CDE

ACKNOWLEDGMENTS

Research for this book would have been impossible without the use of the Interlibrary Loan and computer search systems at our two universities through which copies of publications and articles were provided. We are grateful to Deborah Sayler and Lorretax Mindt of the Interlibrary Loan Service and the staff of the Architecture Library, North Dakota State University; and John J. Dillard and William S. Ogden, librarians at the University of Texas at Arlington, for their efforts in searching for needed books, articles, and computer-based source materials. The diligence and patience with which each of the aforementioned librarians pursued our requests are greatly appreciated.

Throughout the U.S., many individuals, groups, and organizations provided their help and assistance by answering requests for case-study information, drawings, photographs, and other supplemental materials. In many instances, their unusually prompt responses were invaluable to our making deadlines. Trev Albright (North Dakota State University); Craig Amundsen, Architect (BRW, Inc., Minneapolis); David R. Bolton, MAI (David R. Bolton, Inc., Austin and Houston); Dale Bransford (San Antonio Department of Parks and Recreation); David H. Brune, Esq. (Faison-Stone Las Colinas, Inc.); Nancy Curran (Omaha Development Council); Dr. Robert B. Dean (D^2 Associates, Chicago); Phil Eklof, MAI (Grubb & Ellis Real Estate Advisors, Dallas); Martin Flores, Landscape Architect (Redevelopment Agency of the City of San Jose); Elsa D. Flores (University of Pennsylvania); John Fox, Director (Greater Atlantic City Convention and Visitors Bureau); Capt. Robert A. Goldsteen, D.O. (U.S. Army Medical Corps); Alan M. Gordon, Esq. (American Cyanamid Corporation, Stamford); Earle Kittleman, Public Information Officer (U.S. Department of the Interior); John C. Lamey, Jr. (Atlantic County Department of Regional Planning and Development); David K. May (North Dakota State University); Lynn R. Meyer (City of Omaha Planning Department); Dr. Donald C. Royse, Director (St. Louis Downtown Redevelopment Authority and Washington University); Karen Schaar (Urban Land Institute); Donald Turner, Director of Mall Operations (Downtown Denver Partnership, Inc.).

In preparing the manuscript, invaluable assistance was given by a number of readers. Dr. Paul B. Paulus read and commented on the entire manuscript, with particular attention paid to the chapters on psychology and methods. Dennis C. Colliton commented on the historical chapter and provided information related to landscape architecture. Dr. Ard Anjomani reviewed and commented on the design and the methods chapters. Ronald Ramsay provided information and advised on portions of the work. Kimberly Gradney provided assistance in research reviews and suggestions for portions of the manuscript. Paul I. Weisberg (Bloom-FCA! Advertising Agency) provided expert advice about advanced black and white reproduction and printing techniques. Errors of fact, interpretation, and omission remain the authors' responsibility.

    Unless credited, all of the maps, drawings, and photographs are by the authors.

JBG

CDE

1

IDENTITY AND CITIES—SPACES BETWEEN BUILDINGS:

Spaces between buildings, similarity or dissimilarity?; municipal responsibility, motives, participants; geographic identity; land use identity; decisions, distinction, and harmony

Cities across America are changing more rapidly than we realize. Buildings that were landmarks through one's childhood and adolescence are toppled to make way for new glistening structures. Familiar routes are interrupted by the insertion of freeways, and fields are replaced with houses and shopping centers. These changes create new spaces, and favorite spaces are suddenly different. One part of our minds grumbles about the disruption, another part admires the signs of activity. On the whole, such changes are viewed favorably, but they are still usually compared with the comforts of the past. New projects make new spaces, affecting the pathways we follow and establishing new visual meaning for the city. Change—not necessarily growth—is the very nature of cities and towns, challenging but inevitable.

As we face the future, we must pay attention to designing America using our city spaces. Taking our outdoor spaces for granted, we use them heavily, even though many of them are unplanned, unkempt, and still evolving. Streets, parks, plazas, and thoroughfares are used every day on the way to work, school, shopping, and every other destination. Their appearances signal city and neighborhood conditions to residents and visitors. Pleasant, neutral, and disagreeable esthetic experiences are determined as we travel through the spaces of small towns, cities, and urban neighborhoods. Cultural values and norms of orderliness and cleanliness serve every day as the basis of our judgment about the conditions and designs of the spaces and places through which we travel. These values and norms are so strong that even business decisions may be based on city appearances.

People cherish their favorite open spaces, but many of the spaces are changing, and they are insufficiently cared for by the cities. Although some spaces are getting better, many are turning into major civic problems. Newly constructed spaces are being improperly designed to meet the changes of the last decades as well as those forecast by experts. In many cities, revising regulations to adopt new design controls may be an effort that will prove worthwhile as the next half century approaches. New or improved plazas, parks, street designs, or other projects built by governments or private investors need to match social and economic needs better, rather than to become places to avoid as cities change.

SPACES BETWEEN BUILDINGS

If outdoor environments continue to be taken for granted, if we do not plan according to the many forecasts that are made, our cities will continue to decline. With the current emphasis on job creation, social welfare, and other topics with economic implications, urgent and interrelated problems may be expected as cities fail to devote the necessary attention and resources to open spaces. To improve cities and their social and economic conditions, the utmost consideration must be given to the design and construction of spaces and places. The physical environment so strongly affects the economic and social behavior in cities that deteriorating spaces can cause building and land values to plummet. Spaces symbolize conditions, traditions, residents' aspirations, and the business climate. Neglecting spaces or working with insufficient knowledge of the subject are not acceptable alternatives for any developer, architect, landscape architect, engineer, city staff member, or elected official of any city. The spaces between buildings have great impact on the lives of most Americans, and they can be improved. Business conditions can be stimulated or stabilized in cities by learning to utilize sound principles of design and financing to confront the changes expected in the next half century. To ignore the warnings is to risk the grim and drab cities reminiscent of George Orwell's *1984*, the postapocalypse cities of science fiction, or brownish Gotham-like cities from *Batman*. Omens of the future are both bleak and cryptic. Responsibility must be exercised, or intervention abandoned. By either scenario changes in social and economic conditions will affect our futures, forcing us, sooner or later, to pay much more attention to our city spaces. Even when left alone, the spaces between buildings require maintenance. If some spaces are ignored, they will collect refuse, become overgrown and unsafe from the deterioration of their materials. As the fringe areas of American cities develop, new spaces may be built to match the suburbs and spaces in the core city may become obsolete.

Population growth creates even more pressures on urban life. People moving into America's cities create a new urgency to initiate, plan, and modify open spaces and places. There may be little cost involved in redesigning or constructing projects that improve urban and surburban city spaces. Should additional funds be required, they may be more than balanced by the immediate benefits. Places can be changed. There are no excuses for avoiding improving the spaces between buildings.

Many people look back to smaller cities of the past and reflect on the advantages and simplicity of living then. Approaches to city and urban design vary with perspectives about size and the times. Cities over 50,000, for example, present much more complex problems than do cities under 5,000. Our concerns about all sizes of cities are well-founded. Since the turn of the century, when public health data linked disease and death with crowding, lower densities and larger spaces between buildings have been a goal of government. In the larger metropolitan areas, central cities have been partially vacated in favor of the edge city, where space is universal, pervasive, and always available further out. Some people still believe strongly in reinforcing the future of downtowns, while others favor investing in those new areas of cities. Both downtowns and suburbs need intervention by skilled project teams; for, as larger spaces with the lower densities are generally neglected, new kinds of problems emerge.

Most Americans live in cities. The places and spaces of cities therefore cannot be forgotten as a focus of future improvements. Lining a street with trees, adding new park benches and sculpture, or building an office building plaza, and then forgetting about the finished project, has been common. Previously, spaces have been considered merely as amenities, not particularly important to our well-being. Nothing could be further from the truth. Open spaces, parks, plazas, streets, and roads are a system for separate study that will lead to policies, programs, plans, and projects that can successfully affect behavior and greatly improve the urban condition. Those in public service (elected officials, city staff members, and public servants) are failing to properly consider and plan one of the most important aspects of the urban condition, the spaces between buildings. Not only has the body of information about spaces developed and changed over the past few decades, but various disciplines have made important contributions that are buried in recent academic journals, project reports, and conference proceedings.

Neglect may be linked to lower budgets. Many cities are wrongfully turning away from providing effective open spaces for residents. Pleading limited city budgets (which is a spurious argument), officials say that the cost of park maintenance is an obstacle that cannot be overcome in this decade. Economic conditions become obvious. In time the appearances of places decline, and the spirit of the people also declines.

People living in the same city share viewpoints to a remarkable extent.[1] As a result of unique local conditions, an identifiable set of opinions may dominate, and a special tone of the city may evolve. Different cities have different temperaments, racial and ethnic variations, ideological moods, and objectives. Much research has confirmed these differences.[2] For example, some cities favor conservative actions, such as providing private enterprise with freedom to advance their businesses, relatively free from local controls, so that the city will ultimately prosper. By contrast, other cities believe in strongly supporting federal and state efforts in social welfare as a means to train a work force that might attract and promote new businesses, relocations, or expansions. It is, in truth, a double-edged sword. Businesses will bring prosperity to city residents, and city conditions of well-being will bring prosperity to businesses. Such opposing points of view, or their interplay, can create sound situations in different places. No certain dominant ideology or combination of ideologies creates magic bullets for successful cities. At the same time, cities vary in their economic well-being. At times, some may be healthily in the black, and others sorely in the red. Stable cities may remain economically strong and healthy all of the time.

Racial and ethnic variations can be noted also. Detroit and Philadelphia may be predominantly African-American, while San Antonio and Miami are Hispanic, and San Francisco and Los Angeles have large Asian populations. The mood of such cities are often decidedly different, and many of those differences are based on racial, ethnic, and economic variations. A no-federal-funds city, a manufacturing town, an agricultural community, a bedroom suburb, a college town, a tourist-oriented suburban city, a fishing village, a central business district, an office center, a county seat with its courthouse and county business functions, a warehouse and distribution center, a petrochemical production town, a military base city, a mining town, an Indian reservation, a medical center—all describe sets of attitudes, perspectives, and points of view. Without the need to take any action to create one, a collective psyche emerges, or natural factions develop.[3] In linking the fundamental differences of these places to the thoughtful making of spaces and places, future changes and shifts can be accommodated by each city on an individual basis.

Similarity or Dissimilarity?

Seen from a distance, many cities look similar. Rising from flat land, Houston looks much like Los Angeles; as a river port, Detroit looks like St. Louis; and staid old Boston looks like Philadelphia (Fig. 1.1). Wherever one visits, the glass-wrapped buildings, patterns of open space (parks, plazas, and street-sidewalk spaces) provide defining components that create similarities and differences. Though their locations, topographies, climates, and vegetation differ, the skylines are more similar than different. Even the streets and open spaces are almost standardized (Fig. 1.2). Only palms or snow provide an unequivocal clue about whereabouts.

By contrast, singular design responses to local situations have created urban identities for many cities. The responses may have been conscious attempts, unconscious accumulations of decisions, or reactions to unusual circumstances. San Francisco, seen from afar, looks different from Los Angeles, and San Antonio looks different from Denver. Within the cities, streets, open spaces, railroads, and rivers are the base plane, unifying the ground floors of buildings and the areas outside.

Identity is a characteristic combining uniqueness, dissonance, and mystery. Design professionals base their careers on providing their clients

with services that are identifiably different from those offered by others.[4] At the same time, the nature of the apprenticeships that designers undergo tends to bring a sameness to designers' work products. The critics who discuss cities take different views of projects that develop open spaces. Many see a natural evolution of commercial areas and consider retail strip centers (as epitomized in the Las Vegas Strip), drive-in restaurants and banks, regional shopping malls, and other developments as naturally conformist buildings.[5] These products of recent decades are viewed as evi-

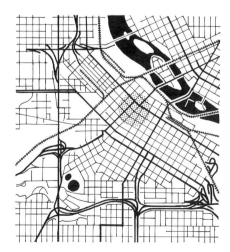 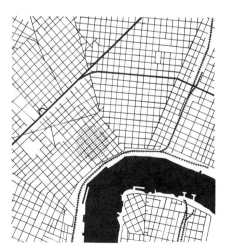

1.2 At opposite ends of the Mississippi River, Minneapolis (left) and New Orleans (right) illustrate the typical alignment of river ports with the banks of the river. Downtown areas are dotted.

1.3 In New York City (top) and Dallas (bottom), similar districts have facades that look much the same. (Top photo by Alan M. Gordon)

dence of present-day life. Therefore, uniformity of appearance is concluded to be inevitable (Fig. 1.3).

In coming to grips with the issue of designing for identity or conformity, investigation into the literature of social psychology, business management, and cultural anthropology is in order. For example, one theory states that people confronted with conflicting views, signals, or situations try to reduce that conflict. When dissonance occurs, there is normally a tendency to reduce it.[6] In making decisions to build buildings to house our daily activities, this tendency probably compels those project teams responsible for their construction to seek more subdued or conservative designs in order to avoid conflicts at many different levels. According to other findings in social psychology, the forces that probably compel project teams to conform to their situations are matters of social comparisons. People compare themselves to others and try to mirror others' behavior.[7] It is no wonder that building projects begin to look alike. Those having strong personalities may wish to build in a manner that makes unique personal statements, but the need to use available building materials leads toward similarities of appearance. Cognitive learning may account for the signals received and intepreted that encourage us to behave in a conformist fashion. Successful projects may influence our decisions and lead us to copy successes. Interpersonal relations affect decisions. "Much of what we know, we know because of others."[8] Trends come and go, and what we see in media or on a trip may become firmly implanted in our minds.

There is no easy answer to the question about whether places should be different or similar. With forces at work that seem to naturally homogenize the appearances of different cities, consciously designing for individuality and identity may be an act that battles against many factors: fashion trends, the sameness of building materials, behavioral instincts, language cues, or attempts at copying financially successful projects in other cities. Taking a position to strive for unprecedented designs of spaces and places is difficult against such strong trends.

Many advantages can be gained by discovering and reinforcing a city's own identity. Small differences may be magnified, special events may be commemorated, designers may seek to set their stamps on projects, and many other motives may embolden efforts to undertake the quest for urban identity. Conversely, cities may wish to add spaces or improve existing spaces in order to become more like other cities; thus, they hope to meet the competition for new sites for corporations or to overcome negative images. The impressions given by vacant lots and empty downtown streets may be changed by visual improvements. Designed from opposite perspectives, improving urban identity can result in similar or unusual spaces and places. Some cities attempt remarkable definition, others emulate neighboring cities, and others are completely oblivious to the outcomes that may result from their own regulatory controls. Whether residents, project teams, city planners, business leaders, or anyone else seek conformity or individuality, standard city regulations exert a great deal of the control of the spaces between buildings and the places defined by them. It is difficult to improve urban identity without first understanding the limits of governmental controls.

MUNICIPAL RESPONSIBILITY

City governments in the United States have the responsibility for the maintenance, protection, and appearance of a large part of the land occupied by the city. Large portions of a city's area will, of course, be assigned for use in connection with major vehicular arteries, the network of parks, and the sites of municipal buildings. In a typical traditional grid of streets, an area of single-family residences, about one-third of the land area is city-controlled as streets, sidewalks, and alleys; and up to a third more may be subject to city regulations governing setbacks required for building

1.4 When city-owned property (black) and setbacks (dots), are identified to be under governmental control, little is left under the owner's control.

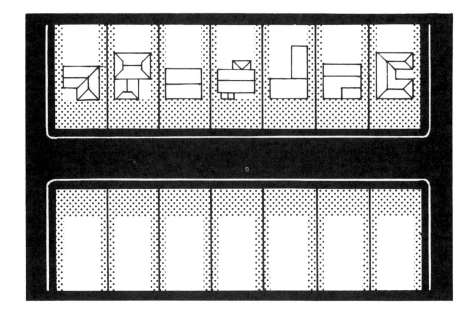

construction and other restraints that are determined by the municipal authorities. Thus, about two-thirds of the land in our cities is actually designed by government. In addition, open space is provided by city ordinances and zoning restrictions that mandate the amount of parking to be provided by most business, office, and housing functions. It is probable that the average American city has at least half to two-thirds of its developed area designated as open space through either city ownership or regulation, and that some degree of control is exercised over about three-quarters of the open areas, even if they are privately owned. (This figure may increase where streams or steep terrain discourage construction.) There are also open spaces provided by the grounds surrounding institutional buildings, such as schools, churches, and hospitals.

In some cases, the city government exercises complete control over open spaces, being responsible for all factors that affect their function and appearance. Maintenance and routine improvements, parks, sidewalks, and spaces around city-operated buildings may require a significant amount of a city's budget. Some spaces, such as the grass areas between curbs and sidewalks in typical residential neighborhoods, are jointly cared for by the property owners and governmental agencies. Other areas, such as those formed by setback requirements, are controlled through city regulations, but are nevertheless the responsibility of the property owners (Fig. 1.4). The appearance of spaces in the second category is usually controlled by the city only insofar as traditional standards of neighborhood uniformity or similarity may be applicable. The provision of lawns or trees is sometimes legislated, and it is customary to require that vacant lots be mowed to lessen the danger of fire. From a distance we may see a city as a skyline, the shapes of its buildings standing tall and sharp against the sky, but within the city the open spaces are most of what we see and provide much of the information by which we characterize the locale.

1.5 Institutions provide many of the open spaces in cities. The formality of this university quadrangle may not affect the behavior of the occupants of the space. Students sit everywhere and cut corners as they walk. Quadrangle at Brookings Hall, Washington University, St. Louis.

The conclusion is inescapable that open spaces are major functional and visual factors in the well-being of American urban structures. From village to metropolis, our dwelling places are embedded in networks of open spaces that strongly influence our work and our leisure, and they largely determine the way we view our everyday environment and ourselves.[9] Parks, plazas, and streets are often the summary elements used to describe a locale that we have visited. Quadrangles, ivied walls, hedges, and walkways epitomize campuses we have known, and they are vital parts of alumni's memories of Old Siwash (Fig. 1.5). Trees, flowers, and lawns give us both initial and lasting impressions of the homes we visit. It is not only the shady, park-like places that stick in our minds with such extraordinary tenacity (Figs. 1.6, 1.7). Clean, bright shopping streets; attractive benches at a bus stop; containers of flowers at a traffic island; and many other small evidences of a community's sensitivity and concern form an aggregate impression, although we may have had no occasion to talk to any of the residents. There may not be a precise ranking of preferences that can be applied in all circumstances, but there is a plethora of evidence, statistical and anecdotal, indicating that people clearly prefer to live, work, and relax in areas that offer them opportunities for esthetic and psychological pleasure.

When neighborhoods are described by both adults and children, parks and streets are mentioned along with buildings.[10] Real-estate agents are well aware that the visual aspects of an area strongly influence the sales potential of a property. In 1960, James Felt, chairman of the New York City

1.6 In a casual arrangement, the railroad station at downtown Durango, Colorado, is closely related to a city park. Building detail and planting scale unifies the setting.

1.7 In contrast with the previous view, Chestnut Street in downtown Philadelphia shows a pleasant breaking of the linear visual perspective by the cross streets, corner plants, and sculpture.

Planning Commission, was quoted in the *New York Times* as saying, "The smallest patch of green to arrest the monotony of asphalt and concrete is as important to the value of real estate as streets, sewers and convenient shopping."[11] It is not only planting that has an attraction for the urban resident. The beautification of a street, even when it does not involve planting trees, can bring new grace to living or shopping there. In fact, current discussion among urban designers, landscape architects, and others who are concerned with matters such as the improvement of streets is about evenly divided between those who favor the "greening" of the streetscape and those who want to "urbanize" it—that is to say, to endeavor to make a thoroughfare as much like a park as possible or to give it over to the downtown panorama of paving and the necessary fixtures (Figs. 1.8, 1.9). Fortunately, neither group proposes one solution as appropriate for all places, and the discussion appears to center on the appropriate occasions for each.[12] Perhaps the best evidence for the vital importance of improving urban spaces and places is historical. Beyond the reports of sociologists, psychologists, and analysts of real-estate activities is the fact that from the times of the earliest cities there is evidence of a basic human impulse to govern streets and open spaces, to make them more useful in

1.8 The central square of Jackson, Wyoming, resembles an isolated woodland area, although it centers on a statue of a cowboy on a horse. (Photo by Alan M. Gordon)

1.9 Stone paving and stone walls dominate Pioneer Square, Seattle. Even though some trees are present, the setting is distinctly urban and composed of hard surfaced materials. (Photo by Robert A. Goldsteen)

the necessary and desired activities of the city and to make them more beautiful and restorative to the citizens of the community.

The improvement of public places comes about in many ways. Paley Park in New York City, surely an American classic that displays the potential to be found in the development of small areas between buildings, was the gift of a wealthy man whose office was only a block away. The park was contributed to the city in memory of the donor's father (see Fig. 2.1). The restoration of Boston's Quincy Marketplace, preserving old buildings for their place in the city's history and relating the city's downtown area to the harbor, was opened in 1976 after the project was instigated by Benjamin Thompson, an architect.[13] An urban planner, Wei Ming Lu, helped initiate

1.10 Fort Worth's Downtown Main Street development, only thirty miles from Dallas' West End, is yet another old district that has been converted to a festival marketplace.

the development of Minneapolis's Nicollet Mall, which transformed and revitalized the city's principal downtown shopping street, and Dallas's West End warehouse district, a project of revitalization and historic preservation (Fig. 1.10).[14] In St. Louis, business executives were the main supporters of the Jefferson National Expansion Memorial, the famous arch on the banks of the Mississippi River. Southwest Bell Telephone, General American Life, and Boatman's Bank were a few of the companies that wanted a "nice front yard" for their downtown office buildings. As a result of their efforts in collaborating with the National Park Service, a series of independent projects were initiated, including the downtown Mansion House project, La Clede's Landing (a restaurant area in a former warehouse district), and the national park that includes the arch that symbolizes the city's history as the gateway to the west.[15] Denver's 16th Street Mall was the result of a study to improve the city's transportation system, and development of the project was largely in the hands of officials of the Regional Transportation District (see Fig. 2.17).[16] Citizens' groups have organized and raised funds for memorial areas that remind us of the sacrifices of recent wars, and of the Holocaust. In addition to such projects of historic preservation, commercial development, and the design of memorials, each year hundreds of governing boards in villages, towns, and cities meet to discuss and take action on the beautification of their communities' streets and the provision of additional plazas, playgrounds, and parks for residents. The movement to improve life in urban areas manifests itself in a multitude of ways.

An army of individuals, real-estate developers, architects, landscape architects, engineers, urban planners, professional design consultants, contractors, construction lenders, permanent lenders, joint venture partners, long-term equity investors, brokers, leasing agents, property managers, public agency regulators, local government officials, lawyers, accountants, corporate real-estate officers, and ordinary citizens (individually or in groups) all participate in making civic improvements happen. A specific project may require the cooperation of all these categories, each having a separate role to play. And each, at the same time, represents the viewpoints of certain social, ethnic, economic, and ideological groups within the community.

Motives

Projects to improve the open spaces of a city can be motivated by many different intentions, and it is seldom only one of these that instigates action. Improvement of a shopping street may be enthusiastically supported by businesspeople of the district, but included in their reasoning is the belief that additional customers will be attracted by making the surroundings pleasant and hospitable for them. A project for creating a neighborhood playground will, quite naturally, be initiated by residents of that immediate area; however, residents of other nearby neighborhoods may support the scheme as an improvement to the entire district of the city. For each improvement and each area of the city there are a variety of motives that coalesce to endorse improvement or beautification.

One of the most obvious motives for the improvement of open spaces is profit. With sound logic, citizens of a city are convinced that the attractive and useful development of spaces leads to more profitable and useful retail and service businesses.[17] At the same time, such improvements are believed to stabilize or improve real-estate values in both residential and commercial districts. The indications that an area is "going downhill" are feared by all property owners and real-estate agents, and the principal evidence of that condition is usually the deterioration and abandonment of the neighborhood's open spaces, which any potential investor can quickly interpret from what is to be seen.[18] Empty shop windows and a series of "For Sale" signs can only be read as harbingers of a dismal future for a neighborhood. In the past, such situations denoted and encouraged flight to the suburbs, but now the suburbs are also infected.

Every city is anxious to entice new industry or businesses to its downtown area or its "industrial park" and to keep its present enterprises from leaving in search of greener pastures. The taxpayers support this activity, because the arrival of new industry will add to the city's sources of revenue and forestall the necessity of increasing tax rates, including those on their residential and commercial property (Fig. 1.11). This tightly woven mesh of municipal finance means that the appearance and, if possible, the reality of a community's economic health is highly desirable to the major elements of local business as well as to the individual taxpayer. The

1.11 New industrial sites are being planned with gracious open space areas, keyed to the scale of the long-haul truck. In many communities, the industrial and office parks are considered the city's most scenic drives. This industrial drive in Plano, Texas, has trees with shrubs at their base, providing a linear element along the parkway.

common assumption that well-developed and maintained open spaces reflect a healthy and happy population also can be taken to indicate that a population of that kind provides a productive and reliable work force for incoming investors. All in all, the visual characteristics of a city become a powerful way for it to advertise for economic advantages, and even a small neighborhood park can to some degree be a part of civic leaders' plans for economic advances, the boosters' enthusiasm that is a fundamental of America's urban life.

The real-estate developer is one of the most common and directly profit-motivated agents of change. There are many ways in which a developer's activities combine with the roles of others, but essentially the developer discovers property which, according to analyses of present conditions and trends, may be made more profitable through construction or by conversion to other purposes. This initial activity of exploration and analysis is followed by the preparation of a general or specific proposal, which must have sufficient plausibility to attract investors. At heart, American developers, like their counterparts in other countries, seek the maximum return on their investments "with a minimum commitment of time and money."[19] Advantages from their investments come from development fees received as contractual compensation for executing a project; a long-term equity position for profits; advancing the reputation of their company through its success; or the personal satisfaction of participating in civic improvement and innovation. It should never be forgotten that developers are business people, always keenly aware of the financial advantages and risks resulting from their design decisions.

Profit from participation in the development of open spaces need not necessarily be monetary. A developer's actions may be very accurately calculated to gain goodwill that will later assist in obtaining special concessions on other projects. A planning official may show special enthusiasm for ingeniously discovering project funding that will strengthen his position and reputation in City Hall and the entire community. A mayor's activities in behalf of a large-scale enterprise can become a political cornerstone of her administration and thus provide a powerful advantage for the next election. In all these examples, the individual is, in reality, doing no more than voters and officials might expect. However, motives of aggrandizement can easily interfere with sound judgment and will often stir the resentment of competitors in business or politics.

Coexistent with such motives of profit and personal advantage, there is the desire of residents to bring greater pleasure into their lives. The worldwide development of city parks and other amenities related closely to the late nineteenth-century reductions in the number of hours in the work week. Earlier, with only one day of each week available for leisure activities and that reserved for little other than religious observances, on the whole the working classes necessarily confined relaxation and amusements to the areas of the city near their homes. Workdays of ten to twelve hours left little opportunity to spend leisure time farther away than the stoop of the tenement or the bleak street in front, and the sabbath was sternly allocated for church-going and devout contemplation. In contrast, today's workweek and the length of the workday leave ample time and energy for both relaxation and leisure activities. The pleasure of a casual stroll, a ball game, or a shopping trip has caused urban populations to investigate more of their environment and to more fully enjoy what they discover. It is apparent that spaces for leisure time will be needed more in the future. Commercial means of relaxation, such as movies, spectator sports, and household television programs fill much of the leisure time of most families, but they permit little opportunity for exercise, socialization, or peaceful introspection. The improvement of streets and the development of recreational spaces invite such activities for all ages. Downtown improvements bring relaxation to the walk to work and other spare moments through the day; they serve as both attraction and relaxation for shoppers.

Our preconceptions about the use of open spaces such as parks are very often misleading or downright wrong. For instance, it has been the conventional wisdom that only about 10 percent of the urban population actually used city parks.[20] This assumption implied that those who could afford it found relaxation in their homes and at commercial places of amusement. However, the report of a nationwide survey, the first study of that scope, disagreed.[21] Seventy-five percent of respondents to the survey were found to have used a park at least once in the last year, and 24 percent characterized their use as "frequent." At present roughly half of Americans live in suburbs, about twice the percentage in 1950, and customarily they are believed to spend their time in the assumed manner of upper-middle-class life, relaxing in their houses and barbecuing in their backyards. The study showed the contrary, that "those with more money and more education are more likely to use [parks]."[22] Gender and ethnic background made comparatively little difference in the use of parks, although it was noted that Hispanic populations used their city parks somewhat more and Afro-Americans somewhat less than the non-Hispanic white population. Children, of course, often go to the open spaces in their neighborhoods and the larger parks are the scenes of family picnics, but it was people between 65 and 74 years old who were most likely to use their local city parks.

The reasons for people's using open spaces is clarified by considering what they say about the benefits that they receive from using city parks. Streets and the downtown plazas are largely visited out of necessity or as part of sightseeing, but venturing out to the neighborhood park is a matter of choice and whim. In the study discussed above, the respondents stated "exercise/fitness" as the top-ranking benefit of visiting local parks, and they believed that to be true for their entire household. Second rank was given, for individuals and households, to a category designated as "relaxation/peace." Third ranking was a category defined, somewhat vaguely, as "open space." An obvious conclusion to draw from this information is that, whether we run, stroll, or just sit, access to open spaces is a treasured release and exercises valuable restorative powers. While some may insist on the desirability of precisely designated activities in parks, it is evident that for most people the major delight is simply the pleasure of being there. "Exercise/fitness" is probably not a factor in the use of downtown open spaces (although early morning joggers are sometimes sighted on Wall Street), and in many cases the category of "relaxation/peace" can only be considered relative to the noise and bustle of the situation. Still, the benefits listed with regard to neighborhood parks also probably reveal much about why people linger in open spaces in the busiest areas of the city.

In 30 B.C., Horace wrote: "This used to be among my prayers—a piece of land not so very large, which would contain a garden, and near the house a spring of ever-flowing water, and beyond these a bit of wood."[23] The same sentiments remain with us, although transformed by the urban conditions of today. Even if one seldom pauses there, observing an open space from a window or hurriedly walking past it makes things feel right. It is not just plants that give this feeling. The breadth of a plaza and the length of an avenue, when seen from an office window, provide a pause as we work. The elderly sit at their windows and consider the activities outside. Visual peace or movement, at different times and in different ways, enrich our spare moments.

These motives for the development of a city's open spaces are most fully satisfied when the quality of their designs results in spaces that clearly establish a distinct identity for each space. Whether they are constructed by the municipal government, a property-owner, or some form of collaboration between the two, another incentive for the provision of urban places is the personal and community pride that they bring about. One observer stated: "When you look at a city, it's like reading the hopes, aspirations and pride of everyone who built it."[24] To all who pass, the presence of a splendid boulevard or an inviting park proclaims the spirit of those who caused it to be built and the pride of the community in which it stands. When we visit other cities, we inevitably compare the ornamental places we see there with those that are in our own city or neighborhood. One of the most convincing evidences of a community's spirit and its future and an incontrovertible proof of the people's pride and confidence, is the visible proof provided by the fabric of the city itself. We sense in a village or a metropolis the degree of self-esteem that is operative in that place. A town may post signs at the city limits that advertise it as advancing economically and affording many desirable physical features, but always there is included a declaration that this city is a "Good Place to Live."

Abstract as it may be, the quality of life is one of the primary characteristics by which communities identify themselves. Some residents may rarely make use of a children's park or a waterfront esplanade. Nevertheless, they speak of them with sincere pride and point them out to visitors. Even if open spaces within the fabric of a city do not correspond to individual needs or desires, their availability for others is viewed as a significant accomplishment of the community. The ability of citizens to collaborate in the improvement of their surroundings—and to do it in a fine fashion—is judged worthy of being pointed out to others and ourselves. With justifiable civic pride, each such accomplishment is respected, and each suggests the possibility of other projects.

It is unavoidable, considering the way in which profits, pleasure, and civic pride interrelate in a city and its government, that all three motives for initiating projects to improve open spaces eventually will become involved before the project is completed. The playground that is a source of pleasure and a functional advantage to its neighborhood is a matter of pride for the residents of that area, the rest of the city, and the municipal authorities. Businesspeople and elected officials view it as an asset to their efforts to attract trade and new industry, and agencies of social welfare also consider it an asset in the conduct of their work. Such unanimity of course, is not always present. Harmony depends largely on the professional and political skills of the groups involved in forwarding the project.

Participants

Planners, city managers, and the staff of different city agencies, at the direction of elected officials, are usually involved to some degree in the early stages of projects. The city's planning staff may originate the idea of improving an open space or a citizens' group may propose a project to its elected representatives in the municipal government or to the planners. No matter where the proposal comes from, one of the first steps is to determine its feasibility and desirability, which is often a competitive judgment since most cities have many spaces, many problems to be considered, and limited funding available for them. The annual budget for improvements is very seldom sufficient to undertake more than a modest fraction of the work under consideration. Occasionally a large project of extraordinary public appeal, a stadium perhaps, will be promising enough to merit a special election on a bond issue to finance its construction. Otherwise, a project must fight its way through the competition for municipal funding or be developed through collaborative manipulations by the city authorities and real-estate developers.

The planning staff of a city has a major responsibility to make certain that projects are coordinated with the comprehensive plan for the entire city, which should also relate the city to outlying communities. The collaboration of traffic engineers, school administrators, and other agencies are included in their work. A major part of their work is the preparation of land-use plans, which designate the functions that may be located in different segments of the city area. These decisions are customarily subject to approval by an appointed planning commission and the board of elected

1.12 The basis of many planning decisions is the land use map (top), which indicates the types of functions permitted in areas. Here, retail uses (dots), multifamily (checks), and single-family residences (stripes) are shown. Free spaces (black) caused by diagonals are challenging opportunities for open space design. Traffic maps (below) depict the number of vehicles per day along certain routes.

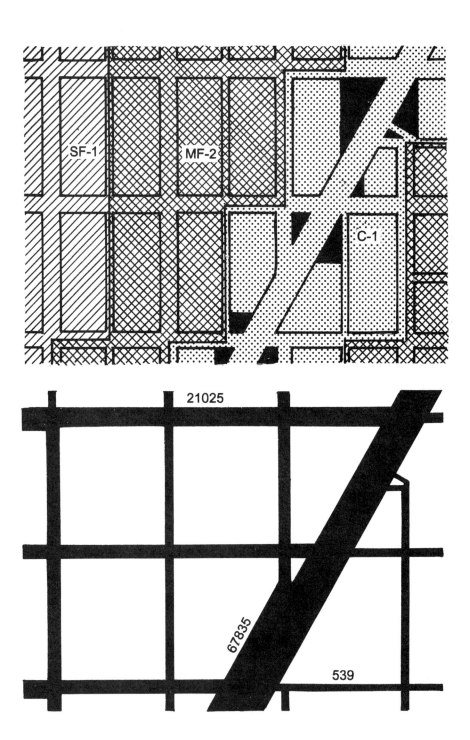

officials that constitute the ultimate decision-making body in the city government. Thus, land-use plans are an embodiment of the aspirations of the city as a whole. For each project, planners must try to foretell the ways in which it could affect the traffic patterns on nearby streets, relationships that might result from the changes they have predicted, and the appropriateness of the suggested location of the project (Fig. 1.12). Depending on the size and characteristics of the planning staff and the project, this municipal agency may undertake to have the project designed by a team within its staff, or it may work closely with professionals and consultants whose services are contracted by city authorities. The planners' participation may include expanding and adding details to the requirements for the design, going far beyond the simple terms of the charge that was provided by the governing bodies. Also, if the project is to be pursued through a partnership of the city and private developers, the financial arrangements will be proposed and negotiated by planners with the assistance of the city's fiscal officials.

Certain kinds of projects involve legal restriction beyond those put into effect by the city government. For instance, waterfront projects, which are extremely common today, are often subject to state legislation and the regulations of several branches of the federal government that are concerned in different ways with the use and protection of the country's coastline. There are always risks of delays that may result from the necessary approvals to be obtained in a process of that sort, and delays add to the time it takes to execute a project and the financial risk connected with it. In addition, questions regarding the public's right of access may arise, causing more delays. The city's elected officials and their contingent of planners are often placed in a difficult position as they try to balance developers' and investors' interests against the frequent opposition of large segments of the local population, a balance that may play off powerful influences in the community against large numbers of votes.

The types of professionals who are to be employed as primary designers or design consultants will, of course, vary according to the purpose and budget of the project. They may in fact be employed by the owners of the project (as when it is the forecourt of an office building or the surroundings of an industrial building) or by the real-estate developers (as when construction is related to the redevelopment of a slum area or the improvement of a waterfront district). When the primary design responsibility rests with professional designers engaged by private parties, their ultimate obligation is to advance the interests of their clients. However, since the goals of all participants essentially are to ensure the quality of the design (as viewed from different perspectives), this common objective can override the fundamentally adversarial relationship among city and private participants.

Architects and landscape architects typically are the professionals who prepare the overall design of the project, whether they are members of the planning agency's staff or contracted participants. Because architectural firms commonly include landscape architects and firms of landscape architects may include architects, both skills may be covered by a single contract. Other alternatives are for the city or property owner to direct that the primary firm associate with a firm providing the other discipline or to engage two firms to collaborate. All of these variations in the format of professional services depend principally on the size and nature of the 20project under consideration, as well as on the characteristics of the professional staffs of the design firms and the city's planning agency as demonstrated by projects that they have executed in the past.

As can be seen by glancing through the credits given in the endnotes for projects illustrated in the next chapter, the number and type of consultants will always vary. Among the possible sorts of consultants, both usual and occasional, are:

■ *Civil engineers*, who provide the structural design of such elements as buildings, walks, drives, and retaining walls.

■ *Lighting consultants*, who plan the general layout of lighting, design special fixtures, and specify the equipment needed to control the lighting system.

■ *Graphic designers*, who prepare a system of sign regulation that will guide visitors through the project.

■ *Sculptors*, who produce sketches and models of proposed sculptures and execute the final works.

■ *Fountain consultants*, who design water displays and specify the equipment and controls needed for them.

■ *Horticultural consultants*, who provide specialized information when highly unusual species are desired or unusual conditions must be handled.

■ *Traffic consultants*, who advise on the layout of vehicular routes within the site.

This list can be expanded for projects requiring advice or creative decisions from designers of mosaics, mechanical engineers, climatologists, and other specialists. For some designs it is desirable to obtain the services of experts in cost estimating and maintenance procedures. The number of consultants can be reduced when projects do not require those forms of specialized knowledge and skills, or when they are adequately provided within the staff of other participants in the design process.

Another sort of consultant and participant is required when the project is a form of financial collaboration between the city government and one or more real-estate developers. The notion of employing financial advantage to attract businesses is at least as old as Elizabethan England—Queen Elizabeth I often attracted skilled craftsmen from the Continent by providing advantages through protective tariffs or exemption from taxes. Today this principle is applied by offering developers such incentives as the city's participation in funding a project, exemption from taxes during the initial years of operation, and choice locations that are made available at lower cost through a city authority. The assumptions are that after the first years, the city will gain taxes from a thriving enterprise (and thus avoid increasing the taxes of its residents) and that the business will attract others and greatly increase the jobs available to residents. The validity of these assumptions is debated often among economists, but rarely among politicians. In some communities, experience has shown that such arrangements are "like selling the children to finance their college education." In other places this arrangement seems to have worked. Nevertheless, this reliance

on the use of incentives has been a complex, but effective, procedure by which an area of the city may be improved. Any project of this nature is subject to societal and economic changes that are, on the whole, unpredictable, and so undertaking such a project can be a matter of remarkable bravery.

In such projects, the city government plays roles as both the collaborator with the profit-making developers and the protector of the population. For example, government is expected to defend the interests of minority group members who might be booted out of their homes to make way for construction and those of competing businesses whose success might be affected by the newcomers. At the same time, they are expected to make sure that the developers' projects will show a profit through the future and that the undesirable district will be improved to attract the kind of customers that the developers envisage (Fig. 1.13). Because all of the fundamental relationships, in such projects, are financial, and the project is essentially speculative, the participation of lenders, investment analysts, and bankers is natural to the situation.

Lenders, from whom funding is sought, hold multiple goals, and they may have different interests in the success of projects. Because the lot and buildings involved in a project serve as collateral for loans, lenders have a fiduciary interest in the project's commercial health. Any potential for increasing the value of the property, including a favorable cash flow, market capitalization rates, and the possible reduction of the amortization period, is heralded as favorable. Even though lenders are impelled by strong profit motives when they participate in the design and execution of open spaces, many are convinced of the commercial value of good planning and design. Long-term equity investors, who may purchase the property after its completion, reap returns that are smaller than those of the developers. Because they are involved for a long period, such investors are particularly concerned about elements of the design that may lengthen the period of a project's successful leasing (Fig. 1.14).

Investors and lenders, design professionals, planners, and the public—all participants in projects to improve a city's spaces—tend to view

1.13 Local shopkeepers in this central district on the island of Maui enjoy the benefits of city investment in the esplanade along the water. For the purposes of keeping tourists for a longer period of time, the rail and bollards provide an edge that is both protective and decorative for people who stop and shop.

1.14 As the effort of a developer, Las Colinas, a master planned community near Dallas–Fort Worth International Airport, contains a number of open-space amenities to hold tenants and attract buyers of sites. Of these open spaces, the most notable are the Williams Square Plaza (W), Lake Carolyn and its waterway, canals, and perimeter monorail (dotted line), and extensive plantings. Also see Figure 2.26.

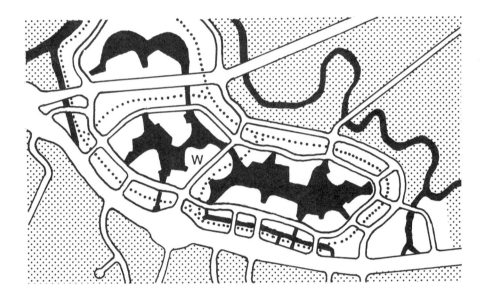

each project as distinctly different from others of a similar nature. After all, who would expect great profits or extreme pleasure from a virtual replication of dozens of other projects? At the same time, success usually can be most accurately predicted by comparisons with previously successful projects. It is in this zone between originality and experience that design takes place. If a project is to be both fresh and successful, it must have its own identity.

GEOGRAPHIC IDENTITY

At the most fundamental level, cities are identifiable in terms of their geographical setting. When their origins are coastal, there was usually a navigable river that allowed people to transport goods to and from the port facilities. Through history the relationships of town and river have often changed in meaning. New Amsterdam was established as a settlement on a point of land surrounded by river and harbor. As it grew to be New York, the populated area increased and it became an island city with connections to the mainland settlements around it. Rivers that penetrated the continent, particularly the Mississippi and the Ohio Rivers, also provided splendid sites for cities, for the United States is a squarish tract of land with much of its most productive farmlands at the center. Elevated areas at these water-related points afforded good building sites, away from the water's edge, which might be plagued with floods and fevers. For example, the town of St. Joseph, Missouri, was built on the bluff alongside the Missouri River, and stockyards occupy the low flat area beside the river (Fig. 1.15). (A computer directory of businesses indicates that in the United States there are thirteen cities with the term "bluff" in their names, and all but one are in the valleys of the Mississippi and Missouri Rivers.[25]) A broad silted and marshy delta or the confluence of rivers sometimes had sufficient economic attraction to warrant town-building at the nearest tolerable point of marshland. Other inland cities were founded on nonnavigable rivers, because railroads often were laid out in order to take advantage of the gentle gradients of the streambeds. On the prairies and other flat land, towns occur at the intersections of railroad routes or the principal roads. Waterfalls, springs, mountain passes, and other geographical features offered practical advantages, and their small communities sometimes became larger. Still more settlements were needed to provide the services needed by local inhabitants. According to the mode of transportation that dominated at a given period and the density of population, settlements rose to provide supplies, markets for crops and other products, and the advantages of government to farmers, miners, and others. At these "nodes," a settlement might be no more than a livery stable or gas station and a general store, or it might include stockyards, grain elevators, and large numbers of commercial establishments.

Each type of geographical location for an urban center contributes to its distinctive character, but there is no simple and direct relationship between the terrain and the street pattern. The preferred American system of subdividing urban land was the gridiron of streets, which made legal description of property simple. Except for informal initial occupation and sites with precipitous slopes, grids dominated street patterns, with the occasional addition of diagonal or radial avenues. On hilly locations, such as San Francisco, the application of a pattern of straight streets made each of them a veritable roller coaster with each upward journey followed by a breathtaking view and downward plunge. (The 1968 motion picture *Bullitt* is remembered for a spectacular San Francisco automobile chase based on this type of visual experience.) When the city sat on relatively flat land, the uniform pattern of the grid would be punctuated only by specific land uses. Except for the placement of a courthouse, school, or city park, such streets are experienced as a drive along the horizontal coordinate of a graph, identifying changes of population density and the character of neighborhoods: the scattered dwellings of the outskirts, succeeded by widely-spaced houses in suburban developments; closely-built bungalows of older middle-class housing, followed by the shabby fringe of a downtown area; the tubular form of streets in the business district; and then a reverse of this sequence as one leaves Flatville.

The grid, with its straight streets, is only one of the patterns employed (Fig. 1.16). In most cases, the oldest portions of the older cities still have the irregular paths of their origins, although they have been somewhat simplified through the centuries. Streets on the banks of rivers, creeks, or even small streams have meandering curvilinear paths, and often wander through shady areas of upper-class houses on large lots. Other irregularities occur at the corners along radial or diagonal boulevards and at the intersection of grids of different orientations. Geographically, the typical city is subdivided into areas of distinctively different visual characteristics. Terrain, street patterns, and the density and placement of buildings do much to inform us of the identity of each of these areas. Beyond the simple terms

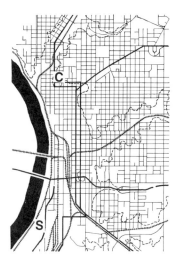

1.15 In St. Joseph, Missouri, the stockyards (S) are situated on low land alongside the Missouri River, while the courthouse (C) and most of the residences are on the bluff, almost one hundred feet above. Bold lines indicate freeways, which are elevated in low-lying areas.

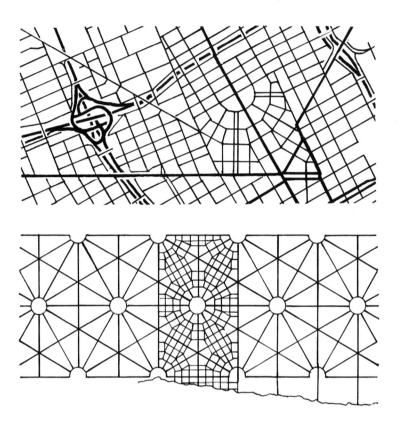

1.16 The current map of downtown Detroit (top) shows fragments of the Woodward Plan (bottom) proposed in 1807. North of this area at McNichols Road, also called Six-Mile Road, this grid shifts to one that is oriented with the cardinal points of the compass.

of North and South, East and West, every community has its vocabulary of geographical references: "up on the hill," "along the river," and "where Main goes into Elm."

Geographic identity does not have a fixed relationship to urban conditions or land use. Oceanfront land may be industrial, recreational, residential, or unused, although land of the last category is dangerously diminishing (Fig. 1.17). Extensive areas of wharfs and piers, with the concomitant sprawl of warehouses and railroad sidings, are often underutilized with present conditions. Established and expanded in the nineteenth century, such developments may acquire inappropriate functions. A 1973 study of about 250 acres of the waterfront in Portland, Maine, showed that 50 percent was occupied by railroads and 12 percent by warehousing. In other locales, parks, beaches, and resort hotels dominate much of the urban waterfront areas. Many metropolitan areas have linear extensions along the water's edge, developments that one observer of California life referred to as "Surfurbia."[26] Riverfront locations may be a major portion of a city's network of parks, for land in the floodplain (areas considered to have certain levels of susceptibility to inundation) is often considered to be unsuitable for building construction and particularly fitting as park land.

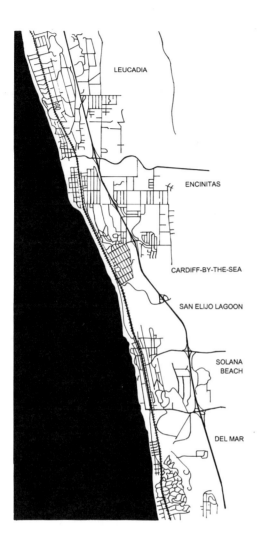

1.17 North of San Diego, the California coastline shows this chain of communities closely related to the attraction of the beaches. Settlement is continuous, although the pattern of streets changes from town to town.

Just beyond such parks, often there are residential areas with splendid views and large trees. Many settlements saw the early development of shipping and industrial fringes that acted as barriers between downtown areas and the water. In most such cities, the response of the last half-century has been to implement urban renewal projects that removed most of the remaining riverbank buildings and replaced them with plazas, parks, or commercial buildings. In the 1940s, St. Louis initiated a program of downtown improvement with the development of Gateway Arch National Park alongside the Mississippi. Farther downriver and years later, New

Orleans converted the riverside Jackson Brewery into a six-story shopping mall equipped with an atrium.[27] Steep slopes are perhaps more definite in their influences on the use of property, but modern engineering practices and the provision of parking spaces in the basements or lower stories of buildings has resulted in many projects that have overcome this handicap.

LAND USE IDENTITY

Land use has become less significant in defining the identity of an urban center. Once cities had cross-sections like those of active volcanoes, densities increasing gradually as one neared the fury of activity at the center. With the advent of automobiles and the highway system, the cross-section was altered. The steep cone spilled out of downtown, lowering the edges of the crater, and pushed toward the rural–urban fringe areas. Nodal concentrations and rings of greater housing densities or commercial development gave cities a more varied and yet predictable visual character. Shopping centers, office parks, and industrial parks appeared along the highways and ring roads, identified by an almost universal architectural language. In this Esperanto of building styles, each function is clearly identifiable, but one place is indistinguishable from others. Except for the possible presence of palm trees, it is hard to tell if one is in the North, East, South, or West. With the national passion for glass-wrapped office buildings and inward-looking shopping malls, the outside spaces between buildings provide the best—perhaps the only—identification of place.

Specific districts of a city, both residential and commercial, possess identities that are more subtly defined. Using visual indicators to interpret a district, conclusions are reached about its characteristics and those of its inhabitants.

> Interpretation, with all the risks it implies, is what we all accomplish every day when we use places. Becoming familiar with a place not only means walking through its streets, memorizing itineraries, but also going beyond the barrier of the streetscape into buildings and engaging with its people.
>
> In the meantime, however, newcomers and visitors have to give meaning to physical places as many statements about a vision of city life. They must explore the dimensions of this public image while assuming that it hides the most private aspect of the town as much as it expresses it. Any unfamiliar city is first a collage of images before the visitor constructs a more integrated mental vision to structure the physical and social characteristics of the entire place. This necessity to infer social characteristics and values from physical appearances is an active and dynamic process which sustains and makes possible a future attachment to the place.[28]

In attempting a quick interpretation of a district, the newcomer calls on a number of clues that suggest the nature of the buildings, spaces, and occupants. A residential area may have broad lawns with wide-spreading trees, multistoried houses of obvious pretension, and a number of cars exceeding those that would seem appropriate for a single family, even a very large family of adults. It can be rapidly categorized as a neighborhood of fine old homes that have been converted to apartments or offices, and discreet signs announcing the presence of law firms or charitable organizations will confirm the latter assessment. The presence or absence of tricycles and bicycles among closely-spaced bungalows will imply the age of their occupants. In different cities, the titles given these districts will be somewhat different, but age, economic level, and function are common terms to be included. In a study of Boulder, Colorado, the terms for neighborhood districts that are to be applied are: residential old town, commercial old town, new town, strip town, university town, hidden town, and nature town (Fig. 1.18).[29] Many of these appellations might be employed in analyzing other cities, but the last three are clearly denotations of the distinctive characteristics of Boulder. As when establishing land use regulations, it is useful if standardized terminology can be employed, but it is also important to recognize the distinctive areas of the city under consideration, the districts that are unique to that city.

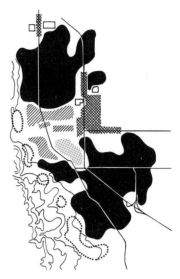

1.18 In Louis Sauer's study of the "town image" of Boulder, Colorado, areas are identified by descriptive terms peculiar to that situation: new town (black); old town (stripes); strip town (checks); university town (dots); hidden town (outlined); and nature town (outlined with dots).

DECISIONS, DISTINCTION, AND HARMONY

With cities so similar and neighborhoods so much alike, the designer must adopt methods that can assist in discovering ways in which a project, when completed, can clearly and appropriately make its identity known. If there is a decision to improve a series of spaces in the city, it may be possible to design all of them with certain details, materials, and other characteristics used throughout. (Since many such multiple projects are executed over more than a decade, changes of taste and officials can sidetrack the original plans.) This technique will afford an opportunity to execute all the projects with a visible unity of design that relates one to another throughout the city or that portion of the city in which the projects are to be located. The specific designs can differ appreciably under a plan of this sort, and savings might be possible in materials, construction, and design services if all are to be constructed at the same time or over a relatively brief period. On the other hand, such savings may not be significant and a greater variation may be considered desirable in order that each location be provided with its own distinctive design, stressing the individuality of the projects over the unity of the series. Neither decision has a clear-cut advantage over the other. The choice between them is best based on the functional similarity of the projects, their proximity to one another, and the character and size of the city. Widely-spaced projects of distinctly different functions can seldom be given an effective appearance of unity and relatedness; demographic differences among locations often call for design solutions that reflect those differences.

How does the designer determine those things that will stress the distinctive elements that will establish the identity of a project? It is easy to begin by assessing the conditions within and surrounding the site in terms of the region, the city, the district, the neighborhood, and the site itself. This analysis must include physical factors, most of which are discussed in Chapter 6. Sunlight, drainage, legal and visual boundaries, and other concrete conditions must be defined and evaluated as both limitations on the project and potential assets in design. Visible characteristics, such as the scale of visual elements and the degree of enclosure, must be evaluated. Inevitably, this consideration becomes largely a matter of making comparisons. Streets are compared with other streets in the city or other cities; the number and varieties of trees are considered; surrounding businesses are categorized according to the height and materials of their buildings. The unusual features, those that make it unlike other places, determine the identity of the site, just as they distinguish one person from other people. Where an area has been cleared of buildings, the site may have only the identity of its surroundings, being itself "faceless."

For instance, if the site or the neighborhood in which a small park is to be situated has the most pronounced slopes in the city, the design team could choose to:

■ emphasize the fact by accentuating dramatic changes of level throughout the project,

■ contrast with the surroundings by making the park into one or more broad level areas, accomplishing drastic changes of level at the perimeter,

■ combine the two aspects with large flat areas having sharp slopes between, or

■ harmonize with the surroundings by maintaining a terrain much like that of the whole neighborhood.

Similar choices can be available for planting, paving materials, and the other decisions that will determine the appearance of a space and the degree to which it will declare its identity. In some circumstances, certain choices will not be feasible. In a downtown vestpocket park it will probably be impossible to harmonize with the scale of surrounding buildings; and the triangular gore remaining at a street intersection may be so small that it cannot strongly contrast with the sidewalks and streets around it by providing extensive planting.

There is no effective formula or logic that can guide a design team's selection among such alternatives. Any of the choices listed above has the potential to result in a solution that would have its own individuality as a single project or one of a series. There is no right or wrong choice. (The best explanation of this design situation is perhaps to be found in the words of an old jazz song, "It Ain't What You Do, It's the Way What You Do It.") Each of the choices, if executed with sound design judgment, can possibly lead to the creation of a place that embodies a distinctive conceptual spirit. To accomplish this objective, every decision should be based on affirmative answers to two questions:

■ Is the choice consistent with the desired overall effect of the project?

■ Is the choice consistent with the other choices made?

These questions require unity of the design in aspects that include functional, visual, and psychological considerations, as well as other factors that may be appropriate to the particular project. This consistency should not be interpreted as mere similarity, for the dissimilar elements and their contrasts could well be a basis for the design of a project. For instance, a park could provide a background of rustic naturalism, against which benches, trash receptacles, and light standards of gleaming modernity might be contrasted. (New York City's Paley Park which is discussed in detail in Chapter Two, exploits this sort of contrast between the shell of the park and its furniture.) Or a starkly stylized plaza might focus attention on a single area of a naturalistic detail. (Williams Square in Dallas, Texas, also discussed in the next chapter, contrasts a severely geometric plaza with realistic sculptures of horses.) Contrast, whether within the project or between the project and its setting, may provide the visual stimulus that can clearly declare the identity of a design as it will be perceived by visitors. In the past, many other terms have been used to describe this quality of individuality. "Character" has often been used, particularly with reference to the exteriors of buildings; "mood" is sometimes applied to the design of interiors; "effect" has always had a connotation of the theatrical and artificial. The word "identity" has distinct advantages when speaking of open spaces, streets, and spaces between buildings, because it encompasses the notion of a specific location and the unique relationship between the place and its context (Fig. 1.19).

Determining the identity desired for the design of a project must include a great variety of considerations. Each of them must be considered in every aspect that seems to apply. (Some of those aspects have been mentioned already, while others will be discussed in later chapters.) Common considerations are:

■ *Function* categorizes the activities that are to take place on the site, the assumed participants, and the times at which the activities probably will occur. (The factors are stated in terms of likelihood, because usually we are dealing with spontaneous responses to the opportunities provided by the project, and they will vary according to moment and mood.) As the design study progresses, functions will be defined in greater detail and the necessary provisions and equipment will be included.

■ *Location* starts to be defined as a point on a map, but terrain, climate, and the qualities of the context are included. The separateness of location and edge conditions are sometimes predetermined, but there may be choices between "soft-edged" designs in which the space extends into its surroundings or "hard-edged" schemes in which fences and gates maintain physical or visual separation.

■ *Users* must be defined, not only in demographic terms, but also according to their relationship to the project. (Is it residents of the project's

1.19 Sometimes there is individual identity and character to the setting, while at other times it is the specific identity of the project. Scattered throughout America, these examples are from Florida (upper left), Texas (upper right), New Mexico (lower left), Ohio (lower right).

neighborhood or does the definition include all citizens of the city who may pass by?) Some users may participate fully in the experience of the space, but others may only observe it as a pleasing landmark along their commuting routes.

■ *Ambience*, probably the most significant factor as one approaches the design phase, is the spirit that is desired. (More than one mood may be desired). Whether peaceful or flamboyant, a determination of the psychological aura must be agreed on by the design team and should be characterized in words or analogies. Because it is not quantifiable and deals with emotional responses, this part of the search for project identity is always most difficult. It goes far beyond agreeing upon single-word descriptions. "Peaceful," "monumental," and "exciting" each have several different definitions in dictionaries, and probably have even more in the minds of the members of a design team.

For any specific project, a list of topics can be prepared, fitting the particular case much better than the above list. But, the last category, "ambience," is inescapable. It is the characteristic that will be most remembered after the design has been executed and used, and it establishes the requirement that must be most firmly satisfied as design decisions are made. No shape should be laid out, no selection made without the designers being confident that their decision is consistent with the project's identity as determined by their preliminary discussions and supportive of the ambience that they believe will be appropriate.

Stylistic determinations follow the clarification of identity. The shapes of things and the geometry of their placement might be fundamentally classical, whether historically accurate or a modern interpretation. Or, at the other extreme, they might be modern and innovative. The layout could be precise and geometric or casual and naturalistically irregular. Certainly, there are sometimes comparatively rigid restrictions on stylistic choices. Rarely would a space designed to be used by teenagers venture into medieval forms, Colonial motifs, or any other historical styles. At the same time, it must be generally recognized that the identity of many projects can be expressed equally well by any one of a variety of stylistic choices. If they were to be successful, each would need to respond effectively to those practical factors that have been identified and to embody those elements of character and spirit that have been decided on as fitting, that have been determined to represent the true identity of the place.[30]

ENDNOTES

1. Ralph B. Taylor, *Human Territorial Functioning* (Cambridge: Cambridge University Press, 1988), 5–8.

2. David Canter, *The Psychology of Place* (New York: St. Martin's Press, 1977), 128–156.

3. Peter Bosselmann, "Experiencing Downtown Streets in San Francisco," *Public Streets for Public Use*, ed. Anne Vernez Moudon (New York: Columbia University Press, 1991), 203–220.

4. Richard Hedman with Andrew Jaszewski, *Fundamentals of Urban Design* (Chicago: Planners Press, 1984), 3–7.

5. Robert Venturi, Denise Scott Brown, and Stephen Izenour, *Learning From Las Vegas* (Cambridge, MA: MIT Press, 1972).

6. Charles E. Lindblom, "The Science of Muddling Through," *Public Administration Review* (Spring 1959):79–88.

7. Peter L. Berger and Thomas Luckmann, *The Social Construction of Reality* (Garden City, NY: Anchor Books, 1967), 173–180.

8. Henry Gleitman, *Basic Psychology* (New York: W.W. Norton, 1981), 334.

9. David Berry, "Preservation of Open Space and the Concept of Value," *American Journal of Economics and Sociology* (April 1976):113–124.

10. Kevin Lynch, *The Image of the City* (Cambridge, MA: MIT Press, 1960), 74–76.

11. "Felt Says Trees Can Make A City," *New York Times*, June 28, 1960, 33.

12. Bernard J. Frieden and Lynne B. Sagalyn, *Downtown, Inc: How America Rebuilds Cities* (Cambridge, MA: MIT Press, 1990), 39–43, 140–141.

13. Frieden and Sagalyn, *Downtown*, 108–109.

14. Interview with Craig A. Amundsen, BRW Planning. Minneapolis. March 14, 1993.

15. Interview with Dr. Donald C. Royse, Director, Downtown St. Louis Development Authority. March 11, 1993.

16. Interview with Donald Turner, Director of Mall Operations, Downtown Denver Partnership, Inc., December 14, 1992.

17. Sandra Hasegawa and Steve Elliott, "Public Spaces By Private Enterprise (Projects in Seattle, Washington)," *Urban Land* (May 1983):12–15.

18. William S. Hendon, "The Park As A Determinant of Property Values," *American Journal of Economics and Society* (July 1971):289–300; and William S. Hendon, "Park Service Areas and Residential Property Values," *American Journal of Economics and Society* (April 1974):175–183.

19. Mike E. Miles and others, *Real Estate Development Principles and Processes* (Washington D.C.: Urban Land Institute, 1991), 12–22.

20. Professor H. Douglas Sessoms, quoted in "Survey Hears Americans Declare Love for Parks," *New York Times*, August 26, 1992, B1.

21. Geoffrey Godbey, Alan Graefe, and Stephen James, "The Use and Benefits of Local Government Recreation and Park Services—A Nationwide Study of the Perceptions of the American Public," *Parks and Recreation* (not published yet).

22. Sessoms, "Survey,"*New York Times.*

23. Horace *Satires.* 2. 6. 1.

24. Hugh Newell Jacobsen, quoted in Barbara Gamarekian, "Two Washingtonians with a Capital W," *New York Times*, May 31, 1984, B8.

25. *Company Profiles 1992.* Information Access Company (computer data base).

26. Reyner Banham, *Los Angeles: The Architecture of Four Ecologies* (New York: Penguin Press, 1971), 37.

27. William Severini Dowinski, *The Malling of America: An Inside Look at the Great Consumer Paradise* (New York: William Morrow and Company, Inc., 1985), 306.

28. Louis Sauer, "Streetscapes in an American City," *Architecture et Comportement/Architecture and Behavior* (December 1990):357–358.

29. Sauer, "Streetscapes," 361–370.

30. Fritz Steele, *The Sense of Place* (Boston: CBI Publishing Company, 1981).

2

PROJECTS:

Projects that succeeded; parks and plazas, Paley Park, Bryant Park, Dearborn Street; monumental places, Vietnam Veterans' Memorial, Williams Square; festive attractions, Inner Harbor, Paseo del Rio; streets, 16th Street Mall, Nicollet Mall; traffic spaces, Gore Park; summary, project possibilities.

Our image of a city is structured from memories of its different parts. In this way, the aggregate of the qualities of spaces are important in creating civic pride, satisfying social needs, and affecting economic behavior. Residents and visitors alike rely on the restorative powers of parks and plazas, which provide proud identity for neighborhoods, city districts, and the city as a whole. How a city looks can also definitely retard or promote investors' interest in constructing new buildings and businesses. And images of the American city arise from a series of open spaces and building projects, executed over a long period of time. Independent spatial images are components that change and can be changed for the better. By deciding upon one or a series of independent projects, planners, developers, city officials, or residents can effectively change city images to better promote social and economic goals.

As new projects are promoted, planned, designed, and constructed, they may vary from adopting a tree-planting program for principal streets to building an impressive public plaza in front of City Hall. In these and other cases that might fall between them in scope, teams become responsible for conceptualizing the need for the project, and team members interact to produce the design. In small towns only one project may be undertaken per year, while in larger cities project activities may be continuous. Some cities always have a number of project teams at work, so their activities will produce a flow of new spaces and places. Viewed as projects produced by project teams, spaces and places may be stylized, based on traditions and conditions, or blend or contrast with buildings. Many of these approaches work.

Urban spaces in America today exhibit a variety of design attitudes. The most formal situations, such as the approaches to major governmental buildings, are still given symmetrical, even classical, treatments in most cases, and many spaces that are adjacent to commercial buildings clearly display reflections of European traditions. In other projects, visible influences of the environmental concerns of our own period may be found, or native plants may be used, with attention paid to local climate conditions. Some spaces have been vigorously overdesigned, with gewgaws and gimmicks that will soon be the embarrassing reminders of yesterday's stylistic enthusiasms. Elements of a whimsical spirit and spellbinding uses of shapes and color may contrast or harmonize with their surroundings. Other spaces display a disarming simplicity that suggest that they should always have been there and will long remain attractive.

It is difficult to formulate precise designations for the styles in which today's spaces are being designed. The variety of uses and users that must be considered in designing open places today makes it difficult for designers to follow the dictates of a stylistic choice so rigidly that the commitment to a certain style is followed strictly and accurately. Architectural styles, or the briefer influences that may be thought as fads or fashions, and their changes, are strong influences on the design characteristics of urban spaces. Buildings comprise the settings for many designed spaces, and their design or even construction customarily precedes the development of the spaces between or around them. Therefore, a relationship of esthetic attitudes in the two arts is prevalent where the built surroundings are closely related to the open space. Where the hard forms of all buildings do not play so important a role, the designers of spaces may feel greater freedom. These conditions, however, do not eliminate possibilities of contrasting their characteristics, such as surrounding classical formality with romantic naturalistic gardens or placing a strict geometry amid irregularities.

The architectural styles are primarily identified by visible and precise forms that are repeated and related one to another. Such earmarks are easily identified in handiwork executed in wood or masonry. In the fixed, hard materials and forms employed in the design of spaces, styles are also identifiable, but in rough stone and growing plants and flowing water the necessary distinctions become more difficult. Clipped hedges and slender poplars may have shapes that predictably follow anticipated patterns, but most shrubs and trees through time declare their independence of precise shapes. Through recent history, many projects for the design of urban places have been required to harmonize or contrast with buildings and other surroundings that display a variety of styles. Indeed, it is not uncommon that a project adjoin thoroughly modern transportation structures, commercial buildings of the late nineteenth century, and some facades that were executed in the 1920s. In such situations, stylistic absolutism is understandably rare.

The last decades have seen a degree of revival of historicism in architecture, graphic design, and other fields that establish the visual milieu of our cities. Historicism in art is an eclectic point of view that derives its forms from the full range of the past, without espousing a single period of history or demanding accurate replication in the use of historical forms. A relatively brief period in which Postmodernism reigned among the avant-garde has been followed by a variety of attitudes, ranging from strict obedience to historical precedents to the combative defiance of all precedents. The results, in some hands, have been ludicrous. Critics and practitioners have used expressions such as "Disneyfication" for the amusement-park mood, "yuppie Baroque" for the conglomeration of classical devices, and "Gunsmoke" for the imitation of the sets of Western movies. The residential fashions exhibited in developer's housing projects have been dubbed with captions such as "MacMansion," "Mount Vermin," and "ranch-burger" to denote the influences of rank commercialism on the design of the houses. There are even "themes" for entire towns, such as "Colonial," "antebellum," "riverboat," "Neo-Traditional," "Spanish," and "Wild West."

At the same time, the broad variety of design characteristics has benefitted from an increased concern about the users of open spaces. Public places are now more consciously organized to provide personal enjoyment for the people who will visit them and to accommodate their activities. Social needs and psychological responses have become as much a part of design decision-making as the physical conditions and visual characteristics of spaces. The recognized quality of environments now is judged not only on the basis of their influence on people when they actually are in the environments, but also on the long-term effects of those environments on people's sociological conditions and ecological well-being. Bombarded by millions of images, we are accustomed to profusion and variety; our notions of beauty and pleasure have become more a matter of here-and-now than of consistency.

Because so many of the decisions regarding public places are made in the arena of civic affairs, all good designs must withstand the vicissitudes of public discussion both before and after they are executed. This critical analysis requires that the project be clearly and effectively presented to authorities and the public. And, in the long run, a design team's choices must be soundly based, for open discussion has a way of exposing affectations and embarrassing stylistic pretensions. The basic concept should be sufficiently sound to survive just criticism and the compromises that are often necessary and sometimes beneficial. Designs for public places must be tested on the bases of esthetics, politics, finance, and public policy. All of these factors are as much a part of their description as any listing of dimensions, materials, and shapes.

The stories of a series of public places follow. They will summarize the events and ideas that led to successful designs of different types that were executed in different styles.

PROJECTS THAT SUCCEEDED

The projects described below are examples of the many public places and open spaces that merit attention, because of the visual qualities they illustrate, the actions of which they are the results, and the attitudes that they demonstrate. Several are now the products of improvements and alterations that have been made to original layouts built decades before. The styles vary, and this variety was an intention in selecting the projects.

Parks and Plazas

Too often in today's cities we feel the poignant truth of the song that says, "They paved paradise/And put up a parking lot."[1] But parking lots, vacant lots, and the other sadly neglected spaces in cities can be rescued. The three projects that follow show ways in which places of very different character have been developed for public use. In the first case a decrepit building was razed to make a midtown place for conversation, relaxation, and the reduction of stress. In the second case an existing park that had become a hangout for pushers and prostitutes was rescued and prepared for use once again by the general public. In the third case the construction of large buildings, both governmental and commercial, led to the provision of large plazas in the midst of a dense downtown area. All three are distinguished by their contrast with their surroundings, fulfilling the primary role of parks: providing places where we can escape from the pressures around us.

Paley Park, New York City: The words "vest-pocket park" have come to be the accepted term for small parks in densely built locations, occupying interstitial areas between buildings and bounded by sidewalks and the walls of existing buildings. Too often such spaces are consigned to interim use as parking lots, but present-day regulations often permit the owners of such parcels of land—not particularly useful or profitable in terms of modern real-estate development—to gain permission to exploit large adjacent parcels more profitably by contributing small areas for use as open space. The classic vest-pocket park is Paley Park in New York on 53rd Street just east of Fifth Avenue (Fig. 2.1).[2] The land (three-quarters of the total cost) and construction funds were provided by William S. Paley, chairman of the board of the Columbia Broadcasting System, as a memorial to his father, who had died a few years earlier. Paley's gift not only included the land and park, but also took care of removing the previous structure and establishing the Greenpark Foundation to provide funds for maintenance of the park. The park opened in May 1967, a 42-feet-by-100-feet space where a famous nightclub of earlier decades had once stood (Fig. 2.2).[3]

A few years before, the park's landscape architects, Robert Zion and Harold Breen, had displayed a similar design in an exhibition, "New Parks for New York," sponsored by the Architectural League of New York and the Park Association of New York. In the catalog of that exhibition, Zion and Breen described their design as "a room, with walls, floors, and ceiling [the branches of trees]."[4] Other features, such as the noise-masking fountain, were included in the description, but the most important innovation of Paley Park was the belief that a park could be less than the several acres that had traditionally been considered the minimum size.

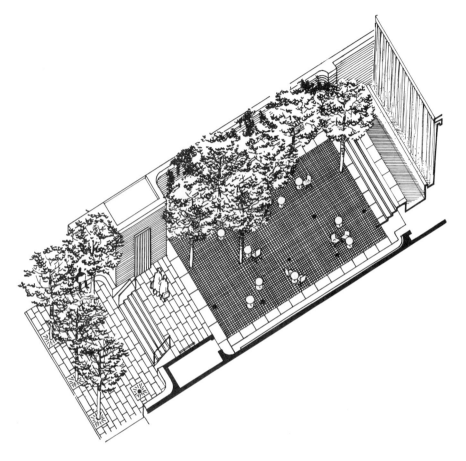

2.1 Highrise buildings and narrow streets surround Paley Park in New York City. Paving textures are used to define major functional divisions of the space, and the entrance from the narrow city sidewalk is interrupted by a change in paving and a small cluster of trees.

The most striking aspect of Paley Park is the fact that it is not striking in its design. Restraint is its most admirable quality. At the early presentations of the design to the client, simplifying alterations were made: a rigid pattern of trees was made more casual; the side walls were changed from a series of arched recesses containing mirrored surfaces to simple planes of gray brick that were to be covered with vines; and a playfully designed refreshment kiosk was removed and those services placed in a discreet

2.2 Unlike many parks, the intimacy of Paley Park in New York City encourages conversation. The sound of street traffic is masked by the sound of the fountain. (Photo by Trev Albright)

2.3 The side walls of Paley Park are covered with vines and a continuous bench is provided at the base of each side wall. Moveable chairs and tables allow visitors to cluster in groups. (Photo by Trev Albright)

location at the park entrance. The rear wall of the space is occupied by a gushing fountain of water falling. On a "floor" of granite blocks are placed white pedestal tables and white chairs—there are no park benches, only seats along the sidewalls. It is the overall sophisticated restraint of the place that has attracted attention. Eschewing the temptation to "knock their eyes out" or to be "amusing," it has ironically come to do just that, in a manner that is truly urbane (Fig. 2.3).

In 1963 the Parks Department divided the city into seventy-four "defined communities" and discovered that nine of those subdivisions contained more than 53 percent of the recreational acreage of the entire city.[5] The Parks Commissioner understandably hailed the vest-pocket park as a device that could contribute to correcting this imbalance speedily. Robert Moses, a strong force in city government and previously Parks Commissioner for twenty-six years, thereupon published his views that these were "ideas that have been tried and discarded, impractical suggestions, and some projects that would be good if money could be found to finance them,"[6] a type of argument frequent in City Halls. In 1992, twenty-five years after Paley Park opened, New York City had 1547 park properties with 350 squares, triangles, and malls. Of them, there were 160 spaces, each under three acres, classified as malls or parks and so possibly qualifying to be designated as vest-pocket parks.[7] Few have been as successful as the first was, but history has proved that no minimum size can be set for open spaces that are meaningful in city life.

Bryant Park, New York City: The southwest corner at the intersection of Fifth Avenue and 42nd Street in New York City is occupied by the New York Public Library, a center of scholarship in the United States. The site has known many uses—it was once a reservoir, once a potter's field, and in the middle of the nineteenth century it served as the site of the first New York World's Fair. The library itself is an outstanding example of the Beaux-Arts style, the neoclassicism that was taught in Paris and popular around the world when it was built. Since the 1880s, the seven acres behind the Library have been designated as a park, William Cullen Bryant Park, named for the famed American poet and coeditor of the *New York Evening Post*. In the spring of 1992, the park was reopened, an event about which many New Yorkers were at the same time enthusiastic and dubious.[8] They were dubious because for many years before it was closed in 1988, Bryant Park had been recognized as the realm of derelicts and drug dealers. At that time occupants of the park were 70 to 80 percent male, which was taken as an unfavorable indicator of its safety.

The new park began with the 1980 formation of a private group, the Bryant Park Restoration Corporation.[9] Fund-raising was difficult, because the most likely contributors already had been asked to assist in the library's project, the construction of an underground storage addition with 84 miles of shelving beneath much of the park area. The restoration of the park was delayed while a pit thirty-two feet deep was dug for the addition—the top of the construction was to be only 2 feet below the park's lawn area. Restoration cost almost $9 million, with two-thirds coming from city funds and the remainder from private sources. Maintenance has been estimated at $1.2 million per year. Of that, 71 percent has been pledged by an organization of the neighborhood's businesses, and the rest will come from the city and revenues of the concessions in the park.

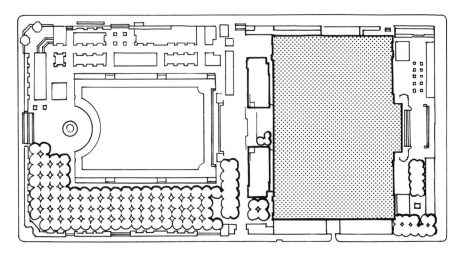

2.4 Bryant Park adjoins the New York Public Library on its west side. Dining facilities have been added along the library wall, and the number of entrances to the park has been increased. The grade level of the park is above street level on the north side, and provisions have been made to increase visibility through the park walls. Ground level is shown in the upper half of the site plan, and the tree cover is shown in the lower. Ground level and tree cover actually are the same in both halves.

The park remains largely the 1930s design by Gilmore D. Clarke, landscape architect, and Aymar Embury II, architect, a spacious lawn surrounded by a shady frame of trees. Restoration of the park and its adaptation to present-day urban conditions was undertaken by Hanna/Olin Ltd., landscape architect, and Hardy Holzman Pfeiffer, architects (Fig. 2.4). The central lawn, edged on two sides by long bands of colorful perennials, occupies a bit more than half the park area, and it is surrounded by rows of trees shading paving and moveable chairs. Those two elements, lawn and paving under a uniform pattern of trees, occupy most of the area, and the open central space is contrasted with the vertical plane of the building facade. The restaurant is along the rear wall of the library, a location that became more difficult when the New York Landmarks Commission and Art Commission insisted that the glass and iron structure of the restaurant be made less prominent and obscure less of the library (Fig. 2.5).[10]

Because the park is above the level of the street, a retaining wall and an existing balustrade (both kept from the 1930s construction) restrict the view from the street into the park. Openings were made in the balustrade and ten wide entrances were provided. Further precautions were taken by eliminating the hedges and shrubs that limited visibility, a method that had proved successful in the renovation of two other city parks (Fig. 2.6). Bryant Park is patrolled by a private security force, and although the park closes at dusk, a floodlight was placed on the forty-fifth floor of an adjoining building.

2.5 Clearly, Bryant Park provides open-space relief to the pattern of grid streets in Manhattan. The park is a long rectangle, and the empty center lawn contrasts with the intimacy of the corners and the places along the sides. (Photo by Trev Albright)

2.6 The directional pattern of the walkways act as a frame to the central open space of Bryant Park in New York City. In contrast with the lawn, seating is provided under the trees, either by benches or by moveable chairs. (Photo by Trev Albright)

Dearborn Street, Chicago: The Loop, the downtown area of Chicago, still has a scattering of buildings that were part of the late-nineteenth-century development of the skyscraper, and among them are also the remnants of other boom periods that the city has experienced. Along Dearborn Street, this mixture includes many tall buildings that exemplify the skyscraper style that predominated around the middle of the 20th century, and three plazas that epitomize the ideas of that period. At that time—and today, for many leading designers—it was believed that a very tall building should be accompanied by a compensating large open space. (By way of contrast, a recent writer complimented a new building in Chicago that rises directly from the property lines: "It's a reminder that cities are made up first of all of streets, and that the prime function of urban buildings is to define these streets."[11]) Within the open plazas were placed pools, low walls, and other simple elements, according to a sparse geometry of painterly quality.

Between Clark and Dearborn Streets, from Randolph Street to Jackson Boulevard, there are five city blocks, three of them occupied by large buildings with related plazas and two of them fully built between the plazas (Fig. 2.7). All three plazas and the buildings related to them were constructed during a period of little more than a decade (completion dates: 1964–1975), a period in which the architectural style of Mies van der Rohe,

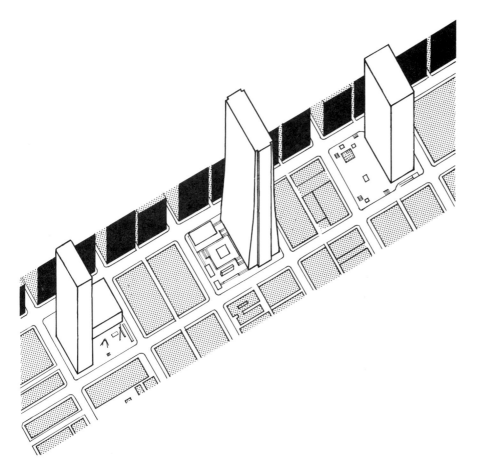

2.7 The three plazas along Chicago's Dearborn Street—the Civic Center (top), the First National Bank (center), and the Federal Center (bottom)—function as shortcuts and building entrances. The formality of the Civic Center allows limited resting places and space for socialization as contrasted with the First National Bank. These plazas were meant to compensate for the lack of open space downtown; however, another point of view would favor continuous building facades to reinforce linear street space.

2.8 The last of the three plazas to be constructed, the Federal Center, has more of its ground area occupied by buildings. A requisite flagpole and an Alexander Calder sculpture occupy the space. (Photo by Robert B. Dean)

who lived and taught in Chicago, dominated in the United States and much of the world. From south to north, the functions that occupy these three blocks are:

■ Federal Center, made up of an office building, a post office, and the federal courthouse that is on the other side of Dearborn Street (Fig. 2.8).[12]

■ First National Bank of Chicago, a single building of sixty stories, housing the banking spaces (Illinois law did not permit branch banks) and rental office areas (Fig. 2.9).[13,14]

■ Civic (Richard J. Daley) Center, a municipal office and court building of about the same height (Fig. 2.10).[15]

All three buildings were designed as large simple rectangular shapes (the bank building tapers toward the top) with curtain wall patterns that combined large areas of glass with the grid of the structural framework. All of them also employed a common architectural device of that time—each one had recessed glass walls on the ground floor that let the plaza paving visibly extend into the lobby area of the building, producing greater spatial continuity.

The designs of the three plazas are quite different, although they have great stylistic similarities. There are flagpoles, fountains, walls, and trees, although the planting never overcomes the fundamental openness of all the plazas. The most eye-catching elements are the works of art displayed on the plazas. In the center of the Federal Center Plaza a steel sculpture by Alexander Calder stands, bright red and fifty-three feet high. The First

2.9 The First National Bank Plaza in Chicago employs level changes to develop a more active atmosphere. Plants and trees are located at the perimeter and major area divisions. (Photo by Robert B. Dean)

2.10 The Civic Center plaza in Chicago is an open design with a monumental sculpture by Pablo Picasso. At the left there is a large square pool in which a pattern of fountain jets are operated at variable pressures. (Photo by Robert B. Dean)

National Bank's two-level plaza includes a large pool and fountain, more planting than is to be found in the other plazas, and a free-standing mosaic wall by Marc Chagall, seventy feet long and fourteen feet high. Not to be outdone, the Civic Center Plaza has flags, a fountain, and a Picasso sculpture, again around fifty feet high.

There have been complaints about the openness of the plazas, a hazard in windy Chicago, and about their great dimensions.[16] Other opinions have queried the possibility of achieving personal scale, considering the size of the building. Nevertheless, the visitor cannot help but be impressed by walking from plaza to plaza, as though walking from gallery to gallery in an art museum. The overpowering size may be suitable for a city famed for its traditions of boosterism.

Monumental Places

The design of memorial spaces is no longer merely a matter of situating a pedestal, placing the appropriate statue upon it, and perhaps planning a plaza around it. For one thing, in recent times fewer monuments have been built to honor individuals, and more have memorialized events. After World Wars I and II, in the United States there was an inclination for communities to construct functional memorials, a solution that resulted in Memorial Halls and Veterans Buildings. The military actions of later years have most frequently been subjects of design competitions in which architects and sculptors have been invited to submit their designs for consideration. This eminently logical method of selection has also led to frequent imbroglios in which the wisdom of the committee's selection is debated and alterations and additions to the designs have been recommended and often executed.

Monuments of a different spirit are being erected in many places. Near the Vienna Opera House roughly carved black blocks of basalt tower over the bronze figure of an old bearded man who kneels on the paving, scrubbing it with a brush as Jews were forced to do by the Nazis.[17] There have been many proposals to move this monument to less prominent locations, so that tourists and citizens of the city need not be so often reminded of Austria's anti-semitic history. Its narrative qualities too clearly and too uncomfortably recall shameful incidents of the past—they do not celebrate a triumph.

Vietnam Veterans' Memorial, Washington, D.C.: After the end of the Vietnam War, a group of veterans began soliciting funds for the construction of a memorial to those who had died in the highly controversial engagement. By the summer of 1980 legislation had been signed that set aside two acres of land northeast of the Lincoln Memorial for that purpose. All funds for construction of the memorial were obtained from the public—individuals and organizations—by a network of volunteers, including the Gold Star Mothers who took care of most mailings. A design competition was conducted, and almost a year after the site was obtained the competition jury selected a winning design. The design, submitted by a Yale student of architecture, Maya Lin, consisted of two walls, sinking into the lawn and bearing the names of all who had died (Fig. 2.11). Inclusion of the names, more than 57,000, had been the only significant requirement of the competition, and in the winning design they were to be placed on polished black stone walls, each more than 200 feet long, that form a wide angle, one pointing toward the Washington Monument, the other toward the Lincoln Memorial. Between the walls, the lawn slopes gently downward until each wall reaches a height of ten feet at the angle where the two meet.

In the six months after the announcement and display of the winning design, objections to the design mounted and became organized. Members of Congress were running for reelection, so some of them postured and blathered about the design; veterans and military brass were irate; and the Texas billionaire who had funded the competition issued threats. There were also supporters—the commander of the American Legion, an organization of veterans, pledged $1 million from the organization and wrote that the design was "a dignified and eloquent tribute."[18] At a hearing held by Washington's Fine Arts Commission (which patiently mediated the bickering), the opposition to the design presented their demands: (1) adding a flagpole, (2) including a dedicatory inscription, (3) using white granite instead of black, and (4) moving the walls above ground (Fig. 2.12).[19] At one meeting the color of the granite was opposed so strongly ("a black ditch in the ground") that an African-American brigadier general rose to say, "I am sick and tired of [your] calling black a color of shame."[20] As debate continued, the addition of a statue of a single soldier was proposed. (It was later enlarged to include three soldiers.) Considerable argument was involved with the placement of the elements to be added, the opponents of the memorial design insisting that the flagpole should be right at the angle

2.11 The plan of the Vietnam Veterans Memorial in Washington, DC, is a simple angle, with one line pointed toward the Washington Monument, the other toward the Lincoln Memorial. Although it has often been suggested that the shape of the plan is a "V" for Vietnam, this symbolism has been denied by the designer. (Courtesy of National Park Service, U.S. Department of the Interior)

2.12 The reflective surfaces of the wall superimposes the visitor's face on the names of the dead. In spite of objections made at the time the design was proposed, the reflected faces have become indelibly imprinted in the minds of Americans. (Courtesy of National Park Services, U.S. Department of the Interior)

of the two walls and the statue in the space between them. If the entire list of changes had been accepted, the character of the memorial would have been drastically altered. It would have been, one writer said, "the esthetic equivalent of turning the Washington Monument into a black sphere."[21] All in all, it was a period of acrimonius argument, an argument of which none of the participants should be proud.

The wall was dedicated in the fall of 1982, and the statue was dedicated two years later.[22] The statue and flagpole were placed in positions somewhat independent of the wall covered with names. As in the original design, the wall was made of black granite—a stone from India was found to provide the desired high reflectivity after it was polished. Reflections of visitors float dimly behind the sand-blasted names, and this image is the one so often conveyed by the media. In spite of all the objections made during its development, the Vietnam Veterans' Memorial, the image of sad faces gazing at the wall and fingers gently touching the letters, has become the undeniable explanation and justification of the original prize-winning design. As the originator of the project stated, "You don't set out and build a national shrine. It becomes one."[23]

Williams Square, Las Colinas, Dallas-Fort Worth, Texas: In 1973 a plan was prepared for the development of a 12,000-acre tract of ranch land in Irving, Texas, a suburb near the Dallas/Fort Worth International Airport. The site included 1,500 acres that the owner had bought almost a half-century before as a cattle ranch and had named "El Ranchito de las Colinas (The Little Ranch of the Hills)."[24] With the name shortened to Las Colinas, by 1991 the development provided hundreds of single-family homes, apartments for about 7,300 people, office space for more than 900 companies, corporate offices and headquarters, over 1,300 hotel rooms, and over 155 restaurants and commercial establishments. Corporations have moved their headquarters there, because operating costs are comparatively low and headquarters can be built as office campuses, occupying 100 acres or more.

In order to pay for the construction and maintenance of the open space, landscaped areas, canals, and plazas, building owners pay special assessments to a modified municipal utilities district. These revenues are used for both existing and new open space projects.[25]

2.13 In the Las Colinas office center, Williams Square (Dallas–Fort Worth), the three towers are connected at ground level by inside and outside corridors around three sides of the plaza. These spaces contrast with the sculpture and the expanse of paving. The paving is the same granite as the facades of the buildings, increasing the feeling of enclosure. Office workers rarely shortcut through the plaza. (Courtesy of Dallas County Utility and Reclamation District)

A focal point of Las Colinas is Williams Square, which was to be defined by a 26-story office tower, fronting on one of the development's 55 artificial lakes and on the square; two fourteen-story buildings at the sides; and a hotel (never constructed) across the street on the fourth side of the rectangle (Fig. 2.13). At the sides there are rows of trees with benches beneath them; in the center there is a square paved with white and pink granite of varying surface textures, a pool, and bronze statues of running horses.[26] At the hooves of the animals, fountains spray splashes of water that are lighted from beneath at night (Fig. 2.14).

Since Williams Square was completed, the statues of the mustangs have steadily attracted visitors. The setting is almost starkly simple. The surrounding forms of the buildings are simple and static. From a distance, the horses seem small within the sweep of the plaza; near at hand, they prove to be half again life-size, powerful and impressive. But the statues are vigorously dynamic, their portrayal of movement providing contrast and excitement. The image, that of a group of wild horses racing through a stream, is inescapably related to the history of the entire region and its folklore. Although the space and the sculpture do not commemorate a specific time or incident, it stirs recollections of the past in much the same manner as do more traditional monuments.

It is apparent that the meaning of monumental spaces is changing or has advanced to a multiplicity of types of expression. The many memorials

2.14 This plaza has a series of viewpoints toward the horses from all sides. The static simplicity of the plaza contrasts with the dynamics of the sculpture. (Courtesy of Dallas County Utility and Reclamation District)

recalling the Holocaust and wars display nothing resembling the triumphant joy of nineteenth-century monuments. Instead, they recall the individual's experience, people not nations.

Festive Attractions

In the first half of the twentieth century waterfront facilities in American port cities were overwhelmed by the increase of shipping activity. In most cases new facilities with up-to-date buildings and equipment were provided farther from the center of the cities. The decline of passenger travel on the nation's railroads in recent decades has led to the abandonment of railroad stations as well as train sheds. Some of these relics of the story of transportation in America were cleared away, others have remained. The romantic aura of such spaces—where once workmen, draft animals, and passengers moved about in a noisy bustling environment—has encouraged their development as attractions for tourists, shoppers, office workers, and townspeople on an outing. In some cases new buildings have been constructed and filled with shops and restaurants of a great variety of price levels. In other cases the original buildings remain with the historical qualities of the locale and its informality carefully protected. The festive environment of such places has been useful to establish once again the nighttime activity that we expect downtown. Tourists and conventioneers provide much of the activity, but local residents also go there for special occasions that call for a festive atmosphere.

Inner Harbor, Baltimore: In the 1950s, many cities in the United States saw their downtown retail areas shrink in the face of suburban growth. The popularity of shopping centers and suburban office buildings drew activity and tax revenues from the cities, and Baltimore, Maryland, was hard hit by these problems. By 1955, the evident deterioration of Baltimore's downtown retail district prompted some local businesspeople to organize a committee charged with finding ways to resuscitate it. In that period many other cities were responding to similar problems, but few have been as successful as Baltimore during these last three decades. In 1963 Mayor McKeldin established a city planning commission, a committee of businesspeople, and a Committee for Downtown, instructing them to work with a firm specializing in planning and urban land economics in the development of a plan for rejuvenating the downtown area (Fig. 2.15).[27] After a year of investigation, their recommendation was that attention be focused on the shoreline location known as Inner Harbor and the development of an office building area two blocks inland, which came to be known as Charles Center. Soon a private nonprofit corporation, Charles Center–Inner Harbor Management, Inc., was formed to negotiate the terms of projects, collaborate with real-estate developers, and otherwise represent the city in the intricate dealings required. (Another development corporation was established to deal with the less glamorous task of improving activity in the downtown areas of shabby office buildings and retail spaces.)[28] Through three decades, $135 million in federal funds were spent, mostly to

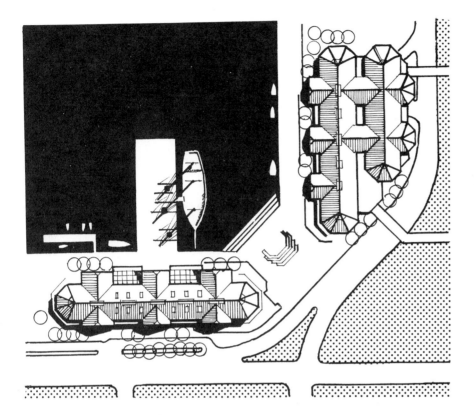

2.15 Festival marketplaces are not always developed in abandoned warehouses or old buildings. Baltimore's Inner Harbor Area is one example. Downtown Baltimore is located directly across the major thoroughfare.

acquire property and clear away pre-existing structures. About seventy-five major downtown buildings were constructed or reconditioned during the 1960s and 1970s. Charles Center–Inner Harbor Management, which operated on the basis of yearly contracts, in 1987 had exercised control over a total of 238 acres of property, had received affirmative votes fifteen times, and had worked cooperatively with six different city administrations.[29]

The Inner Harbor area, through the decades of development, acquired a World Trade Center office building, the National Aquarium, a power plant, and the Public Works Museum/Sewage Pumping Station. Nineteen eighty saw the opening of Harborplace—two buildings full of food and shopping executed under the aegis of the Rouse Company, which had constructed the extremely successful Faneuil Hall Marketplace project in Boston (Fig. 2.16). Harborplace's two buildings, each 300 feet long, were placed at a right angle and fronted on the water. The buildings sit on a strip of land between the water's edge and a traffic artery that runs between the harbor and the downtown area. To prevent their acting as a barrier to the waterfront, several entrances were spaced along the length of each of the Harborplace buildings.[30] They permitted direct passage to the water's edge through spaces between retail areas within the buildings (Fig. 2.17). Boating magazines wrote enthusiastically about Harborplace and the opportunity it offered to tie up in the vicinity of facilities for urban grazing and recreational shopping. It was this dramatic emphasis of the harbor atmosphere that distinguished the Inner Harbor development. From almost any point one could see water and boats, including the S. S. *Constel-*

2.16 This aerial view of the Inner Harbor Area of Baltimore clearly shows the nautical spirit of the project. Visitors can see the mast of the S.S. Constellation from many directions, and upon arrival they can proceed directly to the dock area.

2.17 Note that the buildings of the festival marketplace provide major barriers from the heavy street traffic. Immediately upon entry, the pedestrian at Baltimore's Inner Harbor Area is drawn close to the water's edge. Level changes are handled by ramping of the paving.

lation, a historic sailing ship. At the angle between the two Harborplace buildings there was a simple plaza that made the setting visible to visitors entering from the downtown area, which was at a higher elevation. An arc of seating in the center of the plaza designated a place where mimes and musicians could perform against a background of water and boats. The open views that were emphasized gave the development a feeling of seaside esplanades and wharfs. In its first year, income per square foot in Harborplace was more than twice the level that would be expected from a typical suburban mall.[31] The city's tax revenues from the area increased 400 percent.[32] Crowds filled the area, and local boosters were delighted to find that about half of the strollers were tourists.

Not all reaction to the undeniable success of this concentration on the downtown area was favorable. Although mayoral candidates emphasized that improvements had been made throughout the city, a British newspaper compared the Inner Harbor area to "gold fillings in a mouthful of decay."[33] A city-planning journal commented that since 1970 most of Baltimore's neighborhoods had known "increasing poverty, deteriorating housing conditions and shrinking economic opportunities."[34]

Paseo Del Rio, San Antonio: The Texas city of San Antonio, with a present population of some 1.3 million in the metropolitan area, was established on the river of the same name at a point where the stream formed an oxbow (Fig. 2.18). In almost all parts of the city, the street pattern ignored the curve of the river, whose banks were bordered with "backyards and outhouses."[35] Even though the level of the river was almost twenty feet below street level, floods periodically laid waste to areas along the river, a situation relieved around 1929 when a flood control project was executed, including a channel that was cut across the neck of land within the oxbow.[36] Several times during this period, downtown merchants initi-

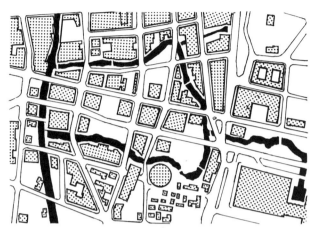

2.18 The San Antonio River's oxbow has survived its conflicts with the grid pattern of the streets. The Paseo del Rio (Riverwalk) development has continued through several decades. Flood control precautions separate the river and the oxbow area and stop any changes in water level, thus protecting the major pathways.

2.19 Whether you experience Riverwalk from the pathways or from the barge, a major impression is the constantly changing patterns of shadow and sunlight. Streets cross overhead at a variety of angles.

ated proposals to provide additional parking spaces or building sites by covering over the stream, reducing it to a storm drain. All such attempts were put down by a stalwart group of women, the San Antonio Conservation Society, which was formed in 1924.[37]

During the 1930s, when the population of San Antonio was about one-fifth its present level, improvements along the oxbow were executed with the assistance of WPA (Works Progress Administration) and other programs under which the federal government conducted make-work projects to alleviate unemployment during the Great Depression. The work was continued in the 1960s when San Antonio's city council appointed a River Walk Commission, which turned to their local chapter of the American Institute of Architects for assistance.

The appointment of the commission was reported to be the result of efforts made in the early 1960s by Cyrus Wagner, a San Antonio architect, and a businessman, David Straus. A bond issue passed in 1964 to support the 1968 HemisFair provided incentives to property owners adjacent to the river to open the lower level rear exits of their buildings to the river. When owners declined to support the design idea, the two sought to find cooperative people to buy those buildings.

A performance team composed of many associations, groups, and citizens effectively improved and changed the river walk to a pleasant, below-grade, well-landscaped promenade, open only to pedestrians. The plan that resulted employed the walks along the San Antonio river to link three major features (Fig. 2.19): the Alamo and its plaza, a shrine of Texas history; La Villita, the restored Spanish village; and two closely-related plazas, one at City Hall and the other in front of the Spanish Governor's Palace.[38] Later in that decade, San Antonio staged the exposition, Hemisfair '68, which was unfortunately upstaged by a long, hot summer of

2.20 In an early section of the Riverwalk, cafes and hotel facades parallel the water's edge. Visitors can experience the length of the Riverwalk by motor barge. (Courtesy of the San Antonio Parks and Recreation Department)

demonstrations against the Vietnam War. But on both sides of the sunken river, meandering pathways were lined with ferns, banana plants, and cypress trees. Because of the winding of the river, the streets above the river walk appear to cross at unusual angles, and overlooks are created at the many protective railings along those cross-streets. In some places, arched pedestrian bridges provide additional vistas and stopping places to look down on the river and onto the almost constant flow of open-air barge taxis with their groups of tourists. The pathways along the river provide shop, restaurant, and hotel access, with many of them double-loaded to provide upper level secondary entrances from the streets above. (Fig. 2.20)

As a component of the 1960s designs, in 1968 the Riverwalk was extended to the site of HemisFair a few blocks away. Through the years, uses of the adjacent parcels have been changed, and after the fair the grounds of HemisFair contained a branch of the National University of Mexico, the Institute of Texan Cultures, and a convention center complex. By the late 1980s a parking garage was added to the HemisFair area and a $53 million bond program added a water park around the base of the revolving high rise restaurant and observation platform tourist attraction, the Tower of the Americas, the visual symbol of the Fair.[39]

In 1988, the river was extended to Rivercenter, a project that combines the spirit of a regional shopping center with a theater, parking facilities, and a large hotel. Recently another hotel has been completed, only a block from Riverwalk, and nearby Houston Street has been closed to all vehicles except minibus trolleys, in a project assisted by a federal mass transit grant.

Because it extends through different kinds of areas and was constructed at different times, the development of the San Antonio River shows little uniformity. However, at all points the effect is that of walking or boating along the bed of a typical Texas creek, a channel of water, plants, and trees sunk below the surrounding plain. In some places the river takes on a park-like character, with grassy slopes beneath trees hanging over the water; in other places restaurant tables and shops border the water. The water and its detachment from the boisterous city life above are powerful thematic strains that unify the different parts of the river walk and also establish a relationship among the principal features of the downtown scheme.

Streets

As much of their population has moved to the suburbs, most American cities have suffered from increasing vehicular congestion downtown and declining occupancy in the buildings of the central area. While shops have emptied, major downtown streets have become noisy canyons, filled with polluted air and carbon monoxide. One of the recognized problems facing cities has been providing efficient transportation to take people from the outlying areas to the established centers of trade and shopping.

16th Street Mall, Denver: To solve the problem of deteriorating central district, Denver adopted a plan to establish two downtown terminals for commuter buses and thus eliminate half the downtown bus traffic. The architectural firm of I.M. Pei and Partners won the competition that was conducted in 1977 for plans to convert thirteen blocks of 16th Street, one of the city's most crowded downtown streets, into a pedestrian mall between the two terminals (Fig. 2.21). Free shuttle buses would run along the mall between the terminals.[40]

The project, which was called the 16th Street Transit Mall and opened in the fall of 1982, acts as a strong center line, unifying the entire mall despite the insets of some building facades and some gaps in the building lines at intersecting streets and vacant lots (Fig. 2.22).[41] In the six center blocks of the mall, its center is occupied by a twenty-two-footwide tree-flanked "pedestrian promenade," narrow lanes at the side for the shuttle buses, and sidewalks nineteen feet wide. The bus lanes and center walk are paved with a rich pattern of granite blocks in light gray, dark gray, and red. As the mall nears the terminals at either end, for several blocks the scheme changes that arrangement to simplify the way in which the buses on the mall approach the terminals.

Emphasis of the street's center line through the use of trees, the paving pattern, lighting standards, and the placement of benches and small fountains creates a unity for the scheme (Fig. 2.23). The buildings, in a wide variety of materials and styles, thus become secondary to the mall. The fact that the elements of the mall, except perhaps for the paving pattern, are simple and familiar avoids conflict between the mall and buildings.

In 1972, federal authorities rejected Denver officials' request to fund a rapid transit system, but several years later the Urban Mass Transit Administration agreed to fund about 80 percent of the construction costs for the mall, the fleet of buses, and the transfer stations at each end of the

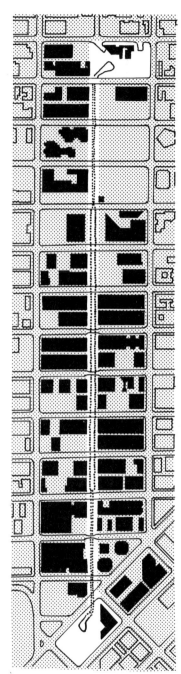

2.21 Location of elements of the 16th Street Transit Mall in downtown Denver are different in the central portion and in several blocks at the ends of the plan. In one arrangement, trees and a promenade occupy the center; in the other, buses are in the center.

2.22 The 16th Street Transit Mall in downtown Denver contains the usual American franchise restaurants. Their sign variations produce a visually interesting counterpoint with the controlled signs of the transit mall. Notice the right-angled intersection and the extension of the same paving. As a result, the spaces of the mall bleed around the corner. (Photo by Robert A. Goldsteen)

2.23 Emphases in planning are accomplished by placing trees in rows. Because the use of a single variety of tree might encourage disease, the city forester required both locust and oak. (Photo by Robert A. Goldsteen)

mall. Much of the management and maintenance of the mall is funded by assessments on the 865 property owners within a 70-block area of downtown Denver. An indication of the project's success has been the 40,000 people who ride the shuttle buses on an average workday. However, after the workday has ended and on weekends, the 16th Street Mall is a lonely place, with few pedestrians or buses making their way along the granite pavers.

Nicollet Mall, Minneapolis: In the late 1940s a few cities in the United States experimented with blocking vehicular traffic from a principal street, an action that was in some cases traditional for certain holidays and local festivals. European cities had long closed streets, but usually because their medieval narrowness made them virtually impassable to modern vehicles. In the 1950s and 1960s, closing streets to traffic became fashionable in U.S. cities, where downtown merchants were confronted with the competition from suburban shopping centers.

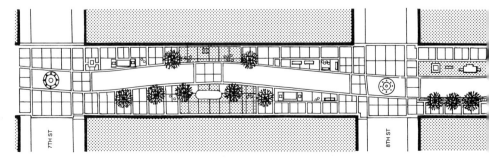

In Minneapolis, the Downtown Council, an organization of retail merchants, engaged a firm of planning consultants to study the problems of the retail core. Their reports in 1957 and 1961 resulted in a decision to focus attention on Nicollet Avenue and convert part of its length to a pedestrian mall while still allowing bus traffic and maintaining vehicular movement on the cross-streets.[42] Nicollet was chosen because it was the major downtown retail street, home to the city's most popular department stores, but between 1947 and 1967 its 62 clothing and shoe stores had been reduced by half.[43] Also, data showed that 80 percent of the vehicles on Nicollet Avenue were through traffic and that only five stores on the street had no delivery access other than the avenue.

Lawrence Halprin Associates, a firm of landscape architects, was selected in 1962 to design and detail the project (Fig. 2.24).[44] In the design they produced, a 24-foot-wide "transitway" is edged with 4-inch curbs and reserved for buses and taxis. (Taxis were not permitted to pass buses.) Following a suggestion in the planning consultants' 1961 report, the driving lanes follow a slightly serpentine path, allowing the width of sidewalks to vary from about twenty to a maximum of thirty-six feet.[45] Trees, fountains, kiosks, clocks, and large medallion patterns set in the paving add detail and reduce the scale of the space. The mall, along with the rerouted buses that ran along it, resulted in an appreciable increase of sales along the avenue, and the addition of the IDS Crystal Court, an extremely successful interior space, sustained the popularity of Nicollet Mall (Fig. 2.25).

From the beginning of the project the city, whose Planning Commission had instigated and encouraged the idea, declined to provide funding. Federal funds for the transportation improvements provided 10 percent of the almost 4 million dollars they cost, and another federal grant for street beautification brought about 12 percent. The remainder was raised by a bond issue to be paid off by assessments on stores in the area. Assessments were based on a complex formula that considered the frontage of each store, its square footage, its distance from Nicollet Avenue if it were on a side street, and its distance from the middle of the eight-block project.[46] On the whole, the cost can only be accepted as a reasonable charge, for Minneapolis has, largely through the Mall, retained an active and profitable downtown area.

In the most recent mall effort, the Downtown Minneapolis Council, which is composed of city council members, tenants, and building owners, found the mall somewhat out of date and in need of improvements after its twenty-three years. The amount of diesel bus traffic had increased to about

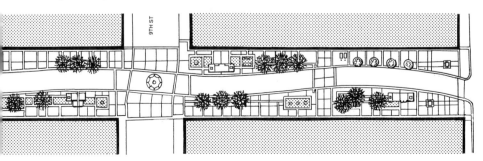

2.24 In the original plan, serpentine cartway and pavement meander down the linear space of the street. Unity is provided by uniformity in the designs of kiosks, bollards, and other elements. The gaps of cross streets provide counterpoint and limit the spatial linearity. Nicollet Mall, Minneapolis.

2.25 (left) Some successful spatial projects require replanning or continuous planning to keep them suitable during changing conditions. Nicollet Mall in downtown Minneapolis serves 140,000 workers, about 84,000 of whom commute by bus. As a result, bus traffic is one of the most important factors that stimulates the downtown retail businesses. (right) The Nicollet Mall provides a sufficient number of street furniture details that counteract the larger scale of tall downtown buildings. (Courtesy of Craig Amundsen, BRW, Inc.)

one every minute and a half. The need to battle the odors of bus fumes, combined with the need to update the appearance of the mall to keep its attractiveness, impelled the merchants and building owners to fund improvements through a special assessment district. As a result, in the late 1980s a number of new, high quality, designer-type specialty stores opened on Nicollet Mall, and they are reported to be generating high sales.[47]

Traffic Spaces

In every city there are wedges and irregularly shaped bits of land—gores—that are left over when streets do not meet in tidy perpendiculars. When they are very small, such places usually consist of pavement interrupted only by signposts; when they are larger a bench, a patch of grass, or flowers may accompany the signposts. But as the dimensions of gores increase there is a greater opportunity for making meaningful city spaces. In the mountain Mexican city of Zacatecas, for example, a triangular area at the confluence of two major routes had long been used as a small park, when improvements were made. One of the long sides already had perpendicular parking, a sidewalk with benches, and a low wall of baroque design. The wall was terminated at one end by an element that was curved in plan, and from this shape was developed the scheme of a paved plaza containing curvilinear planting beds elevated within sloped retaining walls. Pedestrian movement through the area follows no predictable patterns, and the flowing lines of the plan accommodate individual paths. Many other examples can be found to illustrate the great number of traffic spaces that have been converted to usable open spaces for pedestrians (Fig. 2.26).

2.26 At times of low density, the mixing of slow-moving cars and people is a familiar experience offering no great disadvantages, and it can become quite effective as a pedestrian experience. On the main business street in Juneau, Alaska, pedestrians cross the street at will.

Gore Park, San Jose, California: Orchards and farm plots surrounded the city of San Jose in the 1960s, when the city government instituted urban renewal projects that bulldozed much of the downtown area, turning much of the cleared space into parking lots. Twenty years later San Jose had become the center of Silicon Valley, as Santa Clara Valley had come to be known, an area of over a million people, 90 percent of the wage-earners being connected with the industries of microelectronics and telecommunications.[48] With these changes the San Jose Redevelopment Agency was formed and a plan for municipal development was prepared. The scheme that was to guide the city's improvement was focused on the downtown area, including the Silicon Valley Financial Center project, and was in all parts closely related to transportation. As a secondary part of the work, sculptural gateways were to be placed at the north, east, south, and west edges of the central area.

At the south entrance, a large triangle of land was located where two major arterials merged near the center of the city, in an area of low commercial buildings.[49] One of the long sides was emphasized by two rows of trees, with a broad walkway of gravel running between them (Fig. 2.27). The remainder of the gore is occupied by areas of lawn, terra-cotta pavers, concrete paving, and flower beds.[50] Solid patches of color are sharply defined. These horizontal areas are arranged in a pattern that resembles

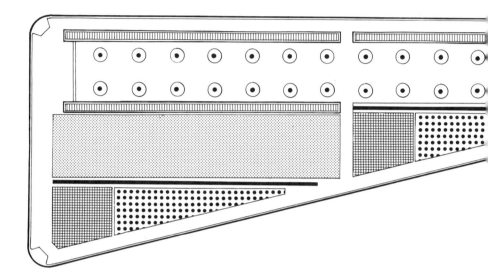

2.27 The shaded walkway is the primary spatial element of this design for Gore Park, San Jose (California), contrasting with the open space created between the low retail buildings. The orchards and fields of the region are reflected in the plan shapes used. The low walls and shrubbery provide containment and visual barriers to the street traffic. The small dots indicate lawn and the large dots flowers. Checked patterns show paved areas for sculpture, and stripes indicate raised plant boxes.

2.28 Three thin granite walls are oriented with the long dimension of Gore Park, San Jose. The neighborhood surrounding the park is composed of low retail buildings. (Photo by Elsa D. Flores)

2.29 The tree-covered walk is separated by raised plant beds from the parallel street. On the other side of the walk, there are raised plant beds and one of the granite walls. (Photo by Elsa D. Flores)

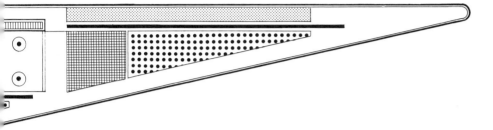

2.30 Between the trees and benches, trash receptacles and drinking fountains are placed. There is a sidewalk of customary width at the curb line to the left. (Photo by Elsa D. Flores)

the abstract compositions of the Dutch abstractionist Piet Mondrian, but at the same time they bear an obvious resemblance to the patterns seen in agricultural plots of the region (Fig. 2.28). This bold arrangement of precise geometries is adapted to both automobile and pedestrian scales of vision. Along the treed walk pedestrians are somewhat separated from the traffic that runs parallel to them, and contrasting rectangles of flowers and paving catch the eyes of passing motorists (Figs. 2.29, 2.30). The entire project was assigned a budget of $200,000, although a city official predicted that it would certainly cost less than that amount. The gore had previously been a park, but in the citywide enthusiasm for improvement the new design was justified by the fact that "it was old and in need of a face lift."[51]

SUMMARY

These examples vary greatly in the problems they confront and the styles in which the solutions are executed. Yet all the projects have created memorable spaces and provided an identifiable landmark in their cities. Each design was the product of cooperative decision making on the part of a group of design professionals and governmental officials and agencies, but the designs have remained clearly focused. Changes in stylistic preferences can be noted throughout the three decades encompassed by the selections; however, a greater influence seems to have been exerted on the designs by the settings in which they occur. Other examples in the chapters that follow will augment the impressions made by this small selection of outstanding work, for there are many other praiseworthy projects, and one can discover them in many unexpected places.

Project Possibilities

There are a number of projects that may be considered by cities to improve their urban identity. They vary greatly, and they may be categorized and typed in a number of different ways. As a checklist or groupings to be used for generating new and unique spaces and places for improvement, the following items may be useful to teams:

■ **STREETS, AVENUES, AND BOULEVARDS**

    Business center

        pedestrian and vehicular limitations

        shopping and display facilities

        grazing/noshing zones

        night entertainment district

        noontime and weekend concerts

        occasional or seasonal fairs

    Business satellites

        district and neighborhood services

        mobile and seasonal businesses

        event and celebration provisions

        demonstrations, both instructional and political

        displays of the arts

    Residential

        low-density walkways and trails

        higher-density walking/driving patterns

        pause points for chats and trysts

        community gardening-and-gathering spots

    Thoroughfare network

entry points
   entrance activity points
   monumental approaches
public transportation transfer points
   bus stops
   rapid transit stations
   cab stands
through-driver services
   individual cars
   truckers
   tour and school buses

■ OPEN SPACES
   Neighborhood
      exercise parks
      children's playgrounds
      solitude parks
      mingling and meeting centers
      sitting place for elderly
   Suburban
      sports fields
      nature walks
      picnic grounds
   Downtown
      memorial squares
      grounds of institutional/government buildings
      open-air lunch stops
      entrance courts
      corner gathering places
      walking plazas
      vest-pocket parks
      outdoor cafes
      "Hyde Park," or orator's corner

■ SPECIALIZED AREAS
   Commercial
      festival marketplace
      historical district
      ethnic shopping center
      farmers' seasonal market

Public
    arts district
    amphitheater and performance centers
    sports parks
    displays for vintage cars, pets, flower growers, etc.

■ GEOGRAPHICALLY DETERMINED

Waterfront
    boating centers
    promenades
    lakeside strolls
    historical or performance/music plazas
    streamside trails
Slopes and hillsides
    winding paths or funiculars
    view points for vistas
    snow slides for children

With this functional variety, it is possible to utilize design devices that can attract visitors, generally or selectively. The objective in some cases may be exhilaration; in other cases, relaxation. Consider the following ideas:[52]

■ Sculpture and fountains, either static or moving, to attract people or merely to provide a resting point for the eye.

■ Passive areas next to active areas in order to encourage "people-watching" in both those situations.

■ Spaces to accommodate distinctive transportation, such as trolley cars, monorails, and specially decorated vehicles.

■ Repaved sidewalks and plazas to provide color and patterns that can afford more interesting visual detail.

■ Decorative kiosks and stalls along walks or on plazas for flowers, food, or educational materials.

■ Selection of benches, litter receptacles, bus shelters, and lighting fixtures to emphasize the desired character of the space.

■ Pergolas and covered walks to provide shelter and accent specific areas and their functions.

■ Emphasis of building entrances with waiting-for spaces and harmonizing fixtures.

■ Awnings, arcades, or plantings to provide shaded places at the edge of sidewalks.

■ Changes in level with ramps or steps to vary viewing conditions or divide types of movement.

■ Bright variegated signs or controlled harmonious signs, according to the spirit of the place.

■ Large-scale fountains for display or several small fountains for intimacy, perhaps with equipment to vary force and lighting.

■ Lighting, from searchlights to tiny strings of bulbs, selected to reinforce the character of a space or a special event.

■ Variation of the above items and types of plantings to distinguish between the spaces of different neighborhoods.[52]

These lists can be lengthened quickly, particularly when design teams meet to explore the potential of a specific space and its purpose. Obviously, many such possibilities can be combined to strengthen the seasonal and age attraction of a design. Since people's tastes differ and seasons change, it is often advisable to allow for changes of mood and weather. The greatest safeguard against considering too few options is the fact that all participants from the public or from the design team will remember places they have seen and enjoyed. And they will also think of things that they have not yet seen.

ENDNOTES

1. "Big Yellow Taxi." Joni Mitchell, included in *Ladies of the Canyon.* Reprise, 1970.

2. Credits: Zion & Breen Associates, landscape architect; A. Preston Moore, architectural consultant; James H. Bigart, real estate consultant; Caretsky and Associates, engineering consultant.

3. Stanley Abercrombie, "Evaluation: A Prototype Left Unreplicated," *Architecture AIA* (December 1985): 54–55.

4. Abercrombie, "Evaluation," 57.

5. Thomas Hoving, "Think Big About Small Parks," *New York Times Magazine*, April 10, 1966, 12.

6. "Tiny Parks Draw Attack by Moses," *New York Times*, May 11, 1966, 51.

7. New York City Parks Department, *General Statistics of the Department of Parks and Recreation–1992*, March 1993; and City of New York, *Parks and Recreation Property Lists for Manhattan, Queens,*

Bronx, Brooklyn, and Staten Island, August 1991, Press Office, Parks Department.

8. Credits: prime consultant: Hanna/Olin, Ltd., Laurie D. Olin—partner in charge; Christopher N. Allen—associate in charge; Craig McGlynn, Beth Myers—project managers; graphics: Frank Garnier; lighting designers: H.M. Brandston & Partners; site civil/electrical & mechanical engineers: Joseph R. Loring; structural engineers: Robert R. Rosenwasser; Garden designer; Lynden B. Miller; park kiosks: Hardy, Holzman, Pfeiffer & Associates—architects; park buildings: Kupiec & Koutsomitis—architects; collaborators: William H. Whyte, Jr.; construction manager: Tishman Construction Corporation; general contractor: LaStruda General Contracting Corporation; landscape contractor: Lewis and Valentine Nurseries, Inc.; Stonework: Pansini Stone Setting, Inc.

9. "After Years Under Wraps, a Midtown Park is Back," *New York Times*, April 22, 1992, B4.

10. "News: Poet's Park," *Landscape Architecture* (March 1989): 13.

11. Witold Rybczynski, "A Good Public Building," *Atlantic* (August 1992): 84.

12. Credits: architects—Ludwig Mies van der Rohe; C.F. Murphy Associates; Schmidt, Garden and Erickson; and A. Epstein and Sons.

13. Credits: architects—C.F. Murphy Associates; Perkins and Will Partnership.

14. Carl W. Condit, *Chicago 1930–1970: Building, Planning, and Urban Technology* (Chicago: University of Chicago Press, 1974), 101.

15. Credits: architects—C.F. Murphy Associates; Skidmore, Owings, and Merrill; and Loebl, Schlossman and Bennett.

16. Harry Weese, "The Chicago Civic Center as Public Architecture," *AIA Journal* (September 1969): 89.

17. Amas Elon, "Report from Vienna," *The New Yorker* (May 13, 1991): 97.

18. "Around the Nation," *New York Times*, January 26, 1982, 10.

19. Christopher Buckley, "The Wall," *Esquire* (September 1985): 66.

20. Hugh Sidey, "Tribute to Sacrifice," *Time* (February 22, 1982): 19.

21. Buckley, "Wall," 66.

22. Credits: Cooper-Lecky Partnership, architect of record; Maya Yang Lin, in-house design consultant.

23. "Hush, Timmy—This Is Like A Church," *Time* (April 15, 1985): 61.

24. Mike E. Howard, "Las Colinas: Selling the Aura," *American Demographics* (April 1990): 46.

25. Interview with David L. Brune, Esq., Faison-Stone Las Colinas, Inc., Irving, Texas, February 27, 1993.

26. Credits: James Reeves of The SWA Group, landscape architect; Skidmore, Owings & Merrill, architects; Robert Glen, sculptor; The Crockett Company and Las Colinas Landscape Services, contractors; Capitol Marble & Granite, consultants.

27. Credits: Wallace, McHarg and Associates, planning; Morton Hoffman and Company, economic studies.

28. John C. Billing, "Baltimore's Past Harbors Its Future," *Landscape Architecture* (September/October 1987): 68–73.

29. Christopher Findlay and others, "In Practice," *Landscape Architecture* (September/October 1987): 75.

30. Credits: Benjamin Thompson and Associates, architects; Gilum-Colaco, structural engineers; Robert G. Balter Company, soils engineering; Poole and Kent, sanitary engineering; Joseph R. Loring and Associates, mechanical engineers; Valley Lighting, lighting; Wallace, Robert and Todd, landscape architects.

31. Gurney Breckenfield, "The Rouse Show Goes National," *Fortune* (July 27, 1981): 49.

32. Grady Clay, "On Baltimore's Inner Harbor," *Landscape Architecture* (November 1982): 52.

33. *Manchester Guardian*, quoted in Clay, "Inner Harbor," 53.

34. Robin Hambleton, "Privatising Urban Regeneration," *Town and Country Planning* (November 1990): 304.

35. James L. Mackay, "Hemis Fair '68," *AIA Journal* (April 1968): 49.

36. Mackay, "Hemis Fair '68," 49.

37. Michael Middleton, *Man Made The Town* (New York: St. Martin's Press, 1987), 205.

38. Mackay, "Hemis Fair '68," 49–50.

39. Robert Cullick, "San Antonio Hangs Tight To Its Dream," *Planning* (March 1986): 4–10.

40. Nora R. Greer, "Finely Furnished Shopping Spine," *AIA Journal* (June 1983): 36–42.

41. Credits: I.M. Pei & Partners, architects; KKBNA, Inc., civil engineers; Hanna/Olin, Ltd., landscape consultant; Phillip E. Flores Associates, Inc., landscape architects; Howard Brandston Lighting Design, Inc.; Barton-Aschman Associates, Inc., transportation consultant; Page Arbitrio & Resen, Ltd., graphics.

42. "The New Street Scene," *Architectural Forum* (January, 1969): 75.

43. Amy Dolnick, "Mall Tales," *Minneapolis-St. Paul* (December 1987): 138.

44. Credits: Lawrence Halprin & Associates, urban design; Barton-Aschman Associates, Inc., urban planning and engineering; K.M. Clark Engineering Co., structural engineers; Evans, Michaud, Cooley, Hallberg & Erickson, mechanical and electrical engineers; Larson & McLaren, Inc., consulting architects; Seymour Evans, lighting consultant. The city planning director, Lawrence Irwin, was supported by the City Planning Commission's urban designer, Weiming Lu.

45. Roger Martin, "Exciting Start with Nicollet Mall," *Landscape Architecture* (July 1969): 302–303.

46. "The New Street Scene," 75.

47. Interview with Patrick R. Siegrist, City Visions, St. Paul, Minnesota, March 12, 1993.

48. "Resuscitating San Jose, Silicon City," *Progressive Architecture* (January 1985): 54.

49. Credits: Kenneth W. Talbot, landscape architect; Thomas R. Aidala, architect and urban designer; Cecily Young and Rachel Rush, design assistants (all of the San Jose Redevelopment Agency); Beals Lechner, consultant for contract documents and project inspection.

50. "Gore Park," *Landscape Architecture* (November 1988): 44–45.

51. City Park Manager Max McClintock, as quoted in "Gore Park Face-Lift Explained," *San Jose Mercury News*, January 22, 1988.

52. A number of these items were developed from lists in "Downtown Dallas: 2010; Toward a Visual Master Plan to Guide Development: A Report of Findings and Design Recommendations." (Dallas: Corgan Associates, architects; The SWA Group, landscape architects; 1989).

3

HISTORY—TRADITIONS OF CITY SPACES IN AMERICA

*European traditions, classical, medieval, Renaissance cities;
avenues, promenades, and streets; bridges and river banks, squares,
parks and gardens; American traditions, growth of America,
influence of transportation, skyscrapers, residential projects,
suburbs, garden cities, formality and grandeur, quadrangles and
courtyards, shopping centers; American values.*

The traditions that led to the adoption of particular patterns and designs for American spaces and places began in Mediterranean Europe. Having evolved over almost three thousand years, the traditions that were brought to America in many ways were responses and adaptations to the local factors found in Europe. For immigrants, their heritage provided an invaluable store of knowledge and a rich design vocabulary. When the first permanent settlements were established in the parts of the New World that would become the United States, European city spaces were being designed with sophistication and significant artistic skill. For example, in the period of the early American communities of Europeans, the massive colonnade of St. Peter's Basilica was erected in Rome, and the careers of the great Baroque architects Giovanni Lorenzo Bernini and Francesco Borromini were drawing to a close. The French king, envying a subject's lavish chateau at Vaux-le-Vicomte, enlarged his own palace at Versailles and began construction of its gardens. The Great Fire of London had been followed by the submission of at least six plans, all rejected, for reconstruction of the city on an orderly pattern, and Sir Christopher Wren had begun the task of designing fifty churches to replace those that had been demolished in the fire, providing the spires that became landmarks of London.

In North America, the settlers were confronted with conditions that were much more primitive. Boston in the middle of the seventeenth century had a population of between 2,000 and 3,000 settled in an area less than 1½ miles on its longer dimension, with many houses of simple wood and thatch (even though frequent fires were factors that had caused many to build new houses of masonry construction).[1] New Amsterdam (New York), a settlement sponsored by the Dutch West India Company, was less populous than Boston and no more developed. Even those pioneer colonial towns that were financially assisted by governments or merchant companies were inclined to take many liberties with the city plans that had been provided by their sponsors.

From the beginning, American settlers struggled to establish their lives and to develop those institutions that assisted in the struggle; they were at the same time aware that their surroundings were far less substantial than those they remembered from their native towns, or those that had been described by their parents. Clearly, the United States lived under the shadow of Europe until the late 19th century. Immigrants' ties to their homelands, the centuries of European culture, and a habit of envying Europeans in all but political matters had combined to establish a European standard of behavior and environment. From the first settlements in North America, the immigrants tried to copy the towns and the city spaces of the countries from which they came, though their attempts were limited by the effort required to scratch a living from their new land and many of the physical characteristics of their settlements were far different from those of their native places. American cities began with the intention of emulating European standards insofar as it was possible, yet the cities could easily be identified as American. By the end of the nineteenth century, the influences began to reverse. Today in Europe and elsewhere, American travelers go from the airport to their hotels filled with amazement at the extent to which all such trips are similar visual experiences. An American influence is clearly evidenced in the newer parts of European cities and American overtones appear even in the oldest parts of European cities. There has been a reversal of influences or, at least, an equalization.

It has long been common for Americans to profess an admiration for the imagery of European cities and villages, and, considering the centuries of magnificent architecture, planning, and artistic work that they demonstrate, the attitude is natural and wise. The spaces, streets, and monuments of Europe are a rich heritage for all the world and most Americans; but, nevertheless, there is a splendid legacy in the urban environment of the United States, a legacy that provides a basis for effective design and that inevitably flavors our approach to other traditions.

> Developers need to educate themselves on the meaning of references to antecedents. Not uncommonly, a designer will say that a space is "like the Piazza San Marco in Venice," that the sequence of movement in a scheme is "just like Rome's Spanish Steps," or that a landscape "resembles the pictorial episodes of Kyoto's Katsura Palace." Developers should familiarize themselves with the elements named, so they can judge the appropriateness of those references to a particular site or

building program. At the same time, they should bear in mind that an architect's final design choice may not closely resemble the antecedent.[2]

The same is true for all those who participate in making decisions about the design of urban open spaces. But, after more than three hundred years, American spaces are equally meaningful. None of the historical examples of either continent can be effectively imitated today. A new reproduction of the space in front of St. Peter's in Rome might be suitable for a movie set, but it would be desecrated by making it suitable for use today. The principal value of knowing about historical examples is that they (1) provide an illustration of the breadth of possibilities to be explored and extended in today's solutions and (2) form a testing ground of ideas with which today's solutions can be compared.

THE EUROPEAN TRADITIONS

The development of European cities and their open spaces relates closely to the gradual urbanization of the continent. From small cities and scattered settlements surrounded by forests and fields (a situation much like that of America in early colonial times), trade and industrialization, in their turns, brought about the concentrations of population in centers that grew larger and larger. Plato declared that the ideal city would have a population of 5040, but at that time all Greece probably had a population of about 2 million, and a very large majority of them lived outside cities. It was the middle of the nineteenth century before England had more than half its population living in urban conditions. At that time only about 15 percent of Americans were urban dwellers. During these centuries of urbanization, the dimensions of cities increased, the density of buildings intensified, and citizens' access to open spaces was diminished.

Classical Cities

Both Athens and Rome were cities that grew haphazardly. In themselves, these cities provide little useful information about the attitudes toward public spaces during classical times, although spaces typical of the two cultures were later inserted within the cities' tangled patterns. One of the first planned communities was the work of the Greek, Hippodamus, who replanned his native city of Miletus after it was burned by the Persians in 494 B.C. (Fig. 3.1). Before that time, Greek cities had been irregular arrangements of buildings and streets, including crude and elementary versions of the kinds of spaces that would be found in later cities, particularly the colonial towns constructed on the Ionian coast of present-day Turkey. It is these planned communities that most relate to later history, since they are the development of forms that existed through the most famous periods of Greek history. The so-called Hippodamian system of town planning consisted of dividing the settlement's area into rectangular

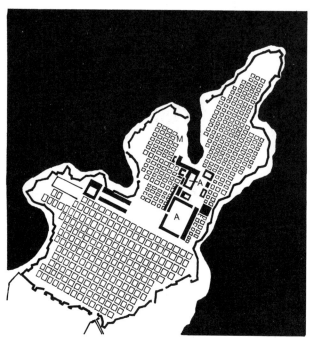

3.1 Miletus. Two principal agoras (A) and market areas (M) are indicated, as well as a trading center at the harbor. They are either enclosed rectangles or linear buildings—open air colonnades—that were open to a view of the water.

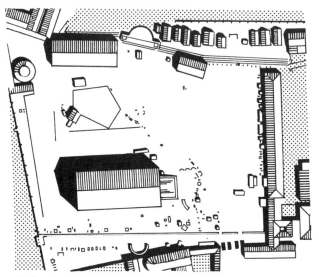

3.2 Olympia, Greece—Temple of Zeus: The entrance (lower right) to a temple precinct in Olympia is directed toward the space in front of the temple. Lesser monuments are lined up along the colonnade at the east side of the area and scattered in the area between the entrance and the principal temple. The other buildings and monuments create unusually shaped spaces around it, and there is little to dictate a visitor's path.

blocks of property (in Miletus only seventy-five by one hundred feet) with a grid of streets. Typically, such cities were surrounded by fortifications that followed the irregularities of the terrain. The spaces remaining between the city grid and its walls were left as open areas or served as sites for theaters and stadiums, where tiers of seating would fit on the steep slopes that were undesirable for construction of most buildings. The highest part of an earlier town's site would be employed as the acropolis (literally "high city") where the principal temples and shrines would be located, but in cities built on Hippodamian principles high land had less significance. Temples were set in the gridded pattern of the town, standing among trees in walled rectangular enclosures (Fig. 3.2). There were usually roofed colonnades along one or more of the sides to protect visitors from rain or to provide shelter for the sick who were brought for a cure. Over time, the open area of a temple precinct would acquire a variety of shrines and monuments, both large and small, that were seldom placed according to a rigid system. If there were a sacred path within the courtyard around the temple, the monuments might be lined along its route, where they could easily be seen by visitors, or most of them might be located in a row before one of the colonnades along the walls.

Within residential areas, the houses focused inward, their rooms opening onto courtyards within the dwelling. Small shops were sometimes built at the front of residences, but along the less important streets one usually saw only solid masonry walls, punctuated by narrow doors opening into the houses and windows in the walls of the upper story. Such streets were rarely paved and usually around twelve feet wide between the walls of the houses, much more hallways than avenues, and they were seldom traveled by vehicles. The streets were noisy, sound echoing between their parallel walls, and often they were crowded with the patrons of food stalls, peddlers and their goods, and pedestrians. Because most Greek colonial cities were built on rocky sloping sites, the courtyards and floors of buildings constituted a series of level platforms, adjacent to each other, and rising along the slope of the land. Pack animals were the customary means of moving heavy goods, and often steps were constructed in the streets where slopes became steep. By imposing a gridiron of streets on a sloping site, many streets in one direction were relatively level throughout their length and those in the opposite direction sloped with the terrain, providing open views as they descended toward the harbor. (The effect must have been similar to that of some streets in San Francisco.) One or two principal streets crossed the city in each direction, as much as twenty to thirty feet in width, and those major streets were more likely to have two-storied buildings along much of their distance.

A primary element of Greek architecture and civic design was the use of a porch, a roofed colonnade along the side of a building, as a weather protection and as an intermediate space between the cool darkness of interiors and the glaring bright sunlight of the outside. This device, which eventually became an earmark of Mediterranean architecture and reached the New World with the French and Spanish colonists, was employed externally around temples and internally around residential courtyards, temple precincts, and agoras. The visual form of the Greek porch was that of one or two stories of white columns, rather closely spaced because they usually carried stone beams. The columns and beams were silhouetted against the sharply contrasting shadows within the interior space or falling on the back wall of the porch. In most buildings, this rhythm of verticals was not interrupted by further architectural embellishment; horizontal contrasts were provided by a few steps leading up to the floor level of the porch, a continuous cornice, and the eaves of a terra-cotta tile roof. This pattern was the main element of the Greek architectural vocabulary and, hence, the basis of the visual effect of the outdoor spaces it surrounded. As a framing device, the porch and its colonnade became a repetitive and richly detailed frame for the events and forms that occurred within a space.

Within the gridiron network of narrow streets that made up a Greek city, an open square would be located near the center of the city or at the harbor. In contrast to the narrow streets, the agora (the name derived from a Greek word meaning "to assemble") became a visual relief from those passageways and commonly occupied the space of several of the blocks made by the grid of streets. In the Ionian city of Priene it was an open area of about 150 by 250 feet, but at Miletus the largest of the city's agoras was about 320 by 620 feet, occupying sixteen blocks of the town grid. Often a major street passed along one edge of the space. The other three sides, customarily in a straight-sided U shape, were occupied by stoas, long market halls with small shops located along the back wall (Fig. 3.3). Whether the stoa was of one or two stories, the side of the market hall facing the square was an open colonnade and the business of merchants and artisans extended into the area outside. Where the site sloped sharply downward, one or two stories of a stoa might be built into the slope, beneath the level of the agora, to provide additional market stalls, opening onto a lower street. If a town were established with a marketplace opening onto the harbor strand, another more formal square might later be built in a more central location. In time, some more formal agoras became increasingly occupied by monuments, statues, and stone platforms from which political leaders spoke to the citizens, but, unlike American courthouse squares, the Greek agoras retained their function as marketplaces. The open space of the agora was the principal civic gathering place. In its vicinity was constructed the hall in which the city's senate met, along with the structure that housed the administrative functions of the city government, and other official buildings. When city populations increased, stoas were often extended along the major street that crossed the agora, and sometimes U-shaped squares, like the original agora, were added on that street. Different functions were designated for these marketplaces; one might be devoted to the constant commotion of handling goods for the lively sea trade of the Greeks, and another might deal only in the finest of wares and be frequented by the most illustrious of the town's citizens. The use of plant materials in classical times is extremely difficult to determine because, unlike the stones and the wooden posts of buildings, trees and shrubs leave little evidence for archaeologists. However, a passage in Plutarch's *Parallel Lives* describes an Athenian general's gift of sycamore trees to be planted in an agora and thereby suggests that agoras, like other Greek open spaces, occasionally may have been shaded by trees.

At the same time, another sort of public space developed, dedicated to that combination of mental and physical well-being that was particularly Greek. The school (or gymnasium) was the place where young men spent time in activities that were about equally divided between the athletic and the intellectual. Here again, the open space needed for races and wrestling (say, around 45 to 135 feet square) was a rectangle surrounded by colonnades and chambers in which philosophical instruction was conducted and sports were pursued. Trees grew between the running paths in the courtyard, and the trees at the academy in Athens led to the phrase, "the groves of academe." The size of even a fully developed Greek city was usually such that there was also easy access to open space along the shoreline, in the rocky hills, and in groves between the town walls and the blocks delineated by the grid of streets.

Although Greek tradition meant that any objects within a space would be symmetrical within themselves, temples, monuments, and sculpture were not centered within a space, although often oriented in harmony with the rectangular form. Even within its enclosure a temple might be off-center, and the gate into the area did not have to be centered either on the

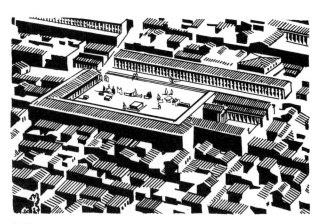

3.3 At the Greek colony of Priene, the sloping site required that the area of the agora be levelled. A major street crossed the agora at the rear of this view, and a scattering of markets and monuments occupied much of the central area. The space is modulated by the through street and the steps in front of the upper stoa.

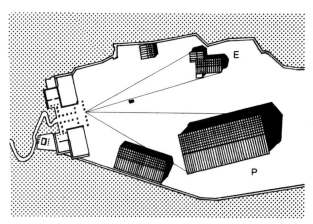

3.4 The gateway building by which one enters the acropolis in Athens establishes the point from which the visitor first views the two principal temples, the Parthenon (p) and the Erechtheum (e). This plan identifies the three-dimensional views of temples that may have been desired by the Greeks.

temple or on the wall of the temple precinct. It has been theorized that the Greeks preferred an off-center approach to buildings in which the visitor would initially experience the building or the volume from an angle that would emphasize its three-dimensionality (Fig. 3.4).[3] Whether or not we accept this thesis, it is clear that the Greek approach would have produced an environment of obvious order, but without a pervasive formality.

A similar spirit is to be seen in the layout of the Greek colonial town as a whole. The blocks of its grid ended irregularly, and beyond them the town's protective wall took paths that made the most of the steep inclines of the rocky slope. Even within the town, the slopes of streets and the cascading pattern of platforms on which buildings were built must have given the simple grid an excitement not clearly conveyed by plans and maps. Only within public spaces might trees be seen and, because of sea breezes and the shadows in narrow streets, their shade may not have been needed elsewhere. The town's contrast with its surroundings may not have been great for the Greeks very early denuded its rocky lands of trees, cutting them for fuel and ship-building.

The Roman inclinations were quite different, although a majority of the basic functional elements of their cities were the same as those of the Greeks. For instance, the dominant public space in a Roman city was the forum, used for both civic and mercantile purposes. The forum was forcefully dominated by a temple (called the capital) at one end, dedicated in early times to the principal gods of the city and the republic, and in later years to the worship of the emperor. In his writings, the Roman architect Vitruvius Pollio advised that the proportion of a forum should be 2:3, but those numbers were not always followed, as the length of the forum at Pompeii was more than three times its width (Fig. 3.5).[4] The forum was customarily located at the intersection of the two major streets in the center of the city, although port cities might place it nearer to the harbor.

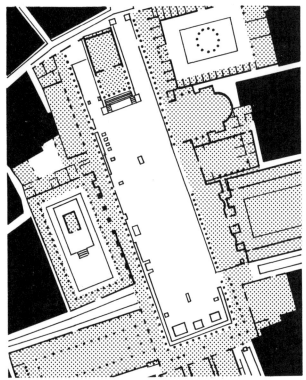

3.5 Trading functions of the Forum of Pompeii were removed to markets at upper left and right. The governmental functions and shrines around the forum were masked by the colonnade along three of its sides.

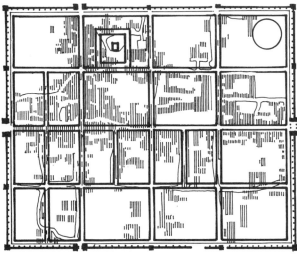

3.6 The Roman town of Aosta, in the extreme northwestern part of Italy, was succeeded by a medieval town, which is shown by the superimposed shaded areas.

Like the Greek agora, the forum was at first primarily a marketplace, and at the same time a political and religious center. It was the traditional place where blood was spilled in the gladiatorial combats that commemorated the burial of leading citizens and the place where placatory offerings were made to the principal deities of the empire. Fronting on the forum were the most important civic buildings (the civil court, treasury, legislative chamber, and various city offices), their disparate masses being masked by the two-story colonnade around the three sides of the forum. This porch provided entrances for all of these governmental buildings and at the same gave a monumental unity to the appearance of the forum. After gladiatorial spectacles were transferred to arenas elsewhere in cities, monuments crowded the forums. The merchants' stalls and wineshops that had been a part of early forums were shifted to nearby streets, where markets might be established with stalls about their courtyards. Temples of lesser importance were placed in their own walled spaces, and Vitruvius recommended that temples to Apollo and Bacchus be located near the theater and those to Hercules near the gymnasium.[5]

Many Roman towns were established as part of the far-flung empire's colonization of its conquests as far away as the British Isles, Germany, and

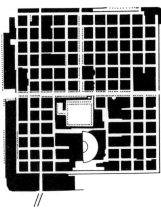

3.8 The Roman colonial city of Timgad in present-day Algeria (founded c. 100 A.D.) had colonnades along the two principal streets that led to the central agora. In some other cities, arches continued the covering of the walkways across the street intersections.

3.7 Most streets in Roman towns had walls of stuccoed brick with few openings. Shadows kept them cool despite the bright sun.

northern Africa. The standard army camp of the Romans was a squarish area surrounded by a wall and made up of a gridiron of streets with the principal streets meeting at the center (Fig. 3.6). (This camp, called the castrum, is the source of the "chester" in the names of many British cities.) The standard plan was varied to meet the needs of different colonial locations, and many of these camps became the basis for the plans of medieval cities.

Roman streets were usually twelve to twenty feet wide (as were Greek towns and American downtown alleys), but the principal streets in Imperial times might be more than three times that dimension (Fig. 3.7). The sidewalks were usually twelve to eighteen inches above a paved street surface, and at the intersections of streets there were stepping stones at sidewalk level, with enough space left between them to let pack animals and the wheels of carts pass. For safety along residential streets, windows customarily were restricted to upper floors, which often projected over the street. In late Roman times many cities built colonnades along both sides of their principal streets (Fig. 3.8). At Palmyra, a colonnaded street 3500 feet long had a roadway thirty-seven feet wide lined with porticoes fifteen feet deep, but this was no spacious boulevard, since the height of the porticoes

3.9 The Arch of Constantine in the Roman Forum (c. 315 A.D.) is a late example of the triumphal arch. Those built earlier usually had only one opening.

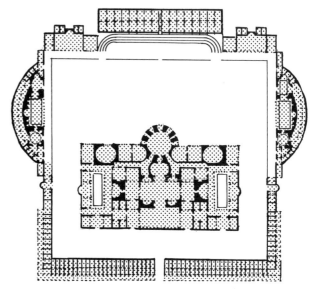

3.10 Walls around the Baths of Caracalla in Rome defined a space around 1000 feet square, and much less than half of the area was occupied by the building itself. Open space within the complex was roughly the equivalent of five or six typical American city blocks.

exceeded the width of the roadway. Such streets were noisy places, especially in Rome, where vehicles were at one time banned during daylight hours (except those used for building projects) and allowed to rumble through the city only at night. The Romans often ornamented their cities with what are called "triumphal arches," although they were erected for several different commemorative purposes (Fig. 3.9). This form (seen in Washington Square, New York, and greatly enlarged in the Arc de Triomphe, Paris) was constructed at the ends of bridges, the gateways of towns, the entrances to forums, and at apparently random locations.

Fields devoted to sports (what we would today call "track and field") and wrestling were still present. Vitruvius stipulated that the periphery of such spaces should attain a specified length (probably to match a standard distance for races) and that within the open area there should be planted "groves of plant trees with walks laid out in them . . . and resting places there."[6] However, the most common places for athletic activities were the open spaces around Roman public baths. The baths were the most popular gathering places in Roman cities. In the African colonial town of Timgad, with a population of about 15,000, there were at least a dozen baths of different sizes. Entrance charges for the baths were very low, and often a wealthy citizen would pay for all citizens' use of a bath for a year's time. Whether in the small baths of a provincial city or the most splendid ones of Rome itself, the ritual of bathing was certainly not the only attraction that drew people to the baths (Fig. 3.10). In small baths exercise and relaxation might be confined to a small courtyard at the back of the men's section of the bath and a garden in the women's section. (Separation of the sexes was accomplished either by constructing two adjoining structures or by scheduling use.) In larger baths, gardens, fountains, trees, and running tracks were lavishly provided. Writings suggest that the gardens may have rivalled the splendor of the architecture. The Baths of Caracalla in Rome included two courtyards within the building (each about 80 by 180 feet) and behind the building was an area (roughly 400 by 1100 feet) that contained gardens, an outdoor swimming pool, and tiered seating from which crowds could watch athletic competitions. Food sellers and peddlers hawking their wares, athletes grunting at their exercises, and carousers around the wineshops caused such noise that Roman writers complained of the disturbance that resulted in a neighborhood. Large baths were built on earth platforms that included complex heating systems beneath their floors. The grounds were surrounded by walls in whose thickness were included shops opening to the surrounding streets and rooms that were part of the bath's activities. All of this was arranged as an extension of the axial design system that was adopted for the plan of the building itself.

Roman spaces were principally formed by the manipulation of walls bearing the play of shadows on columns, cornices, arches, pergolas, and the other ornamental devices of classical architecture. These patterns, in most cases a surfacing applied to the sturdy brick-concrete structures now seen at the ruins, offered an opportunity to establish a consistency among surfaces, having a formality appropriate to the interests of the vast Roman empire. One of the advantages of the methodical approach of the Roman designers was its ease of application; it could be promulgated, regulated, and standardized in a manner that could be followed throughout the empire.

A system of coordinates and axes of symmetry were the primary tools of Roman architecture. Earlier cultures, such as the Egyptian, had arranged temples and their forecourts on an axial line of symmetry, balancing forms and spaces on a centerline that was also the principal line of movement through them. This principle was employed by the Greeks in the design of buildings and, after Greece had increasingly come under the influence of Rome, in the positioning of buildings and spaces. Roman designers extended the fundamental approach of symmetry in a network of major axes and minor axes that developed more complex forms and interrelationships of spaces (Fig. 3.11). As familiar as it is to all of us, this method of ordering designs offers a fascinating combination of various levels of symmetrical spatial connections by which observers can immediately sense the invisible lines connecting the largest objects or volumes, secondary elements, and even those of a third or fourth level of visual significance. Within this axial geometric framework, it is possible to contrast the static qualities of round spaces with the dynamic qualities of long rectangular areas, to organize intricate spatial substructures into subtle relationships, perhaps even beyond the ability of an observer to notice and consciously appreciate them. It is the predictable quality of the Roman-inspired axial system that may be its greatest danger for designers today, but even to those who have experienced or seen it repeatedly there can be surprises when axes are developed with genuine imagination.

3.11 Three complexes in Rome, built by different emperors, illustrate the use of axial composition to relate open spaces and architectural forms.

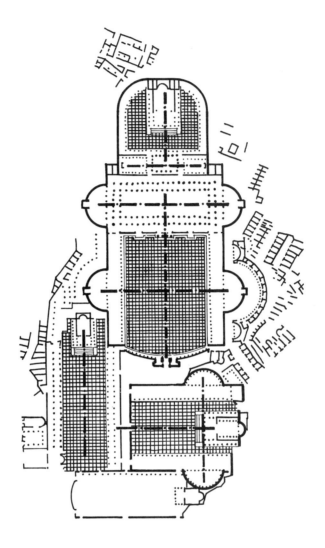

Medieval Cities

The process of urbanization, which had collapsed after the fall of the Roman Empire, was revived in the tenth and eleventh centuries. During that period, some towns grew upon the remains of Roman colonial towns, some developed at sites adjoining feudal castles and monasteries, and still others were located at points that were geographically advantageous, such as crossroads, harbors, and places where rivers could easily be crossed. In towns that were based on Roman gridirons, the street patterns soon became less regular. The haphazard growth of other towns resulted in tangles of streets that appear random and unplanned today, although often a response to the form of high and defensible terrain can be detected. Such patterns were not a considered objective of medieval thought, for new towns of the twelfth and thirteenth centuries were customarily laid out with a rectangular grid of streets and squares carefully selected for the placement of churches and markets. It was necessary that most other towns be

fitted within defensive walls that usually took a generally circular form, except where shorelines or rivers interfered and a semicircle might appear. The construction of city walls, their towers, and their gates was always a matter of great expense, and a circular city required the least wall construction to contain a given area of buildings and open spaces. Until the growth of buildings and markets outside a city wall unquestionably justified the construction of a second wall of greater diameter, the municipal authorities allowed the density to increase within its limited area (Fig. 3.12).

In one sense, we can think of the entire medieval city as a marketplace, much like the central retail areas of our cities today. Most products were sold at the place where they were made. Therefore, the narrow streets were lined with tables on which goods were displayed, windows opened into shops, and stacks of raw materials lay in the streets, waiting to be fashioned into products to be sold there. As the population of a town increased and its trade heightened, traffic in the streets intensified, and at the same time there was a tendency for merchants and artisans to enlarge their quarters by appropriating a part of the open space of the street (Fig. 3.13). Although town governments enacted regulations and officials were

3.12 Gates were important and vulnerable elements in the fortifications of medieval cities, even when the opening only permitted a river to pass through the city (right). When settlements outside the wall grew populous and prosperous, the city government was forced to consider construction of another wall that would include them.

3.13 Shops in medieval towns sometimes consisted merely of an opening into the workshop, above which the owner and his family lived. In other cases, a small area might be rented from the owner of a house. Taken from a fifteenth-century drawing, this view shows (left to right) a tailor's shop, a tavern, the barber's shop, and a grocer's stall.

appointed to control such encroachment, from the city plans of that day one must conclude that the regulations were unevenly and ineffectually enforced.

Medieval streets were narrow, sometimes even narrower than Greek streets had been. Complaints about encroaching construction frequently stated that two men on horseback or two carts could no longer meet and pass. In the typical medieval town, a street of twenty or twenty-two feet seemed a veritable boulevard, but portions of a street might occasionally be intentionally widened to serve as a marketplace. Paving sloped toward a channel in the center of streets, and continued efforts were made to hold households and merchants responsible for cleaning the streets in front of their property. Upper stories of buildings frequently overhung their property lines, and wealthy people might connect upper floors of their buildings on opposite sides of a street, leaving an arched passage through which traffic continued to pass. Since the width of any street was in practice variable and its direction was somewhat flexible, intersections were irregular in shape, presenting the pedestrian with everchanging views. Though certainly picturesque, the medieval street was dark, noisy, befouled with wastes, and permeated by a dreadful stench. Still, the attraction of the street's activity was so great that windows in the principal rooms of residences often opened directly onto the street instead of the workyard or garden behind the house. Because the uproar of marketplaces interfered with the conduct of church services, there were usually at least two squares in a medieval town. (In September 1991 parishioners of St. Louis Cathedral in New Orleans registered similar complaints about the noise of street vendors and performers in Jackson Square.)[7] In one of the squares the church would be situated, placed in traditional orientation so that it was entered from the west. Slightly more open space might be allowed in front of the church, but in some areas of Europe the towering church was encircled by residences and shops that huddled against its walls and left little more than the church doors visible at ground level. The space before the church was usually dedicated to civic and religious ceremonies, although some sorts of marketing might be permitted there.

Not far away, the market square provided space for peasants to sell the products they brought from the countryside and traveling merchants who came with goods from other cities and other lands (Fig. 3.14). Daily

3.14 In the important trading center of Lübeck, the most influential families were those that founded the town and owned parts of the marketplaces. The stalls of resident tradesmen and artisans often were converted into small permanent structures, as shown in this drawing based on medieval conditions.

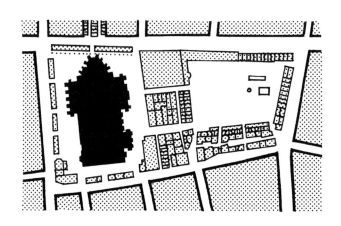

trade was provided for, but weekly market days brought more activity (just as farmers in the United States once thronged to towns on Saturdays). Annual fairs and seasonal markets filled the town and merchants' stalls stretched along the approaches to its gates. In a larger city, several market-places might be developed with regulations requiring sellers to set up their stalls in certain locations according to the goods that they sold and their status as either coming from the city and its immediate surroundings or from places farther away. The buildings around marketplaces and church squares were much the same as those along the streets of a city, although such sites were more valuable and usually merited more pretentious fa-cades. In some areas of Europe, the buildings around a square might have arcades (vaulted walkways set back within the profile of the building), but there was none of the uniformity seen in the Roman forum. As merchants became better organized and more influential, a structure might be built in the marketplace with an open area for vendors beneath a meeting hall for the burghers of the city. From this need for a meeting hall came the city halls that were constructed after the merchants had wrested greater power from the lords and the abbots.

During wars the walls around medieval towns served for defense; in peacetime, they served as tollgates, permitting the collection of fees from all outsiders who wished to sell their goods within the town. Many mer-chants set out their wares just inside the gates without venturing farther into the town. Market areas at the gates, frequently formed by widening streets as they neared the gate, were often designated for the sale of hay, grains, farm animals, and other agricultural products. Outside the walls, where traders waited until the gates were thrown open in the morning, open space was available for trading. Inns, shops, and the residences of some permanent traders came to be established there. When these settle-ments just outside the walls grew sufficiently large and enough farmers and herdsmen flocked to them, it was time for the townspeople to consider constructing an additional wall to protect the new settlers and to gain revenue from them. The traders and other settlers, for their part, had become sufficiently prosperous to consider protection worth paying for through city taxes.

In medieval towns, houses were crowded both internally and exter-nally, and there was little opportunity for privacy. A rule of social behavior advised, "Any time you pass by another person's house, be careful never to look in and never to stop." It is difficult to believe that this rule was always followed, and houses filled with complex groups of family, friends, appren-tices, and servants left few chances for lovers to meet or individuals to be alone with their thoughts. At the gates of a medieval town, buildings crowded outside the wall, but between the gates there was space for orchards. These orchards were valued as places for privacy, as were the cemeteries within the city walls. In fact, one French town denied the wishes of a monastic community to enclose its cemetery, declaring it to be a public place.

The sudden views of spires glimpsed down twisting medieval streets and the twisting lines of buildings' irregular facades are in most cases the results of happenstance, like the surprises and visual pleasures we find in

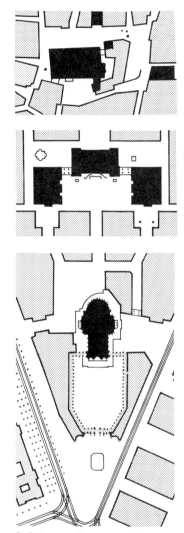

3.15 Camillo Sitte observed the richness of many city spaces with medieval origins, such as central Vicenza (top), where a principal city building had two plazas, both related to a third. He demonstrated how a public building complex (center) might be varied by providing three related spaces. In nineteenth-century Vienna, a vast square was planned in front of the church (bottom), and Sitte proposed that buildings be added in the area, forming an entrance courtyard and two others at the church's sides. Trolley cars converge in front of the church, passing by a grove of trees on the left. See Fig. 3.18, upper left of drawing on right.

nature. Although it is probably impossible for a designer consciously to achieve the charm of such fortunate accidents, medieval spaces merit careful study. During the last half of the nineteenth century the mood of the medieval cities and buildings fascinated a sizeable segment of European and American designers. In opposition to the regularity and orthogonal organization of Greek, Roman, Renaissance, and neo-classical architecture and civic design, the memory of the middle ages was extremely popular, in spite of the fact that a multitude of gloomy and dull interpretations of Gothic and Romanesque designs were built under the influence of the romantic spirit of the time. A foremost student of medieval city spaces was Camillo Sitte, who published diagrams showing the way in which informally related building masses enclosed spaces and directed the observer's eye (Fig. 3.15). His presentations suggested that effective spaces could be designed without relying on axial guide lines, orthogonal grids, or other restraints or that symmetrical elements could be assembled in a complex and dynamic fashion.

Medieval design and that of the centuries that followed in Europe profited greatly from contacts with the Muslim world. From the Moorish domination of Spain and from the crusades, Europe learned of Roman art and science, which had been retained, nurtured, and advanced by Muslim populations. Muslim towns had frequent small squares, and the larger houses were centered on courtyards that reflected the Koran's description of heaven as a garden. Fountains and pools, evergreen plants, fruits, and fragrant flowers offered pleasures for all the senses. These courtyards were virtual oases, treasured by a culture accustomed to regions dominated by a blazing sun and arid landscape.

Renaissance Cities

From the very earliest phases of the Italian Renaissance, theoretical plans for imagined cities are found, and the remarkable similarity of the designs is indicative of the planning attitudes of the time (Fig. 3.16). The plans show cities surrounded by a circle or an equilateral polygon of defensive walls, shapes that enclose a large amount of internal area with a minimum expenditure on the costly construction of walls. Within the walls streets were arranged in a grid, a combination of radials and rings, or some combination of circular and orthogonal geometries. The plans almost invariably have a large central open space, and usually other squares are provided in a uniform geometric distribution that does not designate any specific purpose for them, except perhaps as the site of a church. Although the idealistic generalization of the use of space (shown either as buildings, streets, or squares) has little relationship to the realistic problems of communities, they are the inevitable result of a plan lacking specific requirements.

Later historical periods in Europe are more difficult to elucidate, because of the vastly different characteristics developed by different countries and their different rates of social and economic development. Governments changed, often strongly affected by revolution or the unification of

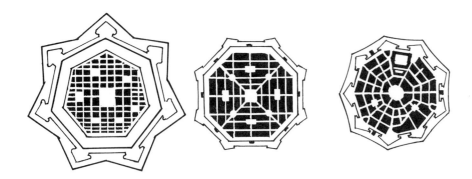

3.16 All three of these city plans were proposed in the last half of the sixteenth century. The one at the right was prepared for actual conditions and, therefore, shows more identifiable elements of the city.

separate small states. Private and public patrons, the socioeconomic groups that have the greatest influence on the outcome of art in a given period, are the products of such variables. For these reasons, urban design of the Renaissance, Baroque, and Neo-classical periods, and even the nineteenth-century developments are best considered under rubrics based on functional categories rather than chronological periods.

Avenues, Promenades, and Streets

At the end of the sixteenth century, the crowds of pilgrims in Rome, which were especially noisy and otherwise troublesome on certain feast days each year, caused Pope Sixtus V to plan avenues that would connect the principal churches and shrines of the faith and include major entrances into the city (Fig. 3.17). Routing pilgrims to minimize disruption of day-to-day activities was the pope's major objective. The task was not always simple in a city famed for being founded on seven prominent hills, and the famed Spanish Steps were built at a point where the terrain prevented an avenue

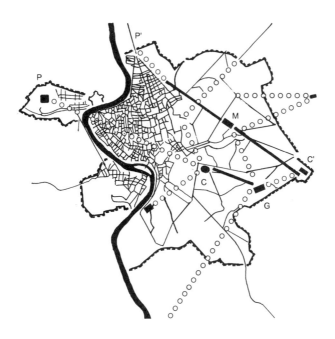

3.17 Pope Sixtus V (1585–1590) authorized the construction of a series of avenues that connected the principal points of Rome, including the major churches, the Coliseum, and the busiest gate that led into the city. Solid lines indicate the avenues that were completed then; rows of circles show those that were planned but were never executed. Some of the points used to establish the pattern were: (C) Coliseum; (C′) Santa Croce; (G) San Giovanni; (M) Santa Maria Maggiore; (P) San Pietro; and (P′) Piazza Popolo, a principal entrance to the city.

from reaching a major gate—the stair was used to connect that avenue to another at a lower level. Between the papal avenues, the city remained a tangle of medieval streets with occasional open spaces of the Baroque period carved out of the thick texture of buildings, usually as forecourts of churches or palaces. Structures, fountains, or obelisks were the focal points where these avenues intersected or terminated. In addition to simplifying the movement of the pious pilgrim throngs, these thoroughfares sped movement within the city and became favorite places for Roman society to congregate and display its coaches.

In other cities, the removal of protective walls provided space for construction of broad streets around the dense medieval core of the city. (The word boulevard is derived from bulwark.) Since late medieval walls were less likely to have been incorporated into the structures built up against them, they were relatively easy to clear away. The third wall around Florence, which was built in the late thirteenth century, was only about 123 feet wide—that width included the wall itself, its moat, and roadways along the inside and outside of the wall.[8] The avenues provided by such removals, broad and often lined with trees, became welcome belts of open space around the dense medieval center and allowed traffic to cross the city without contending with the congestion of the center. This began a tradition that ended as the bypasses and "ring roads" constructed in the automobile era around cities in the United States and other countries. A change in the style of fortification brought finer opportunities. When crossbows were replaced by cannons, stone walls and towers were supplanted by elevated earthen platforms in jagged patterns that afforded positions for firing armament.

In the city of Vienna we see the extreme condition of the removal of fortifications, for in the last half of the nineteenth century the city's defenses had remained with their width equal to the radius of the medieval city center and surrounded by a considerable depth of buildings (Fig. 3.18). This ring of cleared open space, almost a third of a mile in width, provided sites for parks, large complexes of governmental buildings, many apartment buildings, speculative construction, and a broad boulevard, fittingly called the "Ringstrasse."[9] Paris had developed a number of avenues in the seventeenth century, and in the nineteenth century, under Napoleon III, an outer ring was constructed. In other cities, a more typical development surrounded the old city with broad avenues along a band of park space, often with the zigzag pattern of the moat appearing as a serpentine pond within the parks. Railroad stations were located at the outside edge of this band, avoiding the destruction that would have resulted from tracks attempting to reach a central point within the old city, and hotels and restaurants were drawn to places along the avenues. During the day these avenues formed a bypass, speeding traffic to the central area as well as to the suburban growth outside; after dark they became the glittering focus of nightlife, much of it directed toward patronage by the growing number of traveling businessmen and tourists.

The flat tops of fortifications were necessarily provided with walks along which the city's nightwatch patrolled, and the walks became popular promenades where the upper-class citizens of the city might seek fresh air,

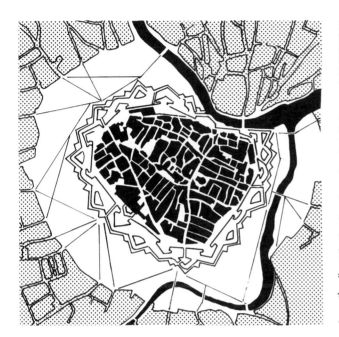

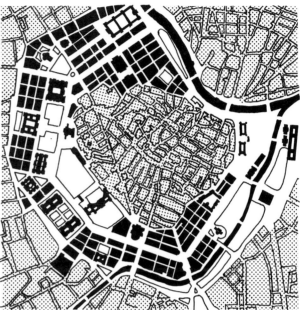

chat with acquaintances, stroll about, and enjoy broad views of the country-side beyond the walls. In some cities the fortifications were planted with rows of trees. In Paris carriageways made drives there even more enticing; fine clothing, marriageable daughters, gilded carriages, and the city's most attractive courtesans were on display daily.[10]

Promenades became important parts of upper-class life in most large cities, with many people walking beneath lines of trees or riding in their carriages along tree-lined routes. As one of her introductions of Italian sophistication to Paris, Marie de Medici established beside the Seine a route nearly a mile long that had a circle at its midpoint. On this prome-nade, the Cours-la-Reine, the gilded carriages of Paris society thronged (Fig. 3.19). Three bands of paving were sheltered by four rows of trees, and it was said that no less than a hundred carriages could be accommodated at one time in the circle.[11] Promenades, called malls or parades in England, became extremely popular after-dinner entertainment. (An event, it ap-pears, resembling American teenagers "dragging Main Street.") Other routes inherited the public fancy in Paris, notably the Champs-Elysées, and

3.18 The gun emplacements (left) protecting the medieval heart of Vienna lay between the city walls and suburban expansion. In the late nine-teenth century the fortifica-tions were razed and replaced with a ring of government buildings and parks (right).

3.19 At the end of Cours-la-Reine, a gateway led to the central and widest of the three avenues that ran between the four rows of elms.

similar fashionable strolling places were built in England and Germany, where Berlin's Unter der Linden remained popular through the nineteenth century.

Narrow streets remained in many of Europe's principal centers. Toward the end of the eighteenth century, Paris demanded that buildings be no more than fifty feet high on streets thirty feet wide; forty-eight feet high on streets fourteen to twenty-nine feet wide; and thirty-five feet high on narrower streets.[12] During the nineteenth century most large cities adopted regulations that employed the principle of relating allowed building height to street width. During the late nineteenth and early twentieth centuries, Paris required a maximum height of about sixty-six feet for the cornices of buildings and the top of the buildings were limited to heights from eighty-two to ninety-eight feet. This regulation encouraged the use of the mansard roof, which contained extra stories of occupied space above a building's cornice. Such requirements are, of course, closely related to the twentieth-century methods of regulating the form of buildings in order to guarantee that a reasonable amount of sunlight will reach spaces at ground level. The concern had been present for centuries (the British use a traditional phrase "ancient lights"), but the introduction of skyscrapers directed fresh attention to it in the early twentieth century.

Bridges and Riverbanks

In medieval cities, bridges had usually been lined with buildings. Much of the buildings' weight cantilevered from the bridge, and they towered several stories over the bridge and the narrow street it held (Fig. 3.20). The banks of rivers within cities were crowded with marshalling yards where the goods from boats were stacked, warehouses where materials were stored, and workshops in which they were prepared for sale. One could walk several blocks along an urban river's bank without more than fleeting glimpses of the water and boat traffic, and streets beside the river or crossing the bridge seemed little different from other narrow streets in the town, except that the activity of carts and draft animals would be more intense. Where there were no buildings between the rivers and the street, marketplaces and the bustle of carts and wagons kept the river's edge a workplace instead of an esplanade.

At the beginning of the seventeenth century, Henry IV provided Paris with Pont-Neuf, the city's first bridge that presented a view of the full sweep of the Seine (Fig. 3.21). The bridge resembled a classical bridge, with two spans connecting the upriver point of Ile de la Cité with both banks of the river. A small square at the level of the bridge was constructed at the midpoint, and in the center of the square an equestrian statue of the king was placed. Throughout Europe, cities began construction of spacious bridges as the increasing volume of traffic demanded. The urge to replace London Bridge and others was understandable because of the weight of buildings on them and the fact that, as one writer has put it, the piers of the old bridges were so large that the bridges were little more than dams with large holes in them. It was the 1750s before the buildings on London

3.20 A 1616 view of London shows the London Bridge and the buildings that were situated on the north bank of the river, the principal location of warehouses and other business enterprises.

3.21 Pont Neuf and the housing triangle behind it were built around the beginning of the seventeenth century to connect the banks of the Seine across the point of the island. This construction, and the moving of the clutter of boat loading and warehousing to other points on the river, did much to make the area become a fashionable residential district.

Bridge were torn down and the bridge, like the new Westminster Bridge, offered a broad view of the Thames.

As density increased in the centers of cities, warehouses and storage yards were moved outward from the center to less valuable sites and the banks of rivers became thoroughfares and promenades from which citizens could gaze at the broad path of the stream and the activities of workaday boats, anchored ships, and royal barges. Channeling the streams and replacing muddy banks with masonry embankments meant that the riverbanks within cities provided an orderly street that combined ease of movement and breadth of view. The Seine and the Thames became the principal ornaments of their cities.

Squares

During the Italian Renaissance, the forecourts of monumental buildings, the kind of spaces in which grand avenues terminated, were most often simply large paved areas. The process of entering a palazzo actually occurred in the central courtyard of the building, so the open area that was in front of the building and framed by adjoining structures was used as a public square. An English visitor to Rome in the 1640s described the piazza facing the Palazzo Farnese as the place where "in summer the gentlemen of Rome take the [fresh air] in their coaches and on foot (Fig. 3.22)."[13] During the seventeenth and eighteenth centuries European cities saw the

3.22 With two symmetrically placed three-tiered fountains, the Palazzo Farnese presented a fashionable facade to its forecourt. Gentlemen of quality strolled about, and ladies lingered in their carriages, where they received visitors.

construction of squares, which were mostly residential in function and with few exceptions built as ventures into real-estate speculation. (We will use the general term "squares," although their plans may show other geometric shapes. Place, piazza, and platz are other terms, employed according to country.) The wealthy owners of estates around which cities had extended quickly sensed the profits that were to be made by subdividing their land for speculation in housing. Some sizeable sites were purchased by speculators, often from needy nobles; and profit-minded collaborations between developers and nobles combined cash and land to undertake large projects. One Paris square, a project combining housing with ground-level retail spaces, was initiated in 1764 by a duke's creditors, who hoped to regain their losses through the development of his real estate. The number and nature of such projects, quite naturally, varied with the economic and political conditions of each country in a period of intense international expansion of trade. Whether built as suburban additions to a city or carved from its dense center, residential squares were laid out in simple geometric shapes: octagons, circles, ellipses, semi-ellipses, or even squares (Fig. 3.23). The facades of the buildings around them were designed as though each side of the square was a single large structure, their division into individual households being identifiable in England only by an observer's noting multiple entrances spaced along the sidewalk or the chimney walls spaced along the roof. Such unity did not signify that the dwellings were identical or even similar on the inside, for often the houses were purchased as vacant shells which could be completed internally as the purchaser wished. Although the projects, particularly in England, might have jumbled rear garden facades that clearly displayed the personal perferences of their owners, their fronts were combined in a manner that gave more prestige and a clearer identity to the square as a whole than to individual facades. Some large squares now have trees and gardens in their centers, but this is often a later addition, and originally most had only paved areas in which carriages wheeled about. In London, many of the less pretentious residen-

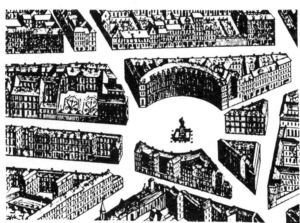

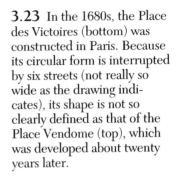

3.23 In the 1680s, the Place des Victoires (bottom) was constructed in Paris. Because its circular form is interrupted by six streets (not really so wide as the drawing indicates), its shape is not so clearly defined as that of the Place Vendome (top), which was developed about twenty years later.

tial squares were built around fenced gardens to which only residents of the square had keys, the squares being little more than widened streets with housing facades facing them. In Paris, a statue of the king was often placed on a pedestal in the center of a square, a design decision that encouraged royal approval of the project.

Isolated squares were less dramatic than a series of spaces that were geometrically connected. One of the most charming of connected spaces is the series at Nancy, built in the 1750s. A large bare square, three sides occupied by the city hall and similar buildings, opens through a narrow street and a "triumphal" arch into a linear space, about nine hundred feet long, with two double rows of trimmed trees standing before houses of a uniform height. At the far end, this space opens into a comparatively small oval space, the forecourt of a building. All of these spaces fell on a centerline: the square, then the long route to an oval with a transverse major axis. This impressive arrangement contrasts with a series of residential developments built in the same period at the English spa, Bath (Fig. 3.24). There a street leaves one edge of a square of houses, farther along enters a circle of houses, and continues at an angle to reach a crescent (actually a semi-ellipse) that opens down a grassy slope. The crescent became a common shape for multistory housing. Many British cities adopted it and added an

3.24 In the British resort of Bath, over about forty years a designer-developer and his son constructed housing areas, in sequence, as a square, a circle (right), and a semi-ellipse (upper left). The Circus and Crescent were immensely popular and led to the development of several housing blocks in serpentine patterns.

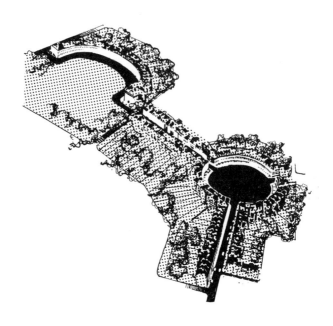

area of planting in its center. During the period when it was the most fashionable place for British society to drink and soak in healthful waters, Bath also saw the erection of housing rows in sensuous irregular curves along streets with gentle slopes.

Parks and Gardens

Public landscape parks were a common development that provided relief from the crowded atmosphere of burgeoning cities in the late eighteenth and early nineteenth centuries. Though spaces so large fall outside the scope of this study, it is useful to note that many were developed from private land holdings of kings and nobles that had been surrounded by a city's rapidly increasing population. As private or public holdings, they were usually large enough to make it possible for scenic arrangements to "disguise the real boundary," making it almost believable that a park in the midst of a thriving city could transport visitors to a rural setting.[14] It was this attitude that thrived with the introduction of the "English garden" (*jardin anglaise*). Gardens had been dominated previously by arrangements that divided an area into a geometric pattern (usually orthogonal); filled the areas with intricate border patterns and arabesques that displayed the color, texture, and dimensions of different plants; and elaborated the composition with three-dimensional elements such as arbors, hedges, walls, and fountains (Fig. 3.25). In contrast, the English garden artfully formed romantic groupings of its features in imitation of landscape paintings, more "natural" than Nature itself. Imitations of architectural ruins and pieces of neo-classical sculpture were inserted as visual accents. Escapism, certainly;

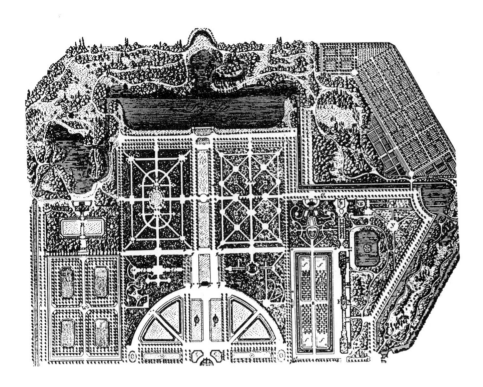

3.25 Part of the gardens of a Bavarian castle show the combination of formal and naturalistic arrangements. The *jardin anglais* at the top of this plan was made more interesting by the hillocks formed from the earth dug to make the lake.

but also an exciting visual contrast to the rigid forms of buildings. The basic principles of the romantic and picturesque designers did not have a direct connection with the physical nature of their designs. Their intention was, first, to evoke memories and associations and, second, to present environments that had the qualities of landscape paintings, virtually a glimpse of Eden. This approach, of course, could easily lead to mawkish sentimentality, and it was much more easily applied to the open sweep of the grounds of country estates than to severely limited urban situations. (In the United States, portions of Central Park in New York City are the best known examples of this romanticism.)

The English garden owed much of its development to the construction of picturesque grounds around the country estates of the very wealthy, but it was also applied to the creation of scenery for the large public parks that most cities built in the early nineteenth century. But promenades and parks were only useful in fair weather. In 1846 a group of Parisian investors constructed a winter garden, the Jardin d'Hiver, as a commercial enterprise—a glass-roofed building of iron structural members that contained several fountains, an artificial waterfall, and an Australian tree that was over fifty feet tall.[15] A few years later the Crystal Palace was built for the 1851 Great Exhibition in London, and after that winter gardens, palm houses, and other planted and enclosed spaces became popular in most major cities of Europe. Many were built in connection with the botanical gardens that were popular additions to city life during the nineteenth century, and all are harbingers of the atriums and gallerias that are popular today.

In the seventeenth and eighteenth centuries pleasure gardens were built and operated as public places of amusement, affording the public

3.26 This view of the Vauxhall pleasure garden shows the broad walks that were the primary organizing elements. Between them, meandering paths led through thickets of trees. The building in the foreground forms an entrance to the gardens and serves as a retreat in case of rain.

opportunities to enjoy the outdoors during the summer season. In most European countries taverns and inns at the fringes of cities commonly had small spaces beside them where their patrons might retire to eat and drink in the open air. Many of the inns built in the outskirts rapidly became surrounded by the city and were no longer far from their patrons' residences. Pleasure gardens were of many types and all levels of formality. In London there were some that attracted those who wished to see cockfights, bear-baiting, or women boxers; others displayed paintings and sculpture and provided evening concerts. At Vauxhall dinner could be served in private arbors, or, if it were a crowded or rainy evening, inside the body of a wheelless carriage (Fig. 3.26). Admission charges for the pleasure gardens were extremely modest, although they were increased for special events such as fireworks or balloon ascensions. Vauxhall occupied an area of perhaps eighteen acres; it contained groves of trees in rectangular groupings, and between them the walks were either broad or romantically narrow.[16] At lines of stalls, food and mementoes could be purchased; an artificial waterfall was turned on once each night; and performances were provided by singers, acrobats, and dancers. Vauxhall's London rival, Ranelagh Gardens, was somewhat more elegant and expensive, with a circular hall 185 feet in diameter in which the eight-year-old Mozart once performed.

Pleasure gardens were also to be found in the guises of German beer gardens (enjoyed in the United States from the nineteenth-century German immigration to the enactment of Prohibition) and, even today, as Scandinavian parks such as the Tivoli Gardens in Copenhagen. English visitors to Paris often compared Vauxhall with the gardens of the Palais-Royal, which were installed in the 1780s by the Duc de Chartres (Fig. 3.27).[17] A long rectangular space surrounded by an extremely repetitive three-story facade of apartments over arcaded shops, the area of about five acres was filled with plants and the stalls of vendors. Because the Palais-Royal was privately owned property, it was protected from police surveillance, and with its central location it soon became a center of activity for all

3.27 The Palais-Royal offered shops filled with the most expensive goods, kiosks, and cafes set among the rows of trees that filled the courtyard. In contrast with these light-hearted frivolities, at three o'clock on the afternoon of 12 June 1789, with some 6,000 people milling about the courtyard, a young man leapt onto a café table and delivered an impassioned speech that was one of the firebrands that started the French Revolution.

classes, the haunt of pickpockets, prostitutes, and veiled ladies out for a lark. It was also a hotbed of political intrigue and the setting for activities that played an important part in the beginning of the French Revolution.

THE AMERICAN TRADITIONS

Some of the earliest American towns were laid out before their settlers ever reached the new continent. Plans were provided by the governmental or mercantile organizations that financed their settlements. However, such plans seldom envisioned a city's full growth, preparing instead for the establishment of a modest and efficient trading outpost. Most of the other towns developed casually with the lay of the land as their sole restraint, in a manner remarkably similar to the development of medieval towns five or six centuries earlier. Except for streets, yards for unloading and stacking goods, and space for drilling a small military force, little area was developed as open space, for outside the settlement there was ample space, though it was sometimes unfriendly. Boston and New York began as uncontrolled developments on complex sites, but in the seventeenth century both cities found it necessary to launch efforts to simplify and regularize their street patterns. Such improvements were on occasion assisted by fires that demolished parts of the town. As a result, regulations were imposed that attempted to put an end to residents encroaching on the roadways and storing or manufacturing flammable goods. In New York, the marketplace was first situated at the water's edge, but by 1660 there was also a forty-day cattle market conducted every autumn at the place where Broadway widened in front of the fort. In Boston a central marketplace was established at the intersection of the town's principal street and the widening of another street that led to the city's principal wharf (Fig. 3.28). In 1658 the Town House, a hall for civic meetings, was constructed in the center of that space

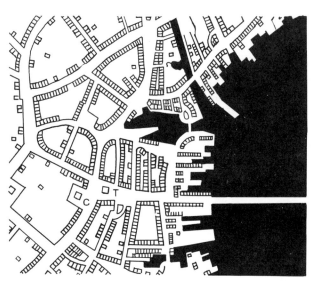

3.28 In early Boston the most active part of the town was determined by the intersection of a street paralleling the waters' edge and another that ran inland from the principal wharf. Here, the Town House, a structure of the city government, was situated, and the nearby church (C). These landmarks reflected the origins of the colony.

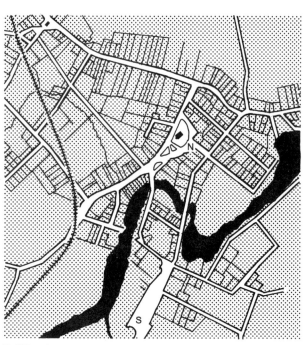

3.29 The north common (N) at Ipswich, Massachusetts, was irregular in shape due to slopes of the land and outcroppings of rock. At the center of this common, on one of the highest points in the area, a church was located, and the south end was the early market place. Another common (S) was situated in the southerly expansion of the village.

with a market area at the ground level and a meeting room upstairs.[18] Altogether, it was a reenactment of the development of markets in many small northern European towns during the medieval period.

In New England, many inland towns began with houses set around an open space, the church sitting within that space or fronting on it. This open space was viewed as property held in joint ownership (hence the term "common") by the original householders, and their sheep and cattle were allowed to graze there (Fig. 3.29). A caretaker might be required during the day to tend the animals on the common, but the space was also popular for evening strolls. On certain days it was necessary to pen the animals so that they would not interfere with drilling the local militia.

As inland transportation advanced, many settlements were located at the intersection of principal trails, the confluence of rivers, or other points where transportation routes assured that trade would be sufficient to maintain a small population. Innkeepers, horse traders, merchants, millers, and toll collectors congregated at such places, forming the nucleus of a growing community. Barring severe limitations of topography, such settlements developed as they do now—aligned beside the road or river, probably more strongly positioned on one side than the other. They extended in a linear fashion until their length demanded transverse routes that opened space behind the sites that fronted on the traffic route. These natural patterns of growth sufficed for Main Street and where the trail entered a town, but as traffic density and speed of transportation increased their simple relationships were no longer sufficient. Once a town grew large enough, owners of farms at its edges found it profitable to subdivide their acreage for sale as building sites.

The Growth of America

The dimensions of North America were awesome. Of the distance from ocean to ocean almost half was taken up in crossing the Mississippi–Missouri River basin, a distance about equal, as the crow flies, to that from London to Minsk. The entire continent was settled, though with extreme variations of population density, during a period of only some two hundred years. Turnpikes and trails, wagon roads that followed the terrain, led over the Appalachians to the center of the Mississippi River Valley. Canals were constructed in the northeast for the efficient shipping of products after settlement was made, and they were often the first leg of a settler's travel westward. Each successive mode of transportation defined and designated important points in a community. For coastal cities or those on navigable streams, the wharf established an area of everyday activity where carts, draft animals, and stacks of goods dominated. A road paralleling the shoreline was often the other determinant that might fix the position of the market.

Such haphazard layouts may have sufficed for settlements so small that the detailed variations of a coastline or a stream were matters to be considered carefully. The orthogonal grid, which had been the basis for planning the colonial settlements of the Greek city-states and the suburban extensions of medieval cities, became the pattern of frontier towns for all but the most extreme conditions of terrain. For one thing, rectangular building sites were well adapted to the traditional and simplest methods of joining building materials. From this background, it is certainly not surprising that the orthogonal grid should become the dominant—almost exclusive—theme of colonial planning in North America as well as other continents. In 1803 the Louisiana Purchase was made—almost a million square miles of land, very little of it settled or mapped. For charting an area so large, its future unpredictable, a grid was the only feasible method.

Many new towns in the West were laid out as simple squares, commonly subdivided into square blocks of building sites (Fig. 3.30). A town would have one dominant street, or two that crossed at the center—probably these would be the country roads that were laid out in the original survey at one-mile intervals. In this rational system a number of city blocks (usually twelve) made a mile, and each thirty-six square miles made another square that was a township (a term that provided a legal description of property rather than an actual designation of a settlement). The active political elements, such as counties and states, might acquire irregular shapes with rivers and mountain ridges making state and county boundaries, but on the whole the "Great American Desert," as it was labelled on

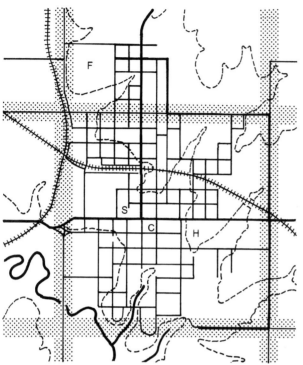

3.30 In Pawnee City, Nebraska, the courthouse (c), school (s), hospital (h), and fairgrounds (f) fit within the grid of streets, which is contained in the pattern of "section-line" roads (indicated with shading). Adjustments were made for the railroad and Turkey Creek.

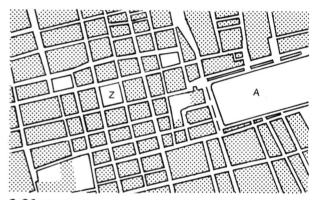

3.31 In San Luis Potosi, a Mexican city with a population of almost one million, the central area shows the elements of the early city. The Jardin Hidalgo or *zocalo* (Z), with its octagonal bandstand, and the *alameda* (A) (right) are accompanied by several other open spaces.

early maps, was settled according to the square-mile grid as the unit of measurement.

An exception to this system might occur when a different orientation was imposed by a railroad, a mountain range, or a river. Rivers in the west often diminished to narrow streams in the dry summers and broadened to torrents when spring brought rain; therefore it was often wiser to place a town on the bluffs at the edge of the wide river bed, while permitting docks, warehouses, and cattleyards to remain in the portions that might be flooded most springs.

Within cities and towns, grids could be oriented in different manners. The streets might be aligned with the cardinal points of the compass, running north–south and east–west (a system particularly common in areas west of the Mississippi River), or one set of streets might parallel the shoreline or riverbank (later the highway or railroad tracks) and the other be set perpendicular to them. (See Fig. 1.16). In the United States, a country in which ninety-degree intersections are almost universally assumed, the intersection of different grids produced geometric adjustments that led to series of open spaces with irregular forms, to triangular "flat-iron" buildings, and to complex traffic conditions.

In addition to Main Street, small towns in America might have two principal types of public open spaces provided: one as the central square associated with business and government; the other as a grove at the edge of town where the summer holidays would be celebrated, tents would be pitched for Chautauqua sessions or religious meetings, itinerant carnival troupes would perform, or families would picnic. In Mexico the distinction is quite clear: in almost all cities, the *zocalo* serves a central function, with government buildings or the cathedral facing the open space, while the *alameda* is a more pastoral setting, containing groves of trees (Fig. 3.31).

Many American towns designated as county seats or other governmental centers made use of the central square. Hispanic influence usually meant that a major building fronted on the open space, while in the United States the courthouse usually occupied the center of the space. In early days it was customary for courthouse squares to be an off-set block so that the dome or tower rose on the centerline of the two principal streets. This was the arrangement in Raleigh, North Carolina, a new state capital that was built at a geographically central site satisfying the battling political factions of the state. As settlement moved westward the survey of government lands had greater influence, and the courthouse square was most often simply a designated block of the town's grid. In a study executed by students at the University of Oklahoma, almost one-third of 585 county seats in that region had centrally located courthouse squares, but only a handful had the building on a central square that interrupted the grid of city streets.[19]

The colonial street was not without activity, even on the Sabbath. Cows and horses grazed there, fowls scratched, and, despite all regulations, hogs served as a primary method of garbage-removal (Fig. 3.32). (In the middle of the nineteenth century there were still complaints about hogs rooting about the streets of many eastern cities.) As the number of vehicles increased, American streets became almost as dangerous as those of European towns of similar size. The busiest street in Boston was paved for a width of twenty feet, and in many cities residents were permitted to place posts in front of their property in order to protect their buildings from damage by carts and carriages.[20]

There were many names for the principal streets of the new towns: Towne Street, Market Street, Broadway, and—most American of all—Main Street.[21] In New England, Main Streets appeared as a route beside the green, perhaps terminating at the front of the local church. As westward expansion continued, main streets not only came to the town, they continued through to towns established later and beyond to the open land that would become future sites for "town-makers." When a Main Street became too long to contain all of the residences and commercial buildings of the town conveniently, lanes were opened to provide access to outbuildings behind those fronting on Main Street.

At the start of the eighteenth century, the city government of Philadelphia instructed all householders to plant one or two "shady and wholesome" trees before their houses.[22] New York required planting along Broadway. Boston made similar requirements, and in Charleston trees

3.32 In colonial towns—this one is early Philadelphia—the streets were wider and less often paved than they were in European cities. Until the middle of the nineteenth century, rooting hogs were usually the principal method of garbage and waste removal in American cities and towns.

were planted for three or four miles along the principal approach to the city.[23] Throughout the United States, the notion of tree-lined residential streets was accepted as a model, with streets that were wide, shaded, and lined with trees that arched overhead. It became assumed that in residential areas and even many commercial parts of towns the city-owned band of property between the curb and the private property line rightly contained a row of trees. In a few places, such as Columbus, Georgia, that distance was made much greater than usual and held a row of handsome trees on each side of the street.

Charles Dickens on his 1842 tour of the U.S. marvelled at the trees to be found in cities here:

> New Haven (Connecticutt), known as the City of Elms, is a fine town. Many of its streets (as its *alias* sufficiently imports) are planted with rows of grand old elm-trees; and the same natural ornaments surround Yale College, ... The various departments of this institution are erected in a kind of park or common in the middle of the town, where they are dimly visible among the shadowing trees. The effect is very like that of an old cathedral yard in England; and when their branches are in full leaf, must be extremely picturesque. Even in the winter time, these groups of well-grown trees, clustering among the busy streets and houses of a thriving city, have a very quaint appearance: seeming to bring about a kind of compromise between town and country; as if each had met the other half-way, and shaken hands upon it; which is at once novel and pleasant.[24]

The appearance of such presuburban residential streets created a design pattern that was unconsciously assumed until the 1960s, when many streets were tragically denuded because of the Dutch elm disease, a plague that demonstrated the dangers of overplanting a single variety of street tree.

Except for suburban developments that have been based on the desire for exclusivism, all American villages, towns, and cities have been based on the enthusiastic assumption of growth. As Daniel Boorstin has pointed out, the nation was by nature populated with boomers, those who lent their enthusiasms and skills to the act of establishing new settlements, and boosters, those who stayed and applied their energies to the advancement of a settlement.[25] Both boomers and boosters were purveyors of unbridled, and sometimes unjustified, optimism. To the boomer, every new town offered an opportunity to gain advantages from colonizing a fresh site, whether it was a frontier cowtown or a Florida enclave for the rich. For boosters, it was an inescapable supposition that their towns would continually expand in ways quantitative and qualitative. Boosters' aspirations were clearly revealed by slogans announcing "Queen City of . . ." "Gateway to . . ." and "Hub of . . ."

Many early towns, including Philadelphia and Savannah, followed the precedent of Renaissance theorists and distributed parks at regular intervals in an orthogonal pattern. As with the Renaissance examples, these open spaces had no designated functions, adopting through time the roles of marketplaces, parks, or sites for public buildings. On a few occasions, some of such reserved spaces might fall at the water's edge (as does Jackson Square, New Orleans), opening onto a view of the water, but it was more customary that the space for handling goods would be gained from the interstices between the straight lines of streets and the irregularities of the shoreline or river bank.

The Influence of Transportation

If parks were too scarce, there were always other open spaces. In the late nineteenth century, street car companies found it wise to build cemeteries or amusement parks at the ends of their trolley lines in order to collect fares during the weekends. At least once a week, the areas in front of churches became meeting places to exchange gossip and renew acquaintances. Schoolyards were gathering places for the young outside school hours. If parks were not provided, there was usually a stream within the town, its unkempt banks serving as the background for the endless fantasies of the young. When there still were town bands, holidays were celebrated by listening to their music at the bandstand in the central square or at the picnic grounds.

Each advance in transportation established a fresh frontier for American boomers and convinced boosters that the expansion and improvement of their town was imminent. Supremely confident that their cities would in time grow to include them, the cities of Bismarck and Oklahoma City sited state capitol buildings in their outskirts.

Some railroads followed rivers, connecting the cities that had developed at bridges or fording points and taking advantage of the gentle gradients of the river valley. Where the tracks ran straight across the plains, the town might be established along them, just as a town might develop along a narrow stream. One side of the tracks usually held the more important buildings of local businesses; the other side was less dignified, having the railroad station, railroad sidings, the livery stable, and the odorous pens of dealers in horses and cattle. In the southwestern states, some towns have planted a narrow strip of right-of-way in the vicinity of the railroad station with palms and flowers, a rare treat for passengers on the train.

The passenger station of the railroad was a focus of city pride, but the more mundane areas around the railroad's right-of-way must be recognized as one of the romantic open spaces of any city early in the twentieth century. Buggies and wagons congregated when trains were due in a small city, and the bustle was constant around the railroad stations of larger cities. The station areas were the haunts of the immigrant groups who built and maintained the railroads (Irish, Hispanic, or Chinese laborers in different parts of the country) and of hoboes. As had long been the case with wharfs, young boys in small towns were warned away from the railroad yards with horrifying stories, but they usually found the switching yards irresistible. Much of a town's contact with the world elsewhere came by rail, and the whistle of the eleven o'clock train was as much a measure of town life as the chiming of the courthouse clock.

Skyscrapers

In the last decades of the nineteenth century, major streets in the largest American cities became hopelessly congested. There had long been grave physical danger for pedestrians from the swarms of skittish carriage horses and heavy draft animals. Along the curbs of Broadway in New York, wooden telephone poles carried as many as fifteen crossbars, each of which held insulators for ten wires. With telephone poles along each side of the street and many wires across the street, the sky was darkened.[26] An ice storm overburdened the wires in 1888, causing most to fall into the streets, and steps were taken to place all the city's telephone wires underground. Soon other cities followed New York's example. Many other developments of urban technology crowded the streets. In 1888 the electric streetcar was introduced in Richmond, Virginia. It replaced horse-drawn and steam-driven public transportation on the major streets, but horses continued befouling the streets. Coal wagons in winter and ice wagons in summer made their deliveries in residential districts; and on downtown streets large wagons loaded with barrels of beer were a major menace to all. When elevated public transportation made some streets even darker and subways provided a deeper and gloomier street below, it was time to be concerned about the growing darkness of downtown streets. In many cases the sun hardly penetrated, and at night store windows were dark, often shuttered, until the incandescent electric light provided a safe method of effectively displaying goods after sundown.

By the end of the nineteenth century, both New York and Chicago had built a significant number of skyscrapers. Then cities began to enact regulations opposed to the continuation of tall-building construction. Some cities restricted the heights or maximum number of stories to which buildings could be constructed; a few cities forthrightly and enthusiastically declared that there would be no limits within their jurisdictions. When skyscraper construction resumed, the area around Grand Central Station in New York had a particularly high density of construction, and that was one of the districts that caused concern about the shadows that tall buildings cast in the streets between them. There had long been requirements in Europe that the height of buildings' cornices conform to restrictions based on the width of the streets on which they fronted. In the United States, where much taller buildings were being built, the concerns were related to general conditions of the real-estate market as well as to shadows.

The approach of the New York Zoning Law of 1916, which designated areas of the city and limited the height and ground coverage of buildings built in them, was so popular that within a decade it was adopted, often with adaptations, by 591 other cities.[27] The restrictions of such regulations provided a three-dimensional boundary within which the actual building was designed. The stepping of the exact shape was usually influenced by reductions of floor area according to the zoning of elevator service.

In order to guarantee sufficient daylight for the street and the windows of other buildings, most cities enacted regulations that established required setbacks at different heights above street level, determining a volume within which the building must be built. Some early regulations prescribed a stepped profile of setbacks. Later, when the Gothic tower became a popular stylistic solution and the shapes of office buildings became more slender, tapered shapes were a popular requirement of city law (Fig. 3.33). The 1916 zoning regulations of New York City designated areas in which office buildings might rise from their lot lines to a distance 2 or 2½ times the width of the street. Above that level, the profiles of buildings had to stay within a slope of 1:5 or 1:4. Towers in the center of such buildings were unrestricted in height; however, their floor area could not exceed one-fourth of the area of the entire site.

A milestone skyscraper project was the design of Rockefeller Center. In October 1929, the same month as the stock-market crash that heralded the Great Depression, architects were chosen, and they began a decade of studies that were required before the project was completed. The site, a large parcel of land belonging to Columbia University, at that time was known principally for its concentration of speakeasies. Rockefeller Center was to be the period's statement regarding urban density. Raymond Hood, the principal architect on the Center's design team, enthusiastically declared:

> [The design] has been founded upon the principle that concentration
> in a metropolitan area for business reasons is a desirable condition. We
> are aware that many oppose that view. Nevertheless the commercial
> success of urban life is dependent upon concentration, which provides

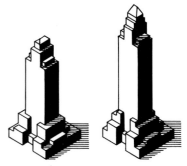

3.33 In the 1930s, the New York building regulations required setbacks and controlled the cubic feet of building volume per square foot of site that might be built in different zones of the city. Here we see the largest shape that a skyscraper might take if 120 cubic feet were allowed for each square foot of land (left) and if 144 cubic feet were allowed (right).

immediate access to those with whom we have to deal. Every large City has its insurance district, its financial district, its garment district, its theatrical district. These are essentials to City life. Decentralization means loss of time and inconvenience.[28]

A centerpiece was sought for the complex of office towers. Early in the studies, an opera house was planned as the central building, contrasting in form with the vertical elements. After that idea proved to be impractical, a bank building was studied for a time. At that point, a stroke of genius and the need to attract the public to the underground level that connected the buildings suggested the present scheme: An open space contrasting with those massive solids; the Plaza—an open space in which the eye is drawn downward in a place where, because of the height of buildings, the eye is irresistibly drawn skyward as well (Fig. 3.34).

There was much criticism when Rockefeller Center was completed, but in recent decades the Center and its Plaza have gained increasing recognition. The American architect I. M. Pei called it "perhaps the most successful open space in the United States, perhaps in the world for that matter." In analyzing the Plaza, Pei also said:

People come here as tourists, they come here to shop, they come here to go to the theaters nearby. So we have a variety of activities right here, day as well as night. In the abstract sense, I would consider Rockefeller Plaza far from ideal in terms of proportion. The spaces are perhaps a little too small for the size of the buildings that surround them. But in a way I am glad that it isn't larger, because it creates a special kind of intensity here, because of this exaggerated proportion. Just as exaggeration is necessary for effect in theater, so I think Rockefeller Center has succeeded in a way as good theater.[29]

Residential Projects

Tenement construction in the early part of the twentieth century introduced a vertical dimension to the crowded residential streets of large cities. In many large cities, tenements were permitted to satisfy safety requirements by installing metal fire escapes that also served as balconies during the insufferable summer months. Streets on which these tenements faced became three-dimensional neighborhood centers as well as trafficways. Children played games or romped in the spray of open fire hydrants, their parents sat on the stoops of buildings or watched and called to them from the windows and fire escapes. In Chicago and some other cities, the buildings that housed European immigrants commonly had multistory porches that generated an active setting for neighborhood exchanges.

Tenements, early in the twentieth century, were usually built to occupy the entire site, except for a small service yard at the back. An indentation of a few feet in each side wall supposedly served as an air shaft onto which windows opened. Because the shafts were so narrow, while they did provide space for the required windows, actually they supplied little air or light. Tenements were principally occupied by poor immigrant

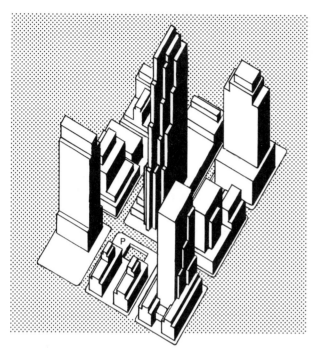

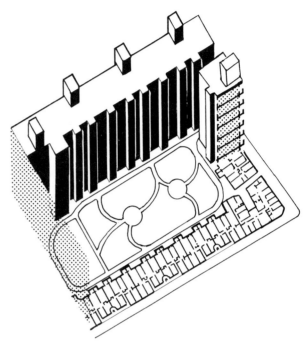

3.34 In the midst of the tallest buildings of Rockefeller Center, the Plaza (P) was placed below ground level. The Plaza's gold-covered statue of Prometheus and the annual Christmas tree placed behind the statue have become national symbols.

3.35 In six stories of small apartments in the Riverside Building, every room opened to air and light—an unusual amenity for low-income housing at that time. All units had access to the central courtyard, but they also opened to the noisy streets around the project.

families. Because of their popular association with their French origins, apartment buildings were at first considered to be suspect, even immoral, by middle-class Americans.[30] In time this prejudice was overcome, and much of the middle-class moved into apartments. Air shafts were wider where rents were higher, but since many of the buildings had elevators their additional height meant that their ventilation was only slightly better than that found in tenements. Building regulations extended the requirements for ventilation in multifamily housing, but they usually were applied only to new construction.

In 1890, a New York developer introduced the "garden apartment" building, so-called because the buildings surrounded a central open space. On a Brooklyn site about three hundred by two hundred feet, the six-story Riverside Buildings extended along the three sides of the site that fronted on streets (Fig. 3.35). The central area was planted with a scattering of trees, including the area that was designated as a children's playground.[31] Around the edges of the courtyard, adjacent to the buildings, there were rows of clotheslines for drying all the laundry that must have issued from over two hundred apartments.

Larger "garden apartment" projects came to involve buildings around a series of quadrangles. In situations where land costs did not demand high-density planning, three-story walk-up buildings were allowed sunnier and more spacious courtyards. Smaller projects, common in the 1920s, were simple U-shaped layouts. Their courtyards opened to the streets, and they often were more an entrance area than a recreational space for the tenants.

Suburbs

Even in England, the leader in industrialization and trade, business offices remained in the homes of their owners until late in the eighteenth century. In the United States the medieval combination of residence and workplace persisted into the twentieth century. The tradition of the "mom-and-pop" establishment, principally an immigrant business venture, included young sons and daughters who were looked after by all those doing business in a typical small-scale commercial area. However, by the nineteenth century advancements in communications and transportation made it possible for the owners and managers of larger enterprises to live at a distance from their businesses. The tradition of the "summer house" to which people fled during the uncomfortable periods of the year was transformed into a full-year separation of home and business. One of the first escapes was New Yorkers' flight to Brooklyn, which began in the 1820s when steamboats first offered ferry service from Manhattan. Commuter railroads, horsecars, and eventually electric trolleys made it possible for people of higher income to live in real-estate developers' projects that extended the fringe areas of a city. Commuting instituted and promoted an American ideal of living in a safe and simple village, while availing oneself of all the financial advantages of metropolitan activities (Fig. 3.36). But commuting was not to be an escape exclusively for the wealthy.[32] Manufacturers relocated their factories outside the city, and they built towns to house their workers. Along the tentacles of the railroad, clerks and artisans, who could afford the daily cost of commuting, escaped from the city. This application of transportation in effect turned the city inside out and by 1930 one out of every seven Americans lived in the outer fringes of cities.

The more scenic sites for suburban development had usually been taken for early higher income occupancy, by those who had been attracted by advertisements inviting them to "live in a park." Picturesque curved streets were the most popular pattern for developments of this sort, often following a stream or ravine so that the houses might have the higher ground and be impressively approached. Later and denser housing groups in the suburbs were often situated on farmland with less scenic quality, but the frequent and continued use of winding streets meant that developers could devote less land to rights-of-way and provide less paving. In addition, curved street patterns often made it possible for a development to achieve some small degree of individual identity, offsetting facades in order to diminish monotony. And complex street patterns kept residents of neighboring subdivisions from passing through an area for which deeds and regulations insured residents of a higher class. Even when a suburban development was built on a treeless cornfield, setbacks might be generous as a symbol of luxury, and twisting roadways seemed to wander aimlessly across the expanse of lawns. New suburbs sprang up everywhere. During two years of the Los Angeles boom in the 1880s, plats were filed for at least 1,770 new subdivisions.[33]

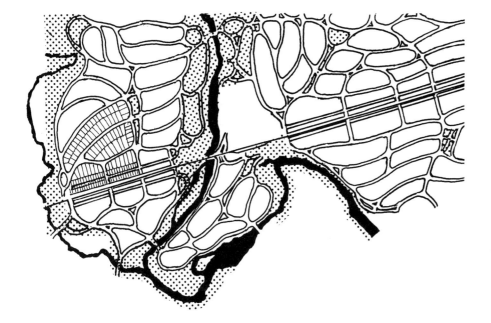

3.36 In 1869, Frederick Law Olmsted, designer of Central Park in New York, laid out Riverside, Illinois, a pictur-esque settlement suitable for the picturesque houses of the time. Dotted areas are park land within the project site.

Garden Cities

After the 1920s, there were movements to apply the intentions of the picturesque residential developments of the late nineteenth century to single-family housing, providing smaller lots for owners with moderate incomes. Fewer through streets were required by use of the superblock, a larger parcel of land with cul-de-sacs providing access to sites in the center. This plan allowed for at least two levels of traffic intensity within these residential areas, although formerly there had been only one. In addition, the traditional alley was eliminated. By this means, whether the pattern was orthogonal or one of the increasing popular irregular patterns, a significant amount of street paving was avoided. At the same time, houses' backyards became a more unified space, and under present-day practices the center of a superblock may include both private backyards and a shared recre-ational space. This latter area afforded an opportunity for the development of an independent network of pedestrian movement, largely separated from vehicular traffic. Just as traditional town plazas had assumed a group-ing of dwelling units alongside a street, this "garden city" system employed groupings about the backyards and pedestrian routes. In this way, streets became not the central elements of neighborhoods, but instead the divi-sions between neighborhoods that were formed around open spaces. This kind of planning allowed a great degree of separation between pedestrian walkways and vehicular streets, a principle that had been introduced in Frederick Law Olmsted's design for Central Park in New York. The Green-belt towns, a small number of commuter villages, built under federal sponsorship during the Great Depression of the 1930s, were the fullest statement of the idea. This scheme was accompanied by and largely based on proposals that the typical house plan be altered to locate social spaces toward the backyard and service spaces toward the street. In effect, this change of attitudes toward residential planning reversed the old pattern in

3.37 Greenbelt, Maryland, between Washington and Baltimore, was one of three commuter towns built under federal sponsorship during the 1930s. Six residential superblocks were laid out within the principal roads. Inside the superblocks, pathways led to community facilities and schools, crossing streets at only a few places where pedestrian underpasses were constructed.

which sidewalks and living rooms faced the street, and kitchens faced clotheslines, garbage cans, and the alley. (The family automobile, which had long been garaged in the place once occupied by the stable, moved to a place adjacent to the street.) In residential developments built after World War II, these changes often meant that the streetscape became one of curbs, lawns, automobiles, garage doors, and housefronts—the few trees that were planted usually were so small that they were hardly visible (Fig. 3.37).

For denser housing locations, the ideas of the French architect and painter Le Corbusier were influential. His city-planning scheme of the 1920s took advantage of the new technologies of elevators and skyscraper construction to place tall apartment buildings among gardens and parks. By building upwards architects eliminated the direct relationship between an area's population density and the degree to which land surface was covered with buildings; if a site that would be completely covered by a ten-story building was used for a thirty-story building, two-thirds of the site could be developed as open spaces that would be conveniently available to the tenants. (The logic and cost of such schemes suffered when the American affection for automobiles was considered.)

Both skyscrapers and garden cities had their limitations as the solution of overall housing problems. Those who dreamed of

> . . . a perfect, cityless, endlessly suburban world, to which anyone could belong who possessed the following qualifications: (a) enough money to build his own house and to operate a car or two, and (b) the right color (once the right religion, too, but that requirement largely passed by) to be allowed to build in that suburbs at all. If one was poor (of whom there were comparatively few in America) or black (there were about the same number), there was no room in the dream-world for him. Since a majority had been able to meet middle-class standards in the United States, it has usually been simply tough luck for those who couldn't; they have never controlled enough power, upon which architecture is ultimately based, to build a reasonable environment for themselves.[34]

Even in the rural slums, a major solution to American housing problems has been the utilization of deteriorated and unsanitary dwelling places.

Formality and Grandeur

The use of monumental avenues gained credence in America with the plan devised by Pierre L'Enfant in 1791 for the new national capital in Washington (Fig. 3.38). For this scheme, desirable sites were selected for the presidential palace and the capitol building,—the latter was about eighty feet above the level of the river. The city was to be covered with a small-scale grid pattern of streets, irregularly spaced, that ran north–south and east–west. Over these streets was superimposed a network of diagonal avenues, and squares and circles were planned at the intersections of these major routes. All of the elements employed in the plan were well-

3.38 L'Enfant's plan for Washington, DC, applied diagonal avenues over a rectangular grid, making special spaces at the intersection of the diagonals. In the center, malls relate the White House (left) and the Capitol (right).

established in Europe, with the gardens of Versailles probably the most significant model at that time. Unfortunately, once the street pattern was set, little more was done to develop the character of the city until the last part of the nineteenth century. An odd medieval-style castle that housed the Smithsonian Institution and the station of the Pennsylvania Railroad were among the elements that had intruded on the Mall, a space intended for sweeping and majestic vistas.

The 1893 World's Columbian Exposition in Chicago was a masterful and eye-catching arrangement of neo-baroque buildings, a gleaming white stage for a temporary show. The chief architect of the fair, Daniel Burnham, announced a few years later that "the time has come for Chicago to make herself attractive" (Fig. 3.39).[35] Over the city's grid, he placed a larger-scale diagonal grid of major avenues, their intersections marked by monuments or principal buildings of civic pride. Similar Burnham plans for cities such as Cleveland, San Francisco, and Manila followed and established the pattern of what came to be referred to as "City Beautiful" planning. An effort to rescue the spirit of the L'Enfant plan in Washington employed Burnham's talents immediately after he completed his plan for Chicago. The railroad station was removed, spaciousness was restored, and buildings of importance were restored to the appropriate dignity.

In many ways it became the most beautiful city in the United States, particularly if you remained within the confines of the major axes and the parks along the Potomac and the creeks leading to it, and if you did not approach it with a disposition to be nauseated by its classicism or its "imperialism." But it was less rewarding if you strayed from the avenues of the northwest quarter.[36]

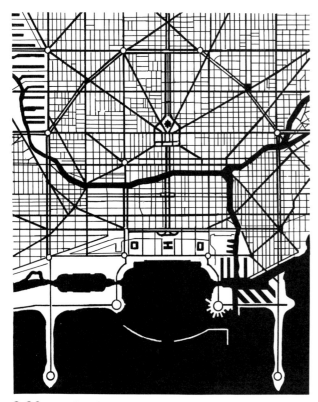

3.39 Burnham's 1909 plan for Chicago employed networks of streets and avenues, combined on a grand scale. The scale of such projects was usually so vast that only portions of them were executed, the most successful being the Mall in Washington.

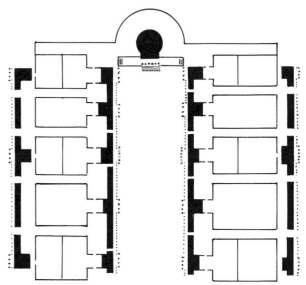

3.40 Thomas Jefferson's design for the University of Virginia flanked the domed library with two long lines of classrooms and professors' residences (black). Outside of these are lines of students' quarters and more professors' residences (black).

Although grandiose to a fault, City Beautiful schemes were remarkably adapted to expansion. Streetcar routes could be extended in the center islands of the major avenues, creating an efficient network of transportation with the city, and sewers and power supply could grow in the same manner. More interesting at this scale are the many triangular open spaces created by the combination of the two grids, where the familiar small street environment of residences met the monumental scale of the diagonals.

Quadrangles and Courtyards

From the village green in New England, American places had often been designed on a theme of open space filled with trees and grassy lawns and surrounded by buildings. Thomas Jefferson's plan for the University of Virginia had assumed many of the characteristics of the Roman forum—the library situated as the temple and students' quarters providing a frame for it (Fig. 3.40). The English precedent for arranging groups of university buildings was the cloister of a monastic complex, but the American pattern became the quadrangle, a rectangle of trees and lawn, its sides made of

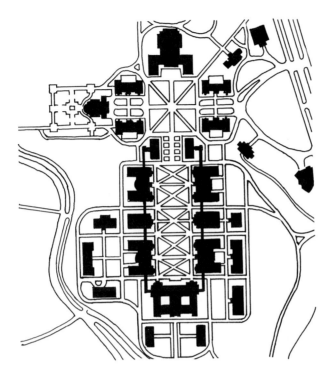

3.41 The plan for Johns Hopkins University, prepared in 1905 by architects Parker and Thomas, involves a series of axially related quadrangles. Typical of institutional planning of the period, the scheme could be expanded by the attachment of additional quadrangles.

four or more rectangular buildings. Institutional plans, except for a few functions such as hospitals, tended to rely on this pattern, linking sequences of quadrangles as they grew (Fig. 3.41). Sometimes the center lawn was ringed by a drive that ran in front of all the buildings. At other times, vehicular access was eliminated from the interior of the quadrangle and was allowed only at entrances other than the formal portico that faced on the quadrangle.

During the first half of the twentieth century, significant changes came about in the ways in which groups of buildings, related in function, were arranged. Previously, the buildings had been set out employing the fundamental principles of Roman axial order. Emphasis might be placed on the central space, on one or more principal buildings and their facades, or on both in different portions of a complex arrangement based on several related axial systems. The most traditional building functions, almost all formal and monumental in nature, were well suited to such schemes. Many of the functions that developed later in architecture, such as office buildings, were seldom provided with more ground space than that occupied by the building itself. But early in the twentieth century, various social and governmental changes caused architecture and landscape architecture to be viewed much more frequently as agents of social improvement. This naturally involved greater activity in the planning of housing complexes, particularly those intended for low-income families and factory workers. In the densest urban situations, housing projects provided no outside space. In other situations, there came to be accepted practices for the arrangements of the buildings and their relationship to the space around them. One of the most powerful influences on such decisions was the growing concern about matters of public health.

The acceptance of the germ theory of disease early in the twentieth century held out the possibility of developing measures that could assist in controlling epidemics and environmental conditions that might reduce the incidence of certain ailments. At that time great faith was placed in the healthful effects of sunlight and ventilation, their curative powers for such diseases as tuberculosis and their preventive powers for many other every-day ailments. Through that period Europe and the United States had many tuberculosis sanatoriums where patients were treated, principally with fresh air and sunlight. It was natural that many architects and public health experts should arrive at an ideal orientation for housing units, one that would call for windows to be placed to admit the maximum amount of sunlight and fresh air. As shown in many of the older public schools in the United States, a common principle of orientation favored windows facing east and west so that all rooms would have equal exposure to the healthful beams of sunlight during the day. Housing was designed with long build-ings that permitted each dwelling unit to have precisely the same, equally beneficial, conditions of light and air, the supposed ideal orientation. The spacing of these parallel bars of housing was set at the distance that would prevent one building from blocking sunlight from the windows of another. To avoid long spaces between buildings, the parallel bars were often kept relatively short and staggered in their placement. This arrangement, when well executed, could result in a continuity of the open area around the buildings without confining it to precise shapes.

By the end of World War II, heliotherapy and precise orientation no longer seemed so essential to successful housing design. Many functional types of buildings, however, were oriented so that the majority of windows faced south or southeast for natural ventilation and sunlight and solar heat were controlled with overhangs or grillage. Such restraints were reduced in importance by the advent of air-conditioning. The emphasis in site-planning returned again to the placement of building masses in a manner that would create spaces that were rectangular, or at least quadrilateral. It may have been due to the influence of Cubistic abstractions and their development of dynamic relationships between shapes, but the buildings were no longer placed symmetrically about the open spaces (Fig. 3.42). Instead, irregular placement of building masses along the sides of the quadrangles left openings of variable dimensions and placement. Thus, in the terms of the time, space and circulation "flowed" from one quadrangle into those adjacent, and still a feeling of containment was maintained within each open space. Design of the areas among buildings arranged in this ambiguous manner was different than when quadrangles had been symmetrical and strictly self-contained. Angled and curved walkways and asymmetrically placed clumps of trees, were the most common solutions to the new problems caused by the new design, and often they proved effec-tive foils to the crisp geometry of the buildings' facades.

If a building is to be placed on a site, the two most basic choices are to situate the building in the center of the space, leaving a significant opening on all sides of it, or to set the building along one or more boundaries of the site, leaving an open area in the center. The first option was brought to America principally by north-European influences, for it has the advantage

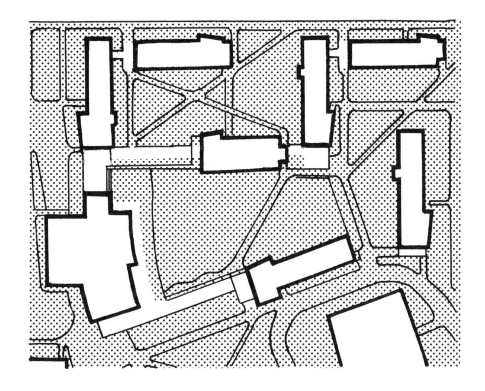

3.42 The Graduate Center at Harvard University (1952) was planned with incomplete quadrangles among the dormitory buildings, space flowing from one area to another and covered walks to connect the buildings and provide a subtle completion of the quadrangles. All white areas are roofed. In some ways, this spirit of site planning embodies the principles stated by Camillo Sitte. Compare the spatial design with that shown in Figure 3.15.

of providing a building that is compact, easily heated, and with enough wall surface to admit much light. A centered building opens much of the surrounding space to public view. The sideyard of one building falls alongside that of the next building, and with the streetscape and the space around other buildings there comes to be a spatial continuity that extends across a multiplicity of ownership, maintenance, and personal preferences in design. This condition has led to the imposition of many controls, both *de jure* and *de facto*, regarding the utilization and development of these areas. Setbacks are customary (except where land values encourage building to the lot line), grass may be required, and regulations may severely limit the provision of fences or hedges. Beyond those restrictions, the desire to coexist comfortably with neighboring landowners usually demands a certain conformity to the typical design norms of the locale. On the other hand, the second treatment, which concentrates open space in the center of the site, requires little regulation, for the privately controlled space is privately experienced and public spaces are clearly public. In America, centralized space is observed largely as the result of Hispanic influences and in regions where hot and dry climates find advantages in shady courtyards and access to breezes.

During the 1920s, interest in some of the Hispanic methods of viewing the open spaces between buildings began to resurface in the United States. Because of population increases in the southwestern states, today known as the "Sunbelt," Spanish influences were a sensible, eclectic solution. Arcades, courtyards, and a limited but effective utilization of planting developed a picturesque character in the design of spaces, in contrast to the English "woodland" notion of the picturesque.

Shopping Centers

Promoters of the earliest suburban divisions soon discovered that retail facilities should in many cases be an integral part of their plans. Sometimes no stores were conveniently near; sometimes the use of existing shops meant that residents of the finer subdivisions would necessarily mingle with the very populations they had sought to escape. In general, the absence of a village center predating the subdivision merely meant that the developers provided one that might at first glance seem to be even older.

With the increase of automobile traffic and construction of high-speed highways, the shopping locations made up of parallel bands of higher-speed traffic, slow-speed traffic, and parking, pedestrian movement, commercial buildings, and service areas at the rear were no longer practicable. An early solution in the United States was the development of one or more blocks in which this same succession of parallel functions was curled within the city block near a busy commuting route—parking around the outside, a ring of buildings and a service yard at the inside. Spatially, this solution, which dates to the early decades of the twentieth century, was little different from today's strip shopping groupings along busy street or highways at the edges of cities. By the 1960s this model had increased in size to become the regional shopping center, a group of buildings located near the intersection of major commuting routes, that is surrounded by vast parking areas, and that has several points at which shoppers penetrate to reach the center of the complex. This form of shopping center, as exemplified in 1952 by Detroit's Northland, prided itself on the series of courtyards between the buildings (Fig. 3.43). Service and deliveries were subterranean, and slightly more than 40 percent of the 165-acre site was used for automobile parking. During the short period in which the Northland "style" was in its ascendancy, considerable attention was given to the development and ornamentation of the courtyards inside shopping centers.

> Generous colonnades, fourteen feet wide, connected the malls and courts. These had sculpture by many artists, fountains and planting of rhododendron, azaleas, flowering cherries and magnolias. . . . Despite the indifferent quality of its art, it was such a magnet that many Detroiters had the habit of visiting it, even on Sunday when only the restaurants were open.[37]

Once shoppers had entered from the expanses of sun-baked or windswept parking lots, the display of charming open spaces was often so effective that it became an embarrassing standard against which downtown spaces were to be compared. By 1975, workmen were erecting skylights over the courtyards of Northland, and the fashion had changed in favor of totally enclosed malls.

Following World War II, shopping centers attracted so much trade away from the traditional downtown retail establishments that many communities felt impelled to mount counterattacks. In some cases, shopping centers (without the vast parking areas) were built downtown. A more

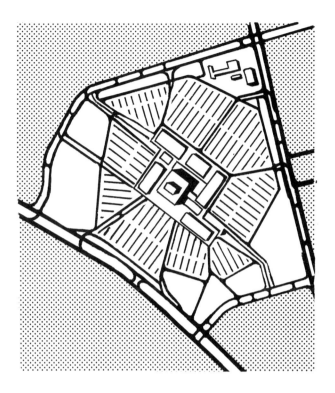

3.43 Northland, a Detroit shopping center, clustered other businesses around the department store that was its major attraction. Underground services and delivery facilities kept the plan sufficiently compact to permit quick access to the center.

common approach was designating certain downtown streets as pedestrian areas, barring vehicular access or providing transportation by small vehicles. These areas were supplied with such amenities as trees, benches, sidewalk cafes, and even glass roofs. Many pedestrian streets were set in areas of charming old commercial structures; others attempted to revitalize old markethalls and warehouses. In general, the designs clearly were focused toward tourists and middle-class shoppers. Boutiques abounded and often quaintness was at a premium. One irate critic snorted at a project, "Corn. Kitsch. Schlock. Honky-Tonk. Dreck. Schmalz. Pseudo-Victorian Junk creating an ersatz San Francisco that never was."[38] Because of economic factors in the 1980s, automobiles were readmitted to many of these projects where there was not powerful support for retaining the ban against them.

AMERICAN VALUES

In about three centuries of town-making and city growth in the United States, some common principles and attitudes have developed—in spite of the fact that the nation encompasses ranges of climate, terrain, and lifestyles that are the equivalent of those across the entire continent of Europe. Of course, the concrete evidence of European traditions is always visible. In the future, no doubt, there will be increasing effects of the Asian traditions. But the average American citizen today is at least two generations removed from immigrant status, and the effects of family association with a homeland is extremely slight. This temporal and social distance does not mean that such associations are negligible. The fact that a surname has certain ethnic associations may be significant, even though in a few generations that relationship may become only a small fraction of the individual's genetic inheritance. Association with the past is necessary, and the massive immigration of the nineteenth century has meant that for many Americans association with the "home country," although not strong, is greater than any personal association with Pilgrims or the Civil War.

Much of American visual values are understandably derived from foreign associations and the many worldwide standards of design that have long been established. Standards such as the grand avenues of Paris were imitated or emulated in Buenos Aires, Cairo, Calcutta, and Chicago. Such repetition across countries occurs for several reasons. From the middle of the nineteenth century well into the twentieth, Paris was accepted as the international center of artistic taste, fashion, and elegance; colonization, governmental or financial, carried with it the standards and aspirations of other countries; and many growing cities developed the same need for larger and straighter thoroughfares that had necessitated their use in Paris in the first place. Government buildings around the world assumed the same bland, repetitive classical appearance, just as today worldwide commercial establishments and transportation centers have an inescapably American air about them.

Just as northern European, Mediterranean, and Latin American traditions have affected American spaces and places in the past, and Asian traditions are increasingly affecting them now, turnabout has occurred with the transplantation of American visual, spatial and functional values. There are distinctly American ideals that have strongly influenced American urban spaces and, it is to be hoped, will become consciously employed by designers in the future. As with all history, past and present, the individual designers may accept such attitudes as admirable and meriting encouragement and enhancement, or they may disapprove and choose to defy them. In practice, such black-or-white purity of decision is seldom possible. Designers more often make choices in which they hope to make the best of an undesirable aspect of American life, dramatize an aspect that they believe is too little admired, or endeavor to find a way in which the positive factors are emphasized and the negative ameliorated.

As do all human beings, Americans suffer from self-frustration. In the words of an old saying, they would like to "eat their cake and have it too." They wish for an idyllic residence in a park-like setting, but to have all the advantages and opportunities of a thriving metropolis available to them without travel becoming inconvenient. The obvious impossibility of this dream has been somewhat mitigated by technological advances in communication and transportation, but it remains essentially unattainable. Fortunately, there remain possibilities of effective compromise through both technological and artistic means.

Those characteristics of public spaces that are particularly American are not matters of basic form. For avenues, squares, parks, and other categories of outdoor spaces came to be used as adaptations of the European traditions of civic design to the nature of the New World. Certain aspects of the historical movements that opened and occupied the land of North America, aspects that also left a clear imprint on American culture, left their mark on the urban spaces of the United States. Although the settlement of the lands that became the United States was dominantly conducted by English colonists before the 19th century, the English influence was tempered by the fact that English traditions had in many ways absorbed and adapted French, Italian, and other European traditions. The early settlements of French immigrants and explorers soon diminished in importance (except for the port city of New Orleans), but the features of French cities had by then influenced design in England. Spanish settlers and the traditions they brought with them remained influential in the southern zone of the United States, perhaps primarily because of climatic similarities, but in Europe they had incorporated many Italian and French precedents.

On this foundation of European traditions were imposed those factors that arose from the distinctive conditions that settlers encountered in the United States and the settlers' responses to those conditions. The contiguous area of the United States is almost as great as that of Europe, and the direct distance ("as the crow flies") from Washington, DC, to Seattle is almost twice that from Athens to London. Even today the population of Europe is roughly three times that of the United States. Furthermore, the westward expansion of culture across Europe took place over a period fully five times as long as the period in which the United States was settled and developed. (Certainly, these data can be disputed, but their general import is unquestionable.) After the earliest years of colonization there was little need for strong defensive provisions in the layout of American settlements, and the image of a typical American city was in no way associated with the crowded conditions that had resulted from European fortifications. Instead, the narrowest streets in American towns were wide compared to equivalent European streets, and as the American settlement moved westward the difference was more pronounced. By the 1930s, streets in small cities had the dimensions of some Parisian boulevards, although they might pass frame houses that were more widely spaced than even the villas of Paris suburbs.

Distance also resulted in a remarkable emphasis on systems of transportation and their routes. As in Europe, American cities were first situated along shorelines and river routes, but North America, certainly that part of it that was to be the United States, has far less coastline than Europe. With the intrusion of the Baltic and Adriatic Seas into the mass of Continental Europe and the protrusion of Italy and Iberia into the Mediterranean Sea and the Atlantic Ocean, no modern national capital was more than about 350 miles from a coastline. (It is about twice that far from St. Louis to New Orleans.) The narrow bands of ports on America's east and west coasts were, of course, important centers of trade, but they were distant from the hundreds of new inland centers that were established as the population moved westward. These cities relied on rivers, trails and roads, canals, and—in the end—railroads, and the distances between cities increased as settlement was extended into the vast western area that at that time was shown on maps as the Great American Desert. Railroad stations and the marshalling yards around them became centers of activity, very similar to the port areas of older cities, and the locations of many new towns were determined by railroad engineers as they mapped the routes along which tracks were to be laid.

Climate, too, caused American towns to differ from those of Europe. Winters in America were longer and colder, and summers were hotter than settlers had been accustomed to in Europe. Those who came from England soon found that the traditional half-timber dwelling could not withstand the shrinking and swelling caused by American winters. The customary methods of preserving foods were inadequate for the extremes of the American climate. In the summer St. Louis reached temperatures higher than those of the Mediterranean coast, and in the winter the city was almost as cold as the Scandinavian capitals. For this reason, trees were planted for shade in summer and as windbreaks for winter. Trees, for which there had been no space in medieval European cities, became an essential element in the American view of the ideal urban environment.

With this broad view of American traditions, roots, and values for spaces, the stage is set for a detailed examination of the spaces themselves—their design factors, qualities, and characteristics. Those forces that are peculiarly American are displayed not in the fundamental forms of urban tradition, but in the manner in which the essentials of tradition have been adapted and changed in expression to respond to the challenging breadth of geography and aspirations that were discovered in America.

ENDNOTES

1. John Reps, *The Making of Urban America* (Princeton, NJ: Princeton University Press, 1965), fig. 84.

2. Michael P. Buckley, "Creative Design Management: Understanding Motivations and The Creative Process," *Urban Land* (April 1990): 21.

3. C. A. Doxiadis, *Architectural Space in Ancient Greece* (Cambridge, MA: MIT Press, 1972).

4. Vitruvius Pollio, *Ten Books on Architecture,* tr. Morris Hicky Morgan, 1914. (New York: Dover, 1960), 5.1.1.

5. Vitruvius, 1.7.1.

6. Vitruvius, 5.11.1.

7. "In the Birthplace of Jazz, It's Just a Little Too Loud," *New York Times,* September 3, 1991, A18.

8. E. A. Gutkind, *International History of City Development*, vol. 4, *Urban Development in Southern Europe: Italy and Greece*, (New York: Free Press, 1969), 331.

9. Carl E. Schorske, *Fin-de-Siecle Vienna* (New York: Knopf, 1980), 46.

10. Mark Girouard, *Cities and People* (New Haven, CT: Yale University Press, 1985), 166–167.

11. Robert Laffont, ed., *The Illustrated History of Paris and the Parisians* (Garden City, NY: Doubleday, 1958), 136.

12. Josef W. Konvitz, *The Urban Millennium* (Carbondale, IL: Southern Illinois University Press, 1985), 82.

13. John Evelyn, *Diary*, November 10 and 12, 1644. Quoted in Girouard *Cities and People*, 124.

14. Humphry Repton, *Repton's Landscape Gardening*, ed. J.C. Loudon, 1840. Quoted in George F. Chadwick, *The Park and the Town* (New York: Praeger, 1966), 23.

15. Georg Kohlmaier and Barna von Sartory, *Houses of Glass*, tr. John C. Harvey. (Cambridge, MA: MIT Press, 1986), 569.

16. James Granville Southworth, *Vauxhall Gardens* (New York: Columbia University Press, 1941), 36.

17. Simon Schama, *Citizens* (New York: Alfred Knopf, 1989), 134–136.

18. John W. Reps, *The Making of Urban America* (Princeton, NJ: Princeton University Press, 1965), 141.

19. *Descriptive and Predictive Modeling of Central Courthouse Square Towns in the South Central United States* (Norman, OK: University of Oklahoma, College of Environmental Design, 1971).

20. Carl Bridenbaugh, *Cities in the Wilderness* (New York: Ronald Press, 1938), 168.

21. Carole Rifkind, *Main Street* (New York: Harper and Row, 1977), xi.

22. Bridenbaugh, *Cities*, 169.

23. Bridenbaugh, *Cities*, 170.

24. Charles Dickens, *American Notes for General Circulation and Pictures from Italy.* (Portsmouth, NH: Heinemann, Inc., 1991), 81.

25. Daniel J. Boorstin, *The Americans: The Democratic Experience* (New York: Random House, 1973), 274.

26. John Atlee Kouwenhoven, *The Columbia Historical Portrait of New York* (Garden City, NY: Doubleday, 1953), 357.

27. Sam Bass Warner, Jr, *Urban Wilderness* (New York: Harper and Row, 1972), 31.

28. Raymond Hood, "The Design of Rockefeller Center," *Architectural Forum* (January 1932), 7.

29. Walter Harrington Kilham, Jr., *Raymond Hood: Architect of Ideas* (New York: Architectural Books, 1974), 170. Quoted in Alan Balfour, *Rockefeller Center: Architecture as Theater* (New York: McGraw-Hill, 1978), 224.

30. Russell Sturgis, *A Dictionary of Architecture and Building* (New York: Macmillan, 1901), s.v. "apartments."

31. Alan Bassett, *Buildings in Construction* (New York: Arno Press, 1968), 280, 312.

32. Joel Schwartz, "Evolution of the Suburbs," in *Suburbia*, Philip C. Dolce, ed. (Garden City, NY: Doubleday, 1976), 21–22.

33. Boorstin, *Americans*, 275.

34. Vincent Scully, *American Architecture and Urbanism* (New York: Praeger, 1969), 173.

35. Speech given by Daniel Burnham to Chicago Merchant's Club, 1897. Quoted in Christopher Tunnard and Henry Hope Reed, *American Skyline* (Cambridge: Riverside, 1955), 199.

36. John Burchard and Albert Bush-Brown, *The Architecture of America: A Social and Cultural History* (Boston: Little Brown, 1961), 212.

37. Burchard and Bush-Brown, *Architecture of America*, 431.

38. Allan Temko on Pier 39, quoted in Michael Middleton, *Man Made the Town* (New York: St. Martin's Press, 1987), 180.

4

REACTING TO SPACES—THE PSYCHOLOGY OF PERCEPTION AND BEHAVIOR

Experiencing spaces, perception, interpretation, order and mystery; personal space; response and behavior in spaces, physical influences, settings, time of day, climate; situations and behavior, purpose of trip, familiarity vs. newness, reputation of a place; choosing paths, way-finding, cue-proximity, distance, broad views vs. narrow views; individuals and groups, interpersonal relationships, home range, proxemics, stereotyping responses, grouping cues, cultural and social responses, role-playing.

People want to live, work, and play in special places, perhaps not within totally unfamiliar forms and materials, but certainly not within a facile, faint variation of a stereotype:

> A deep human need exists for associations with significant places. If we choose to ignore that need, and to allow the forces of placelessness to continue unchallenged, then the future can only hold an environment in which places simply do not matter. If, on the other hand, we choose to respond to that need and to transcend placelessness, then the potential exists for the development of an environment in which places are for man, reflecting and enhancing the variety of human experience.[1]

If we create projects that lack identity, singularity, a sense of place, visual individualism, or character, and those projects fail to evoke people's feelings of pride, surprise, or involvement, then prospective occupants—the renters and buyers of those buildings—will avoid them in favor of other places. Developers of projects often impose requirements for building that result in ordinariness in building facades, site layouts, and landscape development. Imagine this competition: "Bill Jones Place," a complex of mundane-looking office buildings with a few rows of small trees, is in competition with the neighboring "Mystic Harbor Arbors," which has glistening buildings with a water's edge terrace at the rear and an established grove of trees in front.

EXPERIENCING SPACES

The consideration of psychological phenomena in the design of open spaces is not limited to capturing tenants, ensuring profits, recreational purposes, or the relief of stress. Hard-headed real estate developers use these principles, just as sales managers carefully plot the location of different kinds of merchandise along the paths that will be followed by shoppers. Design of spaces around a San Diego hotel was described by one observer:

> To strengthen the relationship between Roger Morris Plaza [San Diego] and the park, the hotel's architect . . . engaged Peter Walker to landscape the building. Walker's first move was to reposition the tower from the north side of the block to the south, moving the tower closer to the park to form a solid edge that helps define the park. This siting also freed 20,000 square feet of land at the north end of the property to become a park along Market Street, a verdant transition space that will draw pedestrians from Horton Plaza into the waterfront park.[2]

All such decisions are based on the mythical "average" person, but it should be recognized that individual responses differ and even average reactions are difficult to ascertain with reasonable accuracy. It is revealing that a standard method by which designers evaluate schemes consists of following an imagined path into and through the plan under consideration, saying. "And then I would turn right until I see. . . ." The results will be somewhat different for each member of a design team that goes through this story-making procedure.

> Experiencing spaces and places is personal. Each person who walks down a street or moves between buildings brings individual sets of expectations to the place and each point and object in it and previous experiences are major factors in determining what those expectations will be. Whether people move between buildings in order to reach another building or to pause in their schedules for a moment in the sunlight, the setting is absorbed and new images, emotions, and behaviors are combined with those of past experiences in similar places. The

responses of individuals and groups in an outdoor space are difficult to analyze and anticipate, because their actions, thoughts, and impressions are influenced by so many factors. Certain of the background influences may be common attributes of the entire groups. Some may be ascertainable characteristics of a majority of the individuals; others may appear as preferences or displeasures of certain identifiable subgroups; and still others are the results of individual and personal attitudes. On a chilly spring morning it is relatively safe to assume that everyone enjoys the experience of bright sunshine; most will appreciate protection from the sharp breeze; children will delight in an opportunity to dance about; and a blind man pauses to listen to the rustling of the trees. In a variety of ways the spatial and sensory factors of a place act upon each of us to determine our experience. In spite of the remarkable range of differences among people, the major objectives for design of a public place are definable. Paramount objectives include the functions for which provision is made (sitting, walking, or play), the evidence of location (semitropical, downtown, and financial district), and the mood (contemplative, hyperactive, or recreational). These aspects establish the identity of the place.

The question to be asked is: What role does the structure of the environment play in cognitive representations and what do people remember about their everyday environment?[3]

One observer has found three principal environmental factors: 1) what you do there—function of the space; 2) where it is—location; and 3) what it looks like—physical form, movement of people, size, shape uniqueness, . . . surface textures, simplicity versus complexity, brightness, isolation from surroundings.

People perceive their surroundings by an instantaneous two-dimensional and three-dimensional sensing, which varies relatively little from person to person (Fig. 4.1). This sameness of perception may initiate similar spatial behaviors among quite different individuals. Young or old, male or female, rich or poor, the same pedestrian pathway probably will be picked or the same parking space will be preferred. It is principally in the

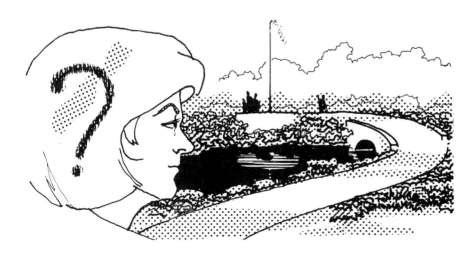

4.1 When viewing a scene in three dimensions, the mind generates a plan-like understanding of the relative placement of objects and shapes.

interpretation of the place that variations occur. In the process of interpretation, the individuals must balance in their minds aspects of order, propriety, and predictability against aspects of disorder, impropriety, and unpredictability. Both of these opposite extremes have certain appeals, and people's individual interpretations vary according to social characteristics, gender, ethnic factors, age, and temperament. The similarity of people's perceptions of places appears to promise a designer a very convenient unanimity of demands that are made on a project; but that happy circumstance is quickly destroyed by the variety of interpretations that will almost immediately follow. There is no simplistic equation that is adequate for design decisions. The temptation to generalize about users' interpretations of a place must be balanced against the recognition that there is a multiplicity of possible interpretations. Diverse interpretations mean that demographic factors help determine an expected majority view, may even establish attitudes of considerable frequency, but the designer's empathetic and artistic understanding of the users' dominant interpretations will determine the extent to which the design of the place will correspond with those typologies or intentionally depart from them.

Spatial voids are temporal. They change with the seasons of the year. Leaves drop in the fall and so the trees lose their canopies. Cold winds make people walk faster, and the scene becomes more animated. People no longer dally in plazas, but seek refuge in warm buildings. In warmer weather, the same urban spaces seem to welcome strollers, bench-sitters, and people-watchers. Going to work and leaving work in the winter is a walk through half-light, but in summer the sky is bright.

How do we experience spaces? Studies of the environment and behavior have provided new findings about how we perceive and react to spaces. The field of social psychology, particularly with its subdivisions of environmental psychology and ecological psychology, is the area in which the greatest amount of investigation has considered the relationships between people and spaces. In these studies, important information has been discovered about attitudes toward the natural landscape, differences based on gender, ethnicity, and other factors. Such investigations have laid the foundation for the study of environmental psychology. So far the field has not produced a discreet package of information that is transferable to the design disciplines. Instead, the findings are at present a sophisticated mix of topics and conclusions for deriving inferences that may be used cautiously.[4]

One of the pioneers in developing the study of person–environment relations was Roger Barker, who derived the concept of behavioral settings in the late 1940s. By following people through their daily acitivities, he was able to record all of their reactions to the objects, spaces, and places around them. As a product of this analysis, Barker discovered that the objects in spaces mold and shape behavior. The inanimate objects were directly utilized, leaned against, written on, moved about. In addition, other people caused the subjects of the studies to adapt their paths to meet or avoid them. This observational study was referred to as contextual research, for people's actions were measured against the physical, social, and temporal

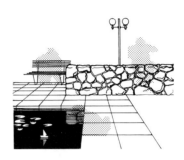

4.2 A view acts as an interaction between the social and physical aspects that are present. The place can be seen as a material construction in which people may be present, or as a setting for human activities.

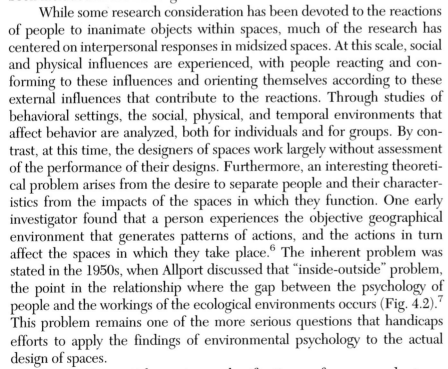

dimensions of their surroundings, rather than with the mechanisms of a laboratory experiment. This approach engendered many studies of people's actions within their behavior settings (defined as small-scale social systems comprised of objects and people that are configured to produce a routine, programmed set of actions within specified boundaries of time and place). Outdoor spaces, such as urban plazas, parks, and sidewalks, have been included in the investigations.[5]

While some research consideration has been devoted to the reactions of people to inanimate objects within spaces, much of the research has centered on interpersonal responses in midsized spaces. At this scale, social and physical influences are experienced, with people reacting and conforming to these influences and orienting themselves according to these external influences that contribute to the reactions. Through studies of behavioral settings, the social, physical, and temporal environments that affect behavior are analyzed, both for individuals and for groups. By contrast, at this time, the designers of spaces work largely without assessment of the performance of their designs. Furthermore, an interesting theoretical problem arises from the desire to separate people and their characteristics from the impacts of the spaces in which they function. One early investigator found that a person experiences the objective geographical environment that generates patterns of actions, and the actions in turn affect the spaces in which they take place.[6] The inherent problem was stated in the 1950s, when Allport discussed that "inside-outside" problem, the point in the relationship where the gap between the psychology of people and the workings of the ecological environments occurs (Fig. 4.2).[7] This problem remains one of the more serious questions that handicaps efforts to apply the findings of environmental psychology to the actual design of spaces.

In pursuing spatial experience, classifications, references, and categories will sometimes be given names other than those commonly employed in the fields of study where the terms were originally developed. Since these terms come from fields as diverse as social psychology, anthropology, sociology, criminal justice, city planning, architecture, and landscape architecture, it seems wise to use the terms taken from this variety of subject areas that are most clear to readers, and select a compromise denotation where the slightly different definitions and completely different captions are used in different fields of study.

Perception

The term perception signifies the reception and identification of sensory stimuli. In walking through a park, one sees an object; the mind perceives it as green, shaped in a curve, straight ahead, probably of cast iron (substitute materials have made many provisional perceptions necessary), and other items of information that identify it—a bench! At the same time, nonvisual information is perceived; the sunshine is warm, there is the sound of children playing, there is the odor of new-mown grass in the vicinity. The combination of messages is matched to one's intentions, purpose, and mood. Interpretation of the perceptions is more a guess; it is an old bench or an imitation of an old bench (again, provisional conclusions are required), sitting there would probably be pleasant, a change of direction will be required to avoid colliding with it. Behavior is actions taken because of the perceptions and the interpretations that are made from them; "I prefer to avoid the person sitting on the bench," "I will turn to my right."

Obviously, objects and people outside a person's immediate vicinity can influence his or her behavior. Signs on rooftops outside of a park and the norms, values, and social perspectives of those working in the buildings around that park can have their impacts. For every environment there are setting programs—groups of transactions among people and objects that are the likely and acceptable choices for any person within that space. These setting programs provide messages that are filtered and begin to affect the perception of a place. Social conventions, the values and norms that are part of American culture, in most cases represent the elements that control the intersections of a person's immediate vicinity and the setting.[8] According to some researchers, both the objects in a place and the place itself act as means of social control, with these setting programs affecting behaviors that are in keeping with society's expectations.[9] There are automatic distinctions made between the fixed elements of a place (buildings, earth forms, trees) and the semifixed elements (benches, trash receptacles, fallen leaves), and at least one significant experimental finding indicates that the small-scale, semifixed features are just as meaningful in imposing behaviors on people as are the fixed features (Fig. 4.3).[10]

The question remains: Can spaces be analyzed without considering the interaction between collective and individual actions and the space itself? Or can they be analyzed without considering objects and social beliefs originating in the background, or far surroundings, of a site? In the words of Barker, the theory of behavior settings is, in fact, an "unfinished business."[11] It has been well established that both place and person regu-

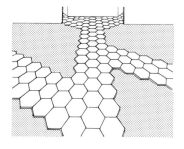

4.3 Physical arrangements present varying possibilities of changing direction. Here, the nearest turn is highly plausible; the next requires strong information that justifies an illogical move. Ahead, the choice requires signs or an arbitrary preference between slight differences.

4.4 This child's drawing represents his trip from his
doorstep, past a mean dog, a parking lot, and a service
station, to his friend's tree house (upper right). Along
any path, certain elements will be noticed more clearly
and, therefore, will figure in the recollection of the path.
The intensity of the forms, momentary interests, and
other factors will determine the memory's view.

late actions. Culture also imposes certain behaviors and thereby influences
human behavior in places.

People instantly react to the visible environment in two different ways
at the same time. They perceive the spaces and objects before them as a
two-dimensional visual array, plan, or pattern. The view in front of them is
seen as if it were a flat picture. Simultaneously, they perceive the place as a
three-dimensional pattern that has unfolded before them. In this almost
instantaneous grasp and comprehension, people look for elements of coherence, regularity, and predictability and also for complexity, deviation,
and the unexpected. There is a concern to understand the arrangement
and to keep one's bearings. When moving, there is a desire to make sense
of one's position as it changes relative to the fixed elements of the scene.[12]

Another reaction of people in spaces is that they become involved:
interpreting the scene, learning it, and becoming stimulated by it. This
sequence is not a certainty. Studies indicate that there are environments in
which a person can both comprehend and be stimulated. Likewise, there
are environments that do not offer any possibility for comprehension or
stimulation.[13] Of course, the relative desirability of either of these responses is part of the analysis of the design requirements.

In the last two decades psychologists and geographers have begun to
investigate the manner in which people comprehend spatial information. A
popular method has been cognitive mapping, a procedure in which participants are asked to draw an illustrated or annotated map of a familiar area
(Fig. 4.4).[14] By analyzing the kinds of objects or situations indicated in the
drawings it is possible to learn much about the kinds of elements that are
sufficiently significant about a place to contribute strongly to people's

4.5 People may walk the same downtown street many times. They may walk obliviously toward their destinations aided by such visual cues as a specific tree at the sidewalk near a shop entrance, or inset storefronts. Chestnut Street, Philadelphia.

recollection of it. Although the participants' unfamiliarity with the graphic techniques of converting reality to a drawn diagram may distort some characteristics, it is evident from these studies that highly imageable components, those elements sufficiently distinctive, remain in the memory, sometimes for a surprisingly long time. Paths chosen consist of an origin and a destination connected by a set of procedural rules such as distance, direction, and orientation.[15] These factors in determining paths are often defined by references to distinguishable physical features, as has been evidenced by studies of the way in which verbal instructions are formulated. While factors of orientation (for instance, the points of the compass, which are commonly used in areas of the United States laid out under the Jefferson survey), direction (usually expressed as "left" and "right"), and distance ("four blocks" and "the second stoplight") are employed, major or supportive elements in such instructions are the landmarks that form an integral part of the path-identification process.[16] Phrases such as "at the brick church," "just past the square," and "before you get to the bridge" make it evident that paths and landmarks are an integral combination, just as lines and points are combined in the entity of a geometric construction. Minor components, such as lighting standards and street furniture, or the general flavor of an area may also serve as identifying characteristics, but they tend to be used only to the extent that they are clearly distinguishable from the norm.[17]

At the larger city scale, reference places may have different significances according to the vantage point from which a view is taken. From the fringes of a city, towers, skyscrapers, spires, and domes identify points in the two-dimensional panorama; in the center of the city, ground-level elements assume greater importance, with building entrances, parks, and

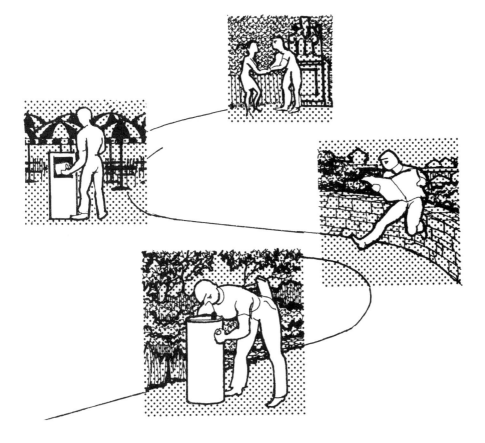

4.6 On a second visit, certain areas and elements will be recalled because of their association with activities on the previous visit.

the planted surroundings of specific buildings acting as reference points (Fig. 4.5). In all cases it is the distinguishability, the significant difference from the rest, that determines which elements will sink into the general texture of the urban scene and which will be remembered.

As cognitive mapping studies indicate, many different visual and spatial features are remembered. Distances between those features are often blurred, so that actual distances become distorted. People may strongly believe that buildings are closer than they are, and they may even frequent businesses in buildings that are more inconvenient and farther away than are competing businesses. In 1963, Thompson initiated studies that established the quality of cognitive distance, a consideration of the relative locations and connections of points. His study focused on consumer behavior regarding the choice of shopping places, but later experimenters have advanced his theory that perceptions of distance dominate shopping behaviors.[18]

Spatial orientation implies an ability to recognize self in relation to sets of points or reference systems existing in the general cognitive map of an area.[19] When people move in space, all parts and points simultaneously shift in direction and distance to and from them according to their specific path.[20] Wayfinding, a term employed by geographers and social psychologists, considers the manner in which such relationships develop and are utilized. Within small outdoor spaces, visibility of the objective point frequently ensures that selecting a path is more a matter of maneuvering to attain the objective, which is a more simple and direct problem than contending with a series of reference points in the true sense of wayfinding (Fig. 4.6). However, all destinations are not readily visible; and when factors of urgency are not involved, points that have been passed are remembered without knowledge of the points ahead. That knowledge is inferred from the relative emphasis given to different alternatives. For instance, although an exit gate may not be visible upon entering a park, a visitor is guided by the width, materials, and linear pattern of alternative paths. On streets, when a pedestrian is unable to see the full size of buildings, the slight setback of a small portion of the facades of some retail establishments may result in a differentiation sufficient to serve as a reference point in spite of the powerful mass of an adjacent office building.

These findings about people's perceptions of places do not make up a firmly knit body of knowledge that is applicable in the design process. However, some of the principles that have been established are useful in making judgments in the planning of open spaces: Places are perceived instantly and similarly by all people. In the process of perception, people gauge their locations relative to memorable visible points, and they are aware of the changes in that relationship as they move through a space. Those points are generally characterized by being different from others. Paths are chosen on the basis of people's perceptions and interpretations of environments, and interpretations vary according to such factors as gender, age, and cultural background.

Interpretation

Perception and interpretation are inseparable, yet interpretations vary. In order to survive and cope with their surroundings, people seek information about and from the environment.[21] When we think about or encounter an environment, perhaps the most important judgment is whether it is interesting, gloomy, frightening, relaxing, or such.[22] The composite of an individual's interpretations of a place and the objects in it produces a general overall assessment, a feeling about that place. One analysis presents eight major feelings that are triggered by experiencing a space. The spatial representation of their relationships begins with quadrants.

arousing
distressing   exciting
unpleasant   pleasant
gloomy   relaxing
sleepy

The scale of perceptual reactions runs horizontal with its two extremes, which are described as "pleasant" and "unpleasant." The vertical scale indicates responses, which range from "arousing" to "sleepy." Thus, a scene may have a stimulating or soporific effect without being identifiably pleasant or unpleasant, and for many people a rollercoaster or a lecture room might evoke such reactions. In the same manner, a situation might be pleasant or unpleasant without causing any response. This situation is particularly clear in cases presenting extreme conditions of light, sound, or smell. The intermediate stages identify pleasant arousal as "exciting" and pleasant sleepiness as "relaxing."

Generally, designers might not want to evoke distressing, unpleasant, gloomy, or sleepy feelings in their spaces, but there might be a reason to do so. The designer must be fully aware that a change on only one scale of the diagram changes the classification of an environment. For instance, the cool and shady nook, clearly "relaxing" on a sunny day, becomes "gloomy" on a dismal rainy day. The "exciting" gathering place, say an amphitheater, can in the absence of music or crowds become merely "relaxing," or even "gloomy." In considering the inescapable changes in conditions that occur in public places, the designer must be conscious of the qualitative changes that may occur as well.

These different feelings about spaces can be expanded to produce fifty-five environmental descriptors:[23]

- adequate size–inadequate size

- appealing–unappealing

- attractive–unattractive

- beautiful–ugly

- bright colors–muted colors

- cheerful–gloomy

- clean–dirty

- comfortable–uncomfortable

- complex–simple

- contemporary–traditional

- convenient–inconvenient

- drafty–still

- efficient–inefficient

- elegant–unadorned

- empty–full

- expensive–cheap

- fashionable–unfashionable

- free space–restricted space

- fresh odor–stale odor

- functional–nonfunctional

- gay–dreary

- good acoustics–poor acoustics

- good colors–bad colors

- good temperature–bad temperature
- good ventilation–bad ventilation
- huge–tiny
- impressive–unimpressive
- inviting–repelling
- large–small
- light–dark
- modern–old-fashioned
- multiple purpose–single purpose
- neat–messy
- new–old
- orderly–chaotic
- organized–disorganized
- pleasant–unpleasant
- pleasant odor–unpleasant odor
- private–public
- quiet–noisy
- roomy–cramped
- soft lighting–harsh lighting
- sparkling–dingy
- stylish–unstylish
- tasteful–tasteless
- tidy–untidy
- uncrowded–crowded
- useful–useless
- usual–unusual
- warm–cool
- well balanced–poorly balanced
- well kept–run down
- well organized–poorly organized
- well scaled–poorly scaled
- wide–narrow

The way in which the feelings in this list come about has a seemingly endless possibility for variation according to a multiplicity of factors. Each individual brings to the problems all the factors that make up his or her temperament, background, and pattern of life.

> To the corporate executive on the fortieth floor of an office tower, the urban landscape may not be aggressively exciting, a symbol of human purpose and power. He may enjoy the presence of trees on the street far below, but that enjoyment may have very low priority with him, especially if he has a lush home in a green suburb. To the clerk leaving an anonymous desk on a lower story, a walk through a park on the way home may be restorative; but he may prefer to elbow his way home by the shortest route to an apartment with a television set and a few potted plants on the window sill, or stop off in the purely social landscape of a local bar. The problem for designers is to determine the particularities in all cases, and to do that they must have a disciplined design imagination, supported by an understanding of not only natural ecology, but human nature as well. As there is no substitute in art for intuition, so there is no substitute for empathy in designing for others.[24]

In urban settings, which are principally human-built environments, different people can hold vastly different viewpoints on their shared environment. The biological basis for these multiple viewpoints lies in the subtle differences in the sensitivity, reactivity, and patience that are inherited, all effecting ultimate personality development. Also, in the process of maturing, people learn to behave in ways expected by their society. Group values are accepted without much reflection and without awareness that others of other cultures may not share those values. Family values exert a similar influence. Male and female differences provide demands and responses that both differ and vary according to social group, and some predictable differences in personality are related to gender. The means of employment relate to educational levels and demands that the individual behave in the manner that society considers appropriate to that occupation, including patterns of speech, dress, and social participation. In addition, each individual has had a different set of experiences, which influence his or her attitudes. Living places, travel, and childhood experiences contribute a flavor to judgments. Subtle and sharp differences in interpretation are possible.

Additionally, people have different combinations of roles, and these roles change through the years. For an individual, one role might be as a parent, another as a commuter, a third as a political activist, and there may be still others. Another individual may share many of those roles, but differ in a few. These roles, often reinforced by socioeconomic status, taint perceptions and promote a tendency toward common behaviors. For example, in a study of people living in Los Angeles, lower levels of education and occupational class, when accompanied by an increase in age, were found to relate to increased preferences for "colonial-style" buildings and decorations and decreases in preference for "contemporary" buildings and decorations. In ethnography and anthropological linguistics, the Whorf-Sapir hypothesis states that a person's language, as related to ethnic background, influences the way in which he or she views time. A parallel might be a hypothesis that language relates to the manner of experiencing space. For instance, Asians have been found to accept the location of slums adjacent to upper-class residences, to prefer brightly lit public places, and to prefer visual and auditory conditions that would be considered chaotic by many other ethnic groups. In Chinese languages there are words that translate literally as "hot noisy." Asian family get-togethers, like those of some other ethnic groups, often feature high-volume competitive speaking.[25]

There are also differences between males and females in their use and interpretation of public spaces. Studies of parks and open space in cities seem to indicate that the fear of rape or attack keeps women from entering parks at night, dawn, or dusk, and makes them want to be only in the parts of the park where there are other women, or where there is a distinct impression of protection. From this research, designers may begin to view portions of spaces as being male spaces, female spaces, and joint occupancy spaces.

Demographic analyses can roughly determine the kind of people who would use a public place, according to current conditions. Time-budget analyses can be made for the place, in order to aid the urban designer.[26] Public environments, our surroundings, are a reflection and a mirror of individual behaviors, social processes, and (at times) clashing community values.[27]

There are so very many differences in the interpretation of spaces that extreme caution must be exercised in developing a picture of the people to be served, and of their interests. It is not a matter of determining who is the average user, for when all major aspects are considered the average may really represent no one. Instead, efforts should be made to satisfy the desires of as large a majority as is possible. It is obviously impossible, and often unwise, to include in a single project all the functions that a significant part of the population might desire. Inharmonious functions must be excluded, but not segments of the population. Achieving this consideration requires that the design team be empathetic, capable of role-playing, and maintain an attitude of inclusiveness.

Order and Mystery

On the one hand, people look for order, security, and a sense of completeness in their immediate spatial experiences; on the other hand, they look for mystery, challenge, and stimulation. The promise of mystery or surprise and the desire for predictability and conformity are desired components of spatial experiences. These seemingly contradictory factors are apparently a part of human nature.

People want to make sense of three-dimensional spaces, want them to be legible. "Safety in the context of space" overlays this desire for legibility, and for that reason people want to be able to organize mentally the ground plane, the space that extends from the foreground to the horizon or discernible distant limit of the area. At the same time, they want the variation that comes from not perceiving the entirety of their surroundings. The strength of these two desires often depends on the function of an open space, the frequency of one's visiting the space, and the characteristics of the people who visit it.

Subjects of research for this phenomenon have referred to dichotomous pairs of words, such as order/complexity, familiarity/novelty, refuge/ prospect (meaning "view"), and protection/openness. All of these words contrast the feeling of comfort and security with that of challenge and adventure. Order and familiarity describe the visitor's feeling of satisfaction in being able to comprehend a space with ease; refuge and protection characterize feelings of safety. In contrast, complexity and novelty stand for degrees of uncertainty, and this uncertainty relates to the feeling of having no control that is represented by prospect and openness. Experiments disclose that order decreases arousal.[28] Regularly spaced items within an open space tend to be ignored. Repeated shapes and forms are ignored because they are expected and anticipated. As a result, carefully arranged and repeated patterns, materials, outdoor furniture, or sculpture may have a dulling effect on the participants in a space or place. Supporting the limited interest in repetitive, regularly spaced items, there are consistent findings that people prefer naturalistic over artificial elements, and that water enhances those scenic qualities.[29]

These terms should not be taken literally. The preference for naturalistic spaces can be interpreted easily as liking irregular forms, as seen in trees, shrubs, and the meandering edges of ponds. Mystery is not necessarily a matter of having a puzzle to solve. Certainly, a drive in the country, with scenes unexpectedly unfolding at every turn, does not lose all interest because it has been experienced once. The process of changing vistas and discovering hidden areas remains exhilarating, even though one has seen it before and is fully aware that the surprise is just behind the trees. One also suspects that opinions about "refuge" and "protection" may have changed with the increase of criminal activity in public places. Where once a nook surrounded by foliage might have been thought safe and an open space a fearsome exposure, it is probable that these classifications have reversed in most urban areas.

It is probable that the meaning of this information to a design team is that the dichotomy signifies a desire for compromise, the mysterious place that is not too mysterious and the orderly place that is not too orderly. Or it may also mean that a contrast is most desired, the stimulating contrast of an orderly arrangement that incorporates some elements of surprise or a naturalistic scheme with certain intrusions of highly regulated elements.

Personal Space

Studies show that the formation, continuation, and furtherance of social relationships generally occur in spatial settings, among which public open spaces are frequent and traditional choices. Necessary activities that are part of daily routine are often the setting in which neighborliness is established and exhibited. Curbside exchanges while parking, alleyway and back fence conversations while mowing lawns are common ways in which suburban dwellers maintain the relationships that are a custom of their culture, while parking lots and building entrances serve the same purposes in the work culture. Since these contacts rely on an accepted cultural supposition of friendliness, they are largely reaffirmations of the fact that the participants share certain characteristics. They depend on the acceptance of specific standards and indicators by the group. The gestures and exchanges have meaning only insofar as they are clearly understood within the group, and consequently they are not completely individual.

Environmental meanings and actions are not solely individual constructions. The individual both defines and is defined by the groups in which he or she participates. The best literature in this area attempts to relate the individual, group, and social-structural characteristics of human responses to threat.[30] The state of being threatened or risking some degree of danger leads to greetings and small talk that hopes to elicit a response sufficiently similar to reassure the individual, through the accepted sociocultural indicators, that the other party to the exchange has like qualifications of similarity (Fig. 4.7). Not all of these indicators are verbal. Mere presence in the same place and making a similar use of the place are often powerful pressures that may convert any initial comparisons that are made.

A comprehensive review of literature on theoretical research related to the actions of people in spaces led Aiello to write, "We treat space somewhat as we treat sex. It is there but we don't talk about."[31]

Early research about responses to spatial conditions was highly influenced by ethnologists and students of animal spatial behavior. Later investigations of topics were pursued by sociologists, ecologists, psychiatrists, geographers, and architects. To identify the study of how people conduct daily transactions and their proximity at those times has often been categorized under the classification of "proxemics," a term coined by Hall in the 1960s.[32] Other terms that have been used are spatial proximity, personal space, and interpersonal distance. It is reported by Aiello that in 1950 Hediger had suggested that every animal is surrounded, conceptually, by a series of "bubbles or balloons" by which it maintains proper spacing between itself and other animals.[33] Personal distance, for Hall, is the dimension that defines the volume immediately enclosing the individual human being and at which the majority of social interactions with others take place. Since this distance is variable, it corresponds to the individual's perceived need for protection and communication. For each relationship between individuals that distance may vary, and people make active use of places to manipulate positions in a way that will achieve their desired personal distances. A more detailed view was taken by Altman and Vinsel:

> Intimate distance ranges from 0 to 18 inches and is characterized by strong and intense sensory inputs. The voice is normally held at a very low level or even at a whisper. Light is a bit distorted, heat and smell from another is inescapable and involvement is unmistakable.[34]

4.7 On crowded streets pedestrians' minds are concentrated on getting from one place to another, and they are not conscious of their surroundings. 16th Street Transit Mall, Denver. (Courtesy of Downtown Denver Partnership, Inc.)

Personal distance ranges from 1.5 to four feet and another is within "arm's length." The voice level is moderate, vision is no longer distorted, and body heat and olfaction are either no longer or minimally perceptible. This distance is more likely to be used by friends and acquaintances.

Social distance extends from four to twelve feet. Nobody touches or expects to touch another person. Voice level is louder and transactions are more formal and businesslike. Public distance extends beyond twelve feet. This distance is more characteristic of speakers and their audience or interactions with public figures. The voice and everything else must be exaggerated or amplified.[35] People prefer interaction distances from others that avoid excessive arousal, stimulation, and the stressors related to distances that are too close for their relationships. Adequate personal space prevents one's freedom of behavior from being threatened by others. The protective function of human spacing runs through the literature and is a common thread of the study of proxemics.

> Once it is acknowledged that humans all have a "spatial mechanism" built in which is behavioral and rooted in our biological past, the acquisition of specific personal space, norms and behaviors is almost invariably explained within the context of cultural experience and with reference to a theory of social learning. That is, through the processes of imitation and reinforcement, children learn the accepted cultural patterns of appropriate proxemic behavior.[36]

Another model of behavior can be applied directly to public places. The conflict or intimacy equilibrium model, as explained by Aiello, was further developed by later studies.[37] This model is adapted from the concept of stimulus-response, and it hypothesizes that any organism approaches and avoids any forces that are in conflict with it. At some distance between the organism and its goal, the forces of approach and avoidance are in balance, and at that point there is stable equilibrium. That point will be maintained, unless events that are the result of the meeting change the conditions. People behave according to this model. There are approach and avoidance forces in all everyday activities and encounters. For example, in the instance of intimacy, eye contact and the amount of smiling may need to be adjusted in order to reach or restore the desired level of intimacy. When this adjustment cannot be successfully achieved or when the character of the relationship is interpreted differently by the two participants, discomfort and maneuvering result.[38] Most of the time, this adjustment is subconscious.

Distance produces changes in behavior. Moving an object to a different location within a place or spatial setting will encourage changes. Hall discusses the naturalistic observations of individuals' actual use of space.[39]

> The kinesthetic code and notational system is based on what people can do with their arms, legs, and bodies. . . . Another person is perceived as close . . . not only because one may be able in some instances to even feel the heat radiating from him, but also because there is the potential for holding, caressing, or being struck. . . . The measured distance depends largely on the size and shape of the individuals involved.[40]

People sit and move closer to people they like than to people they do not like.

> People develop normative patterns of spatial behavior within the context of their effective culture and as a result of their particular socialization experiences, which are strongly tempered by an individual's stage of development, gender, and personality.
>
> However, individuals interact and encounter others not in a vacuum but rather in specific social, situational, and environmental settings. These contextual factors exert their own (additional) influence on the preferred spatial behavior patterns of the participating individuals. For example, the nature of the mutual attraction and liking between interactants, what they happen to be talking about or doing, and whether the activity takes place in one type of environment or another can substantially affect interpersonal spacing.[41]

Even though there are differences in male and female uses of interpersonal distance, exceptions are common. Males use more space for interaction than females do. Women stand closer to close friends than to acquaintances. Mixed sex pairs, such as spouses or lovers, use less space than do any other type of pairing. Yet there are conflicting studies relating to gender differences in investigations of waiting rooms, lines, and spatial invasion.[42]

People of different cultures utilize space differently. Southern Europeans, Latin Americans, and Arabs maintain closer interaction distances and exhibit a higher amount of involvement with others when together. For instance, one study found that Arab college students sit closer together, adopt more direct angles, engage in more eye contact, speak louder, and touch each other more than do American students. In studies with dolls, Greeks placed figures closest, followed by Italians and Americans, with Swedes and Scots placing the figures the farthest apart.[43] Because the

United States is a nation of immigrants, our spaces and places contain multicultural groups of people, each using spaces with different proxemic norms.

The effects of forcing people to intrude on the space of others seem to be most dependent on external factors and is not easily explained by models of a conflict/intimacy equilibrium. Interpersonal distance is best viewed as one of a number of variables used by individuals with particular socialization experiences and from specific effective cultures to establish the desired level of interpersonal involvement (Fig. 4.8).[44]

Age, gender, cultural differences, and mixed sex groups are factors in distances and the ways in which people use space. Racial differences have been noted, also. Very young black children of lower socioeconomic status use less space than middle-class white children, and black adolescents and adults are more distant than whites.[45]

Environmental factors also play an important role in how space is used. Smaller, more confining spaces serve to increase interaction distances; larger or more "overstimulating" environments prompt people to adopt distances that are smaller. But, if a situation occurs where fear is induced, then people will come together, and if there are loud noises, then people will increase their distances.

There are visual and sensual limits to perceptible space. Edges of open areas are defined most typically by building walls and accented by trees, shrubs, fence walls, curbs, rows of street lamps, and roadways. Spatial definers may be any one or a combination of components. When people think about a place, it may be a portion of a facade, the entry canopy of a building or the double row of trees leading to the building entry. In some instances, people more clearly remember events that happened in an outdoor space. Rarely is the two-dimensional or three-dimensional mental map of the spaces between buildings recalled.

People will go to great lengths to avoid invading the interaction space of others and are quite uncomfortable when they cannot help but intrude. How likely a person will be to invade another's space has been found to depend on environmental factors (for example, the amount of room available to go around the interactants; social density level) and characteristics

4.8 "Bubbles" of space for individuals are based on many factors, including background, education, age, and interests. Social settings and events may appreciably expand or contract the bubbles.

4.9 Quiet parks can be used for personal activities such as phoning, gazing, and romancing. No matter what the designers' intended use, activities will conform to the visitor's needs. Monterrey, Mexico.

of the interactants (the sex composition of the group, the status of the interactants, their similarity to the subject, and so on).[46] With so many variables influencing the individual determination of personal space, exact applications are impossible. However, there can be no assumption that even at the most crowded time, all sitting places and all the width of walks will be occupied. Many visitors to a public place will move on rather than put themselves in uncomfortable proximity with others. This kind of distancing action will vary according to the homogeneity of the people who frequent the space. A neighborhood park where there are great similarities among the residents may have a pattern of occupancy quite different from that of a downtown area in which a considerable variety of types of people are present (Fig. 4.9).

RESPONSE AND BEHAVIOR IN SPACES

When a person moves in space, all parts of the environment simultaneously undergo changes in direction and distance to and from her or him according to a family of transformation functions determined by his or her locomotion path. While much of the literature on environmental cognition focuses on the relative stability of key elements of this ever-changing environment (anchorpoints) that are probably well remembered and whose spatial relations are probably well understood, one must also posit that mechanisms exist that update internally represented locations by compensation for movement and rotation. Otherwise, a person could not in general relate to out-of-sight locations even it if was possible to remember how these locations were to himself or herself. This problem is exacerbated in situations of unfamiliar environments.[47]

[*Translation:* You relate your place to the most noticeable objects, and if you didn't adjust that relationship as you change places, you wouldn't be able to go into another room and still remember where the phone is. . . .]

There is a direct and strong connection between people's perception of space and their consequent behavior.[48] Each person responds to a space as a result of perceptions, personality characteristics, and expectations. And, to some extent, personal behavior in a space is a response that is mediated by the physical features that define and identify the space.[49] The arrangement of objects, their shapes, visible details, and social relationships determine behavior. The assumption that one's understanding and comprehension of a place is a determinant of behavior differs from the assumption that served as the basis for the earlier sections of this chapter about perceiving and experiencing spaces and places. That section was based on the fact that a person moving through an environment comprehends the immediate surroundings in a manner that is distinctly individual and could be designed to produce those specific behaviors. The designer can advantageously employ and determine those physical characteristics that are most likely to result in desired responses. To that end, this section intends to develop an understanding of how people behave within spaces, whether they are considered as individuals, participants in the actions of small clusters of people, or members of large groups that respond *en masse*. It must be acknowledged that there is controversy surrounding the extent and nature of the connections between perception and behavior, but social psychologists have established some distinctions and a significant correlation between the two.[50] A solitary pedestrian taking an evening stroll, someone walking with family or friends, or one person among the hundreds leaving a theater or stadium—the behavior of each of these people while traversing the space has been shown to be strongly influenced by his or her perception of that space.

Our evaluations of spatial experiences are affected by the responses of others.[51] If those around us display excitement, pleasure, confusion, or indifference, we are influenced toward feeling the same sensations. If others hurry past us, dashing to the start of the working day, we cannot avoid a feeling that we should walk briskly, although really we may be only idly passing a half-hour before an appointment. And, in response to those harried commuters, we can speed up and spend the time busily or withdraw from the group and observe their rushing as a detached bystander. Either behavior, whether imitating or differentiating, exists as a response to the behaviors visible around us.[52]

4.10 Choice of place is inescapably a choice of the degree of sensory communication one wishes to experience—from a brick-paved passageway, to a small street with parking, and onward to cars, stop signs, and crowds. Albuquerque, New Mexico.

4.11 External characteristics created by noises, smells, motion, and other factors affect our impressions. Many of those impressions may be strongly recalled by cues such as odors, sounds, and events. These sensory characteristics are related to spaces, but they are also related to the people who are there. New York City. (Photo by Alan M. Gordon)

Behavior becomes the result of a composite response, the total of all information gained from the senses.[53] As we move from the busy street to the small park, the sound of trucks is reduced and may even be replaced by the rustling of leaves in the trees; our feet feel the texture of pebbled walks instead of the hard smoothness of concrete; the stench of carbon monoxide gives way to the scent of new-mown grass (Fig. 4.10). But the perceived visual information is the initial and dominant basis of our response. Alone or as members of groups, a person has individual responsive behaviors, which may appear to match the responses of others. Minor variations of behavior due to individuals' personalities may not be apparent, but the behavior induced by the major decisions of site design are such that they seem to cause little variation, leveling the responses across differences that are present because of cultural factors, temperament, physical size, age, sex, and social class.[54]

Odors and noises may reinforce indelible images of an urban space. For instance, the forecourts of downtown office buildings often may be associated with the rumble of traffic and the fumes expelled by engines, but sound from a record store and the scent of a vendor's hotdogs, perhaps being peculiar to one particular place, may become its identifying characteristics, although spatial distinctions are almost unnoticeable. According to individual preferences, the odors and noises, as well as the visual characteristics of a place, cause us to formulate our impression of it (Fig. 4.11). Often this interaction of the senses can lead to complex sensations. A quiet garden near a thoroughfare may seem even more sheltered if the sound of traffic is merely loud enough to remind people that they are removed from it; but a roar of traffic can overpower all the feeling of separation and the pleasant seclusion of the garden.

Although our immediate definition of going somewhere is the process of taking ourselves closer to our destination, much of our effort and attention can be also defined as being absorbed by avoiding collision with those objects that lie between us and the point we want to reach. Just as the streets of a city lead to different points within it, they also go around and

4.12 In spite of common interests that bring people to the same place, divergent backgrounds may make them pay no attention to each other. Downtown Monterrey, Mexico.

surround buildings and capture areas that have not been designated as streets. As we travel through the canyon-like atmosphere of downtown streets and their sidewalks, crowded with people, much of our attention must be devoted to avoiding other people or other cars (Fig. 4.12). Trash cans, other people, and double-parked delivery vans demand our attention and may significantly diminish our perceptions of spaces. Broad suburban thoroughfares, lined with the parking lots of shopping centers, may evoke little spatial experience. The tree-lined sidewalks may serve more as screens than as amenities, and parked cars may act as a fence. The hurrying pedestrian crossing a downtown park may at that time see a bench or a pool merely as an obstruction.

Physical Influences

Settings: The nature of a setting can be characterized in four different ways:

1. *Physical attributes* include the elementary descriptors of landform, dimensions, water, soil, and sky;

2. *Landcover* defines the utilization of the site in terms of those things, such as forests, farms, meadows, and even parking lots.[55]

3. *Information variables* identify the variety of elements, their similarity or diversity, and the clarity or mystery with which they are revealed; and

4. *Perception variables* include the observers' reaction to the conditions in terms such as feelings of enclosure, spaciousness, esthetic pleasure, and peacefulness.[56]

In one study, it was discovered that there was a distinct preference for situations in which the arrangement of a natural setting provided a sense of mystery.[57] In other experiments preferences related clearly to such factors as the ease of movement through a space, smoothness (little variation of contour or topography), and "non-openness."[58] On the whole, in investigations of people's preferences in open spaces, "mystery" has been found more influential than "complexity." While they were determined to be important in some studies, "coherence" and "complexity" failed to prove significant in other studies.[59] Due to the many categories of users and surrounding conditions, there are often directly contradictory findings, as shown by the popularity of both "mystery" and "coherence." Nevertheless, these studies, in aggregate, indicate that characteristics of a setting, when clearly determined and exhibited to the observer, elicit responses. On the other hand, indefinite presentation of the spirit of a place garners indifference.

Time of Day: Almost all public spaces have daily, weekly, and seasonal variations affecting the dominant occupants and their intentions. (See Chapter 5.) In a downtown financial district, the streets and plazas will have heavy traffic early in the morning and late in the afternoon as workers arrive at and leave their jobs. The vicinities of entrances will have one-way movement at those times—the directions reversed as people come to work and head home. (Elevator engineers find that more people crowd on an office-building elevator at five o'clock than at eight o'clock, when they are quite willing to wait for the next car.[60]) In addition, shoppers may arrive around ten o'clock and at noon shoppers will mingle with workers disgorged from the office buildings, perhaps relaxing as they go to lunch and return to work (Fig. 4.13). The frenetic behavior of early morning settles into a mood that is somewhat more leisurely, and the quiet sitting places that were ignored during the morning rush are filled with people eating sandwiches or reading newspapers. Neighborhood parks have similar changes, although they seldom reach the frantic level of the downtown areas. Children pass through the park on their way to school at about the same time that their parents rush to work. This activity is succeeded by a period in which the elders stroll or sit in the sun while babies and toddlers play and children from a daycare center solemnly walk by hand-in-hand. In all of these situations, different people with activities set by the time are experiencing spaces with different actions resulting from what they see and the mission of the hour. The intensity of the time-control varies greatly. The pressure of getting to work on time brings about certain extremely focused responses to the environment, but the relative freedom from schedule that is a privilege of the elderly and the young permits other interpretations and reactions to the surroundings.[61]

Climate: Walking is often considered a "mindless" activity, deserving and receiving less attention than many others, and principally involving automatic and unconscious reactions. It has been found, however, that the speed of a person's walk varies according to the conditions of environment. Heat increases walking speed even more than does fearsome uneasiness in an environment.[62] People walk faster in high temperatures than when it is moderate, and they appear to be more uncomfortable and in worse moods

4.13 The street has been closed to vehicles, and pedestrians of different ages and interests can read, eat, and stare in peace in a crowded place. It takes little more than benches and this kind of setting to designate a place. New York City. (Photo by Alan M. Gordon)

when it is hot.[63] In fact, although one would assume a cold-weather tendency to rush toward protection, it seems that cool conditions actually result in slower movement and warm conditions result in a faster pace.

An extrapolation of this finding suggests that cool weather and the concomitant slower pace of pedestrians makes passersby more susceptible to the blandishments of show window displays and, hence, more subject to impulse buying. This conclusion may relate to the success of air-conditioned shopping malls, where strolling in a cool atmosphere gives ample opportunity for shopping.

Observations of over 1,300 downtown pedestrians in England and Australia demonstrated that walking speed may be a function of city size, with pedestrians moving faster in larger cities than in smaller ones. Other factors of significance were found to be age, sex, density, time of day, and climate. According to these data, however, the variation of walking with city size was far less pronounced than the experimenters had expected—there was only a slight difference.[64] In fact, it can be argued that the difference might result simply from responses to the "fast-paced life of the city," a figure of speech that may refer more accurately to the mood of the population than their movement.

Situations and Behavior

Purpose of Trip: Crossing a space in order to enter a building for a day's work will usually result in a completely different set of behaviors than those produced when one's purpose is rest, recreation, or sightseeing.[65] Walking at a faster pace can be natural when the office starting time or an important appointment is the objective. Those with a fixed objective will concentrate their observation of a space mainly on the routes available and their relative efficiency. If rest is the purpose, a pedestrian concentrates on discovering areas suitable for inactivity, and a sightseer (for whom it is probably the first visit) will search the environment to identify and relate the different visual experiences that are present. Office-workers may seldom pay attention to quiet alcoves until they arrive a little early on a fine spring day.[66]

Familiarity vs. Newness: Many decades ago, according to reports, the horses that drew carts in a London railway station would be unharnessed at the end of the day. Then, in response to a slap on their rumps, they would cross a street, walk up a ramp, and go to their own stalls in the multistory stable—and do all those things all by themselves! Yet most of us have seen horses skittish and wary when led into strange places. Being at home in a space or viewing that space as alien can strongly influence behavior there. At the same time, our feelings about the environment can be influenced further by the population, whether we are alone or in a crowd, and whether the crowd is related to us.[67] For instance, on entering an unfamiliar space alone we may be wary if it does not resemble places in which we have been comfortable. If there are a number of other people who seem of a similar social level, our disorientation is easily overcome as we watch their behavior, but if the other people speak a language other than ours and are of a clearly different social class, their behavior is much less reassuring to us. Dealing with unfamiliar environments is a major part of learning and maturation, and we all develop standards through which a space we have never seen before can be identified as being sufficiently similar to familiar places.[68]

Using a space repeatedly or spending a long time there produces a series of acts that accumulate to develop a bond between people and those places. Time and repetition usually reduce the number of remaining mysteries about a locale, with observation of others' activities identifying the nature and utility of elements of the space.[69] This childlike method of learning shows us that the drinking fountain is operated by a foot pedal and that the top of a low retaining wall will be a reasonably comfortable place to sit when all the benches are in hot sunlight. In addition, repeated visits or a single visit of long duration informs us about the character and attitude of other visitors, as individuals or as archetypes. We realize that we must be wary of certain people or types of people whom we observe in the public place, or we detect similarities or lose our fear of differences. Distinctions among class or status may diminish with time.[70] In the same way, familiarity with the physical elements that are incorporated in the place will clarify the functional qualities of the place, qualities which we were uncertain about when we first entered.

Reputation of a Place: Before visiting a space, we are often informed of its nature and character by the way that it has been mentioned or referred to, or perhaps just by its name.[71] A certain sidewalk may be well-known as the place where farmers bring their products for sale (Fig. 4.14), Capitol

4.14 Many cities of all sizes have farmers' markets. This commercial land-use serves a wide range of clientele. One of its principle advantages is that the necessary shopping trip can turn into a pleasant outing. The metal shed-like roofs, interspersed with paved areas, produce a lighting effect that resembles a canopy of trees. Kansas City, Missouri.

Square can be safely assumed to have a degree of monumentality in its form and its use, and a city's adult entertainment districts are clearly defined in purpose. Such designations predetermine many of our behaviors. Even if the name or reputation of a place has not been made known to a visitor, its visible characteristics can cause typification, the recognition that it seems to fall within an established category and therefore can be expected to have the characteristics commonly associated with that category.[72] Accidentally roaming onto what is clearly a courthouse square, our actions tend to conform to our expectations of events appropriate to the courthouse squares that we have known. However, if we discover that the square is being used as the venue of a noisy protest demonstration or a children's Easter-egg hunt, we will adjust our behavior to the event rather than to the reputation of the place.

Choosing Paths

Way-finding: For visitors unfamiliar with an open space and the objects within it, introductory determination of locations, objectives, and available paths must precede any significant progress through the space.[73] Often, this process accounts for pedestrians' pausing afer passing through a gate or at the bottom of stairs (Fig. 4.15). Selecting a path is a relatively simple matter when a person's destination—perhaps the entrance to a building—is clearly in view. A completely different path is chosen if there is no urgency felt, if little more than a pleasant stroll is intended.[74] Obviously, the intentions of visitors largely determine the methods and results of their way-finding. Whether the primary concern of the pedestrian is efficiently reaching a destination or pleasantly passing time, success is measured in terms of the time and cogitation required to weight the alternatives against intentions.

4.15 How much of traveling is the avoidance of obstructions? Decisions often are made that require a longer walk to avoid special outdoor objects of design. The formality of this small, walk-through vest-pocket park requires many compromises. Downtown Monterrey, Mexico.

Cue Proximity: In open spaces, objects provide the cues by which occupants of the space determine their positions and sense of movement.[75] Each tree, bench, drinking fountain, or store window serves as a marker by which a pedestrian measures passage through a space. Just as ancient seafarers navigated by skirting coastlines and sailing along chains of islands, a pedestrian's progress through a park can be recorded as a series of sightings, followed by evaluation and decisions about the continuation of movement. If objects are situated in an orderly fashion, with trees in a straight line and benches centered between them, observation of the objects results in a determination of the pattern in which they are positioned, and decisions can be made on the basis of the pattern. Irregular placement of objects requires a repetitive routine of sightings, assessments, and decisions. On the other hand, the absence of nearby objects increases the distance to those markers that are available for determining one's position, and reduces the personal association with them.[76] The selection of path can be described as "past the fountain," "down the step," and "to the left of the bench;" but across an open space such as the Government Center Plaza outside Boston City Hall, the path can be described as little more than "across," and simple sailing gives way to the awesome prospect of navigating the broad expanse of an ocean (Fig. 4.16).

In addition to the cues afforded by the inanimate objects set in a space, the variable cues provided by an individual stroller or a phalanx of office workers require a pedestrian's additional alertness. The simple task of orienting oneself among static forms demands little more than an initial analysis and subsequent verification; walking along a crowded sidewalk may require that full attention be concentrated on moving cues, leaving

4.16 Upon arrival at the seaport, a visitor's indecision is accentuated by the expanse of the boardwalk area, which gives the visitor freedom and responsibility for choice of direction. Some visitors have no idea about which way to turn, others dash forward without information or orientation, and still others follow somone else. New York City. (Photo by Alan M. Gordon)

little for visual experiences less important than street intersections.[77] Design for such conditions can become extremely complex at certain times when casual walkways are suddenly filled with rushing crowds.

Distance: Behaviors may be changed by open space designs that affect perception. The same distance can be perceived in different ways as a result of different conditions. For instance, people traveling toward a city believe that the distance is much shorter than people traveling away from the city believe it to be.[78] Extending this experimental finding, it is possible that people traversing open spaces tend to believe that they are making greater progress as they move toward a clearly defined destination, such as the entrance to a building, and that they make less progress as they leave that destination. Longer distances, though perhaps they only seem longer, may appreciably alter the walker's attitude as he or she crosses a plaza and, as a consequence, may alter the rate and manner of movement. This behavior may be manipulated by designs.

In order to encourage more positive feelings in certain situations, unequal distances might be part of the design—there may be a longer distance to be traveled to approach the destination, a shorter distance to leave it. Also, it may be possible to adjust the visual elements so that the view when leaving would present an illusion of a shorter distance, perhaps by presenting views of a scene or object that can temporarily serve as a destination for the exiting path. Many traditional buildings accomplish this illusion by having long walks for the first-time visitor approaching their principal entrances and shorter side entrances that become apparent from the lobby.

Distance and perception can be mediated by either the placement of objects along paths or changing social settings. Temporarily placed chairs, decorations, signs, or street furniture can promote people to change their usual routes. The variations in a known open space can change behaviors there. Maintaining certain distances between observers and objects or other people is often influential in selecting among behavior alternatives. An approaching throng of frisky teenagers may be perceived as threatening by an elderly walker, prompting withdrawal to the extreme edge of the walkway, but an approaching stranger who is apparently of similar age and social condition will usually require no drastic change of path and may even merit a tiny smile and nod.

Broad Views vs. Narrow Views: As pedestrians walk through an outdoor space, their behavior may be shaped by the manner in which the design is revealed or concealed.[79] In an open space that contains few elements to interrupt vision, the visitor is able to comprehend the entirety of the arrangement quickly, determine objectives, and continue walking after only a short period of orientation. If destinations are altered during the walk, the changes are made with a relatively complete understanding of the relative positions of the places to be visited.[80] When a space offers only limited and narrow views, the partial visibility of the space means that only partial planning can be undertaken by the visitor.[81] Trees, shrubs, and slopes may obscure all but a single view that presents a single destination, or two paths may be revealed without any indication of their physical relationship or visual connections. Once an introductory determination is made, a shorter distance can be traversed and a further path can be suggested and finally revealed. The single act of revelation permitted by a broad view enables a pedestrian to formulate a plan, while the narrow view requires the execution of a sequence of evaluations and decisions.[82]

Planting is not the only method by which views may be limited or opened, but studies of behavior in parks reveal useful general knowledge about the way in which reactions may be influenced. Once they distinguished between people's conditions of pleasure (a passive state of satisfaction) or stimulation (an active condition of excitation), experimenters found clear relationships between these states and the characteristics of parks. One report indicates that pleasure increases as the overhead canopy of trees becomes more clearly established and as the ground-level obstruction of shrubbery decreases. Pleasure is apparently associated with sheltering elements that do not hem in the observer. On the other hand, stimulation is aroused by eye-level shrubs that hide many elements of the park and result in a series of intriguing mysteries that are resolved by surprises.[83] People become uneasy when they can't see potential dangers. Since research suggests that people visit parks in search of experiences different from those of their usual environments, there is little uniformity in the impression sought by individuals.[84] Some may seek adventure; others may merely hope for a moment of peaceful meditation. There are means through which each of these purposes may be served in the same space by the provision of alternative routes, each having different characteristics.

Individuals and Groups

Interpersonal Relationships: Research discloses that the relationships within small groups are strong influences on people's behavior in public spaces.[85] Strangers may distance themselves for protection or privacy; close friends, members of a family, or lovers may be expected to walk close together.[86] Business colleagues or elementary school chums may traverse a plaza intent on their conversation and unaware of the visual environment except for those points that demand decisions regarding their route. Socialization can virtually obliterate their awareness of the fountain, benches, or flowers they happen to pass, or if the route is very familiar their response to objects may be somewhat automatic and absent-minded. Fountains, benches, and other details of the design may become invisible as a result of strollers' concentration on each other and the subject of their conversation.

Some people through aggressive behavior, may lay claim to portions of a public space either for the brief time they visit it or on a more or less permanent basis. Strong feelings of territoriality often emerge, on the parts of both aggressors and other users of the space, who may be thereby forced to limit their choices to other portions of the space.[87] Because of their desire to avoid conflict or to assert their presence, different groups may suffer the inconvenience of self-assigned areas within a space, although the nature of their areas may be contradictory to their intended activities there. The identification of areas that are part of such territorial designation is more easily and lastingly arrived at when the physical arrangement more clearly distinguishes between areas. For instance, benches in a U-shaped alcove may be more definitely claimed by a group, and their claim recognized by others, than would be an equivalent length along a straight row of benches (Fig. 4.17). As a result, in a space frequented by the same groups, areas may acquire explicit meaning regarding age, social class, and activities.

4.17 The arrangement of seating and the types of seating provided serve as visual indicators of the designers' objective. Each of these types of seating implies certain interpretations and concerns on the part of a design team.

Home Range: Somewhere between the dimensions of personal space bubbles and perceived territories, there lies a dimension that encompasses the area that individuals sense as their scope of concern.[88] Serving as caretakers, hosts to visitors, and collaborators, they establish a personal jurisdiction over the area. One researcher found that people have little interest in projects that cover large areas.[89] In one instance, groups having a keen interest in street relationships seldom focused their attention on an area that exceeded two blocks in length; subgroups were formed within that limiting distance. Within such precincts, the development of mutual interests and action could advance through small numbers of energetic leaders.[90]

In a classic study of housing that looked at dwelling units surrounding a courtyard, friendships were found to develop more often among occupants of the units on the same side of the courtyard than among those on opposite sides, despite other factors.[91] Another study indicated that in houses along a street, neighborly relations were stronger with neighbors along one side of the street than with those across the street.[92] It appears that face-to-face contact at doorways, mailboxes, and stoops is a greater force for socialization than mere proximity, and similarly the development of group interests is more likely to be instigated in the home range than at the neighborhood level.

Proxemics: Related to the consideration of personal space and territoriality is proxemics—a field of study that encompasses privacy; attachment/detachment; the sense of distance; home range or jurisdiction; and defense against the threatening behavior of other people.[93] In these terms, behavior in public spaces occurs at three distinct levels. At the first level, the fixed features of a city form a network within which human activities take place; the distribution of major elements (large parks, thoroughfares, and the most prominent landmark buildings), the mesh of spaces and smaller buildings that connect them (particularly the vast amount of area devoted to streets and their rights of way), and the designed points of spatial interest. At the second level, there is a constantly changing pattern of changeable objects as automobiles and trains make their way through the city, signs flash, and parking structures disgorge their contents. At the third level, there is the small protective sphere that people visualize around themselves, the bubble of variable radius into which others may not enter.[94] All behavior occurs and is related to these three levels of association. Human functioning is inevitably locus-related and place-associated (Fig. 4.18).[95]

> Surrounding individuals and in some cases even very small groups such as a couple conversing, is a personal space. This surrounding zone or series of zones is an area others are not usually allowed to enter; unwanted [contacts] are usually interpreted as intrusive and may cause the person whose space was invaded to feel uncomfortable and/or annoyed. This surrounding zone is not totally rigid. Rather, it is flexible. We "use" particular zones to distance ourselves from particular other individuals in certain situations. Individuals with whom we have intimate relations can approach more closely before we feel "invaded."

Acquaintances are felt to be invading at somewhat greater distance than close friends, and strangers are felt to be intruding at an even greater distance. Or a particular individual may be approached less closely in a formal than in an informal contest (i.e., at a large company board meeting instead of in a living room at a party).[96]

4.18 People alter their paths in order to avoid invading the personal space of others. Independence Mall, Philadelphia.

Investigations clearly indicate that smaller, more confining spaces cause people to increase their distances of interaction.[97] While the findings are controversial and depend on context, some examples are useful for consideration. When they are in a small alcove, people have a tendency to keep an ample distance between themselves and strangers. Conversely, larger or more stimulating spaces lead people to position themselves closer together. Through the years, a succession of studies have shown characteristics of human behavior on park benches, in restaurants, along sidewalks, at the beach, and at work in an office.[98] Such reports can lead only to general conclusions, because the conditions and subjects are extremely variable. However, by generalization and extrapolation a limited range of expectations can be derived.

In designing a space, likely behaviors can be arrived at from the data that are available from research projects. In applying these data, the designers most typically project their individual experiences and feelings to others, as *individuals* within that space. The responses of groups are often neglected.[99] There are indications that participation in a group lessens the variation among individuals who are members of the group.[100] In *clustered behavior*, small groups make use of a space, experiencing it in unison. Because of this simultaneity and probabilities among members of the group, it is likely that reactions will be similar and differences that occur may be repressed in order to conform to an apparent group attitude. The same may be true in cases of *mass behavior*—for example, when large groups of people are in an amphitheater or walking toward a stadium.[101]

The reason for the assembly of a large group often prescribes strong similarities of interests and social condition, and those differences of response that are present are most often submerged because of a feeling that personal individual expression is futile.

Stereotyping Responses: One approach to designing spaces is to assume that all people will behave the same way.[102] For very fundamental responses such as physical comfort and fear, this stereotyping could be well-founded. Designs that influence choices of direction and determine points of emphasis may also have the same affect on all sorts of users. Beyond those responses, differences in sex, age, nationality, income group, height, or personality may mean that we can seldom be certain that there will be a uniformity of response.

There appears to be a shared belief, valid or not, that natural park experiences are beneficial. It is common knowledge that visiting parks may reduce stress, induce contemplative behavior, stimulate and renew the spirit, and result in peacefulness and tranquility (Fig. 4.19). As mentioned earlier, some speculate that people escape to parks in order to experience an emotion different from those customary in typical urban and suburban locales.[103] In addition to all of the aforementioned factors, "past experiences, current expectations, and previous mood influence affective responses" to spaces and places.[104] One study indicated remarkable unanimity by finding that there were only minor differences in behavior in parks across socioeconomic status, careers, and age.[105] Whatever the experimental corroboration may be, there is undeniable evidence that parks and similar retreats have been developed and enjoyed through many centuries. Although they are certainly not a panacea for a myriad of ills, both social and psychological, there can be no doubt about the public's attitude toward them.

Grouping and Sorting Cues: The same objects that initiate proximity judgments may also cause groups to form and suggest their type of grouping (Fig. 4.20).[106] For example, in an office building plaza, a large number of pedestrians entering the plaza from the subway and bus stops hesitated and formed a cluster before they walked toward the revolving door of the building. When the group grows to seven people, clustering stopped and that group moved together toward the revolving door of the building. People tend to hesitate before or after clearly defined changes in the character of their path, such as steps, gates, sharp angles of movement, and areas that do not exert a direction influence. If smooth and continuous movement of pedestrians is desired, it may be wise to allow an appreciable distance between the incidents of the last step of a stairway, a ninety-degree change of direction, and passing through a gate. Where a steady movement is required, as in entering or leaving a stadium, ramps may be desirable in order to avoid stackups as people hesitate before taking the first step up a stair. In other cases, it may be desirable that places to pause punctuate movement through a space.

Cues within spaces may also serve as indicators of territorial conditions.[107] Meeting places are commonly identified in terms of their spatial

4.19 The choice of place is inescapably a choice of the degree of sensory communication one wishes to experience. Consequently, it can be a place of solitude and introspection or at another time a place of fun and games. You make it what it is. Sitka, Alaska.

4.20 Groups form in different and unexpected places. At the entrance of shops, on sidewalks in front of office buildings, in parking areas, and at transit stops, clusters of large numbers of people may require special consideration. Four people may be assumed as a design factor, but forty requires exceptional concerns. Country Club Plaza, Kansas City.

relationship to objects—"under the oak tree" or "at the gate." Benches may designate the location for "sitters," although there is hardly more commonality to the group. Temporary objects may indicate a designation or even a grouping (Fig. 4.21). For instance, a newspaper or paper cup on a park bench is accepted as perhaps indicating the imminent return of the person who placed them there and that person's claim upon the location. And if both the newspaper and the cup are present, it is evident that claim has been staked on the entire length of the bench. "At the simplest level, for example, territorial markers in public settings indicate that the occupant will return and reclaim the location. Even while a site is occupied, the spread of markers can be used by others as a rough index of how extensive an area the person feels he or she needs for setting-specific purposes."[108]

Cultural and Social Responses: Cultural needs for space vary. Upper- and middle-income users of a space may maintain greater distances than lower-income participants.[109] The same urban park may be used by college-educated white-collar workers as a place to sit and read during their lunch hour, and at the same time it may serve as a conversational and walking area for blue-collar workers. If these are both short-time uses of the space, they may even take place in the same area of a park. Distances and the desire to "stake out" territory may diminish when the place is used only for short periods. If a person pauses for only a moment of rest, she is more likely to share a park bench with a person of different status than if she intends to sit for an hour. Crowding may also discourage "stake-out" behavior, as during a holiday weekend at the beach or in a college library near the end of a term. If there is a nonexistent or low level of acquaintanceship between the individual occupant or small user group, then stake-out behavior will not be evidenced.[110]

Recreational centers, or settings, often seem crowded because our expectations of broad open spaces are contradicted by the presence of crowds, a larger number of people than we anticipated, and a larger number than would be desirable for the activities that we have planned.[111] Some research also indicates that stressful behavior in crowded environments may be determined more by the number of individuals or groups present than by the mathematical relationship of population and area. A common phenomenon is the behavior evidenced by tourists as they crowd the plazas in front of famous buildings. In those situations, there are numerous factors that result in an informal companionship among the tourists. Although they are strangers, the fact that they are forthrightly tourists declares a degree of similarity in income and social levels, cultural background, and familiarity with information about the building. The physical arrangement of the site means that the tourists' attention is directed principally at a single object, with a likelihood that secondary and tertiary foci are similar as well. Such unifying factors commonly overcome unfamiliarities among the group. Research indicates that the density of occupants on a site and their feelings of commonality are more significant indicators of perceived crowding than the experience of direct contact among the occupants—a phenomenon particularly evident among visitors to wilderness areas.[112]

4.21 A sidewalk book sale attracts a different group of people to the spaces between the buildings on that street corner. All unusual events or alterations in a district attract attention and lead to the formation of temporary groups. New York City. (Photo by Alan M. Gordon)

Third-generation Americans utilize spaces in a manner more nearly approaching that of the "average" American than do recent immigrants.[113] With the process of cultural assimilation, there appears to develop a conformity in attitude toward open spaces. Immigrants from certain cultures make use of outdoor places for family and socialization purposes, often disregarding any constraints of climate. Rainy or cold weather may not stop them from the traditional outdoor serenade the evening before a wedding, as is traditional for immigrants from some parts of Italy. Other immigrants may be more inclined to limit family exchanges to the interior of their dwelling units and only utilize exterior spaces for the visual enhancement of the dwelling.

Many researchers have investigated the behavior of different cultures in the same open space.[114] Ethnic variations in levels of exhibitionism and degrees of aggressive friendliness are easily noted. Ethnic groups will often congregate in a particular portion of the space, demonstrating tentative gestures of communication with other groups.[115] Most commonly, such gestures occur between individuals who correspond in age, sex, or evident social level, and they are frequently initiated at the noncompetitive extremes of age, among toddlers and the elderly.

Role-playing: As they walk along a street, people are conscious of other people—both the people they see approaching them and those behind whom they walk.[116] At the same time, it is inevitable and natural that they are aware of inescapably being observed by others. This situation of observing others while aware of being observed sets the scene for role-playing. Beyond the identification provided by apparel and appearance, a certain way of walking, feigned laughter, and other affectations may be adopted in order to convey impressions at various levels of specificity and generality.[117] A messenger may hurry past in a manner that assures the observer of the gravity and urgency of his mission; typists may clearly indicate a mood of ennui; and aging executives may adopt a jaunty and youthful step. Although there are often explicit motives for impressing associates with such trickery, it should be recognized that role-playing is also common before an audience of complete strangers, probably as an act of self-assurance or self-delusion.

Amusing as this behavior may at first seem, public open spaces have a valuable capacity to serve as the background for role-playing and a source of daydreams. The park and the street, particularly when anonymity is afforded, can be stages provided for an escape from reality, a change of environment that may change the personalities seen there.[118]

Even after considering the range of backgrounds and temperaments that are certain to be represented in the users of a single open space at a designated time, a designer cannot with assurance determine that desires and responses will conform to a specific pattern. Moods, weather, and sudden impulses will cause unexpected behavior. So many variables predetermine a loose fit of place and people. However tempting it may be to determine a series of events in which the "average" visitor will participate, remember that there is rarely a truly average individual present. No matter how elegant or fascinating the statistics of reports may be, the behavioral response that is often called average is actually a center of gravity in a galaxy of individuals.

ENDNOTES

1. Edward Relph, *Place and Placelessness* (London: Pion Limited, 1976), 147.

2. Janice Fillip, "San Diego's Marine Linear Park," *Urban Land* (November 1989): 15.

3. Roger Barker and others, *Habitats, Environments, and Human Behavior: Studies in Ecological Psychology and Eco-Behavioral Science from the Midwest Psychological Field Station, 1947–1972* (San Francisco: Jossey-Bass Publishers, 1978).

4. Susan Saegert and Gary H. Winkel, "Environmental Psychology," in Mark R. Rosenzweig and Lyman W. Porter, eds., *Annual Review of Psychology* (1990): 441–477.

5. Urs Fuhrer, "Bridging the Ecological-Psychological Gap: Behavior Settings as Interfaces," *Environment and Behavior* (July 1990): 518–519.

6. Kurt Lewin, *Field Theory in Social Science: Selected Theoretical Papers*, Dorwin Cartwrite, ed. (New York: Harper, 1951).

7. Floyd Henry Allport, *Theories of Perception and the Concept of Structure: A Review and Critical Analysis With An Introduction to a Dynamic Structural Theory of Behavior*, (New York: John Wiley, 1955), 110.

8. Barker and others, *Habitats, Environment, and Human Behavior*, 192–201.

9. Sidney N. Brower, "Territory in Urban Settings," in Amos Rapoport, Irwin Altman, and Joachim F. Wohlwill, eds., *Human Behavior and Environment. Vol. 4: Environment and Culture* (New York: Plenum Press, 1980), 181.

10. Edward T. Hall, *The Hidden Dimension* (Garden City, NY: Doubleday, 1966).

11. Barker, *Habitats, Environment, and Human Behavior*, as quoted in Fuhrer, "Bridging," 533.

12. Stephen Kaplan, "Perception and Landscape Conceptions and Misconceptions," in Jack L. Nasar, ed., *Environmental Aesthetics: Theory, Research, and Applications* (New York: Cambridge University Press, 1988), 48–49.

13. Kaplan, "Perception," 47.

14. Reginald G. Golledge and Robert Stimson, *Analytical Behavioral Geography* (London: Croon Helm, 1987).

15. Golledge and Stimson, *Analytical Behavioral Geography*, 94–98.

16. Refer to the Land Ordinance of 1785 in William Goodman, ed., *Principles and Practice of Urban Planning* (Washington DC: International City Managers Association, 1968), 13.

17. Fritz Steele, *The Sense of Place* (Boston: CBI Publishing Co., Inc., 1981), 14–15.

18. Golledge and Stimson, *Analytical Behavioral Geography*, 75.

19. Golledge and Stimson, *Analytical Behavioral Geography*, 70.

20. Golledge and Stimson, *Analytical Behavioral Geography*, 156.

21. Stephen Kaplan and Rachel Kaplan, eds., *Humanscape: Environments For People* (Belmont, CA: Duxbury, 1978).

22. James A. Russell, "Adaptation Level and the Effective Appraisal of Environment," *Journal of Environmental Psychology* 4:119–135.

23. Julie V. Kasmar, "A Lexicon of Environmental Descriptors," in Nasar *Environmental Aesthetics*, 153.

24. Barrie B. Greenbie, "The Landscape of Social Symbols," in Nasar, *Environmental Aesthetics*, 73.

25. Benjamin Lee Whorf, *The Relation of Habitual Thought and Behavior to Language: Four Articles on Metalinguistics* (Washington D.C.: Foreign Service Institute, 1949). Also, see Benjamin Lee Whorf, "Science and Linguistics," in John B. Carroll, ed., *Language, Thought, and Reality* (Cambridge, MA: MIT Press, 1957).

26. Jan Gehl, *Life Between Buildings: Using Public Space* (New York: Van Nostrand Reinhold, 1987), 147.

27. Relph, *Place and Placelessness*, 137–140.

28. Nasar, *Environmental Aesthetics*, 41.

29. Rachel Kaplan and Stephen Kaplan, *The Experience of Nature: A Psychological Perspective* (New York: Cambridge University Press, 1989), 49; and David M. Woodcock, "A Functionalist Approach to Environmental Preference," unpublished dissertation (Ann Arbor MI: University of Michigan, 1982), 45–46.

30. Saegert and Winkel, "Environmental Psychology," 465.

31. John R. Aiello, "Human Spatial Behavior," *Journal of Environmental Psychology* (1987): 389.

32. Edward T. Hall, "A System For The Notation of Proxemic Behavior," *American Anthropologist* (1963): 1003–26.

33. Heini Hediger, *Wild Animals in Captivity* (London: Butterworth Publishing, 1950).

34. Irwin Altman and A.M. Vinsel, "Personal Space: An Analysis of Hall's Proxemic Framework," in Irwin Altman and Joachim F. Wohlwill, eds., *Human Behavior and The Environment, Volume 2: Advances in Theory and Research* (New York: Plenum Press, 1976), 199.

35. Altman and Vinsel, "Personal Space," 199.

36. Aiello, "Human Spatial Behavior," 393.

37. Michael Argyle and Mark Cook, *Gaze and Mutual Gaze* (Cambridge, England: Cambridge University Press, 1976).

38. Michael Argyle and John Dean, "Eye Contact, Distance, and Affiliation," *Sociometry* (1965): 289–304.

39. Hall, "Proxemic Behavior," 1003–26.

40. Hall, "Proxemic Behavior," 1010.

41. Aiello, "Human Spatial Behavior," 412.

42. Erving Goffman, *Behavior in Public Places* (New York: Free Press, 1963).

43. K.B. Little, "Cultural Variations On Social Schemata," *Journal of Personality and Social Psychology* (1968): 1–7.

44. Hall, *Hidden Dimension*, 112.

45. John R. Aiello and S.E. Jones, "Field Study of the Proxemic Behavior of Young School Children In Their Subcultural Groups," *Journal of Personality and Social Psychology* 19 (3): 351–56.

46. Aiello, "Human Spatial Behavior," 490.

47. Reginald G. Golledge, "Environmental Cognition," in Daniel Stokols and Irwin Altman, eds., *Handbook of Environmental Psychology*, Vol. 1. (New York: John Wiley & Sons, 1987), 156.

48. George A. Miller, Eugene Galanter, and Karl H. Pribam, *Plans and the Structure of Behavior* (New York: Holt, 1960).

49. David Ley, *A Social Geography of the City* (New York: Harper and Row, 1983), 95–97, 102.

50. Although there are many sources that discuss this issue, the most basic explanations may be found in biological studies. See Peter Van Sommers, *The Biology of Behavior* (Adelaide, Australia: John Wiley & Sons, 1972), 29–69.

51. Jean Piaget, *The Grasp of Consciousness: Action and Concept in the Young Child* (Cambridge, MA: Harvard University Press, 1976).

52. Erving Goffman, *Interaction Ritual: Essays on Face-to-Face Behavior*. (Garden City, NY: Anchor Books, 1967), 50–55.

53. Tony Hiss, *The Experience of Place* (New York: Alfred A. Knopf, 1990), 28.

54. Ley, *Social Geography*, 114.

55. Steele, *Sense of Place*, 93–95.

56. Steele, *Sense of Place*, 202–205.

57. Kaplan and Kaplan, *Experience of Nature*, 57.

58. Kaplan and Kaplan, *Experience of Nature*, 68.

59. Kaplan and Kaplan, *Experience of Nature*, 54–57.

60. George C. Barney and S.M. dos Santos, *Elevator Traffic Analysis, Design, and Control*, 2nd ed. (London: Peregrinis Institution of Electrical Engineers, 1985).

61. Kenneth R. Schneider, *On the Nature of Cities* (San Francisco: Jossey-Bass Publishers, 1979), 200–201.

62. Eustace C. Poulton, "Arousing Environmental Stress Can Improve Performance: Whatever People Say," *Aviation, Space, and Environmental Medicine* (1988): 1193–1204.

63. James Rotton, Mark Shats, and Robert Standers, "Temperature and Pedestrian Tempo: Walking Without Awareness," *Environment and Behavior*, (September 1990):668.

64. D. Jim Walmsley and Gareth J. Lewis. "The Pace of Pedestrian Flows in Cities," *Environment and Behavior* (March 1989): 123–150.

65. Edward K. Sadalla, Virgil Sheets, and Heather McCreath, "The Condition of Urban Tempo," *Environment and Behavior* (March 1990): 230–54.

66. Irving Hoch, "City Size Effects, Trends, and Policies," *Science* (1986): 856–863.

67. Ralph B. Taylor, *Human Territorial Functioning: An Empirical Evolutionary Perspective on Individual and Small Group Territorial Cognition, Behaviors, and Consequences* (New York: Cambridge University Press, 1988), 316.

68. Taylor, *Human Territorial Functioning*, 222.

69. Steele, *Sense of Place*, 119.

70. Theresa N. Westover, "Perceived Crowding in Recreational Settings: An Environment-Behavior Model," *Environment and Behavior* (May 1989): 258–76.

71. R. Bruce Hull IV and Antony Harvey, "Explaining the Emotion People Experience in Suburban Parks," *Environment and Behavior* (May 1989): 323–45.

72. Roger S. Ulrich, "Natural Versus Urban Scenes: Some Psychophysiological Effects," *Environment and Behavior* (1989): 523–56.

73. Golledge and Stimson, *Analytical Behavioral Geography*, 93–94.

74. Kaplan and Kaplan, *Experience of Nature*, 55–66.

75. Rachel Kaplan, "The Analysis of Perception Via Preference: A Strategy for Studying How the Environment is Experienced," *Landscape Planning* (1985): 161–176.

76. Taylor, *Human Territorial Functioning*, 318.

77. Kevin Lynch, *Good City Form* (Cambridge, MA: MIT Press, 1984), 146–150.

78. David Canter, *The Psychology of Place* (New York: St. Martins Press, 1977), 97.

79. Kaplan and Kaplan, *Experience of Nature*, 38.

80. Kaplan and Kaplan, *Experience of Nature*, 32–33.

81. Golledge and Stimson, *Analytical Behavioral Geography*, 94–95.

82. Kaplan and Kaplan, *Experience of Nature*, 34.

83. Hiss, *Experience of Place*, 28–32.

84. Hiss, *Experience of Place*, 44.

85. Paul B. Paulus and Dinesh Nagar, "Environmental Influences On Social Interaction and Group Development," *Review of Personality and Social Psychology* (1989): 68–90.

86. Paul B. Paulus, "Group Dynamics," in V.S. Ramachandran, ed., *Encyclopedia of Human Behavior, 1993* (San Diego: Academic Press, 1993).

87. Taylor, *Human Territorial Functioning,* 45–46.

88. Sidney Brower, "Territory in Urban Settings," in Rapoport, Altman, and Wohlwill, *Human Behavior and the Environment, Vol. 4,* 181.

89. Ley, "Social Geography," 105.

90. Taylor, *Human Territorial Functioning,* 171.

91. L. Festinger, S. Schacter, and K. Back, *Social Pressure in Informal Groups* (Stanford, CA: Stanford University Press, 1963).

92. Donald Appleyard, *Livable Streets* (Berkeley: University of California Press, 1981).

93. Robert Sommer, *Personal Space: The Behavioral Basis of Design* (Englewood Cliffs, NJ: Prentice-Hall, 1969), 26–38.

94. Sommer, *Personal Space,* 26.

95. Canter, *Psychology of Place,* 116–17.

96. Taylor, *Human Territorial Functioning,* 97.

97. Andrew Baum and Paul Paulus, "Crowding," *Journal of Environmental Psychology* (1987): 544.

98. Canter, *Psychology of Place,* 116.

99. Canter, *Psychology of Place,* 180.

100. Charles E. Miller, "The Social Psychological Effects of Group Decision Rules," in Paul B. Paulus, ed., *Psychology of Group Influence,* 2nd ed. (New Jersey: Lawrence Erlbaum Associates, Publishers, 1989), 337.

101. Robert A. Wicklund, "The Appropriation of Ideas," in Paul B. Paulus, ed., *Psychology of Group Influence,* 2nd ed. (New Jersey: Lawrence Erlbaum Associates, Publishers, 1989), 417–18.

102. Steele, *Sense of Place* 18.

103. Hull and Harvey, "Explaining the Emotion," 326.

104. Albert Mehrabian, *Public Places and Private Spaces* (New York: Basic Books, 1976), 4.

105. Albert Rutledge, *A Visual Approach to Park Design* (New York: Garland STPM Press, 1981), 125.

106. Amos Rapoport, "Cross-cultural Aspects of Environmental Design," in Rapoport, Altman, and Wohlwill, *Human Behavior and Environment, Vol. 4,* 16.

107. David Stea, "Space Territory and Human Movements," in Harold M. Proshansky, William H. Ittelson, Leanne G. Rivlin, eds., *Environmental Psychology: Man and His Physical Setting* (New York: Holt, Rinehart and Winston, 1970), 37–38.

108. Taylor, *Human Territorial Functioning,* 318.

109. Taylor, *Human Territorial Functioning,* 182–83.

110. Mehrabian, *Public Places and Private Spaces,* 15–16.

111. Baum and Paulus, "Crowding," 543.

112. Theresa N. Westover, "Perceived Crowding in Recreational Settings: An Environment-Behavior Model," *Environment and Behavior,* (May 1989):264.

113. Herbert J. Gans, *The Urban Villagers: Group and Class in the Life of Italian-Americans* (New York: Free Press, 1962), 243–69.

114. John R. Aiello and Donna E. Thompson, "Personal Space, Crowding and Spatial Behavior," in Rapoport, Altman, and Wohlwill, *Human Behavior and Environment. Vol. 4,* 120–130.

115. Muriel Saville-Troike, *The Ethnography of Communication* (Oxford, NY: B. Blackwell, 1989).

116. Hiss, *Experience of Place,* 44.

117. Erving Goffman, *The Presentation of Self in Everyday Life* (Garden City, NY: Anchor Books, 1959), 22–30, 168–170.

118. Goffman, *Presentation of Self,* 238–39.

5

DESIGN–CONCEPTS, ELEMENTS, AND CONSTRAINTS

Elements, points, lines, planes, mass, space; visual qualities, light and dark, color, texture, figure-ground relationships, grids and modules, balance and symmetry, scale, proportion; solutions, paths and walks, automobile parking, steps, ramps, and railings, screens, water, trees, shrubs, and lawns, lighting, fixtures and furniture, summary.

Beyond the obvious functional requirements that are involved, the conscious design of open spaces is also intended to provide esthetic pleasure and satisfaction for the people who experience them. It is this combination of purposes that establishes the fundamental nature of "design." As opposed to "art," which has the function of being beautiful, "design" combines utility and beauty. Anthropologists have provided ample evidence that primitive cultures consciously blended the practical shaping of useful tools and weapons with ornamental considerations, and today all equipment and appliances that have popular use undergo "styling," an activity that combines the principles of art with those of marketing psychology. But the term *principles of art* is applied to a complex mesh of interactions and recognized standards that are physical, experiential, and metaphysical.

There have always been debates on the question of which of three theoretical points of view should govern the creation and judgment of art and design:

1. *Fixed standards*, unchanged through the centuries, can be taken as the criteria for judgment. These standards do not necessarily imply historicism, for the characteristic forms, proportions, and other elements of the past can be captured in other media and details.

2. *Cultural expression* is the conviction that each situation and period generates its own forms. The *Zeitgeist*—the spirit of the time—is accepted as the controlling factor.

3. *Personal expression* values the uniqueness of the individual project or the style of the artist or designer. This expression can become either an accepted interpretation within certain stylistic strictures or a situation that generates its own criteria.

Different periods and different people have been influenced in a variety of ways by these three options. The field of design is strongly influenced by social factors and technological development, so very seldom has only one of these attitudes clearly predominated. The best answer to the question, as seen in realistic terms, is probably "all of the above."

This volume seeks to avoid such philosophical problems and stylistic debates, although participants in design certainly profit from being aware of them. The design of public places is usually the joint efforts of different groups or individuals, whether their function is to create a design, establish its purpose, approve, or execute it. Therefore, the basic elements of form and their execution in materials will be discussed here, while matters of taste, preference, and expression will be left open to variation, according to the spirit of the project.

THE ELEMENTS

The following descriptions of the elements of design (points, lines, planes, masses, and spaces) deal with very simple things that assume complexity through the variety of ways in which they can be utilized. The designers' ideas can boldly emphasize the use of these elements or can employ them subtly and instinctively. In order to become familiar with these elements and some of their more complex combinations, drawings and models can provide simplified and relatively rapid means of experimentation. Inspecting constructed projects or natural settings in terms of the elements can be of even greater assistance in developing a designer's sensitivity. Only a brief survey of the subject can be provided here, but by experimentation and observation designers can expand on the subjects in keeping with their interests and personal attitudes.

One must avoid translating observations of art phenomena into rules. With only a little concentration, it is usually possible to discover exceptions to any such rules or even to find a reasonable logic that would virtually reverse the meaning of the rule. One part of this difficulty is the fact the translation of visual phenomena into a verbal form always risks inaccuracy. For instance in books on this subject it is common to read statements such as "[the square] is a static and neutral figure," which is shortly followed by "dynamic when standing on one of its corners."[1] These statements, although somewhat contradictory, seem plausible when considered in painterly terms, as shapes placed on a flat surface. However, when considered as a plan shape, constructed on the surface on which the observer stands, the

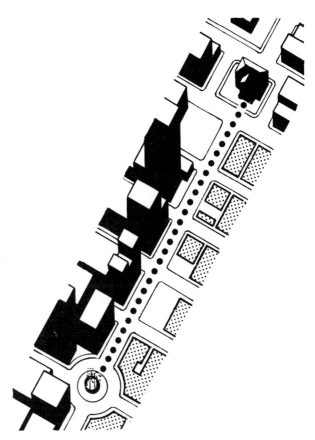

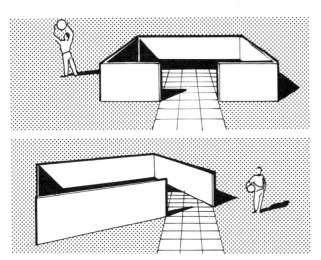

5.1 When approached axially (above), a square seems to be a static shape. But when seen at angle (below), its effect can be dynamic.

5.2 When a street is not strongly defined by buildings, focal points at its ends can maintain the visual linearity of the arrangement.

situation is greatly altered. When approached along one of its center lines, the square is indeed basically static; but approached off-center and at an angle, the effect is strongly dynamic until the observer nears the center of the square (Fig. 5.1). Many of the customary principles have the same tantalizing characteristic of varying in validity according to circumstances. Although this situation means that designers have few iron-clad formulas to help them, it also means that designers actually have a larger number of options than traditional principles would suggest. Nevertheless, it is always wise to be fully knowledgeable about a principle in order to violate it judiciously.

Points: Many spatial compositions rely on overall patterns and their artful variation. But many others are founded upon focal incidents, objects, or loci that are the major events of the experience with transitional areas and secondary points around or between them (Fig. 5.2). This patterning and variation is most clearly indicated historically by the avenues developed in sixteenth-century Rome (as discussed in Chapter 3). Whether an avenue terminated at the forecourt of a church or at a broad and traffic-filled piazza, the place would most often be marked by an Egyptian obelisk, an emphatic vertical that was seen straight ahead as one travelled the length of the avenue. The breadth of spaces, shapes of monuments, or facades of buildings have been employed to identify the objective of travel.

Marking a place is a powerful decision in design. A large object—a monument or a building—is the most forceful method, but the open space itself is a designation both simple and dignified. In either case, that point in one's movement is identified as an objective, and immediately the travel between points becomes secondary to the attainment of the point itself. As a marked objective, the point of destination acquires additional meaning. Excitement or satisfaction is anticipated as the reward for reaching the goal. Even if one has no reason to travel the full distance, the path is characterized as the route from one point to another. Not all routes fall between two significant points. For instance, promenades and esplanades have as their purpose the pleasure of movement and social exchange, and reaching the end of the promenade is merely an occasion for turning around and repeating the trip.

In many cases the point at the end of a route involves an emotional response, the arrival at a point associated with religious commitment, patriotic fervor, or a remarkable visual pleasure. At other times, the point is a practical destination, a functional exchange place for transportation, a center of mercantile activity, or a place of social exchange. One can view the pattern of movement in an urban setting as a web woven between critical points (certainly a prominent historical interpretation), or one can consider that the points are primarily established by the intersection of routes of travel. These factors are essential in one's making decisions about the design of all of the dynamics of motion within urban spaces. When do routes determine points, and when do routes fall between points? Both conditions occur, but they have distinctly different meanings in the degree and kind of emphasis that is appropriate to the points.

Lines: Lines are very long areas, and they are also the edges between areas; hence, a line can be formed by a band of white stone or can be defined by the end of grass and the beginning of pavement. Typical sidewalks present a useful illustration of the nature of lines. The sidewalk itself is a line, its edges are lines, and the transverse scoring of the concrete makes other lines (Fig. 5.3). Each of these examples may have a different visual intensity. A sidewalk that is very wide may seem to be an area as one walks along it while wide stripes of red brick across the concrete of another sidewalk can divide its surface, diminishing its identification as a band of walkway. It is largely the ratio of length to width that leads us to distinguish between lines and areas. In addition, repeated lines can become areas as in the linear pattern of a plowed field. As one looks along a straight line (as opposed to looking across it), one can sense direction and acceleration, for a line is by definition "the shortest distance between two points," and the fastest way to travel between the points. This sensation is influenced by the sleekness or roughness of the line and the augmentation or contradiction that may be provided by other elements in the vicinity. For instance, a residential street may achieve strong directional emphasis through the parallel placement of the housefronts, sidewalks, streetside tree, curbs, and

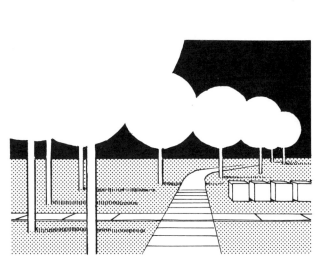

5.3 Walks, fences, rows of trees, and other design features can act as linear elements of the composition, particularly when seen from a distance. Note here that the trees seem to be separate verticals when near to the viewer, but they combine as a horizontal element when farther away.

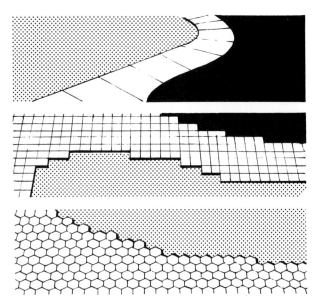

5.4 Curvilinear movement across a lawn and along the edge of a pool can be accommodated by the sweeping curve of a concrete walk or by the irregular edges of square or hexagonal paving units.

even the center stripe on the pavement; irregular placement of different varieties of trees will cause the arrangement to be less emphatically linear.

Not all lines need to have the efficiency associated with straight lines. Sweeping curves or arcs can provide an exhilaration (as in driving along mountain roads), encourage slow meditative walking (as on a woodland path), or emphasize a central area (as a walk circling around the edge of a clearing). By thoughtfully varying the degree of curvature, detail can be included in a curvilinear scheme and so monotony can be avoided. Although the use of curves is most often historically associated with the *jardins anglaises* of eighteenth-century Europe, it need not be limited to naturalistic and picturesque designs. Both formal and informal arrangements can be planned with a repetition of curves or a combination of curves and straight lines. In addition, hexagons, octagons, or other polygonal shapes can be employed to develop patterns that generate curve-like series of straight lines (Fig. 5.4).

Planes: The visually dominant element in the design of outdoor spaces is the ground, a generally horizontal plane that is emphasized through our constant and inescapable awareness of gravity and our standing perpendicular to that plane. In contrast to the planes of floors in multistoried buildings, the ground plan of an outside space is thought to be a portion of the continuous surface that we know is outside the space. Vertical planes may exist as the thin walls of buildings, but at a distance such walls, because they are relatively small elements of the scene, are more often interpreted as being merely the faces of solid masses, than as actually being planes. (This

5.5 Cover portions of the drawing to observe the accelerating (left), shunting (center), and slowing (right) effects of planes placed along a line of movement.

distinction is related to the fact that when we look at an advancing angle of two walls, our interpretation differs significantly if we believe that we perceive the corner of a solid mass or if we know that the walls are simply planes with open space behind them.) Our reactions to planes often vary according to the angular relationship between the surface of the plane and our direction of sight and movement (Fig. 5.5). If we are looking and moving perpendicular to a plane, we recognize it as an obstruction and hesitate as we near it; if we are approaching it at an angle we veer in the direction in which we can continue with the least angular change; and if we move parallel to the wall its size and proximity will determine the degree to which its direction encourages our movement. As we walk among vertical planes, we slow, stop, or turn according to our urgency or speed and the relationship of our direction to the surface of the plane. (It is rather like the movement of rolling balls in some children's toys and pinball games.) If this device is used to excess, it may be resented. However, it can be employed with great subtlety. A typical Italian garden of the Renaissance might have the line of exit from the palazzo perpendicular to a stone railing, which would cause the visitor to pause and look out along the center line of the garden before turning left or right to descend the stairs (Fig. 5.6). Returning from the garden, the center path would lead directly to a massive retaining wall, relieved by the placement of a fountain in a niche, before ascending stairs to the level of the palazzo. The device seldom annoys visitors if the degree to which a plane disrupts movement is appropriate to the relative interest and importance of that point.

The effect of planes depends largely on their dimensions, especially as related to the human eye-level, and the materials of which they are formed. Our response to being confronted by a concrete wall will be clearly different than our response to a plane of foliage, and the impression we

5.6 In this simple version, an Italian garden permits a centerline view of the space from the elevated terrace. An angled view is obtained as one descends to the bottom of the stairs, and becomes a centerline view again at a different level.

receive from the foliage will be different if it is a closely clipped hedge or a roughly-textured wall of branches and leaves. Planes that have horizontal curvature or vertical tapering can become particularly interesting because of their relationship to the definition of spatial volumes. A plane established by a hedge only waist-high is greatly different from a stone curb or a building's wall.

If a path of movement among planes went only in one direction, the manipulation of planes would be relatively simple. Instead, in most cases the design is made much more complex by the fact that two-way movement must be considered and many of the effects attainable with planes have the opposite effect when viewed from the opposite side.

Mass: The fundamental mass that is sensed in open spaces is the mass of the earth, the planet on which they rest. If the project site slopes, a visitor's awareness of the groundmass increases, growing greater as the slope becomes steeper. Very steep inclines cause extreme awareness of the hillside and the hill, and all elements of the project seem to exist primarily in terms of their relationship to the slope. Undulations of the site, such as hillocks and ponds, have similar effects, according to their dimensions, particularly the vertical. Gentle forms lead to subtle effects, but as they become steeper and higher, the actions of berms and mounds increasingly resemble those of vertical planes.

When presented as sharply defined geometric forms, three-dimensional elements usually are provided as architectural and landscape constructions; however, a sharp modeling of the earth, such as a slope turning at a right angle, can have the same aspect from certain points of view. Masses, whether shaped of earth or constructed of masonry, have associations with earth forms. Children have always recognized this quality by running to the tops of small mounds in order to survey the surrounding area. Paths can meander between mounds, just as roads follow the valleys between hills. Caution must be exercised in earth-moving because quite small mounds seem almost ridiculously insignificant and large masses of earth take on a geographical scale that can soon become ominous.

Space: Because it is not in itself visible and concrete, space is often difficult to define visually. Sometimes we can sense the shape of a space more clearly if we are not standing at a point within it, but in a position at the side. This sensing may in some manner relate to people's preference to sit with their backs to a wall, looking out into an open space. Outdoor spaces are much more difficult to sense than rooms within buildings, because they usually have no overhead limit other than the irregular and seasonally variable protection afforded by trees. (The interior spaces of pergolas, arbors, and other kinds of shelter are interesting situations that lie somewhere between the conditions of open spaces and those of architectural interiors.) Hence, the visual definition of outdoor spaces varies according to the degree of enclosure that is provided, and when the feeling of enclosure is less strong than the feeling of horizontal openness, the space is less clearly defined (Fig. 5.7). To a great extent, we see space as the

5.7 The roofed pavilion and the enclosed garden are two distinct spaces and, at the same time, a single area. Note that on the left a larger opening and extension of the roof and floor relate the two spaces more strongly.

volume between things, just as a valley is seen as the volume between two hills. If the hills are low rounded masses, the valley is perceived as a subtle undulation of the earth's surface; if the hills are defined by steep bluffs, the valley has a more precise feeling of enclosure and isolation.

Since a space may have varying degrees of definition, this fact can become a factor in design. The tubular volume of a downtown street may open into the broad area of a monument and traffic circle, and the relationship between the height of surrounding buildings and the breadth of the area will determine the clarity with which we sense the circle. In this way, plans easily can be deceptive. As we study a design, we see a shape in the plan, but we may not actually be able to *read* the shape as we stand within it.

Human vision has been characterized as ranging with relative clarity to thirty degrees from the center line of view; that is, the eye acts as a "cone of vision" with sixty degrees as the angle at its point (Fig. 5.8). Outside that cone, objects are seen with diminishing definition, only as part of a viewer's peripheral vision. Using this assumption, we find that a building facade, screening row of trees, or other vertical element will fill slightly more than half our central vision if our distance from it is no greater than twice its height (Fig. 5.9). (The lower portion of our view is, of course, the ground surface.) At a distance about four times the height of the facade, the vertical surface will occupy about half of the area of our upper vision. These data give some definition to the degrees of enclosure various surroundings may offer, but it is always relatively simple to verify such generalities by finding an existing similar condition and visually determining the influence it exerts on the space adjoining it. There are also influences of the objects within the enclosure. A surrounding wall may be relatively insignificant around a monumental tower, because the height of the tower can overpower that of the wall.

Although vertical planes may not completely surround and define the limits of a space, the mind tends to extend the encompassing surfaces. Two planes may not actually intersect, but in our mental extensions of them a corner is defined. This extrapolation of spatial limits is even more strongly sensed when corners are visible and the mind describes the planes between them (Fig. 5.10). In this way, the suggestions of planes may lead to a space

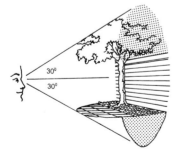

5.8 The assumed cone of vision is about 30 degrees from the centerline of sight. While this visibility is a realistic interpretation of a single view, the perception of a space is a composite of different views.

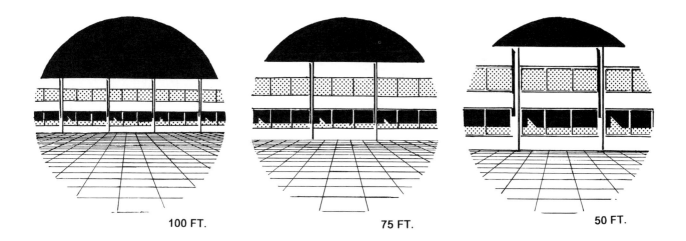

100 FT.   **75 FT.**   **50 FT.**

being interpreted as simultaneously contained within several volumes, each defined by a different set of planes, like the planes within a crystalline structure. Volumes can lie within other volumes and spatial elements may overlap. Grids and modules may be used in this manner, with three-dimensional units forming a pattern that serves as a unifying consistency in a design.

Spaces can be delineated in remarkably subtle ways. If a tree stands only three feet from a fence, there is an identifiable space defined between them, an area through which the space wraps, passing between the tree and the fence. A grassy area between three trees is subtly delineated by the three tree trunks, but you still can almost feel when you cross a line and enter the triangle of space that the trees mark.

5.9 When plazas are larger and the observer stands farther from surrounding elements, the degree of enclosure is diminished. Note that the ground plane is a large part of the view at any distance.

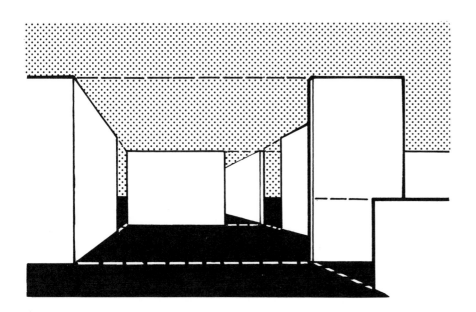

5.10 The observer's eye and mind tend to complete basic solid shapes, although the enclosing surfaces may be incomplete. This completion is most effective when the surfaces present provide edges and corners, and the mind fills in between them.

VISUAL QUALITIES

All our senses are part of our perception of a specific space, except perhaps the sense of taste. The sound, the smell, and the feel of the air on our faces contribute to our understanding of an area. Still, for most people the most powerful experiences are visual. The things we see, including the elements that have been reviewed previously, are both the characteristics of the objects that make up the place and the manner in which they are arranged. Our responses to many of these qualities are strongly influenced by comparison and contrast with surrounding conditions. A red brick walk may draw little attention during the summer when it is surrounded by grass and flowers, but in the winter it will seem bright against a background of snow and gray branches. It is such phenomena that mark the regular and irregular changes caused by time and weather. Objects seem lighter or darker according to the value of the surroundings against which they are seen. Balance, scale, and proportion appear as comparisons of dimensions and positioning. Many aspects of visual experience may have precise scales on which they can be identified, as photographers' light meters determine the amount of light in an area, but visual perception considers the relative amount of light just as photographers adjust their cameras to the conditions within the scope of their lenses.

Light and Dark: The Italians originated the term *chiaroscuro* for paintings and drawings that emphasize the effect of light and dark, and centuries have been spent in artists' experiments on the subject. We see light only in comparison with darkness, and vice versa. As an experiment, notice the ubiquitous silvery-metal lighting standards that are placed along city streets. At the bottom, where the standard is silhouetted against dark trees or buildings, it appears very light; but at the top, where it stands against the sky, it appears a rather dark gray. Similarly, a flowering tree looks brighter when seen against a background of dark coniferous trees, and the shadow within a niche will contrast dramatically with the limestone wall in which it is carved.

The eye is drawn, we find, to the sharpest and most prominent contrast between light and dark (Fig. 5.11). This simple and reassuring statement is beset with many difficulties in outdoor spaces, for seasonal changes, overcast days, and nightfall bring alterations in the light and shadow. Artificial lighting permits us to control nighttime conditions, and the contrasts of overcast days are, except for the sharp edges of shadows, just diminutions of those produced by bright sunlight. It is seasonal change that causes the greatest alteration of values. Although there is little change in the downtown street from summer to winter, spaces where there are plants can change drastically. Dark green trees shed their leaves and show only gray twigs, grass turns from green to tan, and finally the whole scene may be coated with snow. Therefore, places designed with plants often depend on the selection of construction materials and the inclusion of evergreens for value contrast in the winter months, and a narrower range of dark and light is present in winter than during the remainder of the year.

5.11 In drawings, as in observer's views, the eye is drawn first to those places where the maximum contrast of dark and light occur. In the upper sketch, the sharp contrast between a white wall and dark evergreens draws attention to that portion of the view. In the lower sketch, the material of the wall affords less contrast, and the dark material of the sculpture, silhouetted against a bright sky, catches the eye. The contrast between day and night conditions may be important in such cases.

Color: We see the world because of values—the degree of light reflected by surfaces—which we have previously discussed. A black-and-white photograph provides us with essential information, but additional information and design potential comes from color. To describe colors we customarily refer to three characteristics:

■ *hue*, which is the name of the color (for example, blue, orange, or red-violet);

■ *intensity*, brightness or dullness (bright red, burgundy, or an earthen red-brown); and

■ *value*, the lightness or darkness (pale green, grass green, or a green so dark that it is nearly black.)

Generally value and intensity vary together, blue becoming less intense as it becomes darker and pink paint becoming less intense as more white

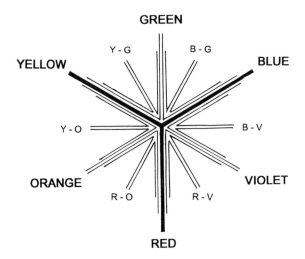

5.12 A traditional color wheel. Complementary combinations are opposite each other (blue and orange, red-violet and yellow-green). Analogous colors are adjacent to each other (yellow-green, green, and blue-green). This is the most familiar of several systems of defining color relationships, each based on different color phenomena.

paint is added to it. Since we are not dealing with wave lengths or colored lights, it is simple to speak in terms of the traditional color wheels, based on pigment colors and the so-called primary colors of red, blue, and yellow. Although the designer's eye should always be the final judge of pleasing color combinations, there are three basic methods of combining colors that are useful as references (Fig. 5.12).

■ *Complementary* selections of colors employ hues that are opposite each other on the color wheel (for example, red and green). Such combinations provide the sharpest contrast of hue, but can be varied in intensity and value (pale pink and an emerald green).

■ *Triads* choose hues that are equally spaced around the color wheel (red, yellow, and blue, but also wine, primrose yellow, and slate blue).

■ *Analogous groupings* of colors utilize a range of hues in the same portion of the color wheel (blue-green, green, and yellow-green, or also deep blue-green, a silvery green, and an olive green).

Triads are more applicable in decorations or paintings than in the design of urban spaces. Complementary arrangements are the most useful because a color appears more intense when set against its complementary color. This is particularly noticeable in combinations of foliage greens and the reds and related earthen colors that are common in construction materials. Analogous groups are common in outdoor spaces because of the interesting range of blues, greens, and yellow-greens to be found in the foliage of different trees, shrubs, and grasses, but much of this color changes in the fall and vanishes in the winter. Consequently, the consideration of color in most public outdoor places is much more complex than the organization and selection of color for a painting or building.

Colors are also sometimes classified as being either cool or warm, although this association is certainly more evident for primary colors (blue as opposed to red and yellow) than it is for the secondary colors (orange, green, and violet). It is often said that warm colors advance (seem to be nearer to the observer), a phenomenon also attributed to colors bright in intensity or light in value. In designing open spaces, color is primarily involved as a selection among available materials, and such principles do not necessarily provide a completely accurate forecast of the visual effects that will be attained. Therefore, sketches should explore possible color combinations, and the final selections should be made by placing samples of the actual materials together in areas roughly proportional to their actual use. The use of color can have a great influence on the effectiveness of a design, and it should be realized from the beginning that the visual impression made by a black granite bench placed on salmon brick paving in front of deep red foliage will be greatly different from that produced by a bench of honey-colored stone set on blue slate paving with dark firs behind. It is not a matter of one combination being more attractive, but that each would display a different mood, emphasis, and relationship with other parts of a design.

Because of the natural colors of plants and many building materials, designers often must work with a palette of colors that are generally low in intensity, with sharp contrasts in hue, intensity, and value providing visual accents to the arrangement. However, when the afternoon sun shines through autumn leaves, those accents may be less striking by comparison. The complexity of such changing conditions has been one of the reasons for designers' traditionally working with a rather conservative palette, although some use the stronger colors made available by modern technologies.

Texture: We understand textures essentially through our experiences of touching and feeling, and we learn to associate the visual appearances of textural conditions with those conditions as actually felt. For one thing, the roughness or smoothness of a surface affects the darkness or lightness we see there. A heavily textured surface may seem darker than a smooth surface of the same material, because each dimple of the material causes a small shadow. However, polished granite seems darker than the rough surface of the stone and wet concrete looks much darker than the dry surface. A pattern of contrasting speckles, such as those found in the crystalline structure of granites, may imply uneven surfaces, although the face of the material has been tooled and polished to a smooth finish and so this is visual texture rather than tactile. For this reason, it is wise always to select colors on the basis of both the color contained within the material and that which will be revealed by the required finish of the surface.

Textural contrasts are often suggested by functional demands (Fig. 5.13). Paving can be smooth or relatively rough, but the range of textures that can be used may well be limited for reasons of safety. Surfaces that

5.13 The textural contrasts between foliage, paving, and pebbles can become powerful elements in creating visual interest as well as guiding visitors' movement through a space. (Photo by Elsa D. Flores)

need to be kept clean are usually smooth, and people will walk closer alongside a smooth-faced wall than beside a rough stone wall. The texture of a vertical surface of fieldstone or rough-sawn lumber will not be so dramatic on the north shadowless face of a wall as when facing the directions where sharp sunlight produces shadows that emphasize the texture. Night-lighting at an angle to a rough surface will display its texture much more effectively than light perpendicular to the surface.

Practical limitations do not greatly diminish our freedom to vary textures for artistic effect. Besides the degree of texture—very rough to polished smooth—there are other textural qualities that are denoted by many words we use, such as spiny, fuzzy, slick, and ridged. Within buildings, architects are often rather limited in the range of textural qualities they can employ, but in designing outdoor spaces there is greater latitude. In general, we tend to associate rougher textures with naturalistic and rustic environments and smoother textures with formal and monumental places, but this need not be the case. After all, in naturalistic settings we often effectively contrast heavy textures with the glistening, smooth, and reflective surface of water.

Figure–Ground Relationships: A basic element of the gestalt psychology of perception is the consideration of the so-called figure–ground relationship. (The diagram in which two faces also form a wineglass is a commonplace illustration of this phenomenon.) We can take a similar point of view as we study outdoor spaces. In designing a small park area, it is reasonable to say that we are planning an area in which people will walk and sit, and that they will be surrounded by planting and other pleasing elements. However, we can also say, and with equal validity, that we are designing an arrangement of walls, plants, benches, and fountains in which people will find it pleasant to be. These very fundamental statements express distinctly different views of what we are attempting. (Fig. 5.14). Which should we employ as our *modus operandi*? (Refer to the discussion in Chapter 6 about "either/or" decisions.)

One valid answer is that we should do both, but a clear picture of the intent of the specific project may instead lead to the choice of only one of

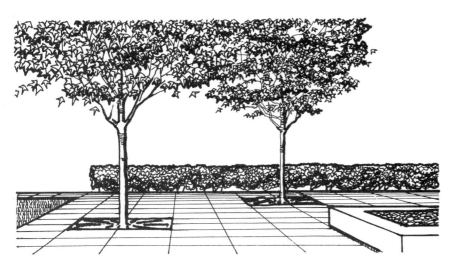

5.14 The character of a space can be more dependent on secondary decisions regarding the design than on the basic layout. The space on top is naturalistic and visitors are almost intruders; the space on the bottom is more evidently intended as a place for people even though it also includes plant materials. However, both spaces have the same plan provisions and site layout.

the alternatives. In the process of designing a place, we do not lay out an attractive walkway and consider the planting beside it merely the leftover space; we do not plan areas of grass, flowers, and shrubs with the paths between them serving merely as interstitial areas. Instead, each area, no matter what its purpose, form, and materials, should be effectively shaped so that the combination of shapes will be strengthened by their relationships.

Grids and Modules: When a project involves a large percentage of construction, rather than earth-shaping and planting, the establishment of a module may be desirable. A module is a repeated measurement, which may be subdivided or repeated to govern the dimensions of a construction. A four-foot module will in this manner accommodate the spacing of eight-inch brick paving, the spacing of columns twelve feet apart, and benches that are sixteen inches wide. In the United States most building materials are manufactured in dimensions that correspond to a four-inch module for

5.15 Divisions of the pavement are used to coordinate the location of benches, walls, and columns. (Photo by Alan M. Gordon)

construction, but design modules are always of a larger dimension. Modules are obviously useful in coordinating materials so that they will meet neatly and accurately. Modules also permit a regularity that may be desirable; stripes dividing a pavement can line up with the columns of a pergola and fit precisely against the edging of a pool. Outdoor construction does not always have the requirement of secure closure that is present in building construction, and many differences of measurements may be absorbed in the intervening areas of plants or lawn. In such instances, modular planning can still provide a pervasive visual organization that is sensed by the observer, an order that binds different shapes and materials together (Fig. 5.15). This visual binding is particularly apparent if the designer chooses to follow a modular grid pattern that is not rectangular. Squares may be combined with their diagonals, hexagons can blend into a triangular pattern, and even circles can be related by the squares that connect their centers. These complex grids permit a geometric relationship among elements in a design, without the rigidity some sense in right-angle intersections.

Balance and Symmetry: As opposed to the static modes of the visual arts, sculpture, architecture, landscape architecture, and the design of public places involve movement on the part of the observer and the changing views that are the result of such movement. In much sculpture, as in certain aspects of other art forms, the sequence of views is the result of a series of points of view, but in most public places the sequence is more usually made up of independent subjects arranged as a continuity—in a way, a sort of choreography. The size and function of a project may largely determine the degree of continuity that should be considered. Surely, a small project may not be suitable for drastic contrasts among its different elements, radical changes of materials and forms, while a large project that encompasses many different activities and conditions might provide an opportunity for including areas and elements of quite different characters. In all cases, transitional portions of the design are critical factors. Should the connecting pattern of walkways dominate, with specialized functions treated as major or minor appendages? Or should the functional locations attract the most attention, and the paths between them be neutral? In small projects visitors' movements may be guided as they are presented with a visible array of options from which to select. Larger projects are often designed so that upon arrival at each critical point a glimpse of one or more of the subsequent points is afforded to visitors, so that they may choose among the alternatives presented. In this way, the visitor can be drawn on in the sequence without experiencing pathways that have unrevealed destinations.

Any planned arrangement of objects and areas probably will have acquired a system of order during the design process. For paintings, some kinds of sculpture, and buildings (both the facades and the plans) the most common distinctions of basic order are made when the designs are created as either symmetrical or asymmetrical. Although in one sense the word symmetry merely means a balanced condition, the term is usually taken to mean an exact correspondence of the elements on one side of a center line with those on the other side (formal symmetry, in another commonly-used term). In symmetrical arrangements, elements occur as they do in a paper-fold inkblot—shapes are repeated on the two sides and they are placed in corresponding positions. The other order, asymmetry, is defined as any composition that does not show symmetrical arrangement, that has objects on the left and right that are either different shapes or not placed similarly. As a matter of fact, there are many inbetween conditions. Even in the center of the most formally symmetrical arrangements, there may be a nineteenth-century sculpture, stiffly erect but holding a sword in one hand and a balance in the other. There are also arrangements in which strong formal center lines are extremely prominent, but visitors must walk well to the side, sensing but never seeing the composition as actually exactly symmetrical. In fact, with the everchanging positions of the sun and the variable walking patterns of pedestrians, it is seldom, very seldom, that any of the compositions appearing to attain formal symmetry when the plan was drawn actually achieve their purpose. Even though we stand at the side of such a space, we mentally determine that it has been laid out in formal symmetry and read its forms on the basis of their relationships to the invisible center line that we have sensed (Fig. 5.16).

Because it is a static arrangement, formal symmetry has connotations of monumentality, seriousness, and conservatism. This image may be more an association with the examples of formal symmetry that we have so often seen, than an indication of an inherent characteristic of that mode of composition. We have all seen gardens with symmetrically determined paths approaching a small fountain in the center, an arrangement that has a certain elegance and simplicity but certainly no awesome grandeur. Although asymmetry is often said to have dynamic qualities, it is relatively easy to remember examples where it seemed as imposing and monumental as did formal symmetry. Therefore, it is both unwise and inaccurate to conclude any absolute relationship between the spirit of a design and the use of a particular kind of balance.

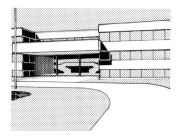

5.16 This view is a symmetrical building on a symmetrical drive, and even though one is not standing in the center, the symmetry is evident.

Scale: At its elementary level the term "scale" signifies the system of reduction that is used in executing a drawing, the fact that a certain unit of length in the drawing consistently represents a much larger unit in the actual project. In design activities the term scale has two other meanings as well.

The first of these, personal scale, is a term used to denote those dimensions in a project that are familiar and have a clear association with the size of the human body (Fig. 5.17). The uninterrupted surface of a large concrete-paved plaza may have a dimension that is so great that it is difficult for a person to comprehend its size. Once the paving is subdivided with prominent bands of a contrasting material, the dimensions are more understandable. If the bands are thirty feet apart the subdivision may still be too large to seem comfortable to a visitor, but a spacing between four and ten feet will usually prove to be a dimension that is familiar and thereby makes the entire surface more comprehensible. The distribution of containers for planting or other three-dimensional elements can also reduce the scale to a more understandable level. This phenomenon is particularly noticeable where a small outdoor cafe has been situated at the edge of a large plaza. The tables and chairs reduce the scale to a pleasant and familiar grouping, and, in contrast, the plaza seems immense as you gaze across it. (See the discussion of "Cue Proximity" in Chapter 4.)

Personal scale is more to be sensed than calculated. There are no formulas or rules that can effectively determine when subdivision is desirable or the size that such subdivisions should take. The emphasis of grid lines often can be useful in achieving a sense of personal scale; however, if the dimensions of the grid are too small, they may result in an overall pattern that does little to counteract vastness. It must be remembered that specific elements may need to be larger in outdoor spaces than they would be in interior spaces. A bench that is six feet long may seem generous in an ordinary room, and twelve feet may be effective in the lobby of a building,

5.17 In its simplest form, the matter of scale is a matter of comparative dimension, but it includes the comparison of dissimilar objects and the visual characteristics of large masses and uninterrupted surfaces. The human body is an instinctive standard of comparison.

but in an open place that dimension may need to be doubled or tripled if it is to have the same effect. Out of doors the objects are set against greater dimensions and the vastness of the sky. For this reason, a careful balance must be maintained between the needs for personal scale and the scale of the setting.

Personal scale may not alway be a designer's goal. In monumental spaces or in order to contrast with small areas, it may be more appropriate to impress the viewer with a grander dimension. The reflecting pool in front of Washington's Lincoln Memorial and the monument itself have very little relationship with personal scale. Instead, their dimensions relate to the grandeur of a concept and the greatness of events. Comfortable dimensions would have been inappropriate to communicate matters of such overpowering solemnity. The concept of scale, like many other artistic principles that apply to the design of spaces, is best learned by carefully observing its effects. Once the character and function of a space has been identified, thoughtful preparation of details can usually enhance the sense of scale that is appropriate to the project.

Proportion: The use of proportional systems in design is based on the belief that:

■ certain mathematical relationships of dimensions are inherently more beautiful than others, or

■ the use of dimensional ratios will contribute to achieving harmony and unity among shapes.

During the Renaissance, architectural theorists often propounded the idea that rooms with dimensions that had simple whole digit relationships were more appealing (for example, 36'w. × 24'h. × 60'l., or 3:2:5). Subsequent systems have favored the use of the ratio of one to the square root of two (1:1.414) or one to the square root of three (1:1.732). Many other proportional systems have been proposed through the centuries, and often there have been comparisons of such systems with musical harmony. Particular attention has always been given to the "golden section," which is mathematically termed the "extreme and mean ratio." This can be most simply understood as the division of a line into two parts so that the smaller part (a) relates to the larger (b) as the larger (b) relates to the entire length of the line (a + b)—or as the proportion a:b as b:(a + b). This relationship proves to be between one and 1.618 (Fig. 5.18). There never has been a contention that a proportional system guarantees the artistic quality of composition. Proportional systems are merely tools that may assist in the process of achieving pleasant relationships among shapes.

One can reasonably question whether such systems of proportion are as meaningful in dealing with outdoor spaces as they may be in the design of buildings, interior spaces, and paintings. Their first weakness is the fact that they are generally developed on the assumption that they are to be applied to planar surfaces in a rectilinear system, and curves and slopes are treated as the diagonals of rectangles or curves, helical or circular, inscribed within rectangles. Certainly, such systems have little application to

5.18 Because adding a golden-section rectangle to a square produces a larger golden-section rectangle, many variations and subdivisions are possible.

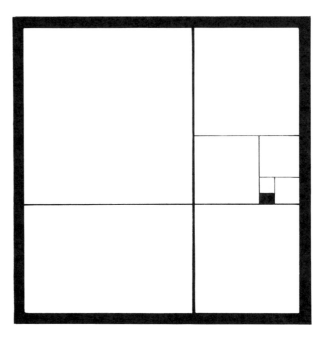

5.19 The same arrangement, based on golden-section rectangles, appears on three planes. The question is: Are the same qualities of a proportional system perceived when it is viewed at an angle?

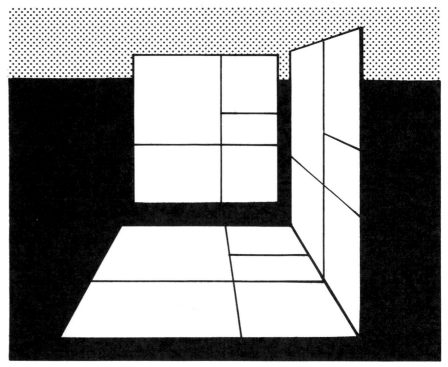

irregularly-shaped masses of planting. A second weakness lies in the fact that outdoor projects usually are set on a site whose shape and dimensions have been determined by legal situations rather than by esthetic judgments. In addition, the major planar surface of outdoor spaces, the ground plane, is very seldom viewed straight on but almost always seen at an extreme angle from which it is impossible to estimate accurately the precise dimensions of areas (Fig. 5.19). It can, however, be argued that the mind, experienced as it is at seeing shapes at an angle, understands the true proportions. Many designers have found proportional systems useful. (The use of proportional systems bears a close relationship to the matter of grids and modules, which has been discussed previously.)

SOLUTIONS

From the abstract and analytical aspects, designers come to the point when the actual features of a project must be considered. The ways in which decisions can be made are discussed in Chapter 6, but many of those decisions will include the systems and objects that are included below. A number of sound reference books provide detailed descriptions of the construction of such features as retaining walls, paving, and pools; professional journals show the materials, furnishings, and equipment that are commercially available. But before such final determinations can be made wisely, it is necessary to ascertain the needs of the situation.

Because the design of outdoor spaces necessarily involves preparing and referring to plan drawings, there is often a tendency to neglect three-dimensional study of the schemes. It is tempting to draw, redraw, and embellish plans, so that the work almost takes on the character of a painting. Color is applied and intricate details are added, until the whole is almost ready for framing and hanging in a gallery. The question remains: To what extent does a two-dimensional plan representation indicate the visual reality of the three-dimensional project that it predicts? Shadows drawn on the plan and certain mapping techniques can contribute a degree of three-dimensionality, but that can at best only convert the flat drawing into a portrayal of a bas-relief that resembles the site as it would be seen when flying overhead. That representation is far different from the many views seen at ground level. Sometimes designers insist that in drawing plans they can clearly visualize the three-dimensional effects that will result; however, many designers of extensive experience and recognized skill assiduously verify such impressions with the study of models and three-dimensional drawings.

When the process of information-gathering is well underway, and the design team begins its consideration of the elements that might be appropriately included in the design solution for the project, many possibilities will be excluded from consideration because they are manifestly unsuitable for the location and the obvious primary uses of the space. Children's play equipment would seldom be suitable for a downtown square in the financial district, and certain water displays may be potentially too dangerous for inclusion in a playground. Much of the eventual design will be made up of familiar elements, but with the observation of some basic principles these time-tested elements are still susceptible to fresh treatments and new effects.

In recent decades, three additional aspects have been stressed in the preparation of designs for outdoor spaces:

■ First, provisions for the physically handicapped are often required by law and are always required by good judgment. (The design of ramps is discussed later in this chapter.)

■ Second, increased attention has been given to those details that might cause physical injury, particularly in the case of children's facilities.

■ Third, demographic trends have made it clear that in the future the use and design of open spaces will be strongly influenced by the increased numbers of the elderly, by an increased amount of leisure time, and by the life-patterns that are observed in families with both parents working or in single-parent families. While these demographic changes do not necessarily call for specific solutions, they should be considered in evaluation of the data gained in the process of information-gathering.

The elements used to make up a design for an open space are often few and basic. It is the skill and sensitivity with which they are selected and developed that brings a distinctive flavor to the place. Two things are usually sought in determining the nature and treatment of the basic elements that are to be included:

■ The relative visual significance of each of the elements should be coordinated with all the other elements according to clearly determined objectives. If the principal purpose of an element is to serve as a walkway, a paving pattern may be suitably eyecatching and other elements more subdued.

■ The selections should be governed by their appropriateness to the overall character intended for the place. Appropriateness does not mean that such elements must be the customary and familiar solutions. Appropriateness is an unquantifiable quality usually discovered through the taste of the designers.

The maintenance of a developed open space is costly in areas where seasonal changes are extreme. In winter, snow must be removed and plants protected; in spring, the toll of winter must be assessed and preparations made for the growing season; in summer, planting must be watered and lawns mowed; and in the fall, leaves must be removed and the space readied for the coming winter. All of these operations are costly, and fully half a park's total expenses may be set aside for the wages of the work crews that care for the park. There are, of course, some devices and machines that reduce the number of workers required. Irrigation systems can eliminate the cost of moving sprinklers, equipment can speed the removal of fall leaves, the choice of hardier and larger plants can effect savings, and the selection of the most durable construction materials can reduce the funds necessary for replacement and repair. However, many of these advances in maintenance procedures demand a sizeable initial expense for purchasing the equipment, and there are continuing expenses for its operation and maintenance.

Herein lies one of the most difficult tasks in the design of public areas: the careful balancing of initial costs and annual costs. Limited funds are usually available for the initial preparation of a project, and it is sometimes necessary to make choices that, it is recognized, eventually will result in expenses that could have been avoided. According to one study, the total nationwide expenditure on parks by local governments grew from 3.8 billion dollars in 1964 to 8.4 billion in 1989.[2] Because maintenance costs vary greatly in different climatic conditions and with different wage scales, the comparison of initial costs and long-term costs is extremely difficult, even for public spaces that involve the use of little plant material. Though general estimates of the expenses may be determined by a city's park system, unusual weather can exhaust overnight the contingency funds that have been set aside.

In recent years much attention has been given to the question of "lifecycle costing," a method by which initial expense is considered in comparison with the cost of annual maintenance and the eventual replacement of materials. With further development of such techniques, it will be possible to select construction materials more knowingly. However, there will still be many projects for which funds simply will not be available for the installation of the most durable and desirable materials. There also will be many projects for which the bid price of contractors appreciably exceeds the funding assigned to the project. In the latter case, it is sometimes possible for the design team to explain the need for durable materials and obtain additional funds. But prices of materials and labor fluctuate, and estimating costs is a devilish experience for both designers and contractors. Even the most conscientious sometimes find themselves confronted with the necessity of reducing the cost or the scope of their design to conform to the funds available. There are two common approaches to this dilemma:

■ First, it is possible to phase the completion of the project, leaving certain parts for execution at a later date. The optimistic implication of this procedure is that the portion that is to be constructed initially will be so successful that the owner will be encouraged to complete the remainder soon. On the other hand, a pessimistic view must consider the possibility that completion will take place much later and might be executed by other hands in a manner inconsistent with the spirit of the original design.

■ Second, the quality of all materials can be reduced and expensive details altered or postponed. With this approach, the entire design can be executed, although it must be recognized that it may lack some of the qualities that were desired and that it will probably deteriorate more rapidly than if executed with the materials initially selected.

In practice, both approaches are usually combined in order to solve the problem judiciously.

The construction of buildings is regulated by a multitude of safety requirements, most of which have originated as fire prevention measures. In open spaces there are few specific legal controls, but reasonable precautions remain the obligation of the designers. All sharp changes of level require railings so that the elderly can traverse them with a sense of safety. All sharp drops need railings, benches, or planting to keep people away from the edge. Paving should, in most places, be sufficiently regular to provide sound footing for those who walk on them. These are, obviously, simple requirements. Not absolutely every part of a public space must be designed for absolutely everyone to use. A small path may be laid in cobblestones and the edge of a pool may be built without a railing, but no handicapped, elderly, or unconfident people should have the feeling that a majority of the attractive elements of a design are barred to them and no listing of prospective users of a space should assume that only the ablest bodies would come there. Even if there are no enforced regulations regarding safety provisions in open spaces, municipal and corporate liability insurance can have a similar effect in encouraging precautions, particularly in the case of play areas for children. While lawsuits that may arise concerning accidents in public spaces are essentially actions against the insurance company, they inevitably have political or public relations effects.

All of these matters must be kept in mind as the general, specific, and detailed decisions progress. One of the most significant steps through these stages of deliberations is the determination of the form that the features will need to take. In our language, basic terms have, quite naturally, a remarkable variety and multiplicity of meaning. If the term "path" can designate routes from the sea lanes across an ocean as well as a narrow passage through a thicket, that situation is an advantage rather than a handicap for designers. The looseness of language can help increase the design options available.

Paths and Walks: The shortest distance between two points is a straight line, but providing the shortest distance is not always the most important consideration. A slight increase in the distance traveled may really make little difference. The layout of circulation should consider the different motives for moving through a space. When you are late for an appointment you will want to traverse a space in the most efficient manner. If you are early, a meandering path can provide an opportunity for a few moments of pleasure, far more enjoyable than sitting in a waiting room and thumbing through ancient magazines. Therefore, the criteria for laying out paths and walkways vary according to the location of the space, its users, and their interests and intentions. However, it is possible to combine these characteristics. A walk with a direct center line can have irregular edges on one or both sides, and the straight route can be emphasized with the use of a smoother paving that is suited to a longer and more hurried stride (Fig. 5.20). (We tend to associate tactile sensation with our fingers and forget the many textural changes we sense with our feet (Fig. 5.21).) A plan may include a straight route that we would dash along during a rainstorm and a twisting path that would be attractive on a sunny spring day. Straight paths can vary by passing under a cluster of trees, and irregular routes can have their destinations emphasized by visible elements at the ends.

As mentioned before, a common device of Italian Renaissance gardens was the establishment of a center line, clearly defined by visual relationships, although the path might only occasionally fall on the center

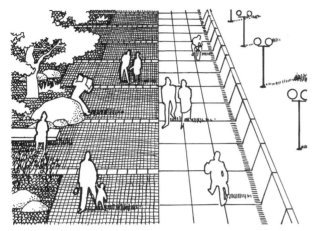

5.20 Visual and tactile characteristics of a walkway can clearly set forth the functional characteristics for which it is planned.

5.21 Fine crushed gravel set beneath the trees provides the walking surface to this principal entrance to the Kimbell Museum of Art, Fort Worth, Texas. The feel and sound of a walk on this material contrasts sharply with walking on the marble entrance platform.

line. By using such subtle differentiations of circulation routes and visual directions, a rich experience can be provided, albeit one that is strikingly susceptible to change through the succession of seasons and the movement of shadows.

The street, being almost entirely a pathway in function, is a particularly challenging example of pathway design. Where downtown traffic is heavy, merchants have discovered that recessing entrances and display windows can cause windowshoppers to step out of the pedestrian traffic and linger longer. The congestion at the entrances to office buildings are reduced if they are recessed, providing an area in which officeworkers exit into the sunlight, pause to orient themselves, and then join the flow of traffic.

The problem of downtown businesses failing and stores left vacant is often addressed by the assumption that beautifying the streets in the area and instituting design controls on the existing buildings will make the street spaces more attractive and, hence, the businesses more prosperous. Closing or partially closing streets, rebuilding with special paving treatment, introducing planting boxes, installing trees, and other measures may be undertaken with that intention. Projects of this nature appear to have succeeded in many cities. In other cases, such efforts have encountered problems. Where the streets have been reopened to vehicular traffic, the improvements that were made when the streets were closed usually have remained as significant enhancements of the district. One suspects that much of the problem with these beautification projects has been rooted in the economy and the distinction between businesses and boutiques.

Automobile Parking: Few problems of site development confront designers and the public with such difficult choices as those related to the parking of vehicles. (These problems may have been true ever since "carriage parks" and parking regulations originated in London during the 1820s.)[3] On the whole, attitudes toward cars are not yet resolved. Most people dislike parking lots, but want to park their cars as near as possible to their destinations. This conflict is largely a matter of numbers. Our own cars parked in the driveways beside our houses are acceptable, convenient, and sometimes even proud displays to the entire neighborhood. All the cars in the block, parked by all the houses in the block, are considered unsightly—unless trees, fences, and shrubs relieve or obstruct the view. Ten cars parked along the edge of a recreational area do not detract, especially if the space they serve is sufficiently scenic to dominate, but one hundred or more cars parked in front of a shopping complex are disturbing. To insist that the American public thinks automobiles are ugly is to contradict the evidence of almost a century of advertising and all the well-attended displays of new models that have been conducted in that time.

To some extent it may not be the cars we object to, but the bare expanses of paving exposed when cars are not there (Fig. 5.22). At least, a filled parking lot offers a variety of colors and forms within an overall orderly pattern. During the ball game or the Christmas sale at the shopping center, people walk among the cars and some cars move along the driving lanes, and when it is seen from a tall building there is a certain majesty about a filled parking lot. When the cars have gone, we see only the asphalt and the emptiness.

The functional aspects of laying out parking areas are dealt with in a great many reference books. In short, parking spaces perpendicular to the driving lane usually use less space per car, but the fact that they are more likely to have cars improperly parked may counterbalance that advantage. Perpendicular parking layouts are often considered more suitable for all-day parking than for parking lots in which cars are continually entering and leaving. Parking at an angle requires the development of a system of one-way driving lanes, but the spaces are usually easier for a driver to enter accurately. Site dimensions may make a certain pattern of parking more economical, but the choice will always be strongly influenced by the fact that parking at a forty-five degree angle may require about 50 percent more area per car than perpendicular parking in small lots. Unless different lots are provided for specific groups, such as employees and visitors, or the project covers a very large area, all parking spaces usually should be available in a tour of the parking lot—it should not be necessary to go back to the street and reenter the lot. Often the need to drop passengers at a building entrance will influence the overall shaping of vehicular traffic on a site and, consequently, determine much of the design.

Paving costs are lower when a parking area is treated as a single broad expanse, uninterrupted by curbs and walks, and this arrangement also greatly reduces snow removal expenses in northern states. Sidewalks between lines of parked cars offer little improvement unless they are wide and their lines are emphasized by rows of trees or lighting standards. The extent of parking areas is usually determined by legal requirements that

specify a mathematical relationship between the square footage within buildings, the function of the buildings, and the number of cars for which parking will be required. The validity of these ratios is sometimes challenged, but proposed changes would hardly make a significant difference in the visual problem of parking spaces. The dimensions are prescribed for maximum requirements, and when fewer cars are present—which is most of the time—barren paving is exposed. In the financial aspects of real-estate development, the high cost of land may at different levels justify the construction of parking structures or parking beneath a building, since the opportunity to build additional floor area within a larger building would offset the increased cost of parking space. As the value of land increases in the future, it may be possible to eliminate surface parking for most building functions. In the meantime, design teams can merely rely on the fact that in such complexes as shopping centers and sports arenas any method of visual subdivision can counteract the forbidding immensity of parking spaces, and that the attractive treatment of the exterior of the structure can serve as an effective diversion.

The service functions of buildings (trash containers, delivery doors, and a stack of debris that seems always to defy the best efforts of building management) are located where they best avoid public notice; but buildings today require thorough utilization of their sites, and increasingly seldom is there a facade that can be accurately termed the "backside." Too often, service areas are eyesores because of the architects' oversight or the fact that occasional requirements have been given the full treatment that is usually accorded busy delivery spaces. For a concert hall with infrequent deliveries, access can be provided by paving units through which grass grows or by two narrow bands along which a truck's wheels can move. For the busy service area of a restaurant, screens of planting or fencing are warranted. (The ubiquitous "Dumpster" should never escape the consideration of a design team.) With rising land costs, no aspect of a building site can be designated as useless or allowed to be wasted by the presence of an eyesore.

Steps, Ramps, and Railings: Changes of level provide the opportunity for the exploitation of distinctly different views of an area, one of our clearest examples of a site requirement which through imaginative design

5.22 The variety of automobiles' shapes and colors can be visually interesting when framed by a system of regular and repeated elements.

can be made advantageous rather than onerous. When a setting is viewed from above, the viewer sees it with an intriguing degree of detachment, as an observer rather than as a particpant. The different formulas usually employed to determine the treads and risers of stairways produce very nearly the same results when applied to the conditions commonly encountered in the design of buildings. Outside, stairs however, are customarily built at a lower angle, perhaps because space restrictions are not so acute and perhaps also because we assume longer strides when walking outdoors. At such relatively low angles of ascent the standard formulas do not concur, and the dimensions of treads relate more to the normal pace than to the size of the average foot. A short pace should be carefully considered in determining stair dimensions, because steps that fall between average short pace dimensions are extremely awkward, requiring that a comfortable stride be either extended or reduced. Many building code requirements for stairways (such as those governing the height of handrails) can be applied to outdoor stairs, but others (such as the provision of additional handrails in the center of wide stairs) are based on the needs of crowds fleeing fires, and do not necessarily apply to outdoor installations.

Certain precautions are always wise to consider and follow unless special conditions make them unnecessary. By lighting, contrast of materials, or other methods, care should be taken to make a run of steps and single individual steps clearly visible to the pedestrian. Single steps or only a few together easily go unnoticed, and their use should be avoided unless extreme measures are taken to make them highly visible. All slippery surfaces, especially those that become slippery in rain, should be avoided on steps—and probably on all walking surfaces. Not all stairs are to be considered in strictly functional terms. The steps leading up to a monument usually must be generous, even if very few people climb them. In part, the dimension relates to the scale of the idea that is being conveyed; in some other cases, broad steps permit a freedom in the visitors' choice of the paths by which they will approach the monument.

Ramps are required for the handicapped; they are essential for those confined to wheelchairs, and much easier for those on crutches. That is not the only reason for their use. The speed of movement for the average pedestrian is much slower climbing stairs than walking along a level surface or a ramp, and there is always a pause when entering or leaving a staircase. For this reason, ramps are commonly used in transportation buildings and stadiums, where smooth continuous movement is necessary if the passageways are not to become clogged. A basic problem in the design of a building's ramp system is that a ramp occupies at least seven times as much area as is required for stairs, and usually much more is required outdoors.

We have all seen small awkward ramps constructed beside entrance stairs to satisfy requirements imposed in the last few decades. It is time to apply fresh thinking to the ways in which we provide for the handicapped in outdoor spaces. In a park, there are seldom restrictions on space for the use of ramps. Gently sloping sidewalks and imaginatively shaped earth may accomplish the change of level without either stairs or ramps, as such; wide

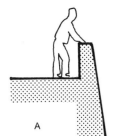 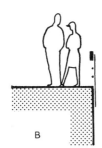   

ramps may provide smooth vertical progressions for all; or the combination of stairs and ramps can serve as alternative routes of different character for the use of almost everybody.

Along stairs and ramps, railings provide a steadying reassurance. For the elderly and the infirm, there is much to be said for designing railings as a continuous surface along which the hand can glide, despite turns and twists in the path followed. Where the railing serves only as a protection at the edge of a terrace, guarding against anyone's falling over the edge, considerable variation is possible. For instance, the railing may be eliminated if a bench or planting even at ground level, prevents visitors from coming dangerously close to the edge (Fig. 5.23). In the same way, a railing may be lower, both functionally and psychologically, if a broad top surface is provided. Such variation is extremely useful when considering the adjustment of sight lines by which views can be obtained from one level to another.

We tend to think of paving materials as providing only a surface for pedestrian and vehicular traffic. In some cases, such as around the bole of a tree or at the base of a retaining wall, it may be desirable to allow water to pass easily through the paving to reach roots or drains below. In other cases, coarsely textured paving may be selected to prevent or strongly discourage people from walking in the area. A wise choice of paving often can do more to control the kinds of traffic than signs or barricades. If broad sidewalks of concrete are edged with wide bands of pebble-surfaced concrete, pedestrians in a hurry will keep to the center of the walk, those stopping for conversations will move to the edges, and grass thus will be protected from trampling.

The differences in the prices and maintenance costs of paving are extreme, and reliable information on local costs and engineering conditions should be sought long before choices are considered. For instance, a brick sidewalk laid on a concrete base may cost eight times as much as a thin asphaltic surface with no subsurface. The impact of these prices, however, will depend greatly on the relative importance of paving in the total cost of a project.

Screens: When it is desirable to provide enclosure or block an undesired view, designers may employ planting, level changes, walls, or combinations of these elements. (In public spaces, it is wise to consider the need for

5.23 Views from elevated terraces can be adjusted through the detailing of their edges. A solid wall (A), sturdy railing (B), or long bench (C), can emphasize distant views and give a feeling of enclosure. Broad low walls (D) and zones of planting (E) conceal unsightly areas at the base of the retaining wall and minimize enclosure of the terrace level.

5.24 While the standing figures can see over the screen wall, the seated figure cannot see out of the enclosure. Seated eye-level is roughly four feet above ground level.

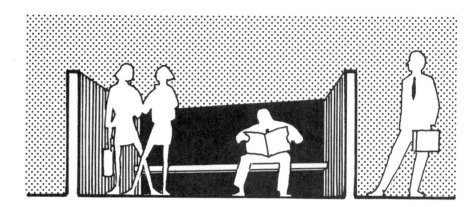

surveillance and the users' feeling of safety. The visibility of an area to passersby and its accessibility to the probing searchlight of a patrol car may be critical factors in a design.) The feeling of enclosure varies with the visual density of the surrounding material and its height. A screen just below standing eye-level can afford an open view to a visitor who is walking, but at the same time create a smaller defined area when seated on a bench (Fig. 5.24). Fences and walls can be designed as louvers to provide varying degrees of visual obstruction or even to change density according to the observer's location. At the same time, openings can allow air to circulate preventing a buildup of heat or relieving oppressive moistness. (This consideration must be weighed against the fact that even small perforations eliminate a screen's functioning as a noise barrier.) Sloped banks with planting may be adjusted to act as screens without rigid physical enclosure, but much may depend on the seasonal changes of the plant materials.

Although we usually think of screening as being provided for visual purposes, the problem is more complex. Screening is also wind-screening, offering the advantages of weather-protection and the problems of heat traps and bothersome eddies of breeze. It offers some advantages by reducing noise, but it usually also presents sound-reflective surfaces that require consideration. The seasonal and diurnal variation of a project's needs makes the design of screening elements a choice among complex but extremely rich design options.

Section drawings (vertical slices through the design) are invaluable when the designers wish to conceal or reveal areas. A parking lot located at the lowest point of a building site is often necessarily visible from almost all parts of the site. By placing the parking lot at a higher part of the site, low walls or planting can screen the cars, and trees become more effective. A high spot offers a view that can visually extend the dimension of a small park area, and for some reason the activity and sounds of a busy street seems less threatening when viewed from a different level.

Water: Whether it is still or moving, water catches the eye. By reflecting or refracting light it can provide a contrasting element, no matter whether the setting is one of great dignity or naturalistic charm. In addition to its visual effects, water can provide a variety of sounds, ranging from the roar of powerful jets to soft gurgling tones of streams running over stones. The cooling provided by fountains or pools, of course, depends largely on the humidity of the location. For the arid southern parts of North America, lowering temperatures in a small area through the evaporation of spray can be most welcome during the summer months.

The precise form of a fountain determines the effect that it will provide. A fine spray, which has a great deal of evaporative surface, will have a pronounced cooling action, will only produce a soft hum of sound, and will be seen as a white fog. A low-pressure arching jet of water will accomplish less cooling, will produce the pleasant sound of irregular splattering, and will sparkle in sunlight. In order to select among the extreme variety of types of fountains the functional and visual purposes should be clearly determined. By installing automatic controls the force of fountains can be altered, varying intensity and sound according to changing needs.

Many of our suburban parks are located to utilize sites considered unsuitable for building because of drainage conditions, and these can afford excellent opportunities for the development of naturalistic water elements. Downtown locations usually do not suggest naturalistic streams or pools unless they have the extended dimensions of New York's Central Park or Boston's Common. Still, paved edges or vessels containing water have the same appeal to the human eye and mind. The variety of presentations seems almost infinite, and even the nineteenth-century stone horse-trough has been returned to some busy streets. It should always be remembered, however, that the use of areas of water demands a commitment to provide the proper maintenance. Once we see litter floating in a pond or a plastic cup among lilies in a pool, the charm disappears, and what was on another day attractive becomes almost distasteful because it has not been respected.

Traditionally fountains often have been associated with sculpture or decoratively formed containers. In such installations, the attraction is still present even when the water has been turned off. Another form of fountain combines sculpture and a water jet, the spray scattering on suitably drained paving instead of falling into a pool. The design potential ranges from delicate sounds to powerful gushes, a range of considerable dramatic intensity.

Trees, Shrubs, and Lawns: Like building and paving materials, plants have many associations for us, but they have several characteristics that are distinctly different from those inert materials. They have a visible pattern and organization that is highly complex. Even when a hedge is clipped to a rigid geometry we perceive the pattern of twigs and leaves, and within the general outline of a tree many elements and a multitude of shapes are combined with an individuality greater than can be found in even the roughest building materials. Being living organisms, plants undergo natural changes through the seasons. A stone wall may weather through the years, but this alteration is gradual, much less dramatic than the annual variation of grasses, shrubs, and trees. We may import plants, just as we bring in building materials, but as living things they require conditions that correspond to their native habitats if they are to survive.

In spite of these variations—or perhaps because of them—plants always have provided much of the richness and variety of public spaces. For one thing, planting provides a remarkably broad palette for the designer. Plant materials can be used horizontally as lawn or ground cover; shrubs can provide screening, hedge barriers, or ground texture; trees can be screens or shades; vines can be grown overhead, on a wall, or on the ground; and flowering plants offer opportunities for seasonal color. Their textures have great variety, and although green is the dominant color, one quickly discovers that there is an amazing variety of greens and other hues. In the early stages of design, decisions can be based on general characteristics of plants—for instance, decisions can be made about the desirable shapes, colors, textures, density, and seasonal changes of trees. These characteristics can be represented sufficiently in drawings or models to allow the basic forms to be experimented with and selected before it is necessary to designate specific varieties (Fig. 5.25).

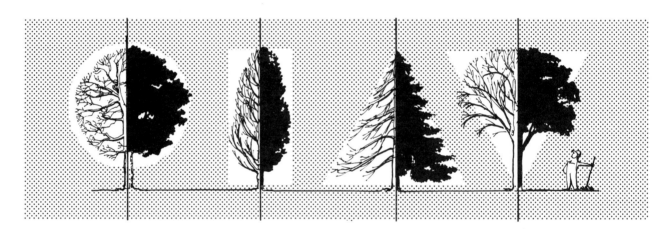

5.25 In early stages of design, trees may be tentatively selected according to their general overall shapes, such as (left to right): spherical, columnar, conical or pyramidal, and vase- or fan-shaped.

Plant materials are largely selected on the basis of the site's climatic and microclimatic conditions. In spite of the most careful selection and maintenance, there is always the chance that some of the materials will not survive. Contracts for the installation of plants can compensate for this possibility by requiring replacement of material that perishes during the first two or three years after they are installed. Some varieties may be eliminated from consideration because of nuisance factors, such as their dropping sticky deposits or their fruit or leaves causing extreme difficulties in maintaining the ground areas around them. Other varieties may be unsuitable for urban use, perhaps because they would be damaged by the salt used on the streets during the snowy season or because they could not withstand the heat reflected by the pavement during summer. A tree's rate of growth can often influence selection. Every variety of tree or shrub has its own characteristic rate of growth, and installation conditions and location can act as deterrents to growth, but usually fast-growing trees do not survive the years as well as the slower-growing varieties. In some cases, it is judged wise to plant fast-growing varieties to provide an immediate effect, removing them after the slow-growing varieties alongside them have matured. An immediate effect of foliage may sometimes be more quickly achieved and little ground space occupied by the use of shrubs or vines.

In planning most projects, a choice must be made between short-range and long-range development of the design. An average type of shade tree seventeen feet high will cost about three times as much as one twelve feet high, and more than ten times as much as one eight feet high. Nevertheless, it is not always most desirable to install larger trees, even if funds are available. Transplanting is more traumatic for larger trees, and often the higher survival rate of smaller trees is an advantage. The total cost of installing a tree, including planting, mulching, wrapping, and attaching guy wires, will approximately equal the cost of the tree itself, and providing a cast-iron grating around the tree's bole will be an additional investment between half and all the cost of the tree itself.

Because of the cost of installing new trees, the time it takes for them to attain mature size, and the cost of felling and removing existing trees, careful attention customarily is given to the condition of existing trees on sites and the possibility of utilizing them in the design that is to be developed. The utilization of existing trees on a site can be handicapped by a need to make strong changes in the contours of the ground, or conversely, existing trees, even those considered to be very desirable, may be taken as limitations on moving earth. A tree's root system, which often is estimated to have a breadth one-third greater than that of the branch system, should be disturbed or diminished as little as possible. When the ground level is to be raised, care should be taken to avoid covering large portions of the root system with several feet of infill. If new trees are planted where paving covers much of the eventual root spread, the tree's rate of growth and ultimate size will be limited.

Street trees, an American tradition, are nevertheless a matter of debate. Some city regulations insist that no trees be located within 40 or 50 feet of an intersection, and others dictate the spacing that should be used.

> Trees should be located in sidewalks at the painted space marks on the street. This location will prevent car doors from hitting trees and will usually be three feet away from parking meters. Since parking spaces are 22 feet long, the resulting tree spacing will either be 44 feet (every two parking spaces) or 66 (every three spaces).[4]

Such regulations are clearly contradicted by such plantings as Pennsylvania Avenue in Washington, D.C., where trees are spaced at fifteen to eighteen feet.[5] The spacing of street trees, which also act as sign controls in commercial districts, determines the degree to which they enhance the view of the drivers and pedestrians and the extent to which an effective separation of sidewalk and street is established (Fig. 5.26).

The ground level of a project is in many ways a determining factor of the design. If planting is to be limited to containers and relatively small shrubs, the project—perhaps a vest-pocket park—will be little different from building construction. Including trees, grassy areas, or more extensive planting means that the condition of the soil, its slopes and texture, must be

5.26 Many trees can be placed along sidewalks without their excessively limiting the places where pedestrians may walk. The tight placement of trees creates a penetrable space that allows direct entry to the office building from any spot along the curb. Trammell Crow Center, Dallas.

carefully considered. When the site has been previously occupied by buildings or other construction, the ground will be virtually replaced with topsoil that must be brought in from elsewhere. Even when the site has not been previously used, the soil must be tested to determine its ability to support plants adequately, and fertilizers, compost, other natural or chemical additives, and perhaps additional topsoil are commonly added to provide adequate nourishment for the plants that are to be placed there.

Fully treating the soil and placing sod over it still costs less than covering it with asphalt, which in most cases is the least expensive paving. However, the annual costs of mowing, fertilizing, and watering grass must be compared with the easy maintenance and low replacement costs of asphalt, a factor very much dependent on weather conditions.

Lighting: There are basically three kinds of lighting, each having its own distinct characteristics and psychological effects. With these three fundamental types of lighting we can create illusions or reinforce reality:

■ *Direct light* is the sharp, high contrast of bright sunlight, the light of a bare electric bulb, the penetrating glare of a car's headlight, the spotlight on a theater stage. Its shadows help us sense textures or steps along a path, and brings shapes into sharp outline. The contrast of direct light makes objects stand out and produces deep shadows.

■ *Indirect light* is the north light of an artist's studio, the ambient light of a cloudy day, and the diffused light beneath a cluster of trees. It causes little glare, it is relaxing, and it is excellent for reading, since its shadows have soft edges and there is only slight contrast between light and dark places.

■ *Specular light* is the sparkle of sunlight in a fountain, the twinkle of Christmas tree lights, and the dazzle of reflections from diamonds or rhinestones. It is associated with excitement and often with luxury.

The secret lies in planning the combination of types of lighting to fulfill the required functions and also dramatize the setting. If a small park area has a splendid view of lighted government buildings, the paths can be lighted by sources below eye-level when standing, permitting nothing to interfere with the view. A plaza near restaurants and theaters could match their mood with lighted fountains and sparkling fixtures; or a contrast could be provided by lights shining upward into trees. The functional requirements are simple. All walkways, steps, and curbs should be clearly visible so that the public can use the park at night; in addition, sufficient general lighting should be provided to make visitors feel safe. The latter function of lighting is principally a matter of avoiding surprise. There is no way that a public area can be guaranteed to have no suspicious-looking visitors, but lighting and planning can be used to reduce the possibility of surprises.

Every device for producing artificial light has its own characteristics of color and diffusion. Most of the systems used in lighting large areas balance their low cost of operation against the disadvantages of their color. Mercury and sodium vapor lighting have dominant portions of the spectrum that distort the natural tones of the human face and the foliage of plants, always startling because we are more accustomed to the yellowish distortion of incandescent lighting. This contrast can be utilized to make a distinction between the street and a park, plaza, or building site. However, designers should be cautious about using lighting effects that are excessively theatrical. Greenish lights shining up into trees and pink light falling on brick paving can quickly produce an artificiality that is unpleasant.

Fixtures and Furniture: The challenges of weather, vandalism, thievery, and other dangers are perhaps most sharply focused on the benches, litter receptacles, drinking fountains, and other furnishings that are necessary for the proper functioning of public places. Every management plan for an open space must recognize in the budget the probable need to replace or repair such features. Nevertheless, careful selection of these features is extremely important (Fig. 5.27). As an illustration, in 1987, when the city council of San Jose, California, considered the purchase of thirty trash cans for a park, skeptics were quick to cite other cities' experiences:

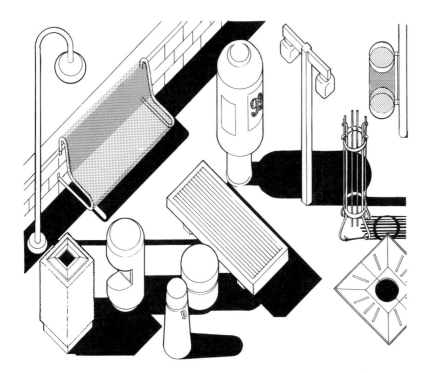

5.27 Completion of the design for an open space requires the careful selection of furnishings and equipment. Evaluation of labor and purchase costs, including maintenance and replacement, are critical if it is to be possible to maintain the space properly. (manufactured by Architectural Precast, Inc.; Dura Art Stone; GameTime, Inc.; Idaho Wood Industries, Inc.; Sitecraft; Sternberg Lanterns, Inc.; and Urban Accessories.)

A couple of years ago, the city of Charlotte, N.C., bought 73 trash cans at $820 apiece. After one winter, the bottoms of the steel cans began rusting away and the chrome-domed tops were pock-marked . . .

In San Francisco, $700 trash cans on Market Street collected almost as much rainwater as garbage, and thieves stole the solid bronze rings off the tops of the fancy cans.[6]

For the reconstruction of Bryant Park, New York, individual moveable chairs in addition to benches were selected. This choice was made with the full realization that some probably would be carried away, in spite of the security guards. The selection was based on the belief that the advantages of individual chairs offset the costs of replacing them.

Many attractive and serviceable fixtures are available from manufacturers, and many, equal in quality, are prepared by project contractors. In either case, testing and conservatism are customary, because of the extreme functional requirements.

SUMMARY

The cost of planting may seem a distant matter, hardly related to the principles of color, but in the design of open spaces the choice of materials is a determination of the medium that will be employed to create a visual effect. Just as a painter might choose a certain watercolor pigment and a paper appropriate to his purpose, designers must select certain materials on a practical as much as an artistic basis. Even a relatively small project requires that decisions be made about the shapes and materials that will respond to the visual and functional demands of the project. These are not simple or isolated choices. Each must be considered in view of the manner in which it may interact with and influence other decisions. Therefore, the procedures by which requirements are identified and decisions are reached—procedures that are discussed in the following chapter—are demanding. In addition, changes may be necessary during construction of a project. Cost estimates, information regarding other materials, and unavoidable situations often cause changes in project plans.

From the initial rough layouts to final selections, the design is developed through drawings and specifications of materials that develop increasing detail as the task proceeds. The idea that began as a rough sketch evolves into accurate drawings and, finally, into construction drawings that are carefully detailed and dimensioned. As decisions are clarified, cost estimates are made periodically, and each one is more precise than the one preceding it. Always, it is a concern that during this process of increasing detail the spirit of the initial design is not lost. The period during which the first designs are prepared and approved may be a matter of several years, as indicated by some of the projects described in Chapter 2. The construction period, particularly in designs in which plant materials play an important role, is followed by several years of maturation, during which small trees grow larger, lawns flourish, and the actuality of the project comes to resemble the design drawings. The design process is in many ways a prediction. Through miniaturization in drawings, models, and recollections of full-scale experiences a prediction is made, and years later the design becomes a reality.

ENDNOTES

1. Francis D. K. Ching, *Architecture: Form, Space, and Order* (New York: Van Nostrand Reinhold Company, 1979), 57.

2. "Survey Hears Americans Declare Love for Parks," *New York Times,* August 26, 1992, C1.

3. Paul Johnson, *The Birth of the Modern, World Society 1815–1830* (New York: Harper Collins, 1991), 174.

4. Urban Trees Group, *Greenstreets: The Street Tree Plan for Oakland* (Oakland: City of Oakland, 1981). As quoted in Alan Jacobs, "In Defense of Street Trees," *Places* (1984): 86.

5. Jacobs, "In Defense of Street Trees," 86.

6. Jennifer McNulty, "Cans of Worms? Critics Say San Jose's Designer Trash Containers Are Foolish," *San Jose Mercury News,* June 30, 1987, 1B.

6

METHODS—SOLVING SPATIAL PROBLEMS

Methods and solutions, visual dominance and neutrality; analysis, terrain, site boundaries, buildings and other barriers, analysis of views, streets and cars, climate, microclimate, noise; user populations, surveys and analyses, self-report questionnaires, interviews, observation, circulation, historical background; methods of designing, visualization, criteria and evaluations, teamwork; the larger team.

METHODS AND SOLUTIONS

Designing a project involves gathering information, generating and testing ideas, and making decisions. The first of these tasks accumulates and organizes data about preexisting conditions and the functions that the project is expected to serve; the second discovers solutions that will satisfy functional requirements, conform to the limitations, and be an asset to the community; and the third tests the possible solutions and selects those to be executed. The order in which these tasks are mentioned does not mean that one is completed before the next begins. In most situations it is necessary to combine the three activities, although one of them probably will be dominant at any particular time during the progress of the design. Customarily, the information-gathering process is undertaken first, and as fundamental information becomes available the first design decisions serve to focus the research. There is always, of course, the danger of limiting research on the basis of some decisions made prematurely and without insufficient evidence at hand. As they start the information-gathering process, participants irresistibly contemplate some of the design solutions that may arise. This preliminary consideration is necessary in order to understand the kinds of research data that will be needed, but early consideration of data should not be allowed to limit the scope of preliminary thoughts about what may be the final design of the project. At the very end of the design work on a project, there may still be minor bits of information that must be secured in order to complete its details. While research is the

6.1 The Tarrant County Courthouse has an axial placement that clearly identifies it as a focal building within the central area of Fort Worth, Texas.

principal need at the beginning, these activities should be viewed as interconnected, not sequential.

Just as the balance shifts from information-gathering to decision-making as a project progresses, design procedures shift from ideation and the exploration of alternatives to a developmental process that fills in the design framework after fundamental decisions have been made. During this process of narrowing focus, it is essential that a design be evenly developed so that a few aspects are not pursued far beyond the level of development that has been given to other aspects. This balance makes certain that a holistic unit is maintained.

The spaces that we are considering—squares, plazas, small parks, streets, regional tubes of space, and the areas between buildings or around them—have definite characteristics and differ greatly in the density of their use and surroundings. For instance, suburban streets are broader and less busy than downtown thoroughfares. Nevertheless, an artery at the edge of an urban area may have even greater breadth and more intense activity than the site downtown. The degrees of pedestrian utilization and vehicular dominance create contrasting situations, but the fundamental manners in which they are approached in design are surprisingly similar.

There are time-tested methods by which the idea-generating and decision-making portions of the project work can be accomplished. Unless the requirements for the project confront the designers with truly remarkable conditions, the solution will be achieved through the use of a familiar palette of devices, such as paving, lawns, plants, water, and trees. It is temptingly easy to accept each of these elements of a solution in the most usual meaning that can be applied. ("Everyone knows what a sidewalk is!") To avoid this tendency toward accepting conventions, architects of the 1920s tried to shake their own and their clients' preconceptions by using verbs such as "eat" and "sleep" to identify spaces so that the traditional definitions of rooms would not inhibit them from taking a fresh view of the problem. The objective, no matter how it may be achieved, is to begin with the broadest interpretation possible of the nature of solutions that are to be considered. Such methods may not be required on those rare occasions when the ideal solution reveals itself immediately to the design team, but on those days when heads have been scratched, brains have been strained, and no powerful concept has appeared, competent professionals fall back on the use of methods to stimulate their thinking, rather than rely on routine solutions. Even if a solution appears in a flash of lightning, design methods are useful in testing the idea and guarding against self-delusion.

Visual Dominance and Neutrality

Traditionally, American cities have had clearly established landmarks, spires, domes, and green areas that have symbolized the religious, governmental, and communal beliefs of the people (Fig. 6.1). With the start of the twentieth century, office buildings became competing landmarks, eventually to overpower the distant silhouette of the city skyline. With more buildings, of a greater variety, clamoring for attention, the urban profile became more a display of commercial passion than an identification of

6.2 Row houses in the Georgetown neighborhood appear to be a single mass forming an edge to the street space. Washington D.C.

people's other values. At ground level, though, the sheer size of the buildings did not have so profound an effect. The plazas, parks, and banks of steps that lead to city halls and churches or the areas of lawn around them retained much of their authority as landmarks and reference points.

There has always been a question of the appropriate prominence of architectural forms. Single-family houses in suburban developments today display imaginative, or perhaps startling, variations of architectural style, but in some suburbs regulations are imposed to require a degree of similarity in forms and materials, a policy often presumed to heighten the value and improve the character of the neighborhood. Cities may also require a designated amount of space and the presence of grass and trees in front of houses. Among row houses or apartment complexes there is often such conformity that intricate systems of building identification are necessary for visitors to find their destinations. Similar standards are applied to retail buildings. Individual businesses along a street are inclined to be highly competitive in the treatment of their storefronts, but identifiable commercial groupings or shopping centers customarily demand a degree of restraint in order that the identity of the group can be adequately displayed. Of course, different sorts of businesses must practice different marketing methods, and bankers will seek a style of identification unlike that of grocers.

A major question is the level at which sensory saturation is reached. There is a certain charm about a residential street along which houses of about the same size vary in materials and precise form and are often unified by a line of trees along the curb. Without the trees and with an extreme variety of sizes and shapes, the effect may be chaotic. Row houses of the same material with no spaces between them become a single building mass (Fig. 6.2). Houses of the wealthy can have extraordinary variations of form and color, but, when widely spaced on palatial sites, the effect is not unpleasant, especially if trees intervene. In residential areas, downtown, and along the highway there is a factor of visual texture, the density and distribution of sensation, that determines the degree of visual stimulation that is attained. The intensity of color and form, in proportion to the amount of interstitial and neutral area, can be thought of as constituting a measure or criterion. If similar nonaggressive row houses fill the entire view with a continuous pattern, a feeling of calm—certainly of nonexcitement—results. But if these houses are individually painted in strong, contrasting colors, the effect will be altered, calm will diminish, and excitement will increase.

The purpose, identity, and context of each place implies a desirable level of visual stimulation. The appropriate contrasts with their surroundings will differ for downtown streets and residential lanes, for monumental plazas and playgrounds, and for major and minor elements of a city's pattern of open spaces. A larger context also influences such decisions. The character of each community, village, or metropolis, and the scale of its visual expression, establish a range within which the hierarchical standing of the space should be posited. A constant danger lies in the inclination of many design teams and their sponsors to strive for a level of overexcitement that may be inappropriate for the specific project. On the other hand, there is sometimes a tendency to believe that the simplistic definition of the place, park or plaza, designates a level of stimulation, without investigating the range of visual stimulation that is possible under the fundamental definition of the design.

This tendency does not actually mean that there is still another set of requirements that must be established for the design team's work. Instead, the decisions that determine the character of the space to be designed are employed as the determinants of where the specific design should fit into the hierarchy of spaces in the locale. A neighborhood park in a developer-built suburban community, built around a dramatic shopping center, would arrive at a level of visual stimulation quite different from that of a quiet village centered around a green (Fig. 6.3). Since the objectives of single-family housing are customarily much the same, the open spaces vary most often according to the upper limit of excitement that is present in the community.

ANALYSIS

A major part of any design approach is the way constraints may be absorbed and whenever possible inserted into positive elements.[1]

The process of determining, analyzing, and describing the conditions of a site, along with determining functional requirements for a project, is a first step of the design process. The things that will be found are, of course, limitations and obstacles to your following certain paths in the design. At the same time, they constitute a framework that can stimulate ideas and assist in developing them. (In other words, the glass is half empty, and it is

6.3 This suburban single-family housing area is planned around a community green with a small lake in the middle. The spaces between and in front of the large houses flow across the central area.

also half full.) Most designers find with experience that there is nothing so difficult as designing something for which there are no limitations. The analytical study of conditions will eliminate many possibilities from consideration, but at the same time it will often suggest alternatives that were not initially evident. For that reason, when they analyze a locale designers search for the variety of conditions at the same time that they concentrate on clarifying a thematic identity for the entire project. One of the major judgments made during these early considerations is determining the ways in which a site is similar to or different from its surroundings and deciding which of these relationships will be useful in forwarding the objectives of the project.

Terrain: There is usually little importance attached to the configuration of the land in most downtown sites. There will probably be no trace of the original land form, except in a large city park or the open spaces of a small town. Usually, instead, the original landform of a project in an area of high density is suggested by little more than the levels at adjoining curbs and property lines. This remainder leaves the designers free to shape the surface within the site's boundaries as they wish. Shaping earth is one of the most advanced aspects of construction technology, and the extent to which levels are altered is seldom limited except by the problem of providing ramps for the handicapped and providing adequate drainage. A few feet of additional soil can raise a bank of low shrubs to form a more effective screen, accentuate a focal area, or increase opportunities to develop internal vistas by adding a vertical dimension.

By contrast, suburban sites often profit from maintaining or even restoring the natural characteristics of terrain. Slopes and curves can increase the visual relationship between the public space and the streets and lawns around it. Because of the expense of eliminating streams and steep inclines, many old neighborhoods were laid out with streets conforming to such strong land features, lending a pleasant distinction and clear identity to the neighborhood. The problem is more difficult when dealing with suburban arterial roads. The alteration of the terrain that was caused by highway construction and the leveling of lots alongside the highway has often virtually obliterated the original lay of the land, but often we can still see the hills and streams behind the screen of a roadside commercial strip.

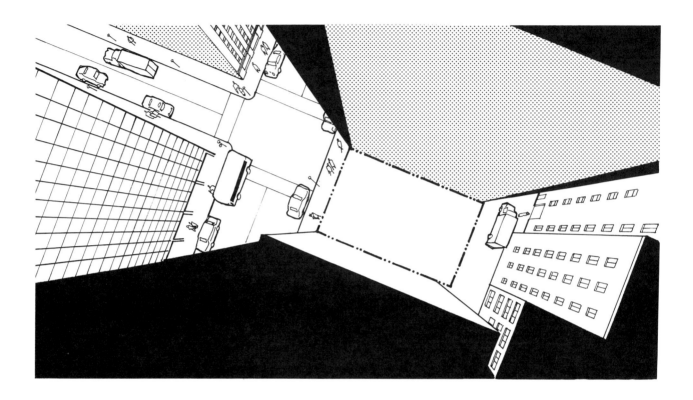

6.4 Visual boundaries of a site go far beyond its legal limits. Here, the black areas are those that cannot be seen from the center of the site, but the remaining scope of vision is much larger than would be expected.

This dichotomy can be interesting in its contrasts, particularly if the relationships of the two kinds of views are made clear by the occasional interruptions of the shielding screens of commercial establishments along the road. Thus the commercial development is clearly identified as a part of a bypass route, contrasting with the surrounding countryside.

Site Boundaries: The legal limits of a site are usually self-evident in an urban setting, but the visual limits, which are usually more meaningful, must be considered as well (Fig. 6.4). Sitting in a small downtown park, a visitor may be confronted in some directions with the solid walls of buildings and in other directions be able to see across a street or look along a distant view that is framed by tall buildings. In a neighborhood, surrounding rows of trees may reinforce the legal limits of the site, although winter conditions make the space more open. No matter where legal property lines are, it is these visual limits that form the enclosure as it is perceived by users of an open space. The designers may decide to internalize the space, isolating it from the surroundings except for the consideration of access, or they may wish to expand the influence of the space by emphasizing its visual extension. In other cases, employing both of these approaches may increase the latitude of psychological impacts, developing contrast inside the enclosure. In weighing such alternatives, a distinction must be made between those vistas that seem certain to remain in the future and those that could easily be altered or obliterated by the construction of buildings. A vacant space between two existing buildings may soon be occupied by another building, but the view down an avenue will almost certainly remain unless air-rights construction interferes.

Along with the consideration of outward views as seen from within the project area, a designer must also consider views *into* the project area (Fig. 6.5). Opening a vest-pocket park to a major street will invite visitors, but that decision can also reduce the park's quality of restfulness and the attraction of its contrast with the street (Fig. 6.6). A common method used to begin the study of the effects of outward and inward views is to collect photographs or sketches of the open site keyed to a plan, that exhaustively record both aspects of the views. For downtown sites, this collection may need to include views from the lower stories of buildings, where office workers will see the space much more frequently than any pedestrians. A series of sketches developed from such photographs usually can lead to an understanding of the way in which the design can enhance or obliterate views.

Buildings and Other Barriers: The maps of a site will usually indicate all the walls of buildings as hard and definite lines, but in visual terms their solidity is highly variable. The brick party wall built on the lot line is the most rigid limit that can be imposed on a space, although in the United States during the 1970s, they were sometimes softened by painted patterns, scenic views, or *trompes l'oeil.* At the other extreme, ground floor walls with large areas of clear glass can enlarge outside space, particularly if planting or a paving pattern extends through the glass. From the exterior, the transparency of a glass wall depends largely on the percentage of light reflected by the kind of glass used, and during the daytime many curtain wall buildings of highly reflective glass are almost as solid in appearance as

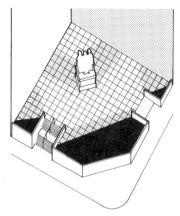

6.5 Changes of elevation and the low eye-level of drivers can severely limit the extent of surveillance by passersby and police controls. Here, shaded areas are obscured from one street, and black areas are hidden from both streets.

6.6 In many situations, consideration should be given to views into public spaces. Walls and level changes may impede surveillance of many areas. Screening vision into a vest-pocket park from busy streets can create feelings of seclusion in spite of the surrounding activities. Trammell Crow Center, Dallas.

brick walls, and they present the illusion that the outdoor space is double its true size as reflections extend into the framework of the building. At night, lights greatly alter this effect.

Along downtown streets, office buildings that have walls recessed on the ground floor or inset entrances can effectively interrupt the solid line of facades; the windows and stoops of row houses form a transition from street to building; and suburban houses with porches and generous spaces between them may serve as no more than a slight suggestion of a spatial limit. Assessment of the extent of enclosure that results from the walls of buildings can involve a complex evaluation of conditions. For instance, glass display windows in a wall facing north will be in shadow but may act as a mirror because of their brilliant reflection of the sunlight falling on the white marble wall of a building across the street; but a solid wall that is interrupted by recesses and made of a dark stone may be relatively unobtrusive as a visual limit.

Every sort of analysis must be considered in combination with others, and this is particularly true of the effect of building shapes and masses on the spaces they abut. The presence of trees before a storefront, light standards along the curb, or even a curtain wall's reflection of an ornate facade across the street can influence the manner in which buildings limit spaces. If such related objects are so near to the building that they are viewed as closely related, they may seem an integral element of the wall, depending on the position of viewers. But there are often ambiguous conditions. A row of trees planted near a building facade may, when seen from certain angles, actually function as an adjunct of the wall; however, on a sidewalk that runs between the trees and the building, the trees and wall will seem clearly separated.

Analysis of Views: The process of identifying and categorizing views of a space from within or from without is commonly considered to be much simpler than actual experience would suggest. Eventually, some evaluation must be made to determine how pleasant or unpleasant each view is, a process that establishes conditions within which a designer must work. Sitting in a quiet and protected garden spot, a glimpse of a noisy and busy street may actually increase our appreciation of the refuge we have found and yet provide the visibility that helped us find the spot in the first place. An intersection that is cluttered and bewildering when seen close at hand may be fascinating when seen from a distance, and at night it may become a pattern of dancing lights. A planted sitting area may provide a pleasant view for ground-level office windows, but still it may confront the office workers with strangers staring through the windows at them. Those views that offer themselves in the urban setting are seldom totally attractive or absolutely dreadful. They are instead a subtle mixture of favorable and unfavorable aspects that must be carefully analyzed with due consideration of all pertinent factors, such as seasons, times of day, activities, and participants.

A method frequently used to reduce the effect of an undesired view (a trick used in every magician's act) is diversion. A row of streetside trees lessens the attention given to the row of cars alongside them; a bubbling fountain or a display of flowers attracts our eye before we notice workers in

6.7 Since a driver, and to a great extent a passenger, keeps vision directed forward, the view from an automobile is necessarily more limited than a pedestrian's view.

6.8 A row of trees effectively screens houses from the view of drivers moving along a residential street. Swiss Avenue, Dallas.

6.9 When someone looks from a house across the street, the spacing of trees does little to screen the view. However, the vertical tree trunks provide a pleasant rhythm to the eye. Swiss Avenue, Dallas.

an office behind them. We see bright areas of light before the shadowy areas are noticed, and the things we see first are usually accepted as the dominant elements of our view. If we are moving through a space, its secondary visual elements merit only a glance, for we concentrate soon on the most prominent feature of the area we are approaching. But if we pause and sit for a while, those lesser features may assume new importance.

Streets and Cars: When they move along a street in a vehicle, the driver and passengers usually view an area approximately forty-five degrees on either side of the line of movement (Fig. 6.7). At such an angle the spacing of trees is visually reduced, and it diminishes as the distance grows greater. If the trees are planted at a customary spacing, people in cars are more aware of the plane of the trees than that presented by the houses' fronts (Figs. 6.8 and 6.9). In fact, the street and the front lawn are distinctly different areas as we look down the street, although they are very closely related as we look across the street from one house to the other. Without trees, fences, or hedges, the house-to-house space is one. With such visual barriers, separations are evident, according to the nature and dimensions of the interrupting barriers.

6.10 When you drive or walk along a downtown street, the space may be perceived as a canyon with little interruption along its distance (left). But where another street intersects your route, the lighting conditions can emphasize the lateral direction (right) as well as the intersection farther along.

Streets downtown, because they are surrounded by taller buildings, are more forcefully tubular in effect. Buildings usually are built right to their property lines, and the principal relief to these rigid limits of the tubular street are the gaps at intersecting streets. Few objects, except perhaps lighting standards, have prominence between the two sides of the space. Even if there are trees, they are stunted and their perceived size is diminished by comparison with the dimensions of the buildings. For that reason, even the slight recess of an office building entrance will be noticed, and the interruption provided by a small park is visually dramatic.

Spatially, the street is a more challenging place than we usually sense it to be as we hurry along. When we look straight ahead, it seems a simple tube, but at intervals perpendicular streets exert a powerful force across our path (Fig. 6.10). (In some cities this effect may be intensified for the pedestrian by a transverse gust of wind.) The tubular form of the street is thus punctuated with lateral spaces, and in Latin American cities doorways along the sidewalk give side glimpses into gardens, storage yards, and courtyards. A typical development in many American towns of the late nineteenth century was the use of corner entrances for buildings at a principal street intersection. This simple device recognized the geometry of the intersection and emphasized the point at which two linear movements crossed.

Cross-section drawings of streets, taken at a series of points and often extended into perspective views, permit the designer to analyze the degree of enclosure and determine the typical views of both pedestrians and vehicular passengers. Consideration must be given to the breadth of vision along streets, for pedestrians looking straight across a street may see little higher than the bottom two stories of a building.

No sound solution has yet been found for the visual effects of automobiles parked alongside downtown streets. Cars have become lower, but where sidewalks are wide, city officials have seemed increasingly willing to permit the installation of sidewalk cafes and other features that force pedestrian movement toward the curb. This problem seems to arise more from mental conflict than from urban design or governmental misjudgment. On the whole, people would like to live in a village park, have a metropolitan center nearby, and drive between the two with a minimum walk between parking and their destinations. Because this expectation defies logic, arithmetic reasoning, and the geometric principles of space utilization, it must be categorized as more a problem of mass psychology than civic design. The common solution at present replaces the downtown street with the suburban shopping center parking lot. Mandating exclusively pedestrian streets has seldom proved a solution. Nevertheless, the complex economic, political, ecological, and psychological problems can be ameliorated, if not solved. The problem, whether real or imagined, certainly merits attention.

Climate: First, a cautionary note: Many designers tend to imagine and draw only the conditions of a splendid June day. By limiting themselves in this manner, they deny themselves the opportunity to take advantage of conditions that might greatly increase the richness and variety of their designs. Except for blizzards, hurricanes, and the most blistering summer days, every kind of weather has its advocates, and it has been said that any region of the United States has two or three months of undesirable weather. To ignore one season is to make a proportional reduction in the performance of the space that is being designed. In fact, a space that is ineffective during two of the chilliest winter months or two of the steamiest summer months may well be viewed as one-sixth a failure. During periods of extreme conditions the sight of a warm splash of sunlight across snow or the cooling sounds of a fountain can do much to satisfy needs for relief from the weather. Traditional practices of gardening serve as an example of the required attitude; the succession of light, color, and mood are carefully considered in the cyclical characteristics of a design. Certainly, in the least pleasant weather people may occupy a space less often and for shorter periods of time, but the benefits they derive from their visits therefore may be much more meaningful.

Weather is a description of the temperature, humidity, sunshine, wind, and other matters that determine environmental conditions and comfort for a particular time and place. Climate is a description for a region's average and extreme conditions of weather over a long period, considered seasonally and comparatively (Fig. 6.11). Summaries of the basic information are available from the U.S. Weather Bureau, but unfortunately they do not include correlative information, such as the wind direction when rain falls in the spring. (The significance of such relationships is indicated by the introduction of wind-chill, derived from temperature and wind velocity, and the temperature-humidity also known as the "sweat index.") Information and—more correctly—opinion, can be sought from natives of the area, but more than one source is advised. Since people's descriptions of the weather are often folkloric, corroboration will add depth to the information. Various kinds of graphs can be made to plot the outstanding characteristics of the climate (such as average temperature vs. average precipitation), and monthly data can be plotted to determine the times when conditions exceed accepted standards of comfort. While such analysis may seem to overly detail conditions, it sometimes reveals pertinent information, and it also sets out all the facts in a manner that makes them easier to utilize in combination with the other factors that must undergo analysis. Usually it is useful to ferret out any climatic infor-

6.11 Two diagrams that assist in studying climate: (Above) Charts show month-by-month changes in temperature and precipitation for Tucson, Arizona, and Portland, Maine, to compare the basics of their climates.(Below) A wind chart shows that prevailing winds in Fort Dodge, Kansas, come mainly from one direction, while in Athens, Georgia, wind directions are quite variable.

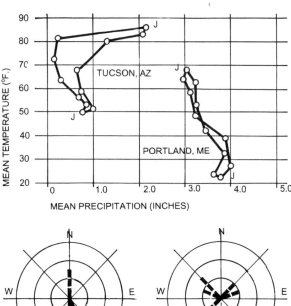

mation that can be had, because the correlative information essential to environmental design is not readily available.

Microclimate: There is usually even less known about the climate within a particular site. For one thing, the designer may start work before a large building is constructed on or near the site, or the site may not yet have been cleared of buildings. Even when conditions on and around the site offer no such problems, it is seldom possible to obtain even one year's measurements. It is necessary, therefore, to use methods that allow the extrapolation of predicted conditions based on established principles regarding the behavior of the microclimate and superimposed on the general climatic conditions of the location.[2]

By simple geometric principles, the shadows of existing or proposed buildings that fall on the site can be determined and charted for different times of the year (Fig. 6.12). Sites that open to the south or north may have equivalent conditions throughout the year, with the west portion sunny in the morning and shaded in the afternoon. Differences in the amount of sunlight falling on part of a site may well be the deciding factor in determining that area's function. It is often found that a critical role is played by a tall building that is not even adjacent to the site but casts a very long shadow. The direction of sunshine is the only element of microclimate that can be determined with accuracy.

Estimating the microclimatic influences of wind is more difficult and uncertain. Downtown plazas have on several occasions in recent times been plagued by winds funnelled in new directions by the addition of buildings in the area; winds have blown paper, leaves, and dust around courtyards beyond any reasonable limit of human tolerance; and, in a few instances, gusts on city sidewalks have been so strong that they have threatened to push pedestrians into the paths of vehicles on the street. No one can solve the problems of occasional extraordinary wind velocity, the gales that turn umbrellas inside out and send hats rolling down the street, but reasonable precautions can be taken regarding the usual hazards. A study using a low-velocity wind tunnel certainly would be essential in the design of a restricted area in a densely-built urban area. (Aeronautical wind tunnels are not appropriate instruments for this sort of study.)

In estimating simpler cases, some basic information must be incorporated in evaluations:

■ It is most realistic to picture winds as being pulled through a space by the negative pressures on the leeward sides of buildings, rather than being pushed by a positive force. A series of housing projects in Great Britain had paved plazas between a tall block of dwelling units and low commercial structures. Trash and dust swirling in the plazas often made it impossible to use them. After wind tunnel tests, the recommendation was that an air passage be provided through the tall buildings at ground level in order to relieve the negative pressure.

■ Shorter buildings have a strong effect because of the air that flows over their roofs, and tall buildings can be judged to influence the wind almost entirely according to the building footprint. For this reason, it is often true that instead of tall buildings sheltering a site they induce fierce microclimatic conditions, much worse than the climate of suburban or open areas.

■ Air velocity, and most discomfort from wind, depends on the difference between positive and negative pressure and the size of the opening through which air must pass. Drawings can be prepared to estimate the movement of wind through a space; blocks can be placed in a moving sheet of water and sand sprinkled or dye dropped to indicate air movement; or fans and smoking sticks of punk can be used.

All of these are relatively crude indicators, but may be sufficiently accurate to determine possibly critical situations (Fig. 6.13). After all, the variable directions of wind, changes in its velocity, and the pressure of gusts mean that even the most precise wind tunnel study can only present an approximate evaluation of a relatively small portion of the spectrum of possibilities. Still, in recent decades so many downtown plazas and building entrances have proved to be disastrous misjudgments of the wind's action that even such primitive investigations have their merits.

Noise: Between a spooky hush and an ear-splitting din there is a level of sound that is in agreement with our mood or activity at a specific time. We do not always seek quiet, for noise is closely associated with many of our pleasures. Parades, rock concerts, and visits to a state fair all combine loud

SUMMER: JUNE 22

SPRING: MARCH 21   FALL: SEPTEMBER 23

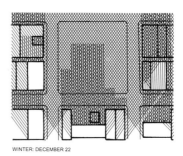

WINTER: DECEMBER 22

6.12 On this hypothetical site, adjoining buildings cast shadows, as shown for the extremes of winter, summer, and the equinoxes at the latitude of Indianapolis. It should be noticed that certain areas are almost always in sunlight and others are dominantly in shadow—a factor that would influence planning of the space. Angles and depth of shadows are calculated for 0800 am, 1200 noon, and 1600 pm. (As in the other site plans and maps in this book, north is at the top of the drawing.)

6.13 When wind encounters a solid object, the air is compressed in order to pass around it. As it reaches the downwind side, the air expands to resume its former direction, and as it expands eddies are formed. This action causes low pressure.

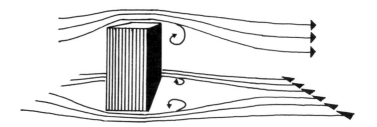

and jumbled sounds with corresponding moods and visual sensations. Any notion that all streets should be hushed or have only the sounds of chirping birds and bubbling streams is impractical and insensitive. Strangely, many people who speak most enthusiastically about the romantic bustle of activity in European marketplaces also complain of the same sound levels in the streets of downtown America. Except for a certain amount of pretension, the problem is largely one of the correspondence of sound and situation. On vacation the repetitious music of a hurdy-gurdy is exciting—one can leave at any moment; outside the office window during contract negotiations it is a totally different matter. In spite of the widely differing sound tolerances of different people, and their strongly held views on the matter, the fact remains that we all want to hear the kind of sounds that we associate with the moment and our feelings at that moment. Considering the variety of people's desires and opinions at any time, the usual solution is to try to keep the sound level as low as possible, assuming that those who want to hear more will listen more sharply or move to a noisier area.

In the simplest terms, the acoustic environment of a place is indicated by two fundamental measures, reverberation and reflection. Reverberation, the tendency to echo and sustain a sound, is related to the volume of a space and the sound-absorptive qualities of its surfaces. Because open air is the most absorptive substance, reverberation is seldom a problem in outdoor spaces. Reflection of sound, a phenomenon much like the reflection of light, is particularly a problem in downtown areas (Fig. 6.14). A sound strikes a wall and, if the wall is a hard surface (as the walls of buildings necessarily must be) a large percentage of the sound's force will be reflected. Thus the sound of an automobile horn can strike a wall, reflect, strike the wall opposite, and be sustained in this manner. The listener hears the sound of the horn directly, hears it reflected once, twice, and on and on. The reflection of sound by a wall is inhibited if there are large variations of surface—insets and projections—that diffuse it, but the small-scale surface textures of rough fieldstone or inset windows are not useful.

There is a mysterious belief that trees and planting will magically soak up sound. This belief is not true. In fact, one study claims that the branches and twigs of trees vibrate with the sound waves and may even enhance noise.[3] Some diminution of the sound of truck noises may result from solid bands of trees that total over one hundred feet in width, and shrubs and a row of trees may work for residential street sounds, but even that improvement is negligible after the leaves fall.[4] On a horizontal plane, grass and ground covers provide a slight absorption of sound, eliminating the sharp

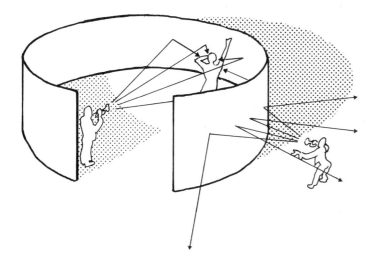

6.14 Convex surfaces scatter sound, and concave surfaces focus the sound. Tilting the vertical face of a wall can direct the reflections upward or downward, eliminating much of this difficulty.

reflection we hear when we boat on a lake. But no amount of planting—unless it approaches the scale of giant redwoods in great numbers—will control a serious noise problem.

Because sound, unlike light, wraps around obstructions, screening elements must be carefully considered. Walls are most effective if they are:

■ solid construction without perforations that let sound pass through,

■ sufficiently long so their effectiveness is not reduced by sound bending around the ends of the wall (one source of information recommends that the wall be at least three times as long as the distance from it to the person being protected from the noise), and

■ sufficiently high and near to the source of noise or the people from whom protection is intended.

Even then a formula for estimating the effects suggests that a wall ten feet high and twenty feet from an automobile would eliminate around a fourth of the noise; if the same wall were only six feet from the automobile it would eliminate about one third of the noise.

Whatever the situation on a particular site may be, there is usually very little that can be done about effectively reducing noise. The masking sounds of a fountain, footsteps, or rustling leaves are often the simplest remedial measure. Certain areas can be surrounded by sound-reflective surfaces to increase awareness of the sound within the area, a solution that risks generating another nuisance. Masonry walls around a children's area can make people more aware of the children's sounds than of the roar of passing trucks. There is also a relationship between the sight of traffic and our awareness of the noise of traffic. One investigation indicates that noise seems louder when its source is not visible.[5]

USER POPULATIONS

The simplest way to understand the population characteristics of a project's locale is to combine residential information from the most recent U.S. Census with self-generated estimates of the numbers of people occupying buildings around the site. Data for the census tracts or blocks surrounding the project can be quickly obtained and summarized. For small cities, for which only tables may be available, the entire city census boundary may be used. In order to obtain similar information about the nonresidential uses surrounding a site, square footages of interior space are employed with acceptable occupancy rates, which are:

■ offices—1 person per 120 square feet net

■ downtown offices, where attorneys may occupy up to 33% of all office space—1 person per 160 square feet net

■ industrial buildings and manufacturing facilities—based on the labor needed for the processes with warehouses—3 to 5 people per 100,000 square feet

■ shopping districts—1 person per 500 square feet

These methods provide only a glimpse of current conditions. In order to predict future occupancies, more complicated methods must be used. Projections, models, and acceptable estimates need to be calculated in order to obtain credible data for design purposes.

> In most cases the process of population projection involves little more than analyzing the nature of past trends for each component of change in the model and extrapolating them. Generally, predictions are made on the assumption that population growth is a self-contained process, and that no significant changes will occur in social, environmental, or economic factors during the period that is under consideration. In this way the possibility of a dramatic event such as war or an earthquake, and also the effects of gradual changes in attitudes, environment, or economic circumstances are largely excluded from these models.[6]

In considering the total numbers of people who will be using the spaces between buildings—and their ages, their ethnicity, their social class, and their gender—an analyst must borrow from the techniques of demographers. Planning for spaces requires knowledge about the expected number of occupants, but projections have been widely accepted as a basis for such decision-making. Too often, designers may assume that a downtown park or a public plaza should be designed for peak lunch-time occupancies or weekend strollers. They may be wrong. Better estimates of either the numbers or other characteristics of occupants could easily lead the project design team to divert its budget from benches to bushes. For this reason, the team must consider the composition of the population (age, sex, ethnic, and racial variations) and the overall growth or decline of an area—activities in open spaces may be limited to certain age groups or populations defined by other social characteristics. Numbers may not affect the design of a space as much as age or social class. Statistics that report educational levels or ages alone may only consider a segment of the population to be served by the project, rather than the total group. Even if data on labor force, household formation, or marital status is available, age, births, deaths, and migration information are necessary to arrive at the most complete and accurate information regarding the total number of people who may use the project.

Population projections can never be accurate. They are only estimates or guesses about how many people will occupy a place at some time in the future. In this respect, population projections are mere images of reality developed to describe a future condition. Generally, population projections represent conditional statements, such as: If the present death and birth rates continue in the future, in the year 2000 the population using our project will be 2,500 per workday, and will average about 320 per hour and about 640 per hour of a peak morning. Given trends will produce a population of a certain size. Changes in population can be predicted by four main components:

POPULATION at the start of the study period
    + BIRTHS during the period
    − DEATHS during the period
    + IN-MIGRATION during the period
    − OUT-MIGRATION during the period
    = POPULATION at the end of the study period[7]

In the widely accepted model shown above, births are considered according to a measure of potential fertility, such as the number of women of child-bearing age. "Live births per 1,000 women" is converted into fertility rates indicating the probability of a woman giving birth over a specified period of time. Population tables can be obtained from the U.S. Superintendent of Documents' most current *Statistical Abstract*. Fertility rates are highly sensitive and affected by many factors.

Deaths are another interest:

> The analyst is mainly interested in those people who survive to form part of the population at a given point in time rather than those who have been prevented from reaching this state by death. Consequently, deaths are measured in terms of the chances of survival rather than the chances of dying. The likelihood of survival is expressed in the form of a life table which indicates the number of people out of a given number of births who would survive in each age category if they were subject to the recorded death rates of the period.[8]

For example, the chances of a boy at birth reaching the age of 80 may be 3963 out of 10,000. Survival rates can vary widely between areas, but, unlike fertility rates, over time in the same area they are quite stable.

Migration is difficult to define and measure. Usually, a migrant is defined as someone whose permanent address on the census date was different from that given on the previous census date. Net change, which examines the extent to which the population of an area changes in a given period as a result of migration, is the migration balance calculated by subtracting the number of emigrants from the number of immigrants.

Surveys and Analyses: The users of an open space to a great extent determine the provisions that designers include in their plans. However, limited financing and constraints on space may also serve as major factors in making design decisions. Usually, long before the designers focus on a project estimates have been made in order to gain approval, and the early phases of design may actually be scheduled as a part of the campaign for approval by municipal or corporate decision-makers. When this happens the design commitments must combine political and planning factors, bringing together elements of "what will sell" and "what is needed." This conflict of interests is inherent, for those who approve are very seldom those who use a project. Therefore, it is wise that the users' input be obtained and analyzed at the same time as, or even before, the approvers' determination of the broad and generalized objectives of the project.

Although there are many ways in which users' opinions may be gathered and assessed, designers cannot abrogate their role in decision-making.

■ First, there is the "child-in-a-candy store" difficulty, the confused and impulsive decisions that often perplex laypeople. Respondents may feel compelled to select their answers without conviction.

■ Second, the political undercurrents of any group meeting may cause the fastest talkers or those with the most authority to override the majority opinions.

■ Third, organizers of sessions to gain public input often phrase questions and manipulate answers in a manner that favors their own views and can give rise to frustration and resentment among the participants.

In general, one can assume that users' responses are most reliable if they are stated in concrete terms, mentioning such things as sand boxes and wading pools rather than "recreational facilities for younger children," and more realistic responses will be obtained when users are asked to choose among or rank alternatives. Such choices provide general recommendations without hampering the designers' work with popular items that could for other reasons prove to be impossible. It is extremely dangerous for a design team to invite firm decisions before they are certain of the wisdom and feasibility of the alternatives that are presented, and conducting a second survey of users may be much less difficult than extricating the group from a commitment made too soon.

In preparing to design spaces between buildings, it is recommended that information be collected and analyzed to describe the social, psychological, and behavioral factors that are involved in each project. When the project is a new space, observations of similar places will prove useful, although caution should be exercised. But when an existing space is to be modified, on-site surveys are usually preferable. All situations require careful design of the research procedures that are to be employed, whether the project designers undertake the work themselves or engage specialists either to prepare the instruments or to analyze and interpret the data that is collected. In order to interpret the behavioral information properly, some sophistication is needed regarding methods of random sampling and appropriate analytical procedures.

There are a limited number of basic methods of collecting social data. Users can be *asked*, either by questionnaires or through interviews, or they can be *observed*. In any case, it is essential that before this task commences a clearheaded decision must be made about what information is actually needed or will be useful for the design, and what kinds of information can be gained from the sources and methods available for that purpose. Trivial, petty, theoretical, and inapplicable items must be discarded from consideration, and attention must be focused on obtaining information that can truly assist in making decisions. For that reason, it is sometimes better to delay these tasks until preliminary design studies have established the fundamental physical feasibilities of the project.

Self-Report Questionnaires: The value of questionnaire results depends largely on the care with which such instruments are prepared and correctly worded to evoke an accurate response. Questionnaire items for the use of field workers in the social sciences cannot be just carefully worded, as if the author were writing prose. Once the questionnaire items have been satisfactorily developed, a form is prepared. Current practice is usually to obtain effectively measured responses through the use of a Likert scale, which is comprised of a range of responses:

■ I strongly agree

■ I agree

■ I somewhat agree

■ I somewhat disagree

■ I disagree

■ I strongly disagree

By having an even number of responses (two, four, or six, never more) the respondent is denied an opportunity to equivocate, which is a natural tendency. A frequency distribution of responses is prepared after the questionnaire is administered to a random sample of respondents. Questions that have strongly skewed responses (say, ten, sixty, three, two, zero, and two in the order of the scale given above) either may be unnecessary or should be changed to a wording that will cause them to yield more useful information. (A more sensitive phrasing of the question would be expected to lead to no less than eight responses in each of the categories offered). Rephrasing the question and pretesting again should provide more informative results, and then the instrument would be ready for use in the field. Caution should be exercised about developing a questionnaire that has more than seven to nine items. After an item is well-developed and believed to be clearly worded, it is recommended that a series of pretests be conducted with randomly selected subjects. This pretesting would determine ways in which the phrasing might be improved or help questioners choose among alternative wordings of the items. In most cases, people will not wish to cooperate if they are interrupted for too long a time, and a questionnaire that includes too many items can lead to results that are inaccurate and unusable.

Interviews: To develop information regarding a neighborhood space it is possible to mail or hand-deliver questionnaires to area residents. A downtown plaza or a space that would be used by residents of all areas of the city may require a different approach, one that would gather the opinions of those who actually make use of the space. This kind of survey can be done by asking passersby questions—usually that would be done by reading items aloud and checking off the response values. If the survey is to be valid, survey development should include far more than casually chatting with a random selection of respondents. The same procedures of pretesting and adjusting phrasing should be followed as in the case of self-report questionnaires, although phrasing for oral delivery may require different language from that used in the written form. Pretests of survey-interviews should be oral, and self-report survey pretests should be administered in written form. Limiting the number of items is most important. A fixed system of selecting respondents should be employed—perhaps every tenth person passing should be interviewed. (Self-report questionnaires also can be handed to every tenth person, to be completed and returned within a few minutes or by mail.) If uncontrolled observations are invited (such as "What is your opinion about . . .?") they should be solicited only after the questions that form the standardized interview document are completed and the responses should be recorded on the uniform scale. Selecting and recording the times at which survey-interviews are conducted is extremely important, for hour by hour there may be appreciable changes in the characteristics of both the setting and those in the area.

Observation: This technique is accomplished fundamentally by "hanging around" the area, seeing what users of the space do, and recording the data. (Here again, the selection of observation times can be important.) At its simplest level, observation may involve merely noting how many walkers turn left or right. A more complex situation may require periodically noting on a plan of the space the location, activity, and classification (child, adult, older adult, for example) of all users at that time. In all cases, notes must be made in a manner that does not risk influencing those who are being observed. Typically, there is a temptation to attempt to record more information than can be done accurately. Therefore, pretesting the notation methods is required to ascertain the procedures and scope of study that will be appropriate. Photography, even time-lapse photography, may sometimes prove to be useful as the primary recording method or as a means of obtaining supplementary information.

Behavioral information about spaces may be elicited also from observations of physical evidence. Even with no users occupying the space, worn areas of paving, the amount and types of trash in bins, and other so-called "unobtrusive measures" can be identified by a sharp eye. (After all, years ago the city of New York found that it could best estimate attendance at parades by weighing the litter swept from the streets.) Using this procedure, conclusions are often difficult to reach. The excessive wear on the treads of a portion of a staircase could indicate greater use of that area, but it might also indicate that those slabs of stone were less durable, a natural variation in the quarry. The Sherlock Holmes method of finding clues ("unobtrusive measures" is a common term) has its risks, but if they are interpreted with caution, the findings can be useful.

The methods of eliciting social and behavioral data will be selected and combined according to the nature of the project at hand and the available resources, both funds and opportunities for implementing certain methods. Basic probability and statistics are concepts that are important in social data collection and analysis. Statistics tell us that, given a pattern of responses, there is a probability that similar people in similar situations would answer the same items in the same way. Any investigation can be no more than a snapshot in time. It is inevitably influenced by the method used, by the time and season, and by a host of other factors. Investigations cannot predict the opinions or behavior that will be present decades in the future. Nevertheless, if the procedures have been carefully planned and the results correctly analyzed, the information obtained is certain to be more reliable than the guesses of an individual or a group. The principle of random sampling assumes that a structured sample of a population will respond in the same way as the entire number; thus, rigorous observation of the accepted practices is demanded for selecting respondents. At the present time, many computer programs devised for statistical purposes simplify the repetitive numerical tasks that were once necessary. Interpreting the numerical results, as well as designing the investigation procedures, are involved procedures, and usually it is advisable to have an advisor or consultant do that work.

Circulation: If a site is already open to pedestrian circulation, it is a simple matter to track users and observe their movements through it. A lookout point in an upper story of an adjacent building can be established and from there records can be made or photographs taken to show the number of pedestrians entering or leaving the space at critical points. It is seldom possible to make an exhaustive analysis that includes different seasons and weather conditions, but adequate information can be gathered, considering the likelihood that parking conditions and business establishments will probably alter many times in the future. The task becomes more difficult when a site is being cleared for a project. Passersby can be tracked to determine if they turn at a street corner in a direction that would be shortened when the project is completed, and counts can be made of the pedestrians on sidewalks in the immediate vicinity of the projects. Sometimes it is possible to stop pedestrians and ask their destinations. Both methods, and perhaps all others that might be possible, give inexact measurements of the circulation that will probably occur within the project site. One would imagine that the ability to count pedestrians could result in planning circulation with great accuracy, but that is not the case. In addition to the possibilities of change, as has been mentioned, there are great variations in the number of pedestrians. Rush hours, rainy days, and even department store sales can lead to significant changes in the numbers of people walking along a downtown street. Nevertheless, a close look at such information can generate assumptions that are reasonably safe to use as estimates of the traffic that will be encountered once the project has been completed.

Vehicular circulation on streets is regularly measured by city traffic engineers, and these data are useful for assessing the conditions surrounding a project site. The provision of roadways and parking on a site is handicapped by the lack of sound standards by which designers can estimate the extent and frequency of automobile use. The choice between using space in a public area for parking and maneuvering cars or increasing the area available for the fundamental purposes of that project is always difficult. Certainly, no one should consider providing enough parking spaces for the few major events of the year. After all, having to search for a parking place is acknowledged to be a sign of an event's success. One solution to the parking problem is the designation of overflow parking, which can be accomplished by such measures as using grassy areas seldom enough to avoid injuring the turf or by constructing basketball goals at the edges of a paved parking space.

Particularly in downtown areas, the layout of a mass transit system will determine specific points at which there will be a concentration of pedestrians. At the same time, those locations can present the design team with a fairly predictable number of people who will be appreciative of a more efficient and attractive place to wait for or alight from public transportation.

Historical Background

Not every site is the birthplace of a hero or the scene of a decisive battle, but it is often possible that a site may have historical connections that are not self-evident or well-known (Fig. 6.15). A review of legal records can determine previous ownership, city directories in the public library will list those who have lived at the address or businesses that may have been located there, and local historical societies are always willing to provide information. In addition, old issues of Sanborn maps, fire insurance records that date back to the 1880s in some cities, show the locations of buildings and indicate their use and construction materials. The historical context may not be an important consideration unless the site has long been identified with a previous use. Even if no historical emphasis is desired or appropriate, however, a basic survey of such information should be made, because at some point in making the many design decisions there may be a historical fact that suggests an approach. The discovery of historical relationships does not require historical imitation in the design of a place. The fact that it is the site of the city's first streetcar barn may clearly merit a plaque, but the park that is developed there need not become a virtual museum.

Everyone is interested in incidental information about their neighborhood or their city. The place where a treaty was signed or a president

6.15 Cities can have an effective mix of old and new spaces. This historic cemetery along the streets of downtown Philadelphia is in sharp contrast with the high-rise housing and office buildings all around it. Although they are often small spaces, historic interests preserve cemeteries as effective spatial amenities.

was born may call for full-force historical treatment, but the fact that a stream was the location of the region's first gristmill or that a street corner was the original site of what is now a national restaurant chain can certainly merit a plaque. By the use of a simple phrase such as "Two blocks west of here" an entire area's history can be explained. Local historians and their organizations stand ready and eager to provide such information.

METHODS OF DESIGNING

There are obvious risks to any procedure followed in initiating a project, and experienced heads are required to determine a strategy and execute it successfully. General proposals have about them an air of mystery that may weaken popular support, while specific proposals can generate objections. Whatever method is followed, once it has succeeded a basic list of requirements will have been developed, albeit probably in a rather disjointed form. If a tentative scheme was prepared as part of the strategy for introducing the project, the requirements on which it was based may have been laid in disarray by events leading to approval. Similarly, the first efforts of a real-estate developer, even if the city's planning staff has collaborated with him or her, probably will have been altered by the process of negotiation. Whether funding is achieved before or after the majority of the design activity takes place, the process must be carefully planned. By its very nature, the design process is an untidy activity. Only after one level of decisions is made can the next level be planned, and details often require a reconsideration of earlier and more general decisions.

Through the centuries, there have been many attitudes regarding the ways in which the work of designing can or should be conducted. Accepted types, the "styles" of art history, evolved slowly through much of that time. Designers made adaptations of older styles, adjusted the forms to local materials and conditions, and competed in improving the styles in accordance with the taste of the time. During the Renaissance, when the notions of genius and originality came to be valued, stress was placed on the work of the individual and that individual's mannerisms of design.[9]

By the end of the nineteenth century, there was general acceptance of the design methods taught in the primary French school of architecture, which was then the most fashionable. Work began with the development of a summary of the requirements. By considering functional groupings of these requirements, a sketch plan that roughly determined the three-dimensional form within which they would be placed was developed. Work continued by developing the design at increasingly demanding levels of detail. The phases of this method, as delineated by later theorists, were usually presented as a sequence: programming, data collection, analysis, synthesis, development, and communication. Analysis, which included the locale and specific site as well as the functional requirements, was customarily followed by a period of sketching and testing several possibilities that led to synthesis and the sketch plan. Because most designs were adapted from historical precedents, this critical phase of the process was principally an exercise of imagination and taste, particularly for traditional open spaces, forecourts, plazas, and parks. Most design during the first half of the twentieth century followed these same procedures, although the small percentage of spaces planned in the Functionalist mode were not restricted to historical precedents.

The 1960s was a period in which much attention was focused on the study of information theory, cybernetics, and other systems that endeavored to rationalize cognitive processes. At that time, it was common for design professionals to describe their work as "problem-solving," skirting the mention of aesthetic and personal considerations or posing these problems as psychological matters. It was felt at the time that previous methods had become inadequate (perhaps because of the need to experience a creative act in the company of engineers and bankers) and that methodology might assist in utilizing the input of nondesigners.[10] The conclusions reached usually were based either on the procedures employed in other fields of activity or on observation of customary methods in the appropriate design professions. Often these studies were represented by diagrams that took the form of branching patterns, inverted genealogical charts, linear routes with attached loops, and even spirals. Few method diagrams actually contradicted the step-by-step organization of the traditional sequence described above. Most included loops where a previous decision might need to be reevaluated before confronting the current problem and interrelationships that indicated that a decision on one aspect of a project would depend on the decision made on another aspect. The methods and the diagrams that represent them are, on the whole, very simplistic pictures of the many decisions that are actually required to execute a project. They are useful in planning an approach to a project and for determining the design's progress at midpoints along the way. The popularity of design methodology ("methodolatry", one writer called it) waned during the 1980s as Postmodernism and historicism appeared briefly.[11] Still, designers often follow a method selected to suit their manner of working and the project.

The study of design methods clearly designated the points at which imagination, creativity, genius, or incredible good fortune were hoped to occur. In the 1960s, the nature of creativity was a focus of study among psychologists. Very early it was found that creative abilities were not necessarily indicated by intelligence. If a group were tested for both IQ and creative talent, the top group as ranked by IQ would include less than half of those in the top group as ranked by creativity scores.[12] Talent in identifying problems and evaluating results were usually included as abilities needed at the beginning and end of the process, although a variety of terms were used.

A common categorization of design decision-making was:

■ *Convergent thinking*, which tends to focus on and believes that there is a single right, best, and most suitable answer to the problem.

■ *Divergent thinking*, which pursues different directions, exploring a variety of possible solutions and finally selecting the best.

Since it is unlikely that every requirement will be satisfied completely, one possible result of divergent thinking involves reexamination of the requirements that started the whole process. For instance, the probability of certain demographic changes in the area around a plaza, though it seemed a minor consideration at first, can easily become the critical factor in making the choice between several design ideas. Sometimes a professional office, when executing a very important project, will assign designers to two or three teams, each assigned to pursue a different plausible scheme; and, through a competitive procedure, a final decision will be made. The linear pattern of convergent thinking has the disadvantages of risking frustration at an advanced phase of the project and requires time-costly loopbacks. The branching pattern of divergent thinking, a sort of "trial-and-error" or "guess-and-test" procedure, which may be more costly, considers a greater variety of ideas and under wise management offers safety.

In actual practice, both of these methods are usually combined. On the one hand, there are no principles and guidelines established for enough of the problems to permit convergent procedures to solve all of the them. On the other hand, the possibilities and their combinations are so multitudinous that a comparative study of them all is virtually impossible and certainly beyond the limits of ordinary professional practice. Often it is the ability to select the situations in which the methods are employed that determines the success of a design team.

To assist in making the necessary choices, intricate methods have been used to rate criteria for their relative importance and to rate alternative designs for their success in satisfying those criteria. These methods can be useful safeguards, but it should always be remembered that such procedures are not holistic in nature. By dividing the design objectives into separate aspects it is possible to determine inadequacies and failures, but this method does not necessarily recognize either unifying thematic strength or the clearly displayed individuality and identity that should be sought. Creative, idea-generating work must accompany analytical work if an excellent solution is to be found.

There are no specific methods that guarantee creative thinking, although certain actions and attitudes have been recognized as stimulating imaginative thinking. The first and foremost is becoming deeply involved in the project, its practical, psychological, and social aspects. Waiting languidly for ideas does not encourage them. At the same time, those who investigate the psychology of creative thinking suggest that flashes of insight often come to people when they are not directly engaged in the project. Many are the stories of inventors and scientists who suddenly realized the solutions to their problems while shaving, listening to a symphony, or otherwise engaging in everyday activities during periods when their other hours were filled with intensive concentration on the project.[13] In such cases, the mind, which has been filled with the problem and the design objectives, suddenly cuts through the mists. Many have cried "Eureka!" since the time of Archimedes, and many apples have fallen since the days of Newton.

Ideas, when they come, are sometimes based on analogies. At one extreme, the analogy may consist of the choice of a similar design and the decision to replicate it, absolutely or with adaptations. At the other extreme, a designer may discover a useful analogy in the pattern of a fabric, a natural terrain, or a mechanical device. Such insights may be founded on actual similarities or may have a heuristic function, serving as an assumption that enables a further study of the problem, and once work has progressed, the analogy may have diminished significance. There are also many tales of technological discoveries made by sensing a solution in some ordinary and familiar device. In the field of design, this kind of imagination usually is stirred by recalling some place experienced in the past. The character desired in the improvement of a street may be recalled as that of a tree-lined country road, the midway of a state fair, or a side street in a city recently visited. A playground may be envisioned as capturing the mood of an illustration in a children's book or a childhood haunt. One or more images of this kind, appearing in the minds of different members of the design team, can be shared and compared to clarify the mood and spirit of the design that is being sought. If the ideas contradict, it may be necessary to execute quick trials in order to choose between them.

Many other techniques have been studied.[14] It should be remembered that all of them are more methods of stimulating the imagination than of problem-solving. Because they do not usually provide specific answers to specific questions, some very practical-minded participants may become impatient, and learning to let the imagination range freely will be difficult for some participants. Concern about the tangibles of paving, parking, and pathways often will seem more earnest and productive than contemplating the intangibles of mood, visual pleasure, perception, and joy. Unfortunately, to many people exercising the imagination hardly seems like an honest day's work, but ideas and creative visions are the labor that determine the value of the practical decisions.

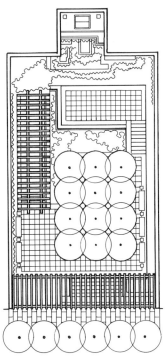

6.16 A plan and a photograph of Greenacre Park, New York City, (left) show the difficulty of relating such drawings to the three-dimensional reality of the executed project. Experience always helps, but sketches (right) are commonly used to assist the imagination in picturing the eventual solution. (Photo by Trev Albright)

Visualization

Our present tools for simulating the full dimensions of reality are sadly limited and must be used with full knowledge of their limitations, as demonstrated by comparing a photograph with a drawing of Greenacre Park, New York City (Fig. 6.16).[15] None encompass the full range of sensory impressions that we experience. Two-dimensional drawings are useful for a small number of purposes, but it requires a great deal of experience to look at several two-dimensional drawings of a space and accurately sense the actual three-dimensional effect. Since plans, sections, and elevations most effectively convey factual information about linear relationships, measurements, and ratios of dimensions, their information is precise and rapidly interpreted. In contrast, though perspectives cannot be measured and seldom provide detailed and exact information, they more closely represent the actual perceptual experience of an observer and are easily interpreted by anyone (Fig. 6.17). One of the inherent disadvantages of perspective drawings is that they are more difficult to construct properly—it is hard to make certain that all the measurements are precise and that the picture accurately shows what a viewer actually would see. Oblique and axonometric projection drawings serve as compromises between these two systems. They indicate three dimensions and can be measured to determine dimensions (at least in the directions of the three axes of the drawing), but they do not show the diminished apparent sizes of distant objects.

The layperson commonly sees only the sketches and models that are prepared in order to explain the completed design to the public. However, there are many additional quick sketches and rough models utilized to describe and test different ideas in order that a decision can be made. These must be prepared by relatively quick methods if there is to be sufficient study of a project in the time available for its design stages. It is not uncommon for a design team to be subdivided into two or three groups,

6.17 A simple project shown with the customary methods used in design and the execution of designs. All except the last drawing can also be utilized at technical stages with dimensions and description of construction added to them.

Plan indicates the manner in which different elements of a design relate horizontally and how the design is adjusted to the site. An indication of vertical relationships can be added by numbers indicating the level of different areas or contour lines that define the slope of the land, either as it is or as it will be altered during construction.

Elevation shows the vertical and horizontal relationships identifiable in a view of only one side. Interior elevations can be shown in connection with sections, as shown below.

Section emphasizes the vertical dimensions of construction and grading as well as horizontal dimensions. Particularly useful for gaining or explaining information about the internal areas of projects, the section clarifies the manner in which slopes and levels may be employed.

Oblique projection of rectilinear forms maintains the angles and lines of the plan and adds verticals. The same or a different scale can be used in drawing the verticals.

Isometric converts the three axes of rectilinear forms to 30-degree slants and verticals. The same scale is used in drawing in any of the three directions.

Perspective is a relatively complex method of constructing a drawing. It most closely resembles camera work or the actual viewing of a completed design. Perspective is invaluable in determining the appearance of a design at normal eye-level.

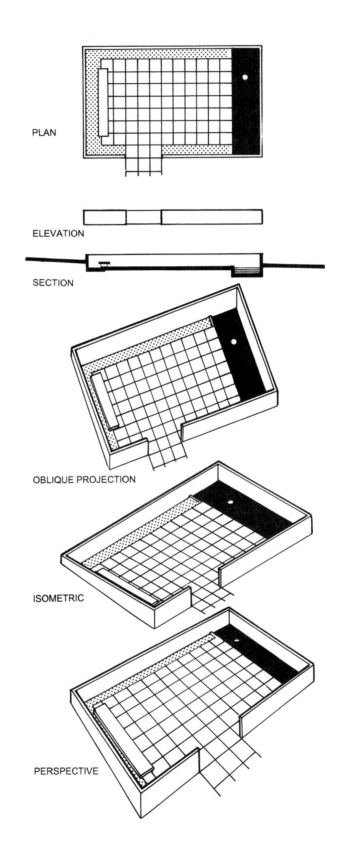

PLAN

ELEVATION

SECTION

OBLIQUE PROJECTION

ISOMETRIC

PERSPECTIVE

each of which pursues a different basic theme for the design solution of a project. In a very short time these groups go through the elementary development of their schemes, and the results are evaluated in a noncompetitive process of consideration. Often the decision is made to combine features of two or more of these studies, drawing a new scheme from the previous investigation. In order for such experiments to be successful, it is necessary that quick sketches and rough models be prepared to provide a basis for the comparison of different alternatives. Usually all systems of visualization are used at appropriate stages: sketching, modelling, producing computer drawings, and photographing the site.

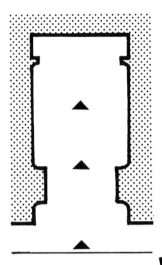

In the development of many large projects, delineators (professionals who specialize in preparing drawings of architectural projects) are employed to provide visualizations of the project and the alternatives under consideration at every stage. Under normal circumstances, architects or landscape architects prepare such drawings. The great advantage of sketches is that they can be quickly prepared—it takes only a few minutes to provide adequate detail for general decisions. Such rapid sketching easily can be inaccurate, showing more the effect wished than what actually would be observed. For this reason, the use of computer graphic systems for accuracy can be combined with rapid sketching. Once existing conditions are established in the computer graphic program, a view can be generated and elements of the design added quickly by the computer or with a crayon.

A useful tool for the visual study of a path through a space or along a street is the consideration of sequential views along the path. Under the rubric of "serial vision," such studies were emphasized in the 1950s in the drawings of Gordon Cullen.[16] To generate a series of perspectives for this purpose, computer aided design (CAD) programs are useful, particularly as a basis for quickly sketching in figures of people, planting, and the shadow areas that might occur (Fig. 6.18). Also a Modelscope attachment may be fitted over a camera's lens or used with a designer's eye to obtain views of a model. The danger of all these methods is that they are usually used merely to record previous decisions in the design process, and not repeated often enough to serve as a true design tool.

It is difficult to imagine a sculptor working without experimenting with the three-dimensional reality of his or her work. Similarly, it is unlikely that a designer of urban spaces can fully study a project without modelling the spaces and the changes that might be made as the design progresses. Unlike the finished model that is prepared for public display, a working model is made in a fashion that can be altered, elements added, and all but the fixed conditions of the site changed to test a sequence of alternatives. Still it must be remembered that the three-dimensional advantage of studying models has certain inherent risks to it. For speed and convenience models usually are prepared as very small-scale replications of the space,

6.18 A series of thumbnail sketches made from drawings describe approaching and entering Paley Park. (See Chapter 2.) Such drawings are usually quick sketches to capture the character of the place, rather than detailed drawings.

and hence they are often viewed so much from above that the more meaningful ground-level views may be neglected. In order to proceed quickly, plant materials and many details are only roughly indicated in models, and therefore a degree of distortion, almost equal to that in quick drawings, is inevitably present. Nevertheless, with imagination the three-dimensional reality can be judged from models.

As design proceeds, visits to the site are imperative. With drawings at hand, a designer can gaze at the existing visual conditions and imagine the forms that might be created. There are risks in this procedure, and it requires extreme self-discipline. Still it offers the flavor of full-scale observation with the sound, scents, and spirit of reality, with the proposed additional features simply fantasized.

Criteria and Evaluations

One useful tool in design is the establishment of criteria. A criterion sets forth a desired result, a measure by which success or failure can be determined. Usually phrased as positive statements, criteria can be ranked according to their relative importance in the project. With numerical values—often percentages—assigned by the team on the basis of this rating of criteria, and individuals rating the alternatives being considered, scores can be calculated for each scheme under view. The scores determined in this manner, consisting of two or three digits, have a seductive suggestion of accuracy and objectivity. However, it should be recognized that they represent only the mathematical treatment of subjective opinions. They may be informative when judiciously reviewed. In the philosophy of science, there is a rule that a valid hypothesis should be falsifiable, that is, it should be capable of being proved untrue. Design criteria should be stated in a manner that permits determination of whether that objective has been achieved. Lists of criteria should be subject to periodic review during the design process. Those that constitute the fundamental mandate on which the project is based are usually immutable, but others may need to be adjusted as ideas emerge.

Many criteria are inevitably subjective. As an example, some subjective criteria for designing spaces are: amenity/comfort, visual interest, activity, clarity and convenience, character distinctiveness, definition of space, views, variety/contrasts, harmony/compatibility, scale, and pattern.[17] Visual quality criteria for spaces might include: fitting within the space's larger setting, expressing of identity, access and orientation, activity support, views, natural elements, visual comfort, and care and maintenance. Still another sort of nonquantifiable criteria for spaces might be: vitality, sense, fit, access, and control.[18] Most such criteria appear to be intuitive only and they are not supported by empirical research. For that reason, the selection of design criteria remains largely subjective, perhaps often opinionated, and always difficult to measure. Among criteria that are more accurately measurable are: environmental adjustment, relationship of massing to buildings, and harmony with existing densities.

Each criterion requires a different kind of evaluation process. For some there may be ways in which tests of models, calculations, comparisons with available analogues, or similar measures can be applied. For others it may be desirable to have the decisions reviewed by peer professionals. But it should be remembered that every professional group is subject to periodic fashions, and that professional standards and enthusiasms are not always shared by the public. If all requirements for the eventual design were included as criteria, the list might quickly become so long that its usefulness would be limited. Concerns that must not be forgotten but are not central to the major design issues can be treated through the use of a check-list. Here, the connections with city services and the many relationships that must be considered may be recorded as insurance against a lapse of memory.

When design decisions are made, frequently the questions are posed as "either/or," choices—either we do one thing or we do another. Choice automatically implies that it is impossible to do both. But if both are reasonably desirable functions, there is a fundamental flaw in choosing between them. Ideally, the design should satisfy both desires, even though the availability of resources, legal restrictions, or other restraints (which must necessarily include the imaginative talents of the designer) may make that solution impossible. One must be careful not to seek the comfort of simple either/or decision-making too quickly, for there is always the haunting suggestion that the choice has been made because of one's personal lack of ingenuity. The danger is simply that a series of either/or selections can improperly eliminate a significant number of needs. Admittedly, such choices may arise for good reasons, but that should be discovered after an honest investigation has been made.

Teamwork

The design of an urban open space is almost always a team effort. No matter which profession takes the leading role, a broad range of expert contributions must be marshalled, and the earlier the better. For that reason this book refers repeatedly to the "design team." Teamwork in decision-making is a difficult process, but only a confirmed egoist would believe that projects can be undertaken and successfully executed by a single mind and its knowledge. Design teams can be assembled, or they can come together naturally without anyone having paid attention to the way in which they can be best utilized. Decisions casually made can quickly alienate members of team and hence reduce the enthusiasm with which they participate in the team's efforts. An erratic system, one that discourages opinions through handling them inconsistently, can quickly put an end to collaborative enthusiasm. Discussions of the techniques of sound group decision-making are common in the literature of business management, and only a modicum of imagination is needed to apply them to the problems of a design team charged with responsibility for an open-space project. The procedures discussed here are planned to encourage participation while maintaining the authority that is inherent in positions of ultimate responsibility. To encourage full participation, major decisions must be preceded by full discussion, with all participants presenting their views.

There are usually two categories of participants in the design of a project. As a core group, the design team has a function that will continue until the project is completed, and it must deal with all aspects of the project. In a peripheral group are the specialists and consultants whose advice will be particularly useful at certain phases of deliberation and whose specialties may relate to broader or narrower categories than those represented in the primary design team. Fundamentally, the design team must include basic roles no matter what the size of the project. The role of management is responsible for ensuring the prompt exchange of information, maintaining a schedule, and providing an efficacious procedure for making decisions. The role of designer-planners is to analyze background information, determine and evaluate different layouts, and propose esthetic solutions. The technical role coordinates engineering information, determines the execution of the project, and monitors the cost of the project. In the design of small projects, these roles are often shared or informally distributed among the participants, but large projects may require that the tasks be subdivided and augmented with additional roles to reflect the more intricate setting in which the work takes place.

A common pitfall is found in the failure to involve consultants early enough. In a typical project of moderate size, consultants might include specialists in subjects as varied as the lighting of fountains, horticultural maintenance, and the behavior of children on playgrounds. A decided majority of consultants complain that they are too often consulted only after project decisions limiting their options have already been made. If they are drawn into the discussions too late, consultants are confronted with what is actually a request to advise on the execution of a largely predetermined decision. Such decisions do not take advantage of the consultants' imaginative powers or their knowledge of innovations. If timely consultation is arranged—and such arrangements are part of the manager's role—the consultants can propose a variety of approaches that will greatly enlarge the options that can be considered by the primary design team. Such exchanges must be initiated by a sensitive and experienced project manager, who can pursue with enthusiasm the task of eliciting the most fruitful input. No consultant performs productively when asked to contribute only after the essential decisions on the subject have been made.

Most studies of teamwork situations have concerned themselves with so-called blue-collar workers, for whom changes in productivity can be determined. Professionals, on the other hand, are usually aiming at qualitative standards rather than quantitative, and their allegiance to a professional group is often as strong as their allegiance to their employers. In open-space projects, members of the design team usually come from similar and related professional backgrounds (such as architecture, landscape architecture, and urban planning), while consultants will come from more divergent fields. Other fields of knowledge may be included in the design team, according to the conditions or focus of the project. Under any circumstances, the design team will be somewhat organized on the basis of seniority and the organization status of the members. Unless the design team has been selected from within a closely-knit unit, it is often wise to anticipate a first meeting by circulating members' resumes, appropriately simplified, in order to inform members of the backgrounds and skills present in the team. However, the influence of these imposed structures may be reduced when certain members of the team are more talented or bumptious than their status would normally indicate or when, as the sole representative of a specific area of expertise, individual authority must be recognized as exceeding official status. Study has indicated that in group activity, members tend to perform at a level significantly lower than that displayed in individual tasks, and this phenomenon increases as the group increases in size (which provides another reason for limiting the size of core groups).[19] A founder-member of an American architectural firm famous for their work as a group described the group as "small enough so that decisions do not have to be made by vote, but only by 'the sense of the meeting,'" and compared such discussions to Quaker meetings.[20] Some studies have noted an "assembly effect" and have described the manner in which one member's ideas can stimulate others.[21]

The composition of design teams depend largely on the talent and experience available within the agency, firm, combinations of firms, or combinations of firms and agencies. Although the variations are many, a few common group structures are:

■ An *acknowledged expert*, acting as chief designer and leader of a number of assistants and specialist consultants.

■ A *capable organizer*, acting as facilitator and manager of the group, although not participating in the design and development activities.

■ *Several members* of roughly equivalent experience and status, none of whom is assigned the role of leader.

■ A *group of promising junior staff members with mentors* assigned within their home departments or firms to provide guidance and reassurance.

Obviously, the size and importance of the project, along with management's attitudes toward staff development, will be external factors that strongly influence the composition of the group. In complex situations, it may be wise to form a small group consisting of representatives of each entity (such as the city planning department, the architectural and landscape architecture firms, and the developer's staff), who are individually and collectively, as the occasion demands, responsible for reporting to and consulting with the entities that they represent.[22]

Brainstorming is a popular procedure for stimulating imaginative thinking by groups. The method was studied and formalized in the 1950s and 1960s. In brainstorming a group verbalizes their ideas without considering details or difficulties. Negative comments are not permitted, and the spirit of the discussion must be one that allows the participants to blurt out their ideas without having prejudged them. The essential rules of brainstorming, as listed by the inventor of the system, are:

1. *Criticism is ruled out.* Adverse judgment of ideas must be withheld until later.
2. *"Free-wheeling" is welcomed.* The wilder the idea, the better—it is easier to tame down than to think up.
3. *Quantity is wanted.* The greater the number of ideas, the more the likelihood of winners.
4. *Combination and improvement are sought.* In addition to contributing ideas of their own, participants should suggest how ideas of others can be turned into better ideas, or how two or more ideas can be joined into still another idea.[23]

Brainstorming may be productive, but only when the procedures are rigidly followed, ideas can flow freely, and group members are made individually accountable.[24] More recent experiments indicate that the effectiveness of groups relates to their members, their context, and the task. While most individuals expect the brainstorming activity to be more productive than solitary individuals in quiet contemplation, actually fewer ideas or items are generated.[25] Having originated in an advertising firm, it is not surprising that brainstorming is more useful for operations that are most easily dealt with by the use of language, rather than the graphic tasks of arranging shapes, fitting them within established areas, and assessing their visual relationships. However, there are ways in which the methods can be varied to adjust to graphic means of expression. Ideas can be presented by sketching them on large sheets of paper; members of the group can sketch individually for five or ten minutes, brainstorming the discussion of their sketches; or the individual can employ a similar technique by rapidly accumulating a series of diagrams, avoiding self-criticism until the time comes for a critical review of the drawings.

Several ideas that have been proposed as standards for brainstorming sessions are also useful for meetings that have other purposes. A guide for negotiation suggests the following measures prior to such sessions:

Define your purpose. Think of what you would like to walk out of the meeting with.
Choose a few participants. The group should normally be large enough to provide a stimulating interchange . . . usually between five and eight people.
Change the environment. Select a time and place distinguishing the session as much as possible from regular discussions. . . .
Design an informal atmosphere. What does it take for you and the others to relax . . . ?
Choose a facilitator. Someone . . . to keep the meeting on track, to make sure that everyone gets a chance to speak, to enforce any ground rules, and to stimulate discussion by asking questions.[26]

One of the most difficult tasks of the facilitator is to generate ideas and items, and to stimulate individual competitiveness without lessening the group participation. An informal atmosphere will deemphasize personal ownership of ideas. You may combine this atmosphere with open scoring, listing the numbers of items generated by individuals.[27] After an individual has come up with several different ideas, it is easier for her or him to give credence to the ideas of others. Because projects at all stages involve the use of maps and drawings, it is usually natural to follow another recommendation: "Seat the participants side by side facing the problem."[28] This arrangement encourages the design team to think of itself as a group confronted with a task, instead of individuals arguing among themselves. For the same reason it is useful to refer to alternative ideas by numbers or descriptive terms, rather than by the names of the participants who initiated them.

In spite of the advantages of group effort, attention should be given to a theory that distinguishes between the tasks appropriate for individual and collective work. It is widely believed that new ideas are most readily attained when a person works alone, while evaluative thinking is more effective in groups.[29] This approach can be advantageously implemented when a group meets to define project limitations and objectives and then disbands to pursue these subjects individually. A subsequent meeting reviews the individual proposals and sets objectives for individual thought before the next group meeting. Where some group members have an area of specialization quite different from the majority of the members, specific tasks for them can be agreed on that are at an equivalent level of specificity. A series of alternations between group and individual work can combine the advantages of solitary idea-generation and group judgment; however, it is wise that the periods of individual work be relatively short in order to avoid individuals' personal attachment to their ideas.

THE LARGER TEAM

Every participant in a project, whether from city or neighborhood councils, the business league, or the design team, has a different notion of what will produce a successful design for an outdoor space and what will indicate the project's success. When "park" is said, each mind holds an image somewhat different from the others, and every adjective used to describe the place that will result has many different interpretations. A municipal project is sometimes proposed in verbal terms, with the actual planning being anticipated after approval has been obtained from voters or officials. If this situation is the case, the debates regarding a project can suffer increasing vagueness. When the project is presented as a concrete proposal, discussions can be more sharply focused. The result may be that those who have not participated in preparing the plans will have concerns that lead to compromise as the team agrees to revise the plans. Under such circumstances there is always a risk that verbal adjustments will be far easier than their physical inclusion in the plans. Similar confusion can occur when city authorities negotiate with a developer. It is therefore wise that all alterations remain tentative until they can be tested graphically.

Each collaborator brings to the design process a clear personal point of view. Since most real-estate developers must necessarily be profit-driven, their point of view will save construction costs and emphasize features that will enhance the profit-making of the buildings they plan. Land-use regulators, representing the city government and the citizens, are concerned with the public safety and maintaining regulations that will continue to control the utilization of land. City planners are vitally interested in the way in which the project may influence patterns of movement and land values throughout that area of the city. A host of city officials consider ways in which changes might endanger or improve the many networks of services, mostly hidden below the ground, upon or around the site. Citizens groups and business interests monitor developments in order to make sure that their interests are protected. The scale of these concerns, their intensity and influence, will vary according to the location, size, and cost of the project. Basically, all such participants exert an understandably conservative influence upon the decision-making. But, at the same time, all are interested in the success of the project. To the design team this means that their confidence must be gained, and they must be convinced that their concerns are understood.

Because many projects take years from conception to execution, changes will certainly be made as time passes. This time period requires that the original design firmly and forcefully state the character that is desired. Subtleties have little chance of surviving the buffeting of years of preparation or use.

ENDNOTES

1. Richard Rogers as quoted in Peter G. Rowe, *Design Thinking* (Cambridge, MA: MIT Press, 1987), 34.

2. A standard reference on microclimatic conditions is Rudolf Geiger, *The Climate Near The Ground* (Cambridge, MA: Harvard University Press, 1957).

3. T.F.W. Embleton, "Sound Propagation in Homogeneous Deciduous and Evergreen Wood," *Journal of the Acoustical Society of America* (August 1963), as cited in M. David Egan, *Architectural Acoustics* (New York: McGraw-Hill Book Company, 1972), 264.

4. David Cook and David Haerbeke, *Trees and Shrubs for Noise Abatement* (Washington, DC: U.S. Forest Service, and University of Nebraska, 1971), cited in Michael Laurie, *An Introduction to Landscape Architecture*, 2nd ed., (New York: Elsevier, 1986), 201.

5. D.E. Aylor and L.E. Marks, "Perception of Noise Transmitted Through Barriers," *Journal of the Acoustical Society of America* (February 1976), as cited in Egan, *Architectural Acoustics*, 263.

6. Ian Masser, *Analytical Models for Urban and Regional Planning* (London: David and Charles, Ltd., 1972), 43.

7. Masser, *Analytical Models,* 19.

8. Masser, *Analytical Models,* 22.

9. Arnold Hauser, *The Social History of Art. (Renaissance), Vol. 3* (New York: Vintage Books, 1957), 153.

10. William J. Mitchell, "Switching on the Seven Lamps," in Henry Sanoff and Sidney Cohn, eds., *EDRA-1* (Chapel Hill, NC: University of North Carolina, 1970), as discussed in Peter G. Rowe, *Design Thinking* (Cambridge, MA: MIT Press, 1987), 111.

11. Alan Colquhoun, "Typology and Design Method," *Perspecta 12*: 71–74, quoted in Rowe, *Design Thinking,* 111.

12. Data cited in Calvin W. Taylor, "A Tentative Description of the Creative Individual," in Sidney J. Parnes and Harold F. Harding, *A Source Book for Creative Thinking* (New York: Charles Scribners Sons, 1962), 174.

13. William Ian Beardmore Beveridge, *The Art of Scientific Investigation,* 3rd ed., (New York: Vintage Books, 1957), 43–46.

14. Geoffrey Broadbent, *Design in Architecture: Architecture and the Human Sciences* (London: John Wiley & Sons, 1973), 272–298.

15. Credits: Sasaki, Dawson, DeMay Associates, landscape architects.

16. Gordon Cullen, *Townscape* (New York: Reinhold Publishing Corporation, 1962), 17–20.

17. Hamid Shirvani, *The Urban Design Process* (New York: Van Nostrand Reinhold, 1985), 121–22.

18. Shirvani, *Urban Design Process,* 122–23.

19. Mel E. Schnake, "Equity in Effort: The 'Sucker Effect' in Co-acting Groups," *Journal of Management* (1991): 41–42.

20. Sarah Harkness in *Architectural Review,* May 1957, as cited in Michael Middleton, *Group Practice in Design* (New York: G. Braziller, 1969), 274.

21. Broadbent, *Design in Architecture,* 357.

22. Paul B. Paulus and Mary T. Dzindolet, "Social Influence Processes in Group Brainstorming," *Journal of Personality and Social Psychology* (January 1993): 575–586.

23. Alex F. Osborn, *Applied Imagination, Principles, and Procedures of Creative Thinking* (New York: Charles Scribners Sons, 1953), 156.

24. Paulus and Dzindolet, "Social Influence Processes," 1.

25. Paul B. Paulus and J.E. Garcia, "The Dynamics of Groups and Organizations," in R.M. Baron and W.G. Graziano, eds., *Social Psychology.* (Fort Worth, TX: Holt, Rinehart and Winston, 1991), 483.

26. Roger Fisher and William Ury, *Getting to YES* (Boston: Houghton Mifflin Company, 1981), 63.

27. Paulus and Dzindolet, "Dynamics of Groups," 578 and Paul B. Paulus, Mary T. Dzindolet, George Poletes, and L. Mabel Camacho, "Perception of Performance in Group Brainstorming: The Illusion of Group Productivity," *Journal of Personality and Social Psychology* (February 1993): 78–89.

28. Fisher and Ury, *Getting to YES*, 64.

29. Michael Middleton, as quoted in Broadbent, *Design in Architecture*, 359.

7

FINANCING—PAYING FOR SPACES AND PLACES

Real estate market, value is created, intervention as a benefit, economics and identity; open space and economic development, goals and economic decisions, economic development organizations; financial basics, funds and grants, donor contributions, federal and state funds, commercial funds, self-funding mechanisms, direct city funds, unexpected revenues, tax abatement, tax increment financing, other methods, public-private participation, special district designation, selecting a financing alternative, funding techniques, city plans, spaces, and timing, plans and budgets, incremental projects, development organizations and teams, design review committees, public-private negotiation, citizen participation balancing interests and equity; economics and esthetics.

THE REAL ESTATE MARKET

In addition to esthetic, physical, social, and psychological reasons, there are a number of financial reasons for promoting improved spaces. By tying spatial improvements to a city's economic future through development programs, neighborhood improvements, and city booster efforts, changes in spaces can help:

    1. create new jobs;

    2. stabilize business cycles and unstable economies;

    3. increase wages through the competition of new employers;

4. hold down increases in city and county tax rates;

5. promote the concept, if desired that "growth is good for the business community;"

6. strengthen the perception of overall city improvement;

7. increase retail sales;

8. increase tourism;

9. increase tax revenues;

10. create higher property values for owners;

11. increase loan business for local banks

Value Is Created

More than 80 percent of all American buildings are the result of investment decisions to build.[1] Therefore, most buildings require an ultimate sale or a reasonable rental income if their developers are to profit. Since so many decisions in real estate are based on return on investment, a primary motive in caring about spaces and places may be the creation of value.[2] Value is a market concept that develops from the interaction of supply and demand. When willing buyers and sellers freely deal in competition with one another, they raise value. Lower supply and higher demand also creates value. In these settings, high occupancies may generate even higher rents and building values if they can be made even desirable by improving their immediate surroundings. To some extent, buildings with low occupancies and low demand can be stimulated by spatial improvement plans.[3] Therefore, value can be improved in either city situation. Buildings that have well landscaped surroundings have higher demand, therefore higher value. If the spaces outside a building make that property attractive, offers may significantly increase. In this way, economics forms an important basis for the spatial conditions in cities of the twentieth and twenty-first centuries. The economic setting of a project embraces the urban design spaces that are considered a part of the buildings, whether they are actually a part of that property or publicly owned. A plaza may act as a setting for the perception of a building, a stage set that will capture tenants or buyers for a very extended period of time. Without a special open space or setting, a project's drawing power may diminish as the building ages. Lifecycle cost averaging is a concept currently employed to explain this phenomenon. As a foreground, the open space may combat or mask the aging process. If the foreground should age and remain attractive, it may stimulate the desirability of the background building.

By contrast to the longer-term advantages provided by improved open spaces, architectural fashions become a component that increase the rapid sale and rent of buildings and help achieve short-term sales goals. New buildings must look new and stylish, and older structures must appear to be in excellent, sparkling condition.[4] When developers enhance the facades of older buildings, the update captures tenants and buyers.[5] Unfor-

7.1 Behind the fence and gate along the sidewalk of Market Street, Philadelphia, the fountain in the entrance courtyard of an office building is the principal visual enhancement of the project.

tunately, this same attitude also speeds obsolescence. If fashion prevails in leasing decisions, new buildings will continually draw tenants from older buildings. This observation is reinforced by data indicating that almost all new multitenant office buildings have the majority of their initial tenants relocating from other buildings in the same neighborhood.[6]

Intervention as a Benefit

Not only are the esthetic experiences available in urban or suburban settings important for day-to-day well-being, but these places promote the feeling that a very special set of city administrators are doing things right. People are proud of their places. And in their appearance the places may progress from current fashion to timelessness. It has been shown that brokers, leasing agents, and property managers can more easily keep tenants in those buildings that have plazas and places relating to them.[7] The ongoing processes involved in managing and marketing the building to prospective tenants, and releasing and remarketing it, depend on many factors for success (Fig. 7.1). Additionally, governmental agencies are critically important in the process of stimulating real-estate investment success. Their programs and policies can work in favor of building owners by providing the needed financial support, design guidelines, and a city-wide plan by which spaces and places are to be constructed, maintained, and coordinated with those in other parts of the city.

In some cities land and buildings that are contiguous to public places have been credited with increases in property values as great as 50 percent.[8] Some buildings are planned and sited to take maximum advantage of an established plaza that has no need for additional design improvements. Their value is increased by location alone. In this way, planners and city governments can produce a web of open spaces, including the improvement of open spaces that already exist, and allowing buildings of average quality to realize value. Rents can be raised after the open-space site construction.

The attraction of new buildings and their syphoning of tenants from older buildings may be slowed or stymied by the quality of an adjacent open space. At the same time, mature trees and shrubs and the comfortable familiarity of an older space can stabilize city neighborhoods. The buildings around Rittenhouse Square, a three-hundred-year-old open space in Philadelphia, are a good example. Because the square is a well-maintained landmark, the buildings facing it are repeatedly renovated, remodeled, and rebuilt to meet changing tenant requirements. Many other examples, including Rockefeller Center in New York, attest to this phenomenon.

There are multiple goals, both individual and shared, that tend to view improved spaces and places as an important economic focus of activity. From a city planner's perspective, the spaces between buildings are a vital part of the entire urban fabric, being one of the components that make the city as a whole a more desirable place, more liveable, and characterized by higher property values. Also, there are reasons for diverse groups and special interests to consider seriously the economic advantages of creating spaces and places or of improving the spaces that already exist between buildings. Some may wish merely to solve simple problems, such as improving the unkempt eyesores between low- and moderate-income housing units. Once those spaces are enhanced, the housing values can stabilize or increase.

Economics and Identity

The media generate mass cultural values. Market analyses on which developers' decisions are based are valid only if one is willing to assume the accuracy of the demographic information, the research designs, and the assumptions on which the studies are founded. Usually uniform buildings and sites are developed, based on the cultural values and assumptions that they will be used by people who have common characteristics, needs, and tastes.[9] The research design may never be disclosed and it may never become apparent, and the demographic data may be flawed. But common beliefs become the basis for decisions. In this view, people become homogenized with an intense desire to be the same, not to be different. This pervasive conformity produces a very predictable pattern of buildings. The spaces between them may be very uniform also. Everywhere begins to look the same, and people begin to accept, even admire, the sameness. By contrast, when there are striking visual spatial differences, an urban district establishes its identity. Tall buildings and unexpected or enhanced spaces clearly denote a business center, and each office building gains leasing success, visibility, and identity by being located in the vicinity of buildings of similar function, just as apartment buildings gain advantages by their

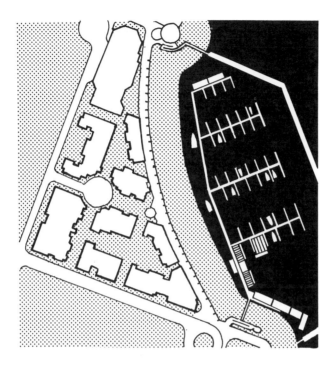

7.2 Riverplace, on the Willamette River, was developed by the Portland, Oregon, Development Commission in partnership with developers. The city severely restricted the building heights allowed in this mixed-use "urban resort" in order that the buildings not block views from the downtown area. The commission encouraged middle-income units by a surcharge on the amount by which the sales prices of units exceeded a fixed level, so that when prices rose, the subsidy decreased.

location in residential districts. Within such single-use areas, or within areas with uniform individual buildings, achieving identity seems easily accomplished by applying facade features rather than designing for interior and exterior spatial experiences or other qualitative characteristics. With the careful planning and patterning of spaces and places, improving urban identity can be achieved much more easily—in spite of these regular building facade patterns produced by mass social and cultural values.[10] Planning for building design excellence is uncontrollable, but planning for the spaces between those buildings can stimulate the economy of a city.[11]

If the project is a full-service urban neighborhood in a low-rise resort waterfront promenade setting, people may be able to walk to work, and new hotels may be built to attract corporate travelers due to the excellence of the promenade's design. Riverplace in Portland, Oregon (Fig. 7.2), and Harborplace in Baltimore, Maryland, are two examples. In those projects, the pedestrian promenades and spaces along the waters' edge are the frameworks for economically successful settings connecting to Marriott, Four Seasons, and other hotels. Docks for yachts can generate additional city revenues from their sales taxes, provide jobs, support restaurants and paid parking, and provide profitable transit stops and new destinations for taxicab patrons. Housing and jobs for low- and moderate-income residents can be incorporated into such settings easily, providing benefits to all income groups. More importantly and realistically, the activities by which the city government secures investors' participation in improving the more fashionable parts of the city may release funds that can be used on projects in the shabbier parts and may even generate tax revenues that can contribute to that purpose. In the hands of adroit politicians with sincere interests in the community's welfare, the pleasures of the well-to-do can be made advantageous to those who have greater need and provide more votes.

OPEN SPACE AND ECONOMIC DEVELOPMENT

According to some authors, political pressures on City Hall grow over time, pushing its occupants to discover additional ways, direct and indirect, to increase the city tax base and accommodate the trend toward rising expectations on the part of the public. Demands for new growth are satisfied by trying to attract the next industrial firm or shopping center, or by stimulating existing companies to grow new jobs and to generate additional tax revenues. All of these activities are grouped under the rubric "economic development."[12]

> Union leaders and business men, wealthy property owners, and minority advocates, if able to agree on little else, can agree on the need for economic growth. Like politics, economic development makes strange bedfellows.[13]

Goals and Economic Decisions

Social factors, issues of community needs, and residents' desires are other forces that demand better designed spaces. For the last few decades, there has been great interest in matching physical forms with social need. These matters and the concerns of economic development usually may be thought of separately, but to those in City Hall they are intimately related. Some believe that the most important challenge facing city administrators is economic development and the creation of jobs, new revenues, and fiscal soundness (Fig. 7.3).[14]

> State and local government officials offer two primary rationales for offering economic development policies. First, they point to the importance of encouraging investment within their communities. Relying solely on private sources of finance would result in an undersupply of capital in these jurisdictions. The profusion of public financing assistance makes possible investment that otherwise would not have occurred. Second, governmental officials argue that financing assistance, and economic development policy more generally, is necessary to forestall other jurisdictions' attempts to lure away their economic base. A jurisdiction that fails to make use of financing incentives will be at a competitive disadvantage relative to more aggressive jurisdictions.[15]

City officials are inevitably placed in the dichotomous roles of enticing, assisting, and collaborating with real estate investors at the same time that they are responsible for regulating their activities and protecting the interests of the community. Adequately and responsibly considering the poverty of some city residents is a constant concern, but a major source of funds for improvements and economic development is long-term and new investors. Considering lower-income neighborhoods and properly funding their residents' needs is not easy. The feat of balancing the two sides of their role requires that the city's planners and other officials employ ingenuity in order to regulate without alienating. If a prospective developer is suspected

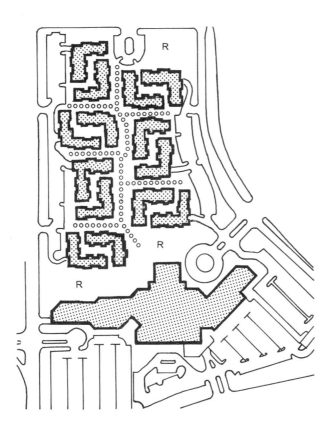

7.3 Although each project contained within the Edinborough complex in Edina, Minnesota, (offices at lower left and right, condominiums in the upper area, seniors' apartments in the bottom center, and indoor park) were separately financed with city assistance, at the same time, each of the developers owned a percentage of the other projects, creating a joint concern about the success of the entire development. Lines of circles are walkways.

7.4 In Boston, the subway exit leads into an open sitting space surrounded by shops. Paving patterns form circles about the subway exit. Coordinating public transportation, open spaces, and retail-office buildings can stimulate vitality and, perhaps, assist in maintaining a stable downtown economy. (Photo by David K. May)

of land banking (that is, of buying and holding a site for future development) a site that is seen as pivotal if a city's future development is to match its expressed objectives, direct negotiation for a public–private partnership may be suggested. A planned multiuse project on suburban land may not be popular with some higher-income groups. As a result, the provision of

7.5 Vigorous promotional activity made the Atlantic City shown in this 1970s photo into a famous recreational center with its many miles of boardwalk. Its revitalization has been stimulated by changes in state laws that allowed gaming. The wooden boardwalk remains the principal unifying spatial element and the major tourist attraction above the beach and the ocean. (Courtesy of Greater Atlantic City Convention and Visitors Bureau)

special open spaces might be encouraged by extensive negotiations to secure development entitlements, negotiated contributions to transportation and infrastructure improvements, tree-saving programs, and recreational features for residents and office workers (Fig. 7.4). If a site is currently zoned for large-lot single-family development, rezoning might be suggested to encourage a developer to help the city achieve its goals. Incentive zoning, or rezoning property to higher densities or more profitable uses, can unleash profits for a developer to use for on- and off-site transportation improvements. Roadways can be widened and landscaped, additional trees planted, and existing trees protected by longer and more expensive alignments of the roads. A sports center with a swimming pool and outdoor basketball, tennis, and volleyball courts can be constructed; day-care centers and tot lots can be built on sites adjacent to existing residential neighborhoods; jogging trails can snake through the development; and building entrances that are more highly pedestrian-oriented may be considered as possible additions to the project.[16]

Economic Development Organizations

Between 15,000 and 18,000 organizations in the United States promote the economic development of cities. These organizations range in size from Chambers of Commerce with no paid staff or budgets to multimillion dollar development corporations (Fig. 7.5). Interest in promoting economic development is very high, and expenditures for that purpose in the United States are estimated to be over $10 billion per year with another $4 billion per year added by federal grants for local economic development. As a standard device to promote urban policies, the federal government gives money to cities to implement national policies and programs. Some of these grants, aid packages, and earmarked funds have been used for shaping urban form. Federal funds have been greater than all local planning funds lumped together.[17] Some cities provide additional direct expenditures for community industrial parks and shell buildings. Other cities provide property tax and occasional sales tax abatements to promote places. States offer tax abatements, individual tax credits, concessions on corporate income tax rates, and loan and mortgage guarantees.[18] These devices can be selected to promote, construct, and control the spaces between buildings.

> We [Logan and Molotch] identify people and organizations with interest in places and how those interests affect use and exchange values. We emphasize the ongoing effort of place entrepreneurs to increase local rents by attracting investment to their sites, regardless of the effects this may have on urban residents. We argue that these strivings for exchange value create a competition among place entrepreneurs to meet the preferences of capital investors. This is our way of showing how local actors link parochial settings with cosmopolitan interests, making places safe for development. It is a system, we indicate, that stratifies places according to the ease with which they can attract capital—a stratification that then alters the life changes of local individuals and groups.[19]

Economic development organizations can operate with a broad or narrow focus to their projects. At times, small businesses can be targeted using relatively low expenditures for open space improvements. Benefits result from the enhanced ability of boosters to market the areas surrounding the places that have been constructed. Certainly, the parcels contiguous to those places rise in value from the investment.[20] The entire neighborhood surrounding the site gains a visual anchor and reference point that adds value to many buildings farther from the site.[21] The Central West End Area in St. Louis contains a fountain plaza that serves as a focal point for the many closed and gated private streets that lead to the large houses of that neighborhood (Fig. 7.6). Businesses such as restaurants, bars, and boutiques may have benefitted from the visitors who are drawn to activity at the plaza. In residential areas near the Central West End, as in other cities, it has been found that the buildings decrease in value according to their distance from the open space.[22]

FINANCIAL BASICS

The primary objective of businesses is to make money, as much money as possible, and those engaged in real-estate development are not exceptions to this desire. If means are found by which a developer can obtain money from a city, profits are more certain. City funds can be transferred in many ways. An outright payment may be possible through direct transfer of funds, municipal bond issues, or loans negotiated with a bank. Equivalents are gifts of land, special roads, or the extension of utilities to the building

7.6 In the 1960s, Maryland Plaza, a street in the Central West End area of St. Louis, was modified as a method of urban redevelopment. The fountain was added, relating the prosperous residential enclave, with its many private streets, to the plaza. As a result, new businesses located on the street and the residents on the neighboring streets benefitted from these improvements. (Photo by Donald C. Royse)

site. Another gift involves the city's giving certain governmental prerogatives to the developer. This incentive is most commonly done through the establishment of an authority that is able to wheel and deal in the manner of businesses and, at times, exercise the power of eminent domain, by which a property owner can legally be forced to sell his land at a low price for the benefit of the developer. The fact that these incentives are provided through a pseudo-governmental agency lends an air of validity to the maneuver.

Instead of giving developers money or its equivalent, the city can exempt the project from normal requirements that are imposed on other businesses. Tax-exemptions are the most common kind of exception granted, and there are many variations by which projects can be gradually phased into full status as a dues-paying participant in the community. Some of these incentives and exceptions have been recently devised under various federal and state acts.

The urban renewal period of 1954 to 1972 was a time when many central business districts and the crumbling areas around them were cleared of deteriorating structures, making sites available below market rates for desired types of projects. Due to the lower purchase prices, more open space improvements were possible and sometimes exploited. At that time, many buildings and plazas were constructed.[23] Urban renewal became synonymous with downtown improvements and new highrise buildings. Low land prices stimulated building construction in many American downtowns and as the lower priced land parcels were sold, many developers purchased deteriorating buildings in the center and edges of downtowns to build office buildings to suit specific tenants or to meet projected demands for office space. High density, highrise suburban office centers became fashionable in the 1960s, 1970s and 1980s, and clusters of office and retail buildings were constructed as self-contained islands within housing subdivisions. In these areas, there were usually larger building sites that permitted parking areas on grade, trees, shrubs, and on-site landscaping. In each situation since the 1950s, new developments and open space projects were tenant-driven due to the need to have lease commitments as a condition for construction and permanent lending. There have been several changes in real estate financing since the enactment of the Tax Reform Act of 1986. Four of the most significant changes were: (1) a reduction in the maximum tax rate for individuals, which means that investors in real estate have their profits taxed at a lower rate so that there are fewer incentives to seek tax advantages from investing in real estate; (2) the treatment of capital gains on investments as ordinary income, meaning that a higher tax must be paid on real-estate profits; (3) the limitation of passive losses, which means that real estate losses are not as advantageous to many investors; and (4) the lengthening of the periods for depreciation schedules, which means that buildings can be depreciated over a longer time period, thus retarding investment interest in real estate. All four items have had a dampening effect on real estate investments, leading to fewer speculative building projects.[24]

Visually pleasing spaces can provide increases in land values around a site, with many of the land parcels and buildings becoming more valuable.[25] Rents, real-estate prices, and the city's tax revenues may thus be increased. If higher occupancies are achieved in an office building, new jobs may be created. Since a typical economic rule of thumb figures fifty to two hundred jobs for every 20,000+ square feet of additional office space leased, that floor area could mean a significant increase of building population, requiring housing and services and paying taxes. If a program to improve open spaces is successful, revenues from sales taxes and ad valorem taxes would significantly increase. This increase is the rosiest forecast. More pessimistic calculations based on the same relationships could arrive at a zero population increase. (The lowest rate of hirings per acre being filled by residents of the city through a "trickle-up" principle that could change with a variation of the birth rate.)

When large amounts of public moneys are invested in a project, cities often must continue pouring money in order to keep it afloat. For example, ten years after the rapid transit system of the San Francisco area (BART) opened, it still required subsidies.[26]

Funds and Grants

Grants and donations are another source of finances for the improvement of spaces and places. In New Haven, the mayor created a task force comprised of forty-two influential residents. The area with which they dealt, sixteen acres known as New Haven's Green was first laid out in 1638, then renovated in 1910 by Cass Gilbert and Frederick Law Olmsted, a

7.7 Now a restoration project, this expansive open space was part of the original colonial plan for New Haven. Funding was secured from federal, state, and local governments as well as from private sources, including historical societies and business corporations. In the New England tradition, the old town centered on an open space upon which all the residents of the houses around the green could let their cows graze. (Photo by Alan M. Gordon)

leading architect and landscape architect respectively (Fig. 7.7). Much of the Green had deteriorated by the 1980s. The task force received a $58,000 planning grant from the New Haven Foundation. By 1986, the task force was transformed into a nonprofit foundation charged with raising $5 million. Although New Haven was at that time the sixth poorest city in the United States, more than fifty major firms contributed $1 million to restore the Green and create the endowment fund. The foundation approached the Connecticut General Assembly for $1.5 million for the Green, which was made available through existing entitlement grants, two special bonding appropriations, and a matching grant from the state department of transportation. These sources were used to obtain $934,000 in federal funds for public transit improvements (such as bus waiting shelters, and seating). By 1990, $3.1 million (63 percent) of the cost of the project came from the local, state, and federal governments, $1 million (20 percent) from corporations and businesses, $425,000 (9 percent) from private individuals, and $375,000 (8 percent) from charitable foundations. The income generated by the permanent endowment fund (about $500,000 per year) was intended for future maintenance expenses. Now that the project is completed, New Haven's Green is used by more than a million people each year.[27]

Donor Contributions

Having a wealthy donor contribute to the construction of a special space or place within a city is an obvious method of financing. Some cities have had a series of contributors fund the construction of spaces, intending them as memorials rightfully to be associated with the family name or dedicated to an event. Local organizations have often collected funds for the erection of veterans' memorials or monuments to prominent local citizens. Sometimes, the contributors are benefactors who stand back and let the city design and build the project. Others may wish to have a hand in the spatial design. Among this type of contributor are developers who wish to enhance their projects. For example, The Trammell Crow Company sought spatial enhancements by having its downtown Dallas high-rise office building (Trammell Crow Center) project design team give their attention to benches, level changes, special outdoor sculptures, and paving surfaces. A downtown open space was provided, which benefits pedestrians as well as tenants. Even though developers do not have to increase their project costs with the addition of spatial improvements, they do so for a combination of reasons: to protect the property from the construction of a potentially undesirable building nearby, for the public good, and to enhance potential investment returns.

Not all observers have views that are so optimistic about the use of financial incentives to encourage economic development. A developer's independent actions may be viewed as a donor contribution in many situations. In the opinion of one: "There is scant proof that economic incentives have real impacts on development and whether program benefits justify program costs."[28] City resources may be better directed to other needs. Many boosters are amazed to discover that a corporation that is considering relocation may attach little importance to some of the financial advantages offered and may be more concerned about the city's educational or park systems, which could make it possible to obtain and maintain specialist personnel in management and research.

Federal and State Funds

Through the decades, federal and state finance mechanisms have contributed to the creation of many special places, usually with the requirement that there be additional commitments obtained from city governments. In 1973, three years before the project opened, developers first became involved in the Faneuil Hall Marketplace, a center in Boston that offers shopping, eating and drinking, entertainment, and socialization. At that time, urban revitalization was usually financed from local funds and federal funds for Urban Development Action Grants (UDAGs), Community Development Block Grants (CDBGs), and grants for historic preservation. In this way, a potpourri of incentives were used. Later on, when the Tax Reform Act of 1986 was enacted, the tax-exempt status of such projects was restricted to local bond issues that assisted private business and "established per-state limits on tax-exempt borrowing."[29] In contrast to the Faneuil Hall Marketplace, when Underground Atlanta reopened in 1989, the city contributed $122 million (85 percent) of the $143 million total cost of the project. These funds came from an $85 million revenue bond issued by the Downtown Development Authority, $21 million from a mixture of sales tax and CDBG funds, $10 million from UDAG money, and $6 million from the Fulton County Building Authority. The remaining $21 million came from developer's private financing.[30]

Federal and state grants relate to a variety of proposals that are successfully presented to Congress and other legislative bodies. In future years the particular purposes for which grants are available (such as parks, low-income housing, and infrastructure) may change or the qualifications may be altered. Departments and agencies of different levels of government may be expected to continue to provide grants, also. Since most projects for the improvement of urban spaces continue through many years of planning and execution, federal and state grants are committed at the time of project approval and made available over a reasonable time period, even when subsequent laws may alter the requirements or eliminate the program entirely.

With the exception of situations where spatial plans are made in a single willful act, making and improving open spaces in cities relies on the economics of project finance combined with local laws affecting land-use controls. Funds and laws can be coordinated toward this end. It is difficult to decide how best to implement spatial improvements, but the use of many legal mechanisms has little, if any, direct costs to a city.[31] Cities can rely on the patterns and specific development of open spaces required by their land use laws. For example, zoning can control the design of the front, side, and rear yards of buildings. This approach to the issue may be too slow in some situations. Attacking change solely through financial techniques, devices, or tricks may be most effective when specific sites are wanted. Sometimes a city can move faster through an economic approach rather than through design controls. In order to avert possible litigation, many cities elect to support their economic approaches with a new umbrella of legal criteria, so that any developer who qualifies can obtain similar financial considerations from the city.

Commercial Funds

Short-term financing for many city open space projects is usually provided by commercial banks. Long-term financing or permanent financing may be obtained from other sources. Some of these sources are Real Estate Investment Trusts (REITS), insurance companies, pension funds, and similar institutions. An REIT pays no corporate income tax, but must meet a series of requirements. It must have more than one hundred stockholders, and the five largest stockholders together must own no more than 50 percent of the stock. The REIT invests the major share of its funds in real estate, and it must distribute at least 90 percent of its profits to its stockholders at the end of each fiscal year.[32] A variation of the REIT is the Real Estate Mortgage Investment Conduit (REMIC) authorized under the 1986 Tax Reform Act. It issues a variety of securities that are secured by mortgages.

Self-funding Mechanisms

Still another method of financing for creating urban identity and the improvement of spaces is a self-funding mechanism. For example, the parking fees for a city-owned lot might generate enough funds to pay for the landscape materials and the rest of a project's costs. As soon as project costs are amortized, the parking revenues can be used for other spatial projects. In another example, admission fees were used to finance a special entrance plaza at the San Diego Zoo. The plaza is one of a series of improvements that have helped maintain the zoo's position as one of the finest and most lauded in the United States for almost a century.

Fort Wayne, Indiana, hired an economic consultant to perform feasibility studies of water parks, ice arenas, and golf courses, and subsequently the city added a four-person marketing division to its parks department. The parks department of Aurora, Colorado, in recent years has earned about $1 million a year in revenues from children's day care programs in their parks. The Department of Housing and Urban Development (HUD) funded sports programs in Aurora's housing projects at $2.4 million. Costs for some types of open spaces, such as farmers' markets and sports facilities, may be balanced by user fees. In 1987, New York City arranged to lease many of the poorly maintained tennis courts in its parks to commercial operators, who would resurface the courts and return them to the city after ten years of commercial operation.[33]

One imaginative method used to obtain an existing golf course before it was sold and subdivided for housing was contrived by officials of Schaumburg, Illinois. Issuing bonds would have caused the city government to exceed its debt limit for general obligation bonds. (This kind of bond is repaid with interest from the general city revenues, its working capital.) The purchase of sites in installments was also impossible as a result of legal restrictions that prohibited leasing when it was connected with the condemnation of land for public use. Under state law (the Illinois Debt Reform Act of 1988) a park district or other nonhome-rule governmental entity—a city with limited law-making powers—could pledge alternative revenue sources. The Schaumburg Park District used alternate revenue bonds to purchase the golf course through condemnation.[34]

Direct City Funds

Not all communities, cities, and other political units are in dire straits financially. Many have excess revenues, which may allow them to choose between investments. Over time, the best investment for a community may prove to be the design and construction of open spaces, which offers a chance to gain both tangible and intangible returns in the long run. Public funds that are invested for the short term provide for safety, liquidity, or return. Studies analyzing the best ways to develop an investment policy for a city are rarely made public.[35]

Sometimes initial construction or major improvements to open spaces is funded through a city's annual budget, with a specific amount assigned annually for new construction or added to a fund that is accumulated for use on projects. The term "capital improvements programming" (CIP) describes this method of apportioning funds for streets, open space, and engineering.[36] This method, of course, may be inadequate for large projects or a coordinated series of projects. For these larger ones, it is possible for some city governments to hold elections that allow them to issue bonds. This kind of election is preceded both by a display of the planning that has been done and by informational campaigns through which the planning department, parks department, and citizens groups present the needs and solutions to the voters. (Preliminary planning funds are often provided through the city budget or contributions of citizens' groups.) The method chosen for city funding depends largely on the overall indebtedness of the city government, the public support available, and the scope of the project that is envisioned. City funding has the obvious advantage of involving established groups of participants, who are usually already familiar with procedures through their participation in other social, cultural, and political activities within the city. As explained later in this chapter, city funding may be employed in combination with a variety of other methods, which include assistance from philanthropic foundations, grants from federal and state government agencies, and the participation of developers and investors.

Unexpected Revenues

Parks and recreation departments often must contend for city funds against the needs of the police and fire departments. At times, financing open spaces may be politically difficult in certain cities. Many parks departments are touted as a "valued and not easily substituted cornerstone of local economies."[37] Even though the open space of the park system may attract outside tourists, the large majority of users are local citizens in small cities like Lawrence, Kansas, with its 50,000 to 75,000 residents. For example, in Lawrence, it was found that the design of the parks greatly influenced the purchases of sports equipment in city stores. The average expenditure for a beginning tennis player had been $150 per summer, but after adding a number of tennis courts this figure almost doubled. Passive recreational areas, such as large parks, can stimulate the economy of rural towns when shopping areas, hotels, and restaurants are provided nearby. Vernal, Utah, serves a large number of tourists due to its location midway between Dinosaur and Flaming Gorge National Parks. Park and recreation areas cause profits indicated by a multiplier that estimates the dollars of merchants' profit generated by each dollar invested in improvements. Multipliers can also indicate the changes of tax revenues, such as sales tax, collected by the city. Such multipliers are high in larger metropolitan areas and low in small and rural areas. If San Francisco's investment in the improvement and maintenance of spaces makes every dollar invested produce $2.00 of profit, the return in a small town like Vernal may be only $0.30.[38]

Tax Abatement

One of the most frequently used ways for a city to encourage economic development is tax abatement, a procedure by which the city government reduces or eliminates an investor's payment of ad valorem taxes, sales taxes, or other forms of taxation for specific periods spelled out in the initial agreement. By steadfastly relating tax abatements to planning objectives, the city can encourage investment in areas of the city that advance its planning policy. If a city decides to utilize the device of tax abatement or to form a tax increment finance (TIF) district (which is only permitted under the laws of some states) to pay for a plaza, park, or open space, it may not be necessary for the city to purchase the downtown land needed for the site. By eliminating some of the taxes that normally would be paid by the developer or the building owners, who wish to construct an income-producing building, benefits may accrue to the city at large at no immediate cost. However, it should always be remembered that this form of short-term economic incentive may lead to higher long-term costs. Thus, the long-term patterns of municipal finance may be in conflict with the relatively short terms of elected officials.

Tax abatement can be used by cities to stimulate change in their physical patterns as well as to create jobs and encourage reinvestment by industries and businesses. In order to be evenhanded and to avoid future legal problems, some cities prepare guidelines and criteria for granting tax abatements. Their tax abatement is usually targeted at special districts, or at somewhat arbitrary boundaries within a city's gray area or central business district.

> The Sugar Land [Texas] tax abatement guidelines are flexible in their criteria. Every proposal for tax abatement is considered on its own merits as long as the capital investment by the proposing company meets or exceeds $1 million and jobs are created by the expansion of construction.[39]

VWR Corporation is a medical laboratory supply company that wanted to consolidate its facilities at one location in Sugar Land's business and industrial park area in 1985. In their proposal to the city, VWR asked to construct offices and warehouse buildings at a cost of $1.2 million, with the promise of twenty-four jobs, eight of which would be new. Since the business and industrial park had high vacancy rates at that time, city officials were enthusiastic about VWR's proposal. After the city determined that the proposal complied with tax abatement criteria, the economic development committee of the city negotiated with VWR about actual tax abatement figures. Accordingly, a cumulative abatement of 340 percent was agreed on. Texas allows a fifteen-year term for tax abatement agreements, but VWR chose a rate of 100 percent abatement for the first three years and 40 percent for the fourth year. In return for the granting of the abatement, VWR signed an agreement with Sugar Land to invest over $1 million and provide new jobs. If VWR does not meet these terms, then all abated taxes are due to the city.

> The total abatement offered using the present tax rate of $.048 per $100 of valuation is $17,584. As a consequence of the location of VWR, the city expects to realize annual tax revenues for personal property in the amount of $7,000, and sales tax revenues of $50,000.[40]

7.8 Tax increment financing was used for the festival marketplace, park, and marina. In this example, an ice skating rink forms the winter-time focus of the outdoor spaces. The marketplace building was designed to protect skaters from the winds off Lake Michigan. Racine On The Lake, Racine, Wisconsin.

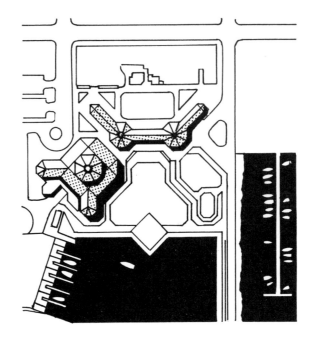

Tax Increment Financing (TIF) Districts

One interesting strategy commences with a city designating a TIF district over a large area. For a limited time, say five years, a prospective developer can be permitted to have reduced tax rates. After five years, the rates could be increased to normal levels. During all of this time, the taxes paid would be placed in a special city fund, which might be earmarked for use only in construction of additional plazas, parks, or other open spaces. As the city or the developers executed these improvements on other sites in the TIF district, funds would be released, and the method would produce a new network of places, raising the environmental quality of the district and the city at large (Fig. 7.8).

Cities institute TIF districts for a number of reasons. Those adopting this method have greater property value increases than others, even after controls for city size, changing population characteristics, property tax millage rates, and other items are considered. It appears that TIFs often are enacted by faster-growing cities in order to fund economic development projects, but it has not been shown that TIFs are a significant stimulus to growth. At present their appropriateness is undetermined.[41]

A locality sets up a TIF district by declaring an area blighted and zoning it for redevelopment. The locality unilaterally freezes the amount of taxes the area pays into the general fund, and the redevelopment agency receives all future tax increments. The redevelopment agency then floats bonds against the increases in tax revenue expected in future years.

Los Angeles has made effective use of TIF, particularly downtown. And in recent years, the city's Community Redevelopment Agency (CRA) has expanded its use into fourteen areas. It's now involved in sixteen projects and operates with an annual budget of $150 million. In fiscal year 1984–1985, the agency expects $55 million in revenue, over 80 percent of it from two high-density commercial sites in the downtown area, Bunker Hill and the Central Business District Redevelopment Project.

"What we've learned in our 30-odd-year history is that only high-density projects bring in high profits," says Ed Helfeld, who was the CRA (Community Redevelopment Authority) administrator until his forced resignation in December. Thus, the agency has used the revenues earned downtown to strengthen the 14 other TIF sites, which bring in only modest increments because they are in depressed residential areas.[42]

Other Methods

Over time, there are broad shifts and major economic changes that lead cities and developers to alternative approaches in financing.[43] A special tax district may be established to fund the construction, and bonds may be issued to finance it. User fees may be the basis for daily operations if maintenance or unusual costs are expected. (Tax increment financing districts were discussed earlier in this chapter.)

Exactions: Exactions—contributions to public facilities—may be required of private developers. Usually, exactions are used for projects such as building sewage treatment plants, widening streets, or other engineering improvements that are the direct results of a developer's project and benefit the city at large. But exactions may be tied to subdivision site approvals to help pay for the design and construction of outdoor spaces.

Impact Fees: Impact fees are payments required to help offset the costs of public facilities, such as engineering improvements. When a building permit is issued, or at the time that the subdivision plat is approved, a developer can be required to pay additional city fees for the development of outdoor spaces.

Enterprise Zones: The enterprise zone is a fairly new concept that can be applied effectively to produce and enhance places and spaces. About thirty states had such zones by the end of 1988, and the 1992 Los Angeles Rodney King riots provided reasons to pass a new federal enterprise zone act. Twenty-five large cities and twenty-five small cities were funded for enterprise zones. Within the specified geographic boundaries of the enterprise zone, a bundle of tax concessions and other incentives are given to win over additional investment by private developers. In most states, property tax abatements, investment tax credits, and sales tax credits are included in the enterprise zone bundle of benefits.[44] Detailed site layout by planning or engineering consultants may be required in enterprise zones as part of the community's planning process.

Public–Private Participation

When private developers are needed to construct a spatial project on publicly-owned land, cautious and complex negotiations are essential. In this instance, cities are forced to become entrepreneurial in order to reduce public outlays.[45] Financial feasibility must be promoted and shown to the developer by clearly linking the important savings provided by the public land contributions. In exchange for the land, the city receives a partnership ownership percentage. Cities can benefit from their investment interest in a public–private project—depending, of course, on the degree of risk. Clearly, a developer will not give up any portion of his or her profits unless it becomes necessary to do so. When city deal makers begin to act like hard-nosed business partners, developers may want to secure a specified portion of a project's cash flow through equity participation with the city, participatory leases, or loan paybacks.[46] The intensity of negotiations and the ability to deal depends largely on the economic climate and on particular market settings.

In preparing to negotiate with developers, methods for communicating public policy objectives should be considered. The long-term goal of constructing open spaces of high-quality design could be the city's principal goal. Unlike the developers, public officials could put money-making at the bottom of their list of goals.

In another strategy, a city participates outright in developers' construction costs for plazas and other spaces connected with a project. Possibly 50 percent of the design and construction costs of the outdoor space might come from a city's general revenues. In larger cities, such a method could be advertised as a system of raising a developer's project rents and occupancy rates in exchange for the city's participation in increasing the developer's tax assessment due to increased building values. Thus, the city government contribution of 50 percent may not be a cost to the taxpayers, but it might provide a net gain in ad valorem tax revenues from the initial occupancy of the buildings.

In order to have a successful public–private partnership, some guidelines have been suggested.[47] The project should contain the kind of activities that could encourage the growth of a positive civic culture, a culture that could encourage citizen participation. Additionally, the project should be related to the long-term employment concerns of the community. The vision conveyed by such spaces should be a realistic and easily accepted image of the community, based on the area's strengths and weaknesses. The public–private partnership should be foreseen as an effective civic organization in which the interests of the developers could mix with the interests of the community. Public–private partnerships should provide a continuity of policy, should adapt to changing circumstances, and should provide a reduction of uncertainty for investors. The most functional form of organization is just as important as developing and maintaining an effective economic development strategy.[48]

Many of these projects by public–private partnerships are very "eye-catching." The most famous seem to be "festival marketplaces." These

7.9 An active downtown area in Seattle has been developed as a festival marketplace using many historic buildings. More often, such enterprises are developed to use derelict structures or pseudo-historic designs. Pioneer Square, Seattle. (Photo by Robert A. Goldsteen)

areas are becoming common social and cultural functions in cities across the country, and can be found in Toledo (Portside), Baltimore (Harborplace), Richmond (6th Street Marketplace), Norfolk (Waterside), Seattle (Pioneer Square) (Fig. 7.9), New York (South Street Seaport), Boston (Quincy Market), Dallas (West End Marketplace), and Los Angeles (Farmers' Market). The Enterprise Corporation develops many of these kinds of markets using a public–private partnership:

> Enterprise typically provides development know-how but requires the city to put up the initial $10 million to $15 million in funding it then lends to Enteprise. Enterprise repays the loan, takes a developer's fee, and, when the project becomes profitable, splits the profits with the city.
>
> "The cities have to see themselves as developers, willing to invest in the resources the city has in order to make possible projects that couldn't otherwise be done," [James] Rouse [Principal of Enterprise] told *Business Week*. . . . Public financing is also needed because festival market places are so expensive to build. Frequently, they need twice the sales of a conventional shopping center to turn a profit . . .
>
> Norfolk is a good example of how the process works. The city had already begun to draw people back to the waterfront along the Elizabeth River. First, the city lured an Omni Hotel to a riverfront site.

Then, to get Waterside going, it lent Enterprise Development $10 million at 11.5 percent interest, using a combination of urban renewal cash, community development block grant funds, and revenue sharing money earmarked for economic development . . .

Norfolk is considered a success. The city is realizing $1.1 million a year in mortgage payments from Enterprise and about $1 million a year in sales tax, and, when the project begins turning a profit, the city and Enterprise will split the funds. Projections show the city's share rising from $100,000 a year in 1988 to more than $800,000 in 1993 and $2.5 million in 1998.[49]

Special District Designations

Municipal design goals for open spaces can be achieved through the use of special district designations. This method selects a specific area for regulatory requirements beyond those applied in other areas that may be similar in land use. In a downtown special district, cities can require more open space amenities to be provided by prospective developers, since their buildings will be so costly anyway. Typically, downtown buildings have larger construction budgets, and they can include the special items demanded by the city with a relatively small percentage of increase in their total costs. For smaller projects and those located in other areas, the cost of paving textures, larger building setbacks, and special street furniture and signs may be exorbitant. For example, some cities, including Portland, Oregon, have downtown zoning ordinances that require at least half of each street-level building facade to be glass with direct vision into the building's interior. To fulfill this goal and make it worthwhile, sidewalks are required to be upgraded, a necessary ingredient for the idea's success. The public purpose is supported by the design and construction of the open spaces in the special district. When profits are potentially higher for developers, such as those within such downtown areas as Portland, stricter regulations may be easily accepted. In many other cases, the design and construction of open spaces and places were required to advance public policy without relying upon private developers or landowners.

Without specific design controls, whether as strong as street closures or as mild as special sidewalk paving, downtown locales—such as New York, Philadelphia, or San Francisco—can become alike and commonplace, like memory chips plugged into a massive computer mother board, with the buildings like chips and the streets and downtown lots providing plug-in slots for buildings.

But such design control schemes are not always successful. The downtown pedestrian streets in Waco, Texas, and Kalamazoo, Michigan, which were begun with great expectations, required high public and private expenditures, yet they failed. As a result, they have been modified and opened to traffic. Planners, architects, city boosters, and many others may dream that the people who work downtown will shop and dine downtown, even if they don't establish any controls. But others believe that without design attention, people will not come downtown or remain there after work. The decades of research that shows how the public behaves when

7.10 Main Street in Grand Junction, Colorado has kiosks, special waste receptacles, benches, large sculptures, and scattered pedestals that hold smaller sculptures. Although vehicular traffic has been allowed, its curved path provides spatial changes for pedestrians and slows traffic.

downtown must be effectively utilized by planners if it is to be useful. Bleak and threatening streetscapes can be avoided or changed by the addition of inviting structures and pedestrian ways. Where the decline of downtown has become entrenched in the people's minds, the change demands much more than a cosmetic treatment of a few shopping and entertainment areas. If the estrangement of downtown and suburbia is to be ended, the beautification process must be considered as part of a total revitalization program.

Capital facilities (streets, utilities, city buildings, and parks) are a responsibility of city government. With the financing and construction of essential services for the general public, cities provide tubes of space as a framework into which individual investors can attach buildings and spaces. At times, as a part of a special district, cities may wish to design and construct a plaza in front of a developer's project. If the site on which that space is to be located is owned by the city, it can determine the design to be constructed. If the site is owned by the building's owner, negotiations may be required to set the design of the space. Collaborations between the city and the owner of the building may be fruitful and, in the long run, save taxpayers' money.

Special districts can also address the problem of vacant downtown stores. It is assumed that beautifying streets in the area and instituting design controls on the existing buildings will make the neighborhood more attractive and the stores more prosperous. Common devices employed for this purpose include closed or partially-closed streets, streets rebuilt with special paving treatments, the introduction of planting boxes, and the installation of trees. In downtown Grand Junction, Colorado, a project of this nature seems to have succeeded (Fig. 7.10) in spite of some empty shops in 1993. Grand Junction has provided planting boxes, trees, street furniture, public art, and sculpture to be scattered throughout its downtown. The spacing of sculpture becomes successful when shoppers are slowed down when walking from store to store. In other cases, such efforts have failed. One suspects that much of the problem with these beautification projects has been caused by the economy and by the operative distinction between businesses and boutiques.

Developers may view a neighborhood as a highly desirable location, but their plans can be too costly without financial incentives. When developers initiate discussions with city authorities, they often begin to bargain. In the past few decades, bargaining for special district designation or advantageous zoning has been a major strategy for many developers.[50]

> [The special district] is an amendment to the text of zoning ordinance creating a new zoning district with regulations that are tailor-made to some particular set of circumstances in a particular area. Special districts are, at least in part, a result of the susceptibility and hostility of neighborhoods to change. Although often an outgrowth or result of neighborhood planning, they generally focus on preserving the status quo.[51]

The use of special districts is very popular in many cities. For example, as of 1990 New York City had thirty-seven separate special districts. Cities are moving away from the single-use district that has been traditional in zoning; that is, an area with only office buildings or only medium- or high-density housing. Cities are now making their zoning three-dimensional. To promote pedestrian traffic in many places, it is required that shops be placed on the ground floors of buildings, especially those buildings that face open spaces. In recent years there have been incentives given to encourage mixed uses, combinations of offices, housing, hotels, and shops in the same buildings or complexes of buildings. Mixed use structures are more common today than is realized, for except for the shops and restaurants in lower floors of these buildings, the other functions have assumed an increasingly uniform appearance.

Suburban special districts are handled differently. They may be designated medical, office, or retail districts. Some are mixed use. All contain one- to three-story buildings or have high-rise office buildings with minor amounts of hard and soft landscaped open space. As the largest single-use land areas in cities, suburban residential districts reflect the public's desire to have a house that is different, but not *that* different. Variation in housing has been based principally on price and the number of features and superficial characteristics of applied facades. Few controls have been enacted to vary the spaces between houses to meet the desires of family groups that are achieving an unprecedented diversification in makeup and aspirations.

City Districts and Economic Concerns: Separate special districts may be created in edge cities or downtown areas to promote different objectives, such as landscape materials, colonnades, covered parking, sitting areas, or fountains. An additional small investment in street furniture and paving patterns may be seen as an effective way to transform a building complex, forced by economies into a bland appearance, into a "landmark" place that might justify higher rents. At The Inn at University Village and Garibaldi Square in Chicago, the developers renovated the streetscape around their buildings in order to outshine the uninteresting facades around them. As a result, the new shops and offices were introduced effectively into the existing low-income housing area and a new retirement-nursing home to create a 7.5 acre island of new, blended facades that have effective transitions to the surroundings.[52]

Planned Unit Development: One form of the suburban special district is the planned unit development (PUD or PD). This suburban zone is a land-use regulatory device intended to promote a three-dimensional system of regulation. Mixed-use projects are usually achieved under the aegis of the PUD. Shops may be built with housing above them, and dwellings may be clustered at a higher density than that usually allowed in a residential district. Prospective developers must present very specific plans about how they will treat the open space that they give in exchange for an allowance to build at greater density. Details are required by planning commissions, who behave as design review bodies. The opportunity to sell part of the land is somewhat frozen once city approvals have been granted for a specific design of the special district. A new owner may not relish investing in townhouses around a lake or providing such amenities as a jogging trail, but the land must be developed in the exact design approved if the density is to be permitted.

The PUD can also encourage or sometimes require the preservation of natural landscape features, such as ponds, streams, or flood plain areas that contain trees and marsh land. The PUD is not very commonly employed because it demands that developers sacrifice business flexibility. In this kind of suburban special district, developers must agree to build projects on PUD-approved land with the same exact uses and building arrangements for which the PUD was originally approved. However, over time, market forces may bring about changes in the desires and intentions of all parties to the project. For instance, the Woodlands in Darien, Illinois, proposed two-story townhouses clustered around cul-de-sacs. The walls of the houses provide the limits of the space; and if the housing designs must be changed to match market conditions, additional city approvals are required from elected officials other than those who gave the initial approval.[53]

Historic Districts: Still another reason for constructing places is the commemoration of historical events and famous people. Designation as a historic site can also be effected by the determination of a historic district. The preservation plan prepared by a city planning agency might indicate officially designated historic structures, sites for which official designation is planned in the future, and proposed plazas, open areas, or parks that support and protect those buildings. The commemoration of the sites could lead to special contributions from interested donors, government funding, or special fundraising efforts. Buildings to be designated as historic sites may be of noteworthy architectural quality, they even may be mundane

7.11 In this historical district, shops and restaurants encircle the town square as in former years. Originally, raised walks protected pedestrians from mud and street debris; now, the streets are filled with cars. Covered sidewalks are not continuous around the square, but offer shade and change of space along much of the perimeter. Old Town, Albuquerque, New Mexico.

buildings that are important because of the events that took place there, or they may typify local activities or population groups. In some communities, they generate high interest and enthusiastic support. Where several blocks of such buildings are in the same area, a historic district can be designated, and this designation affords some protection of the individual spaces between buildings (Fig. 7.11). With this strategy, the spaces between buildings cannot be developed in a manner that destroys the harmony of the designated district.

SELECTING A FINANCING ALTERNATIVE

Preparing a detailed project plan is difficult and time-consuming.[54] There are a number of important items to consider in exploring the economic feasibility of a project to improve or develop an open space. From a regional perspective, decisions about a spatial project should consider its surroundings. One of the most important factors is determining and evaluating its community functions (such as users and social patterns), location (uses surrounding the site), commercial potential, and the likelihood that it will be implemented successfully. The commercial aspects of the project are its revenue-raising potential and its potential to recover the initial costs involved. Three different kinds of studies may be undertaken prior to deciding whether to build a plaza or other open space—market analysis, financial analysis, and cost-benefit assessment.

Three elements must be examined carefully in order to make the market analysis—the project's "product," the total potential market, and the competition. These considerations must realistically include those costs arising from the initiation of the project and its first years of operation. The customary six criteria of lenders are:

> *Term*: When and at what rate will the invested funds and interest be repaid? How does this correspond with the supplier's source of funds and stability? . . .

Risk: What is the primary source of repayment and what is the probability that the invested funds will be repaid from this source? Is there a secondary source of repayment, and what is the probability that the funds will be repaid from that source if the primary source of payment fails to materialize? . . .

Administrative cost: How much time and effort per dollar lent or invested will be required to ensure proper repayment and adequate control? . . .

Return: What is the rate of return to the lender? . . .

Secondary benefits: Will the investment result in the investor receiving additional deposits, new jobs, related business, goodwill in the community, or other tangible/intangible benefits? . . .

Portfolio fit and expertise: Given the policy of the institutions and existing personnel, does the investment fit within the institution's geographic, financial, and professional area of involvement?[55]

If these are the questions that lenders should ask, with minor rephrasing they are the questions that must be asked by the borrowers and cities that would participate in real estate ventures.

After those questions are answered by the project team, an analyst prepares a profit-and-loss statement, cash flow projections, and other evaluations that complete the feasibility study for a project. These materials can be reviewed by independent experts, such as a local economic development advisory committee, the city comptroller, or an accounting firm. It is not easy to attribute profits and losses directly to the development of open spaces. In this preliminary investigation, the economic and social needs of the community must be considered along with the goals and priorities that will govern economic development policy, and the availability of effective leadership and management for this work.[56] Local conditions determine many of the evaluations made in these processes, particularly in the investigation of the various conditions that might arise regarding start-up situations and the reserves needed for contingencies.

Funding Techniques

While a number of private and public funding alternatives were presented earlier in this chapter, governmental funding of open space improvements is more limited and may be received indirectly. Visionary images of the future can be financed or implemented through a variety of methods. Some of those methods involve ways to obtain funds, while others adjust controls and regulations to make investment in a project more attractive. Financing for spaces of any size, such as street districts, tot lots, parks, plazas, public service districts, and historic or other districts should be developed to best suit the characteristics of the specific project. By defining areas, neighborhoods, districts, or sites, cities can place power in the hands of appointed boards that are permitted to issue tax-free bonds, levy property taxes to repay those bonds, and use eminent domain (a legal procedure by which the government may appropriate privately held property for necessary public purposes).[57] Authorities—for example, port or housing authorities—are quasi-governmental organizations that can operate as businesses but have certain governmental privileges. They are especially useful to unify the activities of the many governmental units and administrative agencies that may have different sorts of control over an area. Not only may city and county funds be used, but state and federal funds provide an array of financing possibilities as well. Those methods and techniques to finance directly and indirectly the construction of spaces and places are outlined as follows:

1. Issue bonds (not popular)

2. Direct public funds to finance construction (not popular)

3. Provide subordinated project financing

4. Subsidize loan interest

5. Redirect tax revenues; create special assessment districts

6. Provide direct financing for site preparation (assembling parcels of land, relocating residents, clearing land)

7. Provide density bonuses through zoning ordinances

8. Use the power of eminent domain to assemble parcels

9. Allow transfer of development rights from another site

10. Allow incentives for mass transit stop locations (omit parking requirements in zoning ordinance)

11. Barter assets or swap sites

12. Obtain secured lease-purchase transactions

13. Agree to subordinate ground lease payments to the developer's lender

14. Consider continued city maintenance of project after construction[58]

City Plans, Spaces, and Timing

New or improved spaces and places may be created in cities without public sector expenditures. Regulatory innovations for spaces may be devised to provide incentives for producing them. In some cases, developers may elect to develop spaces at their own cost in order to have the opportunity to gain favor by helping the city further complete its overall plan. In other situations, developers may sense that a plaza will be advantageous for success in leasing office space. They may choose to select their own design team without having municipal participation. In such cases, municipalities may not need to provide tax abatement, condemn property, or otherwise lose tax income from property in order to provide new or improved urban and suburban spaces. In some cities, a comprehensive plan or the designation of a district with special considerations may be all that is needed to stimulate the design and construction of plazas and spaces. Such plans can provide suggestions, cues, and guidelines for investors' actions, and affirm the city's intentions to move in a supportive manner.

Timing is important. Developing new ordinances to control developers' designs may take too long. If a city decides that it needs to stimulate construction and development in a declining neighborhood in the gray area adjacent to the Central Business District, it may choose immediately to condemn land for the public good to provide a plaza, park, or open space. In this case, the outright costs of condemnation (that is, paying a private owner for the land) may begin returning tax revenues to the city much sooner than the time usually required to wait for individual developers to become enraptured with their own special district plans. A year of condemnation time, followed by a design team's planning, design, and construction, could bring public revenues within a three-year period. Millions could come from the reassessment of property values in the surrounding area as a result of the new uses or increased building rents. The city's costs for condemnation and planning might be easily amortized within a five-year period.

The relationship between the spaces of residential streets, sidewalks, and the entrances to houses has changed radically. In most cities there still remain areas in which tree-lined streets—if they were spared the ravages of the Dutch elm disease—are lined with lawns, porches, and bungalows. The streets on which families of moderate income lived usually formed a gridiron, and those for families of higher income might meander through a more scenic area. These evidences of the past are still present, often encouraged by recent gentrification of the neighborhoods. But after World War II the urgent need for additional housing led to new suburban developments, continuing the idea that Lewis Mumford described, referring to earlier American suburbs, as "the suburb . . . as an asylum for the preservation of illusion."[59] Although the primary purpose of such suburban housing was bringing up children, they and their parents were seldom visible as one drove along winding streets. It was assumed that within the houses and in their backyards happy families lived. A few scattered saplings decorated the lawns, and the notion of strolling through the neighborhood was discouraged by the absence of sidewalks.

Recently car-pooling and the popularity of jogging have somewhat increased the visible population of suburban streets. At brief periods in the morning and at dusk we see commuters, joggers, and bikers appear, but many of them may be on their way to a more pleasant outing in a nearby park. The rising prices of land for residential construction promise to cause greater density in suburban developments. With that change there may be a strengthened relationship between houses and life along the street that should unify them.

During the same period the downtown areas underwent the ravages of urban renewal. Areas were cleared of buildings, and the fields of rubble remained until investors could be found to construct buildings on them. Owners of downtown buildings desperately fought to keep business districts alive, despite the attraction of suburban locations for offices and stores. As the downtown population of both workers and shoppers declined, efforts were made to brighten Main Street by barring automobiles

7.12 This developer's unit, limited to one story for elderly buyers, sits on a lot that is 32 feet by 125 feet. A garden-corridor about 10 feet wide leads to the entrance behind the garage. Kitchen, baths, and storage are dotted. (Santa Fe Courtyards, Santa Fe, NM; Phoenix Group)

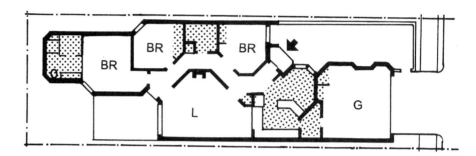

and creating an attractive mall out of the grubby canyon it had once been. Many of these projects failed—often because they were too timid to counteract the powerful forces of suburban growth. Some have succeeded, at least so far.

According to *Builder* magazine, the voice of the National Association of Home Builders, only about 7 percent of families in the United States today are the type on which suburban developments were based—married couples with children, the wife busy at home. As a result of such demographic changes, increased attention has been given to the construction of houses suited to single parents and families in which both parents are employed outside the home, or to sharing adults; houses that are nearer to areas of employment and require less maintenance by the owners. This demand has brought about attempts to offer many of the amenities of subdivision housing with space-saving development of the sites. In order to achieve higher densities, the traditional "front lawn" has often been partially or entirely eliminated. The lot area absorbed in the required front and side setbacks, which often is as much as 40 percent of the lot area in a modest suburban house, can be significantly decreased. By making each dwelling unit narrower and deeper, further economies in land costs can be accomplished. The usual lot in a suburban development once had to be wide enough to accommodate garage doors, an entrance door, and the windows of at least one room, but many recent residential developments have been much narrower.

One method of building narrower houses involves a front facade that is only the dimension of a garage door plus an entrance opening and is placed close to the sidewalk's edge. Second-story bedrooms can have windows at the front and rear, but at the ground level the rooms of the house are located behind the garage. A narrow passageway, enclosed or unroofed, extends from the front property line, past the garage, to an entrance more than twenty feet back (Fig. 7.12). These narrow corridors afford little more space than that required for walking to the entrance, and a few plants in containers can be placed in them. If two or more units are combined the space may be somewhat larger, but still drastically restricted.[60] A San Diego project, winner of an award from the National Association of Home Builders, proposes units placed over subterranean parking to achieve a density of 43 dwelling units per acre. Visitors reach the units through unroofed passageways, termed "alleys" by the developers, that are fifteen feet wide and as long as 200 feet.[61] As efforts continue to

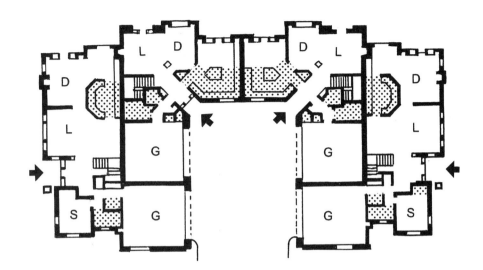

7.13 In this developer's design, four units are clustered around a courtyard that is principally occupied by paving, four garage doors, and entrances for two of the units. Usually a small amount of courtyard planting is situated at the base of walls, and two entrances are outside the courtyard. S indicates study or guest room. (Corte Villa, Tustin, CA; Shleppey Hezmalhalch Associates, Inc.)

accomplish higher densities, such narrow entries will require the development of techniques for designing pleasant passageways to the units.

Another popular scheme compresses the frontage area by grouping clusters of condominiums at the ends of cul-de-sacs. By positioning the entrances and garage doors of several units around the paved turning circle, most rooms in the units can be opened to decks and green areas between the clusters.[62] Thus the lawns are visually separated from automobiles, refuse removal, and strangers. The central space must provide for the maneuvering of several automobiles; therefore, the space assumes a clearly urban appearance, in contrast to the pastoral character of the outsides of such clusters (Fig. 7.13). Little space within the cul-de-sac can be provided for planting, which increases the difference between the two portions of the site. However, the urge to reduce site costs has often meant that cul-de-sacs have opened directly to busy thoroughfares. Without the provision of adequate internal roadways, adults on casual errands and children on bicycles can be forced to enter traffic lanes that are too busy.

The increasing cost of land, as well as the demographic changes that have been mentioned, have encouraged efforts to increase the number of dwelling units that can be placed on a site. Early in the 1980s, the cost of land was roughly 10 to 15 percent of the total budget for a residential project. That percentage has roughly doubled by now, and in the near future it could move toward the 50 percent ratio common in western Europe, if not the 90 percent ratio of Japan.[63]

Plans and Budgets

While cities plan, zone, or develop other forms of building regulations, they usually try to do so in ways that are consistent with their comprehensive plans (Fig. 7.14). Since all property owners must obtain zoning, building, and occupancy permits from the city government, the total number of incremental building projects works toward weaving the city's fabric. Zon-

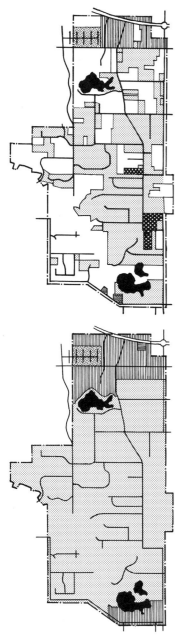

7.14 A land use plan (top) only indicates the intended use of the buildings on specific parcels of land. By contrast, a zoning map (bottom) indicates district designations that contain regulations for height, bulk, and area requirements for building. The zoning map, with its accompanying written documents, can require open spaces, public and private, and stipulate the percentage of the lot that may be built upon.

ing district classifications specify the use of a site, building heights, and allowable square feet, and they designate setbacks as building lines. During any kind of city review, development of the spaces between buildings can be suggested by planning and zoning commissions or by members of the planning staff.

Another method that might be employed to encourage the proliferation of special places is an open-space web plan (Fig. 7.15). In this option, a city develops a master plan for all of its future places. General locations for spatial types could be indicated, coded, or sketch-designed. The map or document that is used to promote the "plan for places" is widely disseminated, since it has the subsidiary purpose of eliciting interest from the development community, individual builders, and neighborhood residents. As a result, the particular city council that initiates the "plan for places" would be credited with having the vision and enthusiasm required to improve urban identity.

There are advantages to coordinating the improvement of all spaces between buildings in a city or a district of the city. A few spaces and the governmental planning policies and coordination required to achieve a multiple site improvement can have a dramatic contrast with the undesigned remainder of a city, and thereby the experience of those places may be heightened. On the other hand, a range of designs with different esthetic perspectives could elevate that city to an extraordinary and exciting level of visual, spatial, and perceptual variety. The advantages of coordinated placement of public places can be seen in the totalities created by the Ghirardelli Square, Fisherman's Wharf, and Cannery projects in San Francisco; Dealy Plaza, West End, and Reunion projects in Dallas; Penn's Landing, Society Hill, and Head House Square project in Philadelphia; as well as by many other series built or now under construction. A total set of well-designed and well-constructed spaces in cities may provide: (1) pleasant sets of experiences; (2) settings for socialization; (3) profits for building owners, developers and the real-estate community; (4) more jobs for city residents; (5) perceptions of increased building value to owners and renters; (6) visual counterpoints and rhythm to contrast with the sameness of other city areas; (7) anchorpoints created as an identifying framework; and (8) a perceived visual coherence resulting from the combination of special places. All of these items are economic advantages that secure and protect investments and promote continued reinvestments.

Incremental Projects

Some cities encourage a series of incremental and individual projects while paying little attention to comprehensive large-scale city design. These projects, built one by one, will each contribute to overall city improvement. Where a comprehensive open-space plan exists, landowners and real-estate developers may request exemption from some of its restrictions that are applicable to their projects, hoping to get leeway regarding such factors as setbacks and height limitations. If these requests are found to be reasonable, they customarily are acted on favorably. Municipal regulations are meant to be broad in application, but when all plausible requests for variations are approved—which is a common practice—the regulations and the city plan are soon gutted. But the step-by-step progress toward completion of a plan makes a city a much better place. Since those writing the regulations (mostly lawyers, social planners, or well-meaning laypeople) may have been untrained in large-scale physical design, insufficient safeguards may have been provided for adequate and effective open spaces.

Development Organizations and Teams

Planning and construction of open spaces, as well as other kinds of improvement projects, may be conducted by teams composed of three kinds of development organizations: governmental agencies, private development organizations, or local interest groups. The use of a government agency as the prime development organization of the project team in larger cities usually involves maintaining a staff within the city administration for the purpose of attracting new jobs and employers, spurring new construction and building renovations, and discovering methods by which city revenues might be increased. These agencies may be called "economic development agencies," or something similar. The private development organization consists of a coalition of business leaders, real estate developers, and boosters. The purchase of land for the development of LaClede's Landing, a historic site on the Mississippi River in St. Louis, was made possible by the Missouri legislature's passing a law that allowed private development organizations to exercise the power of condemnation under specific controls (Fig. 7.16).[64] The local development corporation combines the characteristics of both of the other forms, being based on a group composed of neighborhood leaders, hired city staff, and selected business

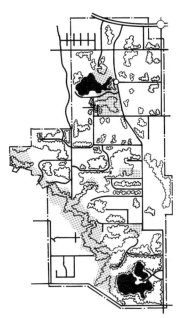

7.15 The open space plan summarizes land occupied by the park system, hike and bike trails, lakes, flood plains, boulevards, and certain amenities.

7.16 In Missouri, under an unusual state law, private developers can condemn land for investment purposes. A plan to add night life to the downtown has been successful on the streets adjacent to the steep sloping banks of the Mississippi River. Grid streets, narrow and cobblestoned, rather than plazas, are the open spaces in this project. LaClede's Landing, St. Louis. (Photo by Donald C. Royse)

leaders.[65] Local interest groups may be citizen-formed historical commissions, labor unions, or environmental action committees.

Also, in attempting to advance economic conditions by improving the city's appearance, city officials' activity in building coalitions is vital. Through the development of alliances, political interests are supported, and the city government develops formal and informal channels that promote the construction of urban spaces and places.[66] When colleagues at City Hall, influential businesspeople, or potential investors see the profits possible through this mode of planning spaces, the use of incentives and penalties becomes a method of holding together their networks of political contacts.[67] Many other individuals or corporations may wish to enhance their own real-estate holdings or promote a broad blueprint for the location of their future investments in buildings. Others may be motivated by altruism, wanting to display support for their esthetic preferences or support for their own charitable interests. Still others may wish to inaugurate a city-wide sense of pride. In any of these instances, despite the fact that the public places are based on economic motives, they still improve the quality of daily experiences, encourage attendance at community events, provide places for rest and recreation, and gain the admiration and envy of people from other cities. A number of cities have developed special and distinct spatial experiences that have created their present-day image. In San Francisco, both the revenues and pleasures coming from a series of projects, ranging from the Cannery to Chinatown, are appealing to visitors, citizens, and businesses. Boston, New York, New Orleans, and Washington have the advantages of their sets of revenue-producing spaces, in which spatial experiences and identifiable places have been developed on a basis of profits. The places not only attract tourists, but provide the backdrop for the daily encounters of city residents.

Design Review Committees

As a device to assure quality, design review committees are sometimes established, so that the city need not rely solely on the determinations of city officials. It is the committee's assigned responsibility to consider the submitted evidence of the developer's proposal and decide whether or not it satisfies legal requirements—at least their intentions, if not their details—and to reach a judgment about its general benefit to the community. One way in which this complex decision is reached is through work sessions with the developers or owners and their design and engineering staffs. It is often required that a site plan be submitted to the planning and zoning commission or the city council as the basis for their considering issuing a building permit, authorizing deviations from regulations, or acting favorably on a request for site rezoning. Open spaces on the site and spaces between buildings thus become factors in those decisions. Where stylistic restrictions are a part of municipal policy, an additional approval may be required from a board appointed to judge the appearance of the buildings and spaces that are part of the project. Recent court decisions have tended to require that the recommendations of such boards be affirmed by the commissions that are charged with ultimate responsibility for general approval.[68]

The decisions required of such boards, commissions, and committees involve factors that are extremely different in nature. Esthetic judgments, problems of the engineering fabric of the city, and financial matters are commonly interwoven into the discussions. It is common for the arguments to become classic "apples and oranges" debates, with an unsubstantiated relationship between economics and esthetics becoming a major factor. Usually these decisions vitally affect the future of open spaces at the site under consideration and will have a citywide effort as well. By their very nature such boards are almost always fundamentally conservative in outlook, for the members are usually attorneys, service professionals (such as insurance agents), politicians, or businesspeople. Many times, the members' on-the-job training and their tendency to consult others who are more familiar with certain matters is sufficient to enable them to reach sound decisions. At other times, the interests and familiar territories of the members may frustrate worthwhile and innovative proposals.

> Communities should note that extensive review processes tend to become more cumbersome and rigid over time. As more parties take part in the review, which often happens, and as more fixed rules are introduced and applied to the next development, costs to the public will go up. Tax monies may be lost and the developer may shift to another location with less burdensome procedures.[69]

Public–Private Negotiation

In spite of all the official and legal methods used, developing projects may involve hard-ball negotiation with developers or investors. In the 1970s Omaha, Nebraska, built an attractive downtown library and a large and handsome park that extends from the library toward the Missouri River.[70] By the 1980s, the city was concerned about economic development. Con-Agra, a holding company that controlled many firms dealing in packaged foods, proposed that it might establish its headquarters in Omaha on cleared riverfront land near the downtown area. Since the downtown area had suffered years of offices moving to suburban locations, the booster groups were excited that ConAgra's headquarters would bring 2,000 jobs to the central city. (Metropolitan Omaha had a population of 621,600 in 1990). The ensuing debate and negotiations between ConAgra, city officials, the Omaha Development Foundation (an arm of the local Chamber of Commerce), and the public mainly involved the corporation's insistence that Jobbers' Canyon, a six-block area of turn-of-the-century warehouses that was listed on the National Register of Historic Sites in early 1987, be razed to provide a view from the corporate headquarters and through the park to the downtown area. (The CEO of ConAgra referred to the warehouses, fitting symbols of the reason for Omaha's growth, as "some big, ugly red buildings."[71]) Since they had competitive offers from other cities,

7.17 Steep slopes and stone outcroppings at Sugar Hill, N.H. prevented the use of standard street layouts for these houses clustered around cul-de-sacs. They are single-family detached residences in a community that has a condominium system of ownership; that is, each house does not have its own lot. The project is landscaped to make use of the natural terrain, using native wild flowers and grasses.

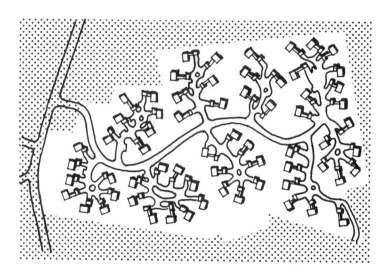

Conagra demanded that the Foundation make the riverfront land available by a deadline, and negotiations were rapidly concluded. One opponent of the project referred to the project as having been "conceived in fear, negotiated in secret, and executed in haste."[72] The results are a riverfront area occupied by corporate offices in buildings of no architectural distinction on grounds of ungainly design, oddly contrasting with the high quality of the work that had been executed in the adjacent park and in a nearby festival marketplace that had been developed some years earlier.

In the suburbs, detailed ordinances having specific requirements that add to the sales prices of houses are not liked by speculative builders.[73] Negotiations that take place when the ordinances are drafted may need to be just as firm as they are when downtown situations are their subject. Suburban setbacks, patterned paving, and sidewalks will cost more and raise prices, which certainly will affect sales (Fig. 7.17). The uncertainty of economic effect is a factor during the adoption of these kinds of regulations. However, in most places residential spaces remain subject to a moderate level of public regulation. Subdivision standards, land use, and building height, bulk, and area requirements all affect open spaces. The zoning administrator in City Hall customarily is the key contact for the real-estate developer. This administrator interprets the ordinance for all who build, and applies the ordinance requirements to the projects they propose. Suburban residential districts are usually regulated, but the specific requirements tend to be less demanding than they are downtown.

Most new developments in the future are expected to be located in places now identified as suburban (Fig. 7.18). The present patterns and expected future suburban conditions require continued public-private negotiation:

> "I'm not sure I know what a suburban area is," said Wayne Ratkovitch, a Michigan developer. "Some areas that we used to think of as suburbs are bigger than our downtowns."

7.18 In such places as the Detroit area, office centers (dots) in suburban locations have become new downtowns. Recent data indicate that the dominant mode of commuting is from suburb to suburb, rather than from suburbs to the old riverside downtown (shaded area at river).

The Detroit area provides a perfect example: two suburbs—Southfield and Troy—each offer more square feet of office space than the CBD [central business district], and nine separate suburban markets exist. "Development is going to be less concentrated," Ratkovich says. "We'll have clusters of concentration in a variety of areas as opposed to a single, strongly dominant area. You can hardly call such areas suburban anymore, because they're urbanized." . . .

Traffic congestion, pollution, environmental, and growth concerns will all contribute to a basic change in the way we use land. More than one use—several uses—will be placed on the same parcel of land or in the same zoned area, as opposed to our traditional patterns of separating uses and then reconnecting them with the automobile.[74]

Citizen Participation Balancing Interests, and Equity

Still another means of constructing open places involves teams made up from the planning department and residents for the purpose of developing a comprehensive plan or special open-space plan for the entire city or a particular neighborhood. The plan could be officially adopted using the customary processes of public hearings. As a result, all residents and prospective developers would become aware of the city's intentions. With the backing of elected officials, residents, and influential individuals and organizations, the open-space plan as originally proposed could have a continued life over a long period using standard professional planning practices. By adding the open-space considerations to the city's comprehensive plan, perhaps calling that element the "spatial framework" of the comprehensive plan, another important dimension of the city's future can be delineated. Certainly, the snapshot in time represented by the comprehensive plan can clearly indicate the design intentions for the physical, social, and economic future.

If a city is to achieve the desired snapshot in time, the comprehensive plan requires both economic and other methods of implementation. Zoning, subdivision ordinances, and special district ordinances could be very successful, even if used alone, but some cities may need to be more assertive in making their plans a reality. Stimulating economic activities can initiate some projects. For example, a city may work with a private developer to engage their planning department's design team with the developer's design team. Both parties together may find richer solutions to the design of targeted spaces. The planning department can espouse its broader views, and the developer's design team can promote specific needs. With this collaboration, cities, townships, or counties can quickly raise the quality of the spaces between buildings. This approach suggests that multiple viewpoints that include developers' financial desires can improve the quality of a space. Planning and zoning commissions, planning departments, or city councils, through collaboration with developers, can discover the most effective methods to get those spaces completed. While city officials become concerned with a myriad of public welfare issues, developers focus on project finances, and their collaborative involvement in planning spaces may effectively combine idealism.

Special care must be given to the planners and developers who become advocates for lower-income groups. Now that court orders demand that public housing agencies provide improved open space for low- and moderate-income residents, special designs to satisfy those needs are being mandated for cities all over the country.[75] Issues that have been raised successfully in the courts have included improving muddy playgrounds through better maintenance, planting additional trees and shrubs, and adding play equipment and park benches to common areas. Low- and moderate-income residents have become quite vocal in their demands that their neighborhoods look as good as others. Because their residents have less money to spend, some city neighborhoods may have a larger share of unkempt lawns and sideyards and they may lack trees and shrubs. In these neighborhoods, planting street trees, landscaping street medians, and maintenance programs can provide important improvements. Additionally, court orders may require open-space improvements to be completed over short time periods, creating fiscal stress. Proper planning can spread these improvements over a more comfortable budgeting period.

Smaller houses, apartment buildings, or townhouses require lower construction costs per dwelling than do other types of housing. As a result of the savings obtained from creating closer building spacing, the leftover space may be best considered as positive space requiring special design attention. Through such an attitude, the design of housing and the spaces and places outside them can provide important opportunities for pleasant personal experiences, such as meeting neighbors, sitting alone on an outdoor bench and reading, thinking, or conversing with others across an outdoor chess table. Clearly, paying attention to low- and moderate-income residents allows the entire city area to be improved. The public welfare is considered more evenhandedly, and the nature and intent of federal, state, and local housing regulations and court decisions are promoted more easily. Street planting designs, open courtyard improvements, street median changes, and other improvements are projects that are important for the large expanses occupied by low- or middle-income residents. Paying attention and paying for capital improvements for these disadvantaged neighborhoods is quite political, but it is essential in order to avoid any higher future penalties that could be imposed by the courts in response to charges of negligence or discrimination.

The rising demand for the rehabilitation of existing recreation and park facilities was the largest projected need that parks agencies reported in one study about projected parks and open space budgets. Local parks departments were demonstrated to need to invest about 50 percent of their capital funds in the construction and development of new recreation and park facilities. Land acquisition and rehabilitation each demand about one half of that portion. On a more mundane note relating to city open spaces:

> It is at the state and local levels that inner-city, economically disadvantaged youth and families are going to be reached. It is recreation, close to home, that is desperately needed if America is to provide alternatives to crime and drugs and if it is to promote the doctrine of wellness and quality of life to individuals who cannot buy golf clubs and tennis racquets and cross-country skis.[76]
>
> A new boom in urban and rural development is underway. It is consuming almost 500,000 acres of wetland yearly, along with 750,000 acres of farms and forests. Older parks in many states and communities have deteriorated facilities and landscapes that need major repair or replacement. And only through strong state and local park systems can America's social issues, ranging from drug abuse to day care shortages, be adequately tackled.[77]

One experienced planner's research concludes that planning for projects will "work only in communities where it is made a major point in every election campaign."[78] Candidates receive campaign funds and political support between campaigns from businesspeople; therefore, they need to be concerned with profits and the overall economics of the city. Such advantages were instrumental in the reelections of Henry Cisneros in San Antonio, Anthony Alioto and Dianne Feinstein in San Francisco, and in many other mayoral races.

ECONOMICS AND ESTHETICS

Not only are there social advantages to be found in effectively designed spaces and places, there are also financial benefits arising from renewed interest in the immediate surroundings of the designed place and the knowledge that one piece of the city's checkerboard of land and buildings has been revitalized. Design improvements to spaces between buildings enhance the rental and occupancy rates of the surrounding buildings. Taking action improves city revenues in many ways. As teams work diligently on projects throughout America, our country slowly improves by producing new places for a new century. Although good design, effective circulation, and pleasant places are something people can learn to live without, we can imagine cities filled with a new spirit of America. And that spirit is important.

For example, even if the project is merely a small square in a high-density city, a spot like Paley Park in New York, the private project design team creates interest, stimulates users, and can provide a refuge from the sidewalks for office workers and tourists. Coming into the park, pedestrians can find a chair and table and move them into a comfortable position. By being able to choose to experience that space or to relax within it, it becomes easier to manage living in New York. Without Paley Park, Seagram's Plaza, Riverside Park, the wide setback of Saint Patrick's Cathedral, and Rockefeller Center Plaza, you would have one of the easiest places in the world in which to get lost—repetitive linear canyons following the streets. And the advantages of Paley Park promote economic value for the buildings near it. As stated in Chapter 4, we move through cities by these cue proximity perceptions. A lamppost provides a possible minor cue; an open space could provide a major one. Spaces do enhance buildings. Buildings house tenants who pay rents to live and work there. The links between occupied buildings and job creation are well documented. To boost a city's economy, enhancing the spaces between buildings enhances the buildings themselves. The outside areas around an office building entrance may become the most memorable in comparison with facades, interior designs, or interior spatial features. Since thinking about cities, whether downtowns or suburbs, evokes images and visions of hard surface materials or soft landscape materials, tenant appeal is the key to supply and demand, and generating tax revenues, jobs, and overall improved social conditions. Boosting buildings through spatial enhancement does not mean improving urban identity for a select few businesspeople. All income groups in cities and towns benefit. Again, all levels of society benefit. Isn't this advantage a clear reason for understanding the benefits of improving urban identity?

Any kind of building development can create small leftover parcels with unsuitable geometry.[79] Not all available land can be developed. From this perspective, maximizing spatial design to stimulate the economy of a city is a very reasonable activity. Without attention paid to spaces and places, the leftovers are not tasty. Many cities have other problems that intermix to affect their visual quality and appearances. For instance, crime rates may make a certain part of a city undesirable as a location for any kind of development. From another point of view, it may be desirable to improve that area with the hope of lowering the crime rate. The buildings cannot be changed easily or economically, but the spaces between the buildings can. Appearances are important and spatial construction programs that add landscape materials and other elements can create a Hawthorne effect, signaling to local residents and visitors that city government cares about this neighborhood. Even if crime is not mitigated significantly, the visual improvements may be worthwhile to the city at large. An entire city may be avoided by investors because of its crime rate, visual images, or other factors. The more design considerations of a city's open spaces, the lesser the potential for social problems. Properly designed spaces can inhibit and suppress crime.[80]

People seem to prefer new buildings to old ones. One set of studies examined about 350 physical, social, and economically observable items for downtown and suburban office buildings, hotels and motels, and strip shopping centers to uncover this factor of desirability and newness. The results of these studies indicated that area features rather than building features were the strongest predictors of high rents and high occupancies.[81] Also, newer buildings had higher occupancies, but the newer ones with special open space treatments had even higher rents and occupancies. Preferences about the external appearance of buildings are linked to fashion, consumerism, and advertising. Novelty is a major element of marketing in our culture, and the leasing or sale of buildings is conducted in much the same way as the sale of consumable merchandise. Over time, building occupancies in the older areas of cities tend to decrease. Managers of real estate projects try to sell their new products, fashionable buildings, to the present occupants of these older areas. Rental projects, either commercial or residential, usually make less profit during their earlier years, when the interest portion of the mortgages are highest. A little more profit is made during the middle period when only minor expenditures are necessary to keep the building competitive with others. The most profitable period comes after maintenance is virtually abandoned and the financing has been completed. With such a cycle at work, absent positive physical improvements to a neighborhood, old tenants become new ones somewhere else. Well-designed places with a high-profile can stabilize neighborhoods, making businesses want to remain at their "good address."

When a series of special spaces are stimulated, residents' perceptions of their city change. According to many studies in social psychology, people attribute this perception to the political leaders in power, even if their overall perception has really been created by a series of private developers' actions.[82] People from all walks of life and all sorts of careers become committed to the city and make a number of decisions that can make things there better. For example, if the perception of a city is closely associated with its spaces and places, then new investors may attempt to develop their projects to mimic the success of others. Another example might be that developers begin regularly to provide plazas in exchange for additional floor areas because they know about the success of a nearby project that did the same. Even if a city only intends to stimulate a few spaces with strategically placed funding, the examples might be so positive that other funding may not be required. More buildings may get constructed due to developers' awareness of the success of other spaces and places.

Beautiful and pleasurable spaces are not accidents, nor are they only achieved when a few brilliant designers work with lavish funding. Care and attention to physical planning can lead to many specially designed places that provide social and economic benefit to any city, whether the city is growing or declining in population. There are no excuses for cities and their political leaders to fail to work with enthusiasm at the task of financing, developing, and improving their open spaces.

ENDNOTES

1. William L.C. Wheaton, "Public and Private Agents of Change," in Melvin Webber, *Explorations Into Urban Structure* (Philadelphia: University of Pennsylvania Press, 1963), 154–96.

2. Halbert C. Smith, Carl J. Tschappat, and Ronald L. Racster, *Real Estate and Urban Development, Revised Edition* (Homewood, IL: Richard D. Irwin, Inc., 1977), 39.

3. Thomas R. Hammer; Robert E. Coughlin; and Edward T. Horn, IV, "The Effect of a Large Park on Real Estate Value," *Journal of the American Institute of Planners* (July 1974): 274–77.

4. William Fulton, "The Profit Motive," *Planning* (October 1987): 6–10.

5. One example of this phenomenon is provided by the Renaissance Tower in downtown Dallas. A sleek, mirrored rectangle containing 1,701,591 square feet, the 1974 building obtained a 95 percent occupancy rate in the late 1970s. By the mid-1980s, occupancies had decreased to under 70 percent. Over the few years following the renovations, occupancies rose dramatically. By 1992, a few years after Prudential Insurance Company completed a $40 million renovation of the lobbies and a complete facade renovation of this fifty-six-story structure, occupancies rose to 83 percent. See *Black's Guide to the Office Space Market—Dallas* (Rockville, MD: Black's Guide, 1992). Also from an interview with staff, Premisys Real Estate Services, Dallas, Texas, March 25, 1993.

6. Richard B. Peiser with Dean Schwanke, *Professional Real Estate Development: The ULI Guide to the Business* (Washington, DC: Dearborn Financial Publishing, 1992), 214.

7. G. Edward DeSeve, "Financing Urban Development: The Joint Efforts of Government and the Private Sector," *The Annals of the American Academy of Political and Social Science* (November 1986): 64–65.

8. Interview with Phil Eklof, MAI, Grubb & Ellis Real Estate, Dallas, Texas, March 17, 1993.

9. Edward Relph, *Place and Placelessness* (London: Pion Ltd., 1976), 92.

10. J. Richard Recht and Robert J. Harmon, "Open Space and the Urban Growth Process," *Research Report 31* (University of California at Berkeley: The Center for Real Estate and Urban Economics, 1979).

11. Robert E. Coughlin and Tatsuhiko Kawashima, "Property Values and Open Space in Northwest Philadelphia: An Empirical Analysis," *RSRI Discussion Paper Series No. 64*, July 1973 (University of Pennsylvania: Regional Science Research Institute, 1973).

12. Herbert H. Smith, *Planning America's Communities: Paradise Found? Paradise Lost?* (Chicago: Planners Press, 1991), 49.

13. Smith, *Planning America's Communities*, 7.

14. Jeffrey S. Luke, Curtis Ventriss, B.J. Reed, and Christine M. Reed, *Managing Economic Development: A Guide to State and Local Leadership Strategies* (San Francisco: Jossey-Bass Publishers, 1988), 225.

15. Richard D. Bingham, Edward W. Hill, and Sammis B. White, eds., *Financing Economic Development: An Institutional Response* (Newbury Park: Sage Publications, 1990), 30.

16. Frank Spink and others, "Fair Lakes," *Project Reference File* 18:5 (Washington D.C.: Urban Land Institute, 1988), 5.

17. Smith, *Planning America's Commnities*, 9.

18. John M. Levy, *Economic Development Programs for Cities, Counties, and Towns*, 2nd ed. (New York: Praeger, 1990), 1–6.

19. John R. Logan and Harvey L. Molotch, *Urban Fortunes: The Political Economy of Place* (Berkeley, CA: University of California Press, 1987), 13.

20. Sandra Hasegawa and Steve Elliott, "Public Spaces by Private Enterprise (Projects in Seattle, Washington)," *Urban Land* (May 1983): 12–15.

21. David H. Vrooman, "An Empirical Analysis of Determinants of Land Values in The Adirondack Park," *American Journal of Economics and Sociology* (April 1978): 165–77.

22. Interview with Phil Eklof, MAI, Grubb & Ellis Real Estate Appraisal Group, Dallas, Texas, March 11, 1993.

23. Michael Southworth, "Theory and Practice of Contemporary Urban Design: A Look at American Urban Design Plans," *Working Paper 510* (Berkeley, CA: University of California, 1990), 2–3.

24. Logan and Molotch, *Urban Fortunes*, 13.

25. Charles L. Siemon and Michelle J. Zimet, "Public Places as Infrastructure," *Environmental and Urban Issues* (Winter 1991): 4.

26. Guy Benveniste, *Mastering the Politics of Planning* (San Francisco: Jossey-Bass Publishers, 1989), 232–33.

27. Sanford Parisky, "Restoring Public Parks with Public Help," *Parks and Recreation* (January 1991): 52–56.

28. Alan Rabinowitz, *Land Investment and the Predevelopment Process* (New York: Quorum Books, 1988), 32.

29. Nicole Achs, "Putting the Fun(ds) Back in Downtown," *American City and County* (June 1991): 67.

30. Achs, "Putting the Fun(ds) Back," 67–68.

31. Harm-Benefit Theory relates to constitutional issues of eminent domain. See Daniel R. Mandelker, *Land Use Law*, 2nd ed. (Charlottesville, VA: Michie Company, 1988), 24–30.

32. Barbara Miles, "Housing Finance: Development and Evolution in Mortgage Markets," in Richard L. Florida, ed., *Housing and the New Financial Markets* (New Brunswick, NJ: Center for Urban Policy Research, 1986), 19.

33. Jennifer Carlile, "Packaging a Park: The Economics of Recreation," *American City and County* (January 1991): 24.

34. Illinois Debt Reform Act of 1988, Section 186, No. 48.

35. Bonnie R. Kraft, "Developing Investment Policies," in Ian J. Allan, ed., *Cash Management for Small Governments* (Chicago: Government Finance Officers Association, 1989), 137.

36. Joseph H. Brevard, *Capital Facilities Planning: A Tactical Approach.* (Chicago: Planners Press, 1985), 116–19, 327–31.

37. Carlile, "Packaging a Park," 20.

38. Richard E. Klosterman, *Community Analysis and Planning Techniques* (Savage, MD: Rowman and Littlefield, 1990), 194–200.

39. Teresa Stankis and Susanne G. Barrett, "Sugar Land, Texas Adopts Tax Abatement Guidelines," *Government Finance Review* (April 1989): 26.

40. Stankis and Barrett, "Sugar Land, Texas," 26.

41. John E. Anderson, "Tax Increment Financing: Municipal Adoption and Growth," *National Tax Journal* (June 1990):155–63.

42. Ana Arana, "Planning Practice: Doing Deals: How California Communities Mix and Match Financing Techniques to Pay for New Development," *Planning* (February 1986):30.

43. Jeffrey S. Luke, Curtis Ventriss, B.J. Reed, and Christine M. Reed, *Managing Economic Development: A Guide to State and Local Leadership Strategies* (San Francisco: Jossey-Bass Publishers, 1988), 20.

44. John M. Levy, *Economic Development Programs for Cities, Counties, and Towns,* 2nd ed. (New York: Praeger Publishing Co., 1990), 107.

45. Ralph J. Basile, "Negotiating Public/Private Deals in Tough Times," *Urban Land* (February 1992): 26–30.

46. Basile, "Negotiating Public/Private Deals," 27.

47. Edward J. Blakely, *Planning Local Economic Development: Theory and Practice.* Vol. 168. Sage Library of Social Research. (Newbury Park: Sage Publications, 1989), 261.

48. Blakely, *Planning Local Economic Development,* 262.

49. William Fulton, "The Robin Hood of Real Estate," *Planning* (May 1985):4–10.

50. Richard F. Babcock and Wendy U. Larsen, *Special Districts: The Ultimate in Neighborhood Zoning* (Cambridge, MA: Lincoln Institute of Land Policy, 1990), 1–2.

51. Babcock and Larsen, *Special Districts,* 3.

52. Maryann Holway, "Small-Scale Urban/Mixed Use Development Award—Garibaldi Square," *Urban Land* (December 1991): 19.

53. Frank H. Spink, Jr., and others "The Woodlands, Darien, Illinois," *Project Reference File* 18:8. (Washington D.C.: Urban Land Institute, 1988), 3–4.

54. Blakely, *Planning Local Economic Development*, 224.

55. Blakely, *Planning Local Economic Development*, 225–36.

56. Blakely, *Planning Local Economic Development*, 256–57.

57. Smith, *Planning America's Communities*, 31–32.

58. Basile, "Negotiating Public–Private Deals," 29–30.

59. Lewis Mumford, *The City in History*. (New York: Harcourt, Brace, and World, Inc., 1961), 494.

60. "Carefree Living," *Builder*. (August 1991): 70.

61. "Builder's Choice: A Leaner, Cleaner Market Out There. This Year's Builder's Choice Winners Show Just How Beautiful Bottom Line Building Can Be," *Builder*. (October 1991): 100.

62. "Merit Award," *Builder*. (October 1991): 115, 122.

63. "The Land-Price Squeeze," *Builder*. (July 1990): 139.

64. Missouri state laws 353, 99, and 100 provide the right for private corporations to obtain tax incentives and take eminent domain actions. Also, see Thomas W. Garland, Inc., City of St. Louis; U.S. Court of Appeals, Eighth Circuit, 1979. 596 F.2d. 784.

65. Blakely, *Planning Local Economic Development*, 257.

66. Benveniste, *Mastering the Politics of Planning*, 156–57.

67. Benveniste, *Mastering the Politics of Planning*, 184.

68. Daniel R. Mandelker, *Land Use Law*, 2nd ed. (Charlottesville, VA: Michie, 1988), 387–89.

69. Credits: HOK Architects; Lawrence Halprin, landscape architect.

70. "Historic District At Issue In Omaha: Company's Plan To Relocate Headquarters Is Assailed By Preservationists," *New York Times*, December 13, 1987, 43.

71. Jim Schwab, "Omaha Held Hostage," *Progressive.* (May 1989): 36.

72. David A. Dowall, "Effects of Environmental Regulation on Housing Costs," in Donald G. Hagman, *Public Planning and Control of Urban and Land Development,* 2nd ed. (St. Paul: West Publishing, 1980), 464–65.

73. Matthew Kiell, "Looking to the 1990s: Developers Take a Long View and See Subtle Yet Surprising Changes in the 1990s," *Urban Land* (December 1989): 12.

74. Debra Walker and others vs. U.S. Department of Housing and Urban Development et al.; Civil Action No. CA3-85-1210-R., U.S. District Court, Dallas; and following City of Dallas City Council Resolution 90-1120, approved March 28, 1990.

75. Suzanne McCormick, "Funding the Next Five Years," *Parks and Recreation* (January 1991): 62.

76. McCormick, "Funding the Next Five Years," 59.

77. Smith, *Planning America's Communities,* 5.

78. Robert S. Cook, Jr., "Fixed Zoning Rules Can Conflict With Urban Design Goals," *Nation's Cities Weekly.* (August 31, 1981): 6.

79. Levy, *Economic Development Programs,* 107.

80. Oscar Newman, *Defensible Space* (New York: Macmillan, 1972).

81. Joel B. Goldsteen, "What Fills An Office Building? Its Neighborhood or Its Design?" *Urban Land* (April 1989):2–5.

82. Robert J. Waste, *The Ecology of City Policymaking* (New York: Oxford University Press, 1989), 82–84, 146–56.

8

CHANGES IN AMERICA—FUTURE AND FORECASTS

Population; technology; business and finance; infrastructure; the constants

Shaping spaces has the potential for creating massive change in many ways. Land values, overall economic conditions, job creation, and social improvements can benefit from improved urban identity. For those reasons, improvements to city spaces are essential for creating livable cities of the future. Whether residents desire and seek their own urban identity or a visual similarity to other cities, coping with change means different actions and different designs for open spaces that must be matched to particular purposes.

This change can be accomplished through different strategies. For example, entrepreneurial cities (those containing large corporations and industries and many business boosters) should promote the design and construction of many different, independently designed plazas at the entrances to major buildings, strategizing a series of spots within the total city area. Spots of attractive space, or places and plazas, will begin to indicate the blossoming of civic pride and interest, and create an individuality of appearance that becomes a polka-dot program for success. The businesspeople who initiate the design of such spaces delegate their tastes, and thus gain personal satisfaction from their financial decisions. Even though every space may turn out to be different, the independent mushrooming accomplishes the goal of improving urban identity. For cities that do not have this entrepreneurial potential, a few large, idealistic, or visionary open spaces might be designed and constructed. In this case, the city could allocate portions of its capital improvements budget for the construction of the spaces. Over time, a small number of spaces could become visionary images or passive green parklands, eloquent statements of the city spirit of its residents and well worth the expense. In other cities, another strategy might be employed. Streets and thoroughfares can be enhanced through amendments to current ordinances to require specific plant materials, spacing, varieties, and sizes. By strong regulations and changes in zoning, subdivision, or the creation of special ordinances for districts of a city, pervasive change can be achieved over a period of time. Typically, change through regulations takes many years to become significant. Each time a construction project is initiated, the approvals needed for a building permit may require compliance with special district regulations. A decade or more may be required before change is clearly evident, but an overall beautification can affect every street and every block.

Only by clearly stating the city's intentions and strategies to improve urban identity can the many members and various factions of a community work in concert to implement changes by designing spaces with an eye to future conditions. Most social studies stress the importance of physical designs matching human needs, but rapid changes can make this goal extraordinarily difficult to achieve. A city's comprehensive plan, zoning ordinances, subdivision ordinances, and special district ordinances can be effective vehicles for continued alertness to change in American cities. The annual reviews of their effectiveness, which are common monitoring devices, permits citizens to steer their city through changing currents. By contrast, if coordinated citywide master plans are not desired, even one improved space or network—even an additional plaza—provides residents of the city with a special place that has unique characteristics planned for a future America. In times of mushrooming growth and much social change, the necessary alterations to city regulations may make these two strategies much the same.

> The only time frame within which planning can take effect is the future. However immediate the actions which follow our planning decisions, follow they must. In relation to those decisions they are therefore inevitably in the future. We cannot avoid taking a view about the future, even if it is simply that the future is totally unpredictable.[1]

Cities are dynamic; and their cultural, societal, and physical changes are always difficult to predict. Nevertheless, many projections, forecasts, and perspectives that have been expressed by researchers and well-regarded visionaries are useful and well-founded estimates of what the future may be. Planners, designers, and others who make decisions regarding the urban fabric of the future should consider these forecasts as suggestions of specific factors that can prove helpful in designing the physical being of urban areas. Demographic changes, population projections, and employment shifts must be considered with the realization that there will be a concomitant alteration of the social and cultural characteristics of the groups discussed in the predictions. Forecasts of financial, governmental, and environmental issues must be viewed with a recognition of the certain alteration of the systemic and technological contexts within which they will operate.

It must be clear by now, based on our past experience, that any single forecast has a high probability of being wrong. There are so many uncertainties within our understanding of the current situation and our grasp of how it might develop that we would be naive to believe any single forecast. More realistically, and with some greater chance of accuracy, we can suggest probable ranges of values and situations that must increase in amplitude the further into the future we look, because time makes more room for variation.[2]

Predictions necessarily provide the basis for the actions of many politicians, businesspeople, scientists, and professionals. Beliefs regarding the future are usually strong and deep, even though some are developed by little more than gazing into a crystal ball. The status, charisma, or persuasive powers of the predictor are always the most important aspects of the prediction, determining the degree to which a prediction is accepted by groups of people.[3] The public is hungry for such prophecies, anxious to discover a basis for the modification of their behaviors in order that they may improve their prospects. Broad predictions, global or regional, often have merit, even though their extrapolation into more detailed and limited situations invariably involves even greater risk. The scenarios of all forecasts have a surrealistic quality about them. The eerie experience of considering, at the present time, the changes that may accumulate through many decades and the resultant changes in our lives, inevitably brings with it the feeling of participating in science fiction. But the scenarios proposed by forecasters gain credence from the fact that many of the people who read them have indeed experienced in their lifetimes unexpected events and conditions that they had not anticipated.

Few, if any, of the changes that are brought forward preclude our using the land as we now do, in performing work, recreation, and other activities. Regardless of the importance and implied inevitability of so many of the forecasts, they do not appear to reduce or contradict the desirability of distinctive identities for different urban locales. Nor do they appear to diminish the desirability of emphasizing those identities as a reason for increasing the effectiveness of open spaces within cities. In order to plan properly for their future, cities base their decisions on the known facts about existing conditions, the spirit and objectives of their residents, and shared visions about the manner in which each city should develop.[4] Plans for buildings, plazas or parks, for transportation systems, or for the entire city must presuppose a future setting for each such project once it is completed and during its useful life. During the process, neighborhood groups tend to discover similarities in their goals, unify their interests, and, over time, achieve unity. Horizons are necessary for planning. Without some foundations for our views of the future, we cannot design places that provide functional and visual satisfaction, although those foundations may have little basis. Trends shift; motives change. Economic and social factors may exhibit considerable stability in one period, but waves of behavior can affect future behavior in unexpected ways.[5] Therefore, the horizons of planning must include adaptable components and unpredictable aspects.

A cautious point of view would picture the future of the United States fifty years from now as much the same as it is now, perhaps with minor scientific and technological innovations. A more expansive perspective

8.1 The spaces created by the separated buildings of this shopping mall on the island of Maui are complemented by the use of native plant materials. Due to the mild climate of Hawaii, the shopping center could be successfully designed by integrating indoor and outdoor spaces.

would envision sweeping and profound alterations of economic, physical, and social conditions, accompanied by extraordinary advances of technology. Either of these fundamental views can be argued passionately and successfully. Change, of course, may be slow or fast. In the last two centuries, two changes dramatically affected the nature of open spaces in America: 1) Nineteenth-century increases in people's available leisure time and improvements in public transportation led to the development of parks; and 2) the twentieth-century development of the automobile led to an increase of the area taken up by roadways and parking spaces. The first of these changes was gradual; the second was a matter of only a few decades. The events that can be foreseen, whether systemic or technological, may result in drastic changes in some kinds of spaces and gradual, almost imperceptible, changes in others. It is most likely that changes in the use and development of open spaces will come about through combinations of factors. For instance, the inexorable increase in U.S. population that is predicted for the oncoming decades could mean that population densities will increase in urbanized areas. But the effect of this change might be influenced decidedly by a gradual reduction of people's attachment to the single-family isolated dwelling or a rapid adaptation of a technological advance that altered the accepted relationship of building volume and land utilization—as occurred with the invention of the elevator at the end of the nineteenth century. Governmental policy, economic conditions, and a multitude of other factors always can be expected to exert similar influences. A shift in the present-day enthusiasm for the acquisition of possessions or the alteration of marketing procedures might do away with shopping centers, freeing large areas near the intersections of major travel routes.

Tangible and intangible aspects must be considered in any prognostication regarding the future value of open spaces for public use, for intangi-

8.2 The shopping mall has been transplanted from the suburbs to downtown. River Center in San Antonio depends on drawing buyers through an alley infill space, the pedestrian river walk, and a main entrance.

ble factors may sometimes prove to be the more urgent and meaningful elements. At first glance, it might be assumed that individuals' desires and preferences will change little in the next half-century, and parks, gardens, plazas, and street-spaces will be needed for purposes that are much the same as now. But, upon reflection, we recall that in little more than four decades the shopping mall has become a major economic and social factor in the United States and other American nations (Fig. 8.1). The shopping arcades of past centuries have been revived and have multiplied, with clear indications of the classes, economic levels, and other group characteristics for which they are intended (Fig. 8.2). Similarly, greater interest and awareness might make open spaces more heavily used. The recent recognition of stress as a significant factor in health and productivity suggests that the opportunity to sit beside a fountain and watch others stroll across a plaza may have greater practical purpose than has been previously recognized. Consequently, scientific research finds converts to a widespread belief that recreation should be viewed as restoration, and pleasure can become pragmatic.

POPULATION

Much has been written about the future, yet changes that portend the future have not been fully grasped (Fig. 8.3). In the United States, many places and spaces between buildings are often used by racial and ethnic groups that are not the stereotypical Caucasians. In spite of this obvious fact, many of us continue to imagine spaces as being filled with people of European descent. One population prediction forecasts 356 million people

8.3 The population of the United States according to the decennial censuses.

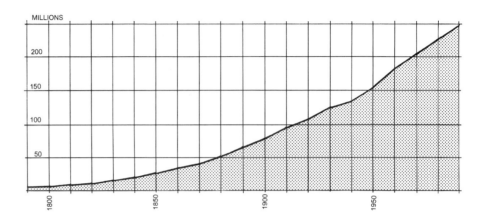

MILLIONS

200

150

100

50

1800   1850   1900   1950

in the United States by 2040 and 383 million by 2050. Given a population of 255 million in 1992, that forecast exceeds a 50 percent increase in population in just fifty years. Thus, there could be more than half as many more people in our U.S. metropolitan areas. Foreign-born citizens, who represented 8.6 percent of the population in 1990, are expected to rise to 14.2 percent in 2040. Immigrants arriving after 1991 or children born to those parents will amount to 21 percent of the population in 2050. For example, the number of Asian-Americans is expected to reach 35 million by the year 2040 and 41 million in 2050. This increase is spectacular, considering that there were about 7 million Asian-Americans in the United States in 1990. Hispanics, 24 million in 1992, are expected to nearly triple in number, reaching 64 million and surpassing African-Americans sometime before the year 2010. By 2020, there will be 49 million Hispanic Americans, and by 2050 there will be 81 million.[6] It is projected that there will be only 2 million Native Americans in 2050—the same number as in 1990. Even though non-Hispanic white residents are predicted to remain the majority (211 million in 2040 versus 187 million in 1990), this forecast means that over one in three people will not be a non-Hispanic white—in fact, almost every other person will fit that category.[7]

The accompanying graph illustrates this prediction of major ethnic and racial changes in the U.S. population during the fifty-year period that follows the 1990 census (Fig. 8.4). Although these data forecast a 43 percent increase in national population and a 13 percent increase in the non-Hispanic white population during this period, that group would drop from 75 percent of the U.S. population to 59 percent. If this prediction proves to be true, the African-American population will have increased 47 percent, at a slightly higher rate than the rate of increase for the country's population as a whole, and the non-Hispanic white population will have increased at less than a third of that rate. The Asian-American and Hispanic groups are shown as increasing to about five and three times, respectively, their present numbers, which would represent increases of more than three times and two times, respectively, of their initial proportion of the total population. These increases would combine the generational growth of the present population and, principally, the arrival of new immi-

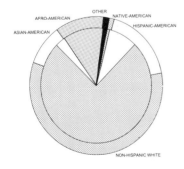

OTHER
AFRO-AMERICAN   NATIVE-AMERICAN
ASIAN-AMERICAN   HISPANIC-AMERICAN

NON-HISPANIC WHITE

8.4 The inner circle shows the ethnic distribution according to the 1990 U.S. census; the outer circle forecasts the distribution as it will be 50 years later.

8.5 Although areas of shops are established primarily to serve certain ethnic populations, they draw customers from a cross section of social and ethnic groups. Sidewalks and streets that were recently designed for other purposes have become open air markets. This phenomenon is associated with the globalization of cuisine. Vancouver, British Columbia.

grants. This information suggests that over one in five people in the United States in the year 2050 may be here as a result of migration during this fifty-year period.[8]

It is not surprising that so many of our spaces and places contain users of diverse races, ethnicities, and ages.[9] Probably more and more spaces and places will come to contain additional social, ethnic, and minority cultures, and many new spaces are to be designed with consideration of those groups in mind (Fig. 8.5). Slowly, spaces will begin to appear even more distinctive, through their design matching special perceptions and behaviors. Therefore, some spaces that are comfortable for some today may not remain comfortable for them. Users may change, and modifications may be necessary. Changes in population will modify the character of our towns and cities.

These and similar predictions of population change might seem to herald a coming need in the United States for the design of open spaces in keeping with the cultural backgrounds of Asian-Americans and Hispanics.[10] However, matching may be a simplistic conclusion. Open spaces serve populations of regions, cities, or neighborhoods. Therefore, the ethnic implications of a design will reflect the overall makeup of those geographic units, and people's desires will vary according to the extent to which distinct ethnic groups are isolated geographically. It often has been argued that urban concentrations of ethnic and racial groups are more a result of economic stratification than of cultural focus.[11] On this basis, if one assumes immigration that is largely motivated by poverty, newly arrived groups might be expected to both live and work in the same places that immigrants live now. The progress of "Americanization" in foreign lands, America's affect on other countries' language and taste, future immigrants' relative desire to undergo assimilation, and their economic opportunities may all challenge, in varying degrees, the nineteenth- and twentieth-century assumptions regarding the locations and preferences of immigrant populations.

There is considerable risk in generalizing design responses to ethnic and racial variation. Hispanic traditions in the design of buildings and open spaces were firmly demonstrated in the southwestern states and Florida early in the twentieth century. Under the influence of stylistic eclecticism, the use of Hispanic styles was probably more a matter of the historical background of the locale, climatic adaptation, and real-estate sales than of population characteristics. In most foreign countries, the most accepted spatial expression of grandeur and dignity may spring from the Parisian boulevards that were constructed by local or colonial governments about a century ago. The determination of a response to ethnicity is indeed more than tourists' recollections or a cursory glance through the *National Geographic.* It involves empathetic investigation, both of traditions and of the present-day outlook of the immigrants who will utilize the space.

Julian Simon, professor of business administration at the University of Maryland, anticipated an increase of immigration into the United States by 2000. He also believes that the average age of the work force will rise and that the ratio of the number of workers to the number of elderly retirees will decrease (Fig. 8.6).[12] If genetic research provides the wealth of medical information that is predicted at present, some of it will certainly prolong lives. More older people will be visible and participate actively in community affairs. Scientists such as Leroy Hood, biology professor at California Technological University, stated in 1990 that within fifteen years biologists will have designed a protein that will bind specifically to lung cancer cells and destroy them.[13] A further prediction suggests that scientists will identify at least one hundred genes that predispose people to diseases.[14] It is possible that genetic engineering could make people more able to tolerate specific pollutants, thus reducing their effect—to the benefit of some industries. Many forecasts see the major cities of the future as polluted with dangerous air and hopelessly congested with automobiles and pedestrians. Despite these problems it would be highly desirable to maintain and increase the number of open spaces as a concomitant of the elderly population. It is interesting to note that Americans over 65 now have the highest household net worth of any similar age group, the highest average after-tax income, and the lowest poverty rate.[15] If these facts remain true as time goes on, it is possible that institutional environments may be more accessible to the elderly, and it is also possible that they will be able to remain longer in their familiar neighborhoods. The development of "gray ghettoes" would call for the development of open spaces particularly adapted to the needs of the elderly. On the other hand, neighborhoods in which the elderly are intermingled with other groups will require that consideration

8.6 Density, congestion, and their environmental results do not necessarily make for unlivable cities. The common assumption that city problems will be aggravated can be answered by more and better spaces in cities. New York City. (Photo by Trev Albright)

of the elderly (which may not be greatly different from the consideration of other groups) influence the design of public places within neighborhoods.

It is expected that the elderly in the future will become an increasing proportion of the users of open spaces. The postwar babies born from 1946 to 1968 will become retirees in the period between 2005 and 2035. Recent enactment of laws extending worklife before enforced retirement would seem to reduce the number of retirees, but financial provisions have encouraged early retirements. It is predicted that in the 2030s the elderly, those sixty-five or older, will be 30 to 40 percent of the population. Germany and Japan at that time can be expected to have half their populations above the age of sixty-five.[16] Some of today's acid rock fans, gray-haired and walking with canes, will listen to their music through earphones as they doze in the park. Advances in geriatric and preventive medicine may mean that more of the elderly instead will be riding motorcycles and playing softball. The stereotypes of tottering oldsters must be abandoned in assessing the influence of "elderly" users of open spaces, even of those spaces built in the near future.

Unfortunately, a rise in the crime rate is predicted worldwide by the *United Nations Survey of Crime Trends.* They predict that from 1975 to the year 2000, for every one hundred crimes now recorded there will be 160, and during the same period the number of adults in prison will have doubled.[17] Designing for defensible spaces will become a more urgent concern. Fences, gates, and bright lights may become routine elements in many public areas. In some projects, sightlines for observation of spaces by patrols and the placement of electronic surveillance equipment may strongly influence the basic layouts.

8.7 The workplace need not be stressful. Visual and spatial relief for workers can be provided in the spaces between buildings. Their elements can be very calming. Park Plaza, San Jose. (Photo by Elsa D. Flores)

TECHNOLOGY

The full adoption of advances in telecommunications suggests that the efficiency of exchange will significantly offset the traditional requirements of physical proximity. Warm-body contact is no longer viewed as a requisite for negotiation or agreement on financial topics.[18] Some prophecies that are largely based on technology and its consequences conclude that much clerical work, and other jobs that involve office work, will soon become home-centered, eliminating for many workers the daily travel between their homes and their offices, whether downtown or in the suburbs. This shift of the workplace certainly would alleviate some pressures on the transportation networks of cities, although workers in manufacturing, retail sales, and some other fields theoretically would continue to commute. If this change in workplaces took place, there might be a much greater need for neighborhood open spaces where home-workers could easily find respite from the stress of employing a single site as both residence and workplace (Fig. 8.7). Even if working at home does not become common, telecommunications will permit business offices and corporate headquarters to continue their present tendency to disperse within the city framework. No longer is it necessary for offices dealing in paper, faxes, and bytes to be clustered in financial districts that deal with specific commodities. The strength of this tendency can be measured by the increasing frequency of press predictions that stock and commodities exchanges, the ultimate centers of finance as a contact sport, will be replaced by twenty-four-hour electronic trading systems. Suburban office parks and office estates, situated as the country homes of the rich once were, will have the open spaces developed around them as an essential advantage of their locations. It remains to be seen if this inclination, which is largely the result of the lower

8.8 High-rise housing and office buildings with sufficient and well designed open spaces surrounding them may solve many of the problems that cause people to move to the suburbs. There may be no reason to move to larger, undesigned spaces in the suburbs, if well designed spaces are everywhere. New York City. (Photo by Trev Albright)

cost of suburban land and employees' migration to the suburbs, will stir the proliferation of small open spaces among those office buildings remaining in downtown areas. There are indications that this change also means the parallel dispersal of hotels, for their success is dependent on the attraction of business travellers who seek lodgings that are near the businesses they wish to visit.

The dramatic changes that have been wrought by the rapid and seemingly limitless development of science and technology naturally have given rise to a belief that those fields can, under the right conditions, solve all problems. Experience, sometimes bitter, has shown how misplaced that view is.[19] If technical improvements drastically reduce the number of workers required, industrial activity may move to isolated locations or zoned clusters, far from residential areas that might suffer from its noise, release of fumes, and disposal of refuse (Fig. 8.8). Or, the development of robotic assembly methods and the miniaturization of electronic devices might permit certain kinds of light industry to be adjacent to other activities, perhaps even be combined with housing and office functions in mixed use complexes. Under judicious legislation and strict enforcement, segregated industrial sites can be surrounded by greenbelts of recreational land. At the same time, many industrial plants concerned with the assembly of parts that were manufactured elsewhere require large areas of relatively inexpensive land for parking, extensive warehousing, and facilities for shipping goods by truck or rail. The first modes of zoning as a land-use control were based exclusively on the distinction between industrial and nonindustrial activities, but the future could see significant changes in those acceptable factors that are employed in regulating the uses and their locations within cities and within the suburban development around them.

It is possible that the continued exploitation of natural resources and the often-predicted climatic changes will seriously limit the extent and

8.9 A trip to the riverfront is not the same as a trip to the beach, but the convenience of an artificial setting close to home can compensate for the possible reduction in the numbers and quality of natural areas. This kind of substitute space appears to be essential for frequent experiences of the residents of America's future cities. Delaware River, Philadelphia.

quality of the nation's park system. Staving off such calamities, as well as dealing with the overall problems of air and water pollution, will in many ways depend on political events, particularly on the actual relationship between government, social controls, and business. Whatever the outcome, any diminution of the quality of national and state park systems, any damage to the countryside, will necessarily and dramatically intensify our dependence on urban spaces. In time, the family vacation at a national park may be supplanted by a visit to the fabricated novelty of commercial amusement parks or the scenic design of urban places (Fig. 8.9).

BUSINESS AND FINANCE

The gap between cultures of technology and cultures of coping is widening as we watch.[20] It has been forecast that the globalization of business and technological innovation may result in a limited number of international consortia strongly dominating certain fields—with perhaps as few as eight to ten of them in telecommunications, five to eight in the automobile manufacture, and maybe as few as three to five dealing in automobile tires.[21] Global companies, which tend to hold quasi-governmental roles, could strongly affect the internal organization of cities and the activities of

8.10 At first glance, the colonnade appears to be a unique space created by a special historic building, but actually it could be part of a residence, hotel, restaurant, office building, or almost anything else. There are certain devices and styles that are nonspecific symbols of luxury and pleasure. Universality in design reduces the visual identity of projects. Worth Avenue, West Palm Beach, Florida.

people within them.[22] These prospects suggest that such events would be accompanied by extensive "internationalization" of behavior and taste around the world and in the United States, a new aspect of the "Americanization" of past decades. Should such factors of increasing cultural sameness appear, there may be an accompanying uniformity displayed in the character of urban public places. The international spread of amusement parks may serve as a descriptor of this tendency (Fig. 8.10). On the other hand, it is also possible that in specific projects the display of local identity may become more desirable. At present the appearance of the newer downtown areas, with their glass-clad facades, are extraordinarily uniform throughout the United States and around the world, while the residential fringes of cities retain local color. This phenomenon may indicate what will prove to be a dichotomous relationship of home and workplace, or it could prove to be the result of different rates for acceptable change in the two settings.

Few actions have concrete results as rapid as those arising from changes in financial procedures, particularly those relating to taxation. One of the primary functions of tax policy is the encouragement or discouragement of certain conditions or activities. By exempting mortgage payments from income tax, home ownership is encouraged; by limiting the exemption to a family's primary place of residence, the ownership of second houses would be discouraged. In this manner, many sections and paragraphs of tax legislation are directed toward the attainment of social and economic goals. Actions of this nature vary from local special taxes on restaurant charges and hotel bills that fund the development of tourist attractions to national policy that might distinguish between corporate investments in buildings and the profits from the sale of goods. A city might effect an appreciable change in its downtown area by applying one tax rate to buildings built more than twenty-five years earlier and a higher tax rate on newer buildings.[23] Although such legislation would not forbid the construction of new buildings, as a zoning restriction would, it can alter significantly the fiscal viability of projects that would refurbish existing structures. Since property taxes are generally viewed as the exclusive purview of local government, cities are able to respond to local situations, adjusting tax rates and determining exemptions that might increase owners' and developers' interest in projects that would, in the judgment of the cities' planning authorities, most strongly forward the objectives of improving the visual and economic condition of the city. Such tactics are as applicable to the provision of open spaces as they are to buildings. Distinctions may be made in tax rates in order to encourage the development of public places together with the construction of buildings.

All similar methods of employing the tax structure as a means of city improvement depend on the political actions that determine the roles that will be assumed at the city, state, and federal levels. During the 1960s large amounts of federal funding were available to cities, and federal urban renewal activity was the basis of many of the examples shown in this book. In contrast, in the 1990s federal funds have been less available. Cities were forced to rely largely on themselves for improvements of the urban fabric, as well as for other governmental activities. Since sole reliance on local funding offered greater economic and political risk, alternative funding methods were developed, which combined federal, state, and city revenues with the advantages to be found in various relationships with real-estate developers. In the last years of the 1980s, the funding capabilities of real-estate developers were severely reduced. These radical changes have occurred and fluctuated over relatively short periods. A change in the dominant attitude of government at any level is capable of very rapidly altering the kinds of urban improvement projects that can be considered and the methods by which they can be funded. This most unpredictable factor, the vagaries of political, financial, and popular interest, is also the most volatile, and it can increase the unpredictability of other factors.

INFRASTRUCTURE

Given the further deterioration of the urban infrastructure of streets and water supply and sewage treatment systems, there will be an opportunity in the future to link those tasks of reconstruction to the visual improvement of open spaces and streets.[24] Improvement of the urban framework and visual enhancement of public areas are both inherently related to the economic objectives of city boosterism. These factors, relatively constant through the

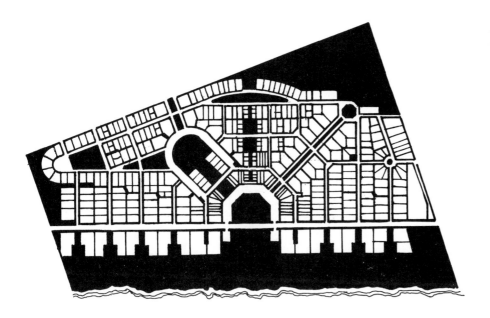

8.11 The term "neo-traditional town planning" became fashionable as a result of this developer's project. Strict building design controls and gridded streets seek to represent small town middle-America. Curvilinear, suburban residential streets could be supplanted over time. Seaside, Florida.

centuries, offer a stabilizing counterbalance to the volatility of political and tax outlooks. The improvements of open spaces are justifiably viewed by most communities as an important aspect of the economic aspirations of urban areas. For that reason, they will often be viewed as investments rather than expenditures. If the competition to attract investment becomes more intense among cities, there may be greater attention paid to the development of open spaces. Furthermore, as future demands for a stable and capable work force become more pressing, potential investors may come to value the quality of neighborhood spaces as well as the more impressive downtown and suburban spaces.

It is difficult to imagine appreciable changes in the present layout of the urban infrastructures of streets, rail lines, utilities, and subdivision patterns. Over time, the current patterns of infrastructure will represent increasingly high financial investments, so high that altering them will become more costly and more difficult. Inner cities in the past have contained high densities in grid patterns, and suburbs have been characterized in recent decades by curvilinear collectors and minor streets. Variations of the two forms are possible in some places.[25] A revival of interest in the use of grid patterns for suburban developments, stirred by the design of Seaside, Florida, may encourage the use of grids in new spots of land use (Fig. 8.11). Curved streets have provided the visual interest to be found in a variety of angles from which structures are viewed as a street turns and the buildings are oriented either uniformly or according to the changing line of the street. Similar effects can be obtained by combinations of key-patterned lots, zero-lot-line construction, and variations of the permitted building heights and densities.

Economy of construction for minor streets and major routes will probably remain a matter of straightening routes in the future. And the accompanying land purchases and earth-moving associated with handling heavy traffic and irregularities of routes, will be associated with low levels of expenditures. However, population growth in cities and the rising value of urban land can alter the prospects of specific streets over time. Volumes of traffic and prices of real estate are inevitably altered as cities grow. These changes will offer opportunities for open spaces—particularly where new construction abuts existing conditions. Growth in many Mexican cities has led to the erection or interconnection of downtown plazas. By routing streets beneath the enlarged open spaces, cities such as Monterrey have been able to provide large park areas in downtown locations. Similar projects could be fostered elsewhere in America by city growth.

The extremely high rate of population growth, urbanization, and increasing densities in Mexican cities have also led to many projects that place parking facilities beneath central plazas. In that country, relatively low construction costs may have made such solutions more available than in the United States and Canada, where fewer parking structures have been built beneath open spaces. By example, this trend toward upper-deck open space and plazas appears to be a model that could be translated easily to U.S. cities. Surface parking areas in the United States occupy a large part of urban open space, probably second only to streets, roads, and their rights-of-way. There are a variety of ideas about what will happen to the automobile in the future. Some predict that the problem posed by cars will be solved by improvements in the vehicle, perhaps by the use of electric automobiles; others see relief through the development of rapid transit within and between urban areas; still others believe that certain patterns of urban dispersal may alleviate troublesome conditions. Most forecasts, even those that take on a *Star Trek* aspect, involve some combination of the three prospects mentioned along with several others. The reality of a future problem is indicated and supported by the fact that between 1970 and 1990 the number of cars (as distinguished from "trucks") in the United States grew at more than twice the rate at which the population grew.[26] The outcome in fifty years would seem to require, no matter which prediction is followed, the utilization of considerable amounts of open space for urban transportation. The cost of all transportation systems, whether they involve rapid transit, highway construction, or the provision of parking spaces, is high, because designers and project teams must satisfy maximum demands even though any of the systems may be underused most of the time. Staggered hours of work can afford a degree of relief, but comparatively little. Needs in coming years will include the discovery and testing of methods by which portions of transportation spaces can be utilized for other worthy purposes at the times that they are not needed for their basic purposes. Elevated routes, despite their tendency to act as barriers at ground level, offer a solution for some problems, and subterranean systems may be of use, particularly in cities that have connected underground retail passageways. On the other hand, the problems of transportation and parking could be vastly simplified by deserting the downtown areas, a movement that is already underway. In the long run, instead of attempting the premature renewal of central urban areas, there may be wisdom in accepting a theory that the areas of growth and activity in a city are at its near edges, just as a "fairy ring" of mushrooms appears at the edges of a fungus beneath the ground. When certain levels of density and congestion are

8.12 Restoration and preservation of traditional American settings can add value to both residential and commercial neighborhoods. At the same time, the simplicity and restraint of design in these neighborhoods may be the fact or that keeps people from choosing only the latest trend in housing. The restraint of these sidewalk details illustrates a cultural tradition seldom seen in modern works. Society Hill, Philadelphia.

exceeded, it may be natural that the center city be deserted or become a tourists' curiosity, frequented by traditionalists. Activity moves outward to the rings established by the ring roads and highway bypasses of previous decades. Frantic efforts to sustain the vitality of the center city may in the end prove to be pointless and wasteful.

THE CONSTANTS

Throughout this chapter we have considered the possible changes that years will bring and the ways in which they may affect urban open spaces and public places. Some of the predictions that were presented probably will prove to be untrue; others could come about with astounding rapidity or so slowly that the change will be virtually imperceptible (Fig. 8.12). Since open spaces are authorized and designed in response to the factors that may change with time, it can be expected that even the more rapid changes will be evidenced in construction only after some time has passed. Taxation and finance may be susceptible to relatively sudden reversals, but social attitudes of geographic units change slowly—except where there are massive demographic changes. Highway construction and the clearance projects of urban renewal can move or disperse neighborhood populations, but years are necessary to determine the neighborhood's succeeding identity.

Designers of open spaces are fortunate that the fundamental human demands on their designs are immutable. Recreation for the body and spirit can be expected to continue to be desired by the public, as has been the case through millennia. If anything, through the centuries there has been growing importance attached to the availability and quality of open spaces. Urbanization and the decline of outdoor employment has increased the demand for plazas and open spaces, and the development of market-places and department stores and the improvement of transportation has increased the use of downtown streets. Even the present-day predictions involving population dispersal do not foresee densities so low that they would significantly reduce the demands for open spaces.

The primary purpose of most open spaces is simply the provision of space. The natural adaptability of humankind ensures that pleasure and relaxation can be found almost anywhere that there is a place that can be designated or appropriated for that purpose. By merely drawing a hop-scotch diagram, small children make a limited playground. When benches are not provided, we sit on steps or on the grass. In spite of inconvenience, it is usually possible to improvise a place that satisfies the functional needs, although probably it would neglect the esthetic needs of the public.

The culture of the United States as it materializes in the future will certainly maintain, improve, and increase the number of public places of every sort. Population growth and other demographic influences will largely determine the needs, and the economic and social conditions will influence those needs that are more fully satisfied. Although there will be a degree of activity across the board, political and social attitudes will, as always, deter-mine the favored groups. Gathering places and quiet retreats will be fashioned within our cities, no matter how the cities change.

If the future sees even greater mass production and uniformity of objects, still differences in climate and terrain and the spirit of people will make certain that urban open spaces maintain their individuality. That individuality will become more precious in its contrast with uniformity. Urbanization and increased population densities will make the restorative powers of parks more meaningful and will demand the visual pleasures of well-designed streets and plazas. The trends we observe today require that we heighten the social and esthetic effectiveness of our spaces tomorrow. City identity, spaces, places, and streets provide the real focus for design-ing America.

ENDNOTES

1. Graham H. May, "The Future of the City," *Futures* (July–August 1989): 608.

2. May, "Future of the City," 609.

3. George A. Miller, Eugene Galanter, and Karl H. Pribram, *Plans and the Structure of Behavior* (New York: Holt, 1960); and Kenneth E. Boulding, *The Image: Knowledge, Life, and Society* (Ann Arbor, MI: University of Michigan, 1969).

4. The typical planning process is explained clearly throughout F. Stuart Chapin and Edward J. Kaiser, *Urban Land Use Planning,* 3rd ed. (Urbana, IL: University of Illinois, 1979), 77, 90.

5. George W. Fairweather and Louis G. Tornatzky, *Experimental Methods for Social Policy Research* (New York: Pergamon Press, 1977).

6. Robert Pear, "New Look at the U.S. in 2050: Bigger, Older and Less White," *New York Times,* December 4, 1992, A1, A10.

7. Confirmed by Peter Morrison, demographer: Rand Corporation and David Heer, demographer: University of Southern California; in Lucinda Harper, "Census Bureau Lifts Population Forecast, Citing Fertility, Immigration, Longevity," *Wall Street Journal,* December 4, 1992, B1, B9.

8. See Jennifer Day, "Population Projections of the U.S. by Age, Sex, Race, and Hispanic Origin: 1992 to 2050" (Washington D.C.: Bureau of the Census, 1992); and Bureau of Statistics, U.S. Treasury Department, *Statistical Abstract of the United States, 1986 to 1991* (Washington D.C.: U.S. Government Printing Office, 1991).

9. Thomas G. Exter, "In and Out of Work," *American Demographics* (June 1992): 63.

10. Howard N. Fullerton, Jr., "Outlook: 1990–2005—Labor Force Projections: The Baby Boom Moves On," *Monthly Labor Review* (November 1991): 31–44.

11. Christopher Jencks and Paul E. Peterson, eds., *The Urban Underclass* (Washington D.C.: Brookings Institutions, 1991).

12. Julian L. Simon, *The Economic Consequences of Immigration* (Oxford: Basil Blackwell, 1989).

13. Daniel J. Kevles and Leroy Hood, *The Code of Codes: Scientific and Social Issues in the Human Genome Project* (Cambridge, MA: Harvard University Press, 1992).

14. "Today's Leaders Look to Tomorrow; 126 Thinkers From Around the World Tell How the Years Ahead Will Transform Our Lives," *Fortune.* (March 26, 1990): 30–158, 96.

15. Joseph G. Altonji and Thomas A. Dunn, *Relationships Among the Family Incomes and Labor Market Outcomes of Relatives* (Cambridge, MA: National Bureau of Economic Research, 1991).

16. Harper, "Census Bureau Lifts Population Forecast," B14.

17. United Nations, *Global Outlook 2000: An Economic, Social, and Environmental Perspective, 1990* (New York: United Nations, 1990), 320–324.

18. George W. Rathjens, "Global Security: Approaching the Year 2000," *Current History* (January 1989): 4–8.

19. Eugene B. Skolnikoff, "Technology and the World Tomorrow," *Current History* (January 1989):5–8, and Eugene B. Skolnikoff, *Science, Technology, and American Foreign Policy* (Cambridge, MA: MIT Press, 1967).

20. Alvin Toffler, *Power Shift* (New York: Bantam, 1990).

21. Riccardo Petrella, "World City-States of the Future," *New Perspectives Quarterly* (Fall 1991): 59–64.

22. Petrella, "World City-States," 62.

23. Although it has been repealed, the federal Tax Recovery Act of 1982 did provide such a tax advantage to owners of old buildings; however, this act was an instrument of federal policy.

24. Willfred Owen, "Mobility and the Metropolis," in Richard V. Knight and Gary Gappert, eds., *Cities in a Global Society.* (Newbury Park, CA: Sage Publications, September 1989), 246–253.

25. Urban Land Institute, *Project Infrastructure Development Handbook* (Washington, D.C.: Urban Land Institute, 1989).

26. Economics and Statistics Administration, *Americans and Their Automobiles* (Washington, DC: U.S. Department of Commerce, Bureau of the Census, 1992); and Marin Wachs and Margaret Crawford, eds., *The Car and The City: The Automobile, The Built Environment, and Urban Daily Life* (Ann Arbor, MI: University of Michigan, 1992).

INDEX